A HALO FOR GOMEZ

A HALO
FOR GOMEZ

By John Lavin

PAGEANT PRESS
New York

COPYRIGHT, 1954, BY JOHN LAVIN

PUBLISHED BY PAGEANT PRESS, INC.

130 WEST 42ND STREET, NEW YORK 36, N. Y.

First Edition

LIBRARY OF CONGRESS CATALOG CARD NUMBER: 54-12341

MANUFACTURED IN THE UNITED STATES OF AMERICA

FOREWORD

As a result of all the idiocies and hoary legends that have been repeated over and over again, Juan Vicente Gómez, soldier and dictator, stands before posterity as a sinister figure, the most falsely maligned man in all Venezuelan history. What little has been published on his life, in rambling memoirs and a sole biography, has been eulogistic flattery, bitter condemnation, or distorted truths; myth has been pyramided upon myth until the real Gómez is portrayed as either a fiend incarnate or a patriot as great and noble as Bolívar. Somewhere between these two extremes lies the truth.

A man of complex attitudes and contradictions, Gómez was a paradox within a paradox, but certain salient facts stand out. His wisdom was profound and his mastery of men was superb. Like Joseph Vissarionovich Stalin, whom he resembled in many ways, he was unscrupulous, cunning, and cautious. Not once during the entire twenty-seven years of his rule did he ever know the humility of defeat.

What makes the saga of Juan Vicente Gómez so remarkable is not so much the brazen outrageousness of the myths about him as the fact that there should be any myths at all; Gómez's life had been so picaresque, no one need have resorted to invention to endow it with color. His political career was so replete with dramatic episodes and exploits that it may at times read like some bizarre novel of eighteenth-century adventure. His is the drama of a leader born in the twilight of feudal strife, who gathered up the people of a nation into his own person and drove them along the cruel road of his vision. His was a way of life that, like the guerrilla wars of his country, has vanished into the memories of yesteryear. Gómez belongs to the vanishing age of absolute Latin American dictators: Díaz in Mexico, Rosas in Argentina, and Leguía in Peru; in his own bailiwick, each was a king

v

who held the power of life or death over his subjects, and whose every wish was law.

This biography does not aspire to be an academic work. The chronicling of contemporary Venezuelan history would fill many volumes and could best be done by a scholar fitted for the task. I do not profess to be such. What I have written is primarily the story of an extraordinary man and his times; the history of the men and events that evolves in the telling is incidental, yet vital, to the story.

To the best of my ability I have attempted to dispel the legends without creating new ones, to show Gómez as he was, a passionate human being who strove mightily to reach a niche among his country's immortals. To try to sift the truths from the many falsehoods and correct the many unintentional errors has been a long and difficult task. By careful checking I believe I have cleared up most of the errors, and what is more important, I can repudiate the most heinous of the lies; this biography disposes once and for all of the charges that Gómez was illegitimate, illiterate and an atheist. Often I found the truths to be self-evident. Wherever possible, however, I referred to written records. As to hearsay, where feasible I have reported it as such, for no mortal can judge who has told the truth and who has stretched it.

In the preparation of this book I have received valuable assistance from men who knew or served Gómez. They have no ax to grind, nothing to gain by wanting to set matters aright, but they have preferred for political or family reasons to receive no mention. To each one of these contributors goes my heartfelt thanks. To Venezuela's venerable elder statesman, Eleazar López Contreras, I am indebted for his permission to recount the many highlights of his career. Without his help this book would have been woefully deficient. I am also greatly indebted to Gómez's sons, Juan Vicente and Florencio, who furnished much information and many photographs. May this book alleviate their fears that I would do them and their father harm. My gratitude must also be expressed to Julio Gómez, Isidro Antonio Torres Gómez, and others of the Gómez clan who desire to remain unnamed; to Juan Cova, Ernesto Velasco, Anthony Picardi, and Adalberto Villegas; to the United States Embassy and Consular staffs; and lastly to the many other kind persons whose assistance has helped to make this book possible.

CONTENTS

PROLOGUE

As the warm tropical night became diffused with the first light of dawn, activity stirred within the mottled walls of the fortress of *El Libertador* which guards the approaches to the Venezuelan port of Puerto Cabello on the Caribbean. The precise day and year do not matter, for the scene we are about to witness has taken place countless times. *El Castillo El Libertador,* a crumbling colonial fortress which gained notoriety even before the War of Independence, has served as a penitentiary for the governments of Venezuela for over a century.

From the barracks on the upper story the blast of a bugle and the thunder of drums usher in the day with a roaring welcome. At the burst of sound the sea gulls take off in flight from the rocks of the island fortress. The rhythmic tramp of heavy feet resounds from worn floor boards. *Mestizo* soldiers in thin faded khaki take to the benches along the four sides of the veranda overlooking the square patio. For their edification and amusement preparations are being made for a macabre spectacle. The performance for this morning is called a *pela.*

No wonder that the two inmates of cell number nine have to be dragged into the patio by a squad of soldiers. After days of hunger and torment they know at last what has been held in store for them.

A lieutenant orders them to remove their clothes and to sit on the ground. As further resistance would be futile, they submit resignedly. One man's legs are drawn up so that his knees reach almost to his chin. With his arms around his knees his hands are tied together by the thumbs. A rifle is pushed through the crook of the knees so that it balances evenly on the man's arms. Another rifle is inserted under

1

the arms against his chest. His arms are firmly locked now. He can neither raise nor lower them. His companion is put through the same procedure. Then the men are tipped over on their knees, their heads bowed to the ground.

The supporting actors in this bloody drama stand around nervously awaiting their cue from the veranda. Above, the chatter of a group of officers subsides to a hush as General Rito Paulino Camero, the prison warden, airily waves his hand.

The harsh music of a fife, drum, and cornet rends the air. There is something catchy about the grotesque melody of tunes that arouses a tapping of feet. General Camero relaxes in his wicker chair, his face a cold, unsmiling mask.

Two husky trusties, bare to the waist, raise thick, black bull whips which have been soaked in pails of sea water. The spectators cannot hear the whine of the wet leather flailing the air but they can hear the lash of the whips striking flesh. They cannot hear the groans of the victims but they can surely sense the sharp pain that racks those helpless bodies. The whips, handled dexterously by experts, rise and fall rhythmically on immobile flesh . . . two . . . three . . . four . . . five . . . Long red streaks appear on the skin.

On the veranda there are mixed expressions of feeling. A few of the younger, untried soldiers wince at each lash of the whips. Some, who have witnessed the *pelas* many times before, look on impassively. Others—tough, seasoned veterans of prison tortures—are deeply absorbed in the spectacle. An officer taps his swagger stick against the railing in time with the fall of the whips. Another complains that the performance does not compare with a bull fight. But what else is there to do? Entertainment is scarce. Other officers remain silent; theirs are expressions of satisfaction and pleasure, a sadistic enjoyment being fulfilled by torturing of human beings.

Eighteen . . . nineteen . . . twenty . . . the whips rise and fall in unison. Two bodies fairly hug the earth and pray that God will let them sink into it and escape forever the firebrands that lash them. From a light tint covered with ever darkening streaks their backs are slowly transformed into a vivid palpitating red, a soft mass of opening furrows from which crimson oozes and drips to the ground. But the whips continue to rise and fall.

Thirty-two . . . thirty-three . . . thirty-four . . . the music is becoming raucous and monotonous now; the officers are becoming bored. In the east the sun is rising fast and the heat hangs heavy in the air. The executioners glisten with sweat and their strokes fall in a slower tempo. Their trousers are specked with blood.

Camero notices with scorn that a young soldier has averted his eyes from the sight. His face has taken on a sickly pallor. So he is sick to his stomach, is he? Well, let him sit there until he vomits! It's like smoking the first cigar, isn't it *muchacho?* No matter—he'll come back for more and like it!

No longer is there any recoiling motion in the victims as the whips strike. Their heads hang heavy on the ground. They have sunk into thankful unconsciousness. No longer is it the skin of man that is bared to the heavens. The backs and buttocks of two human beings have been transformed into masses of raw meat and exposed muscle. Yet the whips continue to hammer the inert bodies in time with the barbarous music. Not until Camero gives the sign will the torture cease.

At last Camero raises his hand. Over the raw flesh they spill some of the salt water. Balm for their throbbing wounds! Each body is dragged by two guards and deposited on the damp, dirt floor of a single, windowless cell. And to finish it off, a blacksmith appears and adds his little bit of devilish torture. Each ankle is sheathed in iron bands riveted to a heavy bar. Let them try to walk, if they can, with sixty pounds of iron on their legs!

Thus these two suffering souls remained, unattended and forgotten, to emerge hours later from their tortured sleep, crying for water to quench their thirst. No need to plead for medicine or bandages. No doctor would be available to administer to the likes of them. They would get their water . . . and that would be all.

Two, or perhaps three, days later—one can't be exact as to names or dates, *as no written records were kept in the prison*—two bodies were carried across the patio. No one could supply the names to which those bodies answered in life. Or perhaps no one cared to remember. After all, two, three, and sometimes four dead men were carried out of the prison every day. Suffice to say that Pedro Ordoñez and José Rodriguez—the two victims of the *pela*—were never seen again. Yet it is almost certain they were carried to a nameless grave in that mysterious burial ground where thousands of Venezuelan prisoners found a final resting place.

What had those two men done to warrant such brutal torture? Not much. Pedro Ordoñez and José Rodriguez had committed petty crimes and had been taken to *El Libertador* prison without trial. Like other common criminals they worked at menial jobs to earn their keep. And like the other common criminals they were not shackled with heavy irons as were the political prisoners. As reward for good behavior they were made trusties. They carried the pails of rice, beans, and plantains to the cells of the political prisoners; they cleaned the foul-smelling latrines and they carried away the dead.

In time the political prisoners came to know and have confidence in these trusties. This was particularly true of the inmates of the cell known as "The Forgotten One." This cell, built into the thick wall of the prison, was an arched chamber ten by twenty feet located at the far corner of the patio. As its name implied, its thirty-five inmates were the most neglected.

Yielding to pleas from the prisoners, Ordoñez and Rodriguez had carried messages to and from other cells. Short, harmless, heart-rending messages they were—a request for a medicine or the names of the latest prisoners and the news they brought from the outside world. Sometimes there was a desperate entreaty to the warden from a dying man who begged for a last reprieve so that he might succumb in the arms of his loved ones. One day both Ordoñez and Rodriguez were caught carrying messages scribbled on scraps of paper. Both knew that writing materials were forbidden to all prisoners. For one week they were confined to a cell without food or water. Apprehension over the punishment they knew was in store for them added to their misery. Then on that fateful morning, when they were weak and exhausted, came the *pela*.

Some prisoners said General Camero was a sadist capable of killing a man daily until the end of his days. There were others who said he acted only on orders from higher up—from "the old man in Maracay"—a suspicion which Camero himself to a certain extent confirmed the day he visited "The Forgotten One" to see a prisoner.

This prisoner was a nineteen-year-old boy from Valencia by the name of Francisco González Salas. He had been imprisoned for telling a joke in a bar gathering, a joke which had involved Martinez Méndez, President of the State of Carabobo and brother-in-law of the President of Venezuela. González had remarked that Martinez

Méndez—who boasted of speaking perfect French—had mistakenly said in that language *hommenage* instead of *hommage*. It was an innocent joke, but a government spy took advantage of the opportunity to denounce him to the authorities. Stripped to his underwear, he had been shackled with sixty-pound irons and left to rot in the overcrowded cell. The filthy living conditions, the abominable food, and especially the heavy irons worked such a hardship on him that he began to lose his senses within a few weeks. Rather than face the prospect of complete insanity he sought means to commit suicide, but there was nothing in the cell to help him, not even a shirt tail with which to hang himself. The news of the young prisoner's desperate plight was brought by a trusty to General Camero, and he visited the cell block to investigate.

When the heavy door to "The Forgotten One" creaked open, the murmur of voices within suddenly ceased and a brawny, unkempt figure in khaki filled the doorway. A cigarette smouldered between his thick lips and a week's growth of black beard half covered a bulldog face that eloquently testified to his vocation. Of humble Indian stock, General Rito Paulino Camero had risen rapidly from the ranks. Promotion, however, had not come by deeds of valor—he was a prison warden and executioner by profession and a soldier by circumstances.

Camero listened coldfacedly to the prisoners' entreaties that the boy's irons be removed before his mind broke completely. He dropped his cigarette to the ground and thirty-five pairs of eyes watched longingly as its pale blue smoke spiraled upward in the shaft of sunlight. Then, slowly, in his thick Indian accent, Camero said: "You must understand that I am but an instrument here, because everything that is done here—whether it be for the good or for the bad—I am ordered to do from Maracay. Even to the weight of the irons for each prisoner, I have to take orders from there. I have already been threatened that if I dare remove, on my own account, the irons from a prisoner . . . I shall have to wear them myself."

Hearing the negative reply—which was certainly a direct accusation against "the old man in Maracay," none other than Juan Vicente Gómez, President of Venezuela—Francisco González Salas pleaded: "If you cannot reduce the weight of the irons, then shoot me . . . shoot me four times!"

Camero's expression was a picture of pity. *"Muchacho,* you ask for something which I cannot do. I repeat . . . everything that is done here is ordered by Maracay and without such an order from Maracay I can do nothing. Now, if Maracay were to give me the order to shoot you all, I would shoot you all, like that. But without this order I will shoot no one, even if he begs me. So don't ask me again, because I am unable to do it." And Camero went out, taking with him the ray of sunshine and leaving in its stead a bitter resentment which festered into a virulent hatred as González's mental illness worsened and he was taken away violently insane.

The time had long passed when sly, implacable Camero could fool his prisoners with such talk. For all his chicanery, they knew him for what he was and had been for nearly twenty years—a sadist and murderer. When it amused him to see men suffer, he would torture them; if they died, it was the inevitable consequences to the act —like the dishes that must be cleaned up after a hearty meal. Compassion and leniency were not in Camero's make-up. Yet among the officers of the prison there were some who possessed the conscience of a man and they carried out their assignments in a humane and responsible manner. Captains, most of them, they settled minor complaints of the prisoners and did not antagonize the men with punishments or visits of wanton destruction—the latter carried on under the guise of "inspections." But these good captains lasted but a short time, and it seemed as though the eyes of Camero had been watching all the while, as though his malignant spirit resented the kind deeds. Camero could not accept condescensions with the prisoners. His criterion in this respect was decisive. "A prisoner is a prisoner," he would say vehemently, "and the prisoner is dung! To the enemy you have to show the bone—that's the advice of the *Jefe!*"

Yet, when Camero said: *"Even to the weight of the irons for each prisoner, I have to take orders from there,"* he spoke the sober truth. From his comfortable retreat in Maracay, President Juan Vicente Gómez took a personal interest in meting out penalties for political prisoners. Whether they suffered, lived, or died—their fate depended almost entirely on this tyrant's whim and pleasure. Venezuela was steeped in clandestine intrigues and seething hatreds, its liberties fettered by shackles it could not throw off. Its people lived in the shadow of fear.

The Spanish Inquisition had been abolished in Spain in 1820, but, until 1935, it still endured ingloriously in a republic which had overthrown the last vestige of Spanish power in 1821, a republic where men were being imprisoned without formal charges, where men languished and died in loathsome cells without benefit of trial and sentence, a republic where medieval tortures were still in practice in the twentieth century. Unbelievable but true, and in a country which, in its constitution, guaranteed all citizens freedom of assembly and religion, the inviolability of the home and private correspondence, and the inalienable rights of life, free press, free speech, and trial by law. In the fight for independence, the blood and sweat of thousands had been spilled for naught. Article thirty-two and its clauses so sacred to the hearts of Venezuela's sons had been expunged from the Venezuelan constitution. For twenty-seven years a tyrant held undisputed control over the lives and destiny of a torpid and befuddled nation.

The fabulous tale of Juan Vicente Gómez is one of cheating, robbing, and killing on a huge scale. He vented his lust on the cream of the nation's womanhood, and fathered more than one hundred and fifty bastard children. Yet he successfully presented to the outside world a false front of benign benevolence and democratic rule. Until he died in 1935 at he age of seventy-eight, he was still the absolute of dictators, still the arrogant and avaricious Don Juan. To this day, thousands curse his name, but by a strange paradox there are some who knew him who revere the memory of Juan Vicente Gómez almost as a saint.

CHAPTER ONE

The Rustic of La Mulera

Juan Vicente Gómez possessed such an extraordinary combination of traits that his role as dictator was almost inevitable. The long absolute rule of this man was so unique it would be difficult to find his counterpart in modern history. He was the archetype of the modern Fascist dictators, possessing their salient strong characteristics, yet unharassed by the weaknesses that inevitably bring on the fall of the great.

All elements of his life and character—his shabby heredity, backward environment, hidden ambitions, ruthless cruelty, and a peculiar intellect, devoid of learning but savoring of mysticism—prepared Gómez for his future role. But his first thirty-four years were bucolic, uneventful, and uninspiring.

He was born on July 24, 1857, at La Mulera, a small, prosperous hacienda near the little Andean town of San Antonio close to the Venezuelan-Colombian border. Contrary to popular belief—which was strongly influenced by the many published works of his enemies who took a fierce delight in calling him a bastard—he was the legitimate son of Pedro Cornelio Gómez and Hermenegilda Chacón, *mestizo* peasants of Spanish and Indian stock. His grandfather, a Spaniard, had migrated from the Canary Islands.

Juan Vicente was the first-born. The other eight Gómez children, in the order of their birth, were Indalecia, Juan Crisóstomo, Elvira, Emilia, Ana, Regina, Pedro, and Aníbal.

The principal products of La Mulera were coffee, horses, and cattle. By dint of hard work and many sacrifices, Pedro Gómez managed to accumulate enough wealth to be considered well-to-do by local standards. Thus he was financially able to be joined in the holy bonds of matrimony by a church wedding [1]—a ceremony many couples did without, professedly for economic reasons. It being the practice of the Andino of the peasant class to take into concubinage the woman of his fancy, the allegations as to the illegitimacy of Juan Vicente Gómez have been accepted for years as fact. Perhaps, too, Gómez's supposed aversion to the Church also lent credence to public opinion. The first, but by no means the last, visit he made inside a church was when his godmother, Carlota Nieto, carried him into the church of San Antonio to be baptized; in manhood he visited the church many times, but only for the purpose of giving away his many daughters in marriage. Strange as it may seem—as he himself never went through a marriage ceremony—he always reprimanded his children and grandchildren if they failed to attend church on Sundays. He himself could not attend, he said, because an old battle wound prevented him from kneeling or from standing for long periods.

His birthday happened to fall on the anniversary of the birth of Simón Bolívar, the Liberator, whose memory Gómez actually venerated. It has been said that during his lifetime he idolized only three persons: his mother, Símon Bolívar, and Juan Vicente Gómez. July 24, therefore, was made a day for double national observance, but to the people at large it was endured as just another one of Gómez's subtle innuendos that he was the reincarnation of that venerable soldier, and they refused to be convinced.

Gómez had his mother's imperturbability and cunning—common characteristics of the Andino Indian. From his father he probably inherited his love of women, his ambition, and his toughness of character that was not so much genuine strength as a persistent stubbornness in overcoming weaknesses.

La Mulera was a one-story stucco building of five rooms, with wooden *rejas* at the windows and a wide veranda which extended along the front and two sides. The parents' bedroom contained the only bed; the children slept in hammocks—the four boys in one bedroom and the five girls in another. Their nourishment consisted of the daily *sancocho*—a thin stew of boiled yucca, meat, and plantains —or perhaps *arepas*—griddle cakes of corn meal—washed down with

---

[1]Although Venezuela is almost totally Catholic, it does not recognize the legality of the church wedding, which must be preceded by a civil ceremony, provided without fee.

thick black coffee, heavily sugared. School was not for Juan. His mother taught him his numbers, and a neighbor's daughter, expounding the alphabet to the children of the neighborhood, taught him reading and writing.

It was not until 1870, when Juan Vicente was thirteen years old, that free and compulsory primary education was established in Venezuela. Although such an educational law had been proposed to the disinterested congress of the previous regime, it remained the good fortune of President Guzmán Blanco to sanction it dictatorially. (Heretofore, primary education had been left to the provinces and municipalities, many of which were riddled with corruption and were either too poor or too unconcerned to educate the illiterate.) To pay the costs of such education, Guzmán signed a second decree whereby all documents, such as contracts, invoices, etc., should carry a fiscal stamp in proportion to the amount involved. The first decree read: "Wherever ten children can be gathered together, there shall be a schoolteacher to teach them reading, writing, and the fundamentals of arithmetic; if there be no building to accommodate them, school shall be held under a tree if necessary . . . so that not one Venezuelan shall remain who cannot read the Constitution of the Republic."

It was a simple and beautiful program which, after eighty years, has not yet been entirely completed. In any case, for Juan Vicente it came too late.

From the time he could walk he had his share of the chores to do: harvesting the coffee, tending the cattle and horses, helping his parents to shell and grind the corn and dry the coffee beans in the sun. Then there was the water to fetch from the stream which ran by the house. But this was a task that Juan Vicente soon was able to delegate to his younger brothers and sisters. Before he was ten, he had helped his father herd cattle to market in San Cristóbal and Cúcuta over the border. By the time he reached eighteen he knew every road and path across the mountains for miles around. Later on, this knowledge of the mountain region would stand him in good stead.

About his childhood very little is known. There is no official biography covering the period. Once he had attained power, Gómez, taciturn to the last, was reluctant to reveal anything concerning those years. We only know that his beginnings were humble and his life hard, that he took it all in his stride, never complaining, always observing. Life taught him lessons, early, that proved useful later on.

Nature itself made some amends to the boy for his drab and weary homelife. Fruits and plants were plentiful and grew all the year around in the cool, invigorating air. The mountains abounded in game of all kinds. These healthy surroundings contributed to the strong physical constitution of the future revolutionist. The countryside was also proverbially rich in legend. Patriots had fought here against the Royalists. Bolívar had marched through the valleys with his heroic army to do battle with the Spaniards. Folk song and story told of the famous Andean guerrillas. In folklore, these brigands were often popular heroes: *mestizo* cavaliers who fought against the colonial governors and despotic military rulers, people's avengers who exacted tolls from the privileged rich and gave to the poor and downtrodden. Their hiding places were in the unsettled and almost inaccessible mountains from which they would swoop down to the roads to trap their enemies. A good part of this folklore was based on facts. The entire mountain region on both sides of the border was, even in those days, infested with guerrilla bands and smugglers. The whole land would resound with tales of raids on rich haciendas and isolated caravans. Looting and shooting affrays in villages were still common occurrences. The poor and downtrodden still paid with their lives for stupid interference. Most of these exploits were unmitigated banditry to be sure, yet they were not without romantic appeal. To the boys playing bandits on the fringe of "no-man's land," these local Robin Hoods offered examples to be imitated.

Even as a boy Juan Vicente showed a distinct penchant for leadership. He was naturally cautious and taciturn, qualities which earned him the respect of his playmates. Though others may have surpassed him in agility and daring, it was to him the boys looked to settle their arguments. Girls, too, noticed his streak of self-assertiveness. Perhaps it was for them that the tall, brown-eyed youth learned to strum the *tiple* and sing the plaintive ballads of the mountains. By the time he reached manhood and became the dominant figure in the Gómez household, Juan Vicente had fathered children of his own. His craving for sexual indulgence was to remain unsatiated until the very last year of his life.

As a youngster, Juan Vicente displayed quiet confidence and

strong nerves. Even a severe earthquake failed to rattle him. On that morning of May 18, 1875, two months before his eighteenth birthday, the entire Venezuelan-Colombian border area trembled and shook in the throes of a violent earthquake.[2] On this occasion, humans dashed from their houses for the safety of the open, but La Mulera, although well within the radius of destruction, was spared. Fifteen kilometers away, the Colombian towns of Cúcuta and El Rosario were leveled to the ground with a tremendous loss of life. In San Cristóbal, San Antonio, and other frontier towns, the toll of the dead and injured was heavy, and Juan Vicente and his brother Juancho [3] were called upon to render aid.

Early one Sunday morning in the spring of 1879, the brothers Juan and Juancho mounted their horses and set off at a canter on a side road to the south. They passed through the little village of Rubio drowsing in the sun and pulled up an hour later at the hacienda of Manuel Antonio Pulido Pulido. They had come to confirm the incredible reports that Sr. Pulido, an enterprising *hacendado,* was processing in a homemade still a lighting fuel (kerosene) from a thick black liquid he pumped from a shallow well. Twenty years had elapsed since the drilling of the first oil well by Colonel E. L. Drake at Titusville, Pennsylvania.

The year before, Sr. Pulido had announced the first petroleum deposits in Venezuela. Forming the company *Cía Petrolia del Táchira,* he obtained from the government of President Linares Alcántara the concession rights to his property. This was an important legal fomality as, since colonial times, the principle had been maintained—as in the majority of Latin-American countries—that ownership of all subsoil minerals is vested in the nation, and its control is effected through the government. The laws of the Indies, in 1602, which were applicable in the Spanish colonies of the New World, authorized the royal governors of the Spanish colonies to apply the mining laws of Spain throughout the colonies. The mining ordinances of New Spain, in 1783, made deposits of petroleum in the Spanish colonies of the New World the property of the Royal Spanish Crown, and these or-

---

[2] Severe earthquakes are not uncommon in Venezuela; the town of Cumana, for example, was destroyed three times in as many centuries.

[3] Christened Juan Crisóstomo, this was later shortened to the familiar Juancho.

dinances were sanctioned, ratified, and made effective in the "Gran Colombia" (which included what is now Venezuela, Colombia, Panama, and Ecuador) by a decree of Simón Bolívar issued at Quito, Ecuador, on October 24, 1829.

An article in the said ordinance of 1783, ratified by the Liberator, read: "Likewise, I concede that there may be discovered, solicited, recorded, and denounced in the manner aforesaid, not only the mines of gold and silver, but also mines of precious stones, copper, lead, tin, antimony, calamine, bismuth, rock salt and any fossil matters, bitumens, or juices of the earth, and proper provision shall be made for the acquisition, enjoyment and development thereof."

The first Venezuelan Code of Mines, 1854, had revoked such of the mining ordinances of New Spain as infringed on the laws and dispositions of Venezuela, but it firmly established the principle that mines, of whatever species, are the property of the State and are conceded by means of *denuncios*.

Sr. Pulido showed his astonished visitors the well from which a peon was pumping petroleum laboriously by hand into a wooden barrel. They inspected the small refining plant (it distilled only fifteen barrels of petroleum daily) and when they left for home they took with them a small calabash of kerosene.

Although crude in the extreme and offering only a slight conception of the intricate workings of the petroleum production and refining industry, the scene created a profound impression on Juan Vicente Gómez which he was to remember in later years in his dealings with foreign oil companies.

That Sunday night, the household of La Mulera—accustomed to homemade tallow candles—stood around agape while Juan demonstrated an innovation, the kerosene lamp.

When his father died a few months later, Juan Vicente was twenty-two. He stood five feet ten inches, well above average height for an Andino. He was a strapping specimen of a man, ready and willing to assume full charge of the clan. Daybreak would find him overseeing planting in the fields or driving cattle to market in San Cristóbal, where he did some shrewd trading. Occasionally, there would be a wave of border smuggling or cattle rustling. Juan Vicente was much too clever to be caught redhanded in such activities, yet by devious means he prospered and salted away sizeable sums.

When at last he found the woman he was looking for, sturdy and mature Dionisia Bello, he installed her in his house as his mistress. No matter that she was married, the wife of a merchant in the city of San Cristóbal. All his life he obtained what he wanted, be it by cajolery, bribery, or stronger methods. He had a strange fondness for Dionisia and she was his favorite mistress for almost thirty years. Of the many dozens of children fathered by Juan Vicente Gómez, hers, and the children of a later union were the only ones he legally recognized.[4]

By 1883, now a man of substance and some influence in cattle circles, Gómez was often seen on the streets of San Cristóbal—a five hour ride on horseback from La Mulera. Occupying a large and distinct place on the map, this provincial town boasted less than five thousand inhabitants, mostly of pure Indian blood. It was a white-washed *pueblo* of red tile roofs and narrow cobblestone streets, and it nestled in a wide mountain-girdled valley on an alluvial terrace above the Torbes River, which flows south to the great Orinoco basin. Through San Cristóbal flowed shipments of coffee and tough lean cattle from the southern ranges. As one of the natural gateways to the western *llanos* and the main artery of traffic to the sister republic of Colombia, San Cristóbal was to become the terminus in western Venezuela of the great trans-Andean highway.

Small wonder that the majority of its inhabitants were illiterate and ignorant; the nights were long and read-less in this Andean city of no lights. When the sun went down, one could only sit and gossip. A thriving, bustling town by day, by night it had the aspects of a quiet rural village, with men in chairs propped up against the wall on narrow sidewalks, the lights of their black cigars punctuating the darkness. There was much to talk about during those interminable evenings—the depression and declining markets, politics and revolutions, and the latest innovations in Caracas, the country's capital.

Until 1870, Caracas—already three centuries old—was still a colonial town of only 47,000 inhabitants. Situated in a fertile valley 3,000 feet above sea level, this birthplace of Simón Bolívar, Francisco de Miranda, and Andrés Bello enjoyed an ideal climate; yet this gar-

---

[4]This involves the registration of each illegitimate child with the civil authorities and a formal declaration by the father that the child is eligible to bear his name and share in the family inheritance.

den spot of eternal spring endured such names as "The City of Earth-quakes" and "The City of Tortures." By 1883, its population risen to 57,000, it could almost be called modern, though perhaps too French in its architecture, thanks to cosmopolitan President Antonio Guzmán Blanco [5] and his long dictatorship. But it was open to innovations.

Guzmán, a pompous, bearded individual who spent money with a lavish hand, had built a new Federal Palace and embellished it with elegant furniture from Paris. The Guzmán Blanco Theater, the last word in rococo architecture, was the talk of the country. In 1881 the first mule-drawn trolley cars appeared in Caracas between Plaza Bolívar and Candelaria, and in 1882 the telegraph system was extended across the sun-blistered, dusty *llanos* and towering Andes to the Colombian border. English capital and technicians had entered Venezuela in 1881 to start construction on short railroad lines from Puerto Cabello to Valencia and from Caracas toward Petare, but it was not until June 27, 1883, that the first locomotive of the La Guaira-Caracas railroad chugged in to the Caracas station. It covered the twenty-two grueling miles from the seaport of La Guaira in three hours and fifteen minutes. Three months later government buildings were being illuminated with gas (while North American cities were installing incandescent lighting), and a railroad spur had been completed to the Caracas suburb of El Valle—both accomplished with foreign capital. Quickly converted to this comparatively rapid and comfortable mode of travel, Guzmán promptly decreed two more railroad lines: one to Antímano, where, by coincidence, was located the President's largest hacienda; and the other to the shore resort of Macuto, where, by another coincidence, Guzmán rested for a few months each year.

Yet these few belated innovations did not spell progress and prosperity for the land of Bolívar. While Caracas was to continue as the hub for anything new and novel that struck Guzmán's fancy, the country's inland towns and hamlets, isolated and forsaken, were to remain stagnant and colonial. There was another reason why Venezuela would have to await the advent of the automobile and air-

[5] The double name is a combination of his father's and mother's surname — a custom which is still in popular use. For the sake of brevity, G.B. will be referred to henceforth in this book as Guzmán.

plane before the curtain of isolation could be lifted. She learned quickly, through the costly experience of French and English railroad companies, that rail systems do not pay off when a population of 2,075,245 (census of 1881) is scattered over an almost impassable and poorly productive terrain of 352,000 square miles.

For Venezuela, 1883 was a noteworthy year in one more respect. It marked the definite arrival of a major depression. The price of coffee and cattle had been declining steadily on foreign markets and, as if it had been an ominous warning of impending disaster, the country was plagued with locusts. In June of that year the good citizens of the capital were horrified to see their little valley invaded by these marauding insects, which stripped their gardens and plazas clean. In the fall, the government sorrowfully admitted that the production of gold in El Callao—which had revived the legends of El Dorado when it was discovered in 1864—was declining alarmingly; revenues were insufficient to cover current expenditures and meet the interest on the internal and foreign debts; and although the national treasury still possessed a surplus (less than 1,000,000 bolivars), all government employees (with the exception of the President of course) would be obliged to undergo a cut in salaries.

Although the years 1883 and 1884 ended peacefully enough, the depression and the locust invasions continued. Many business houses, including the country's sole paper mill which had opened but two years before, closed their doors. Then the government cut salaries for the second time. In a last act of desperation it decreed the free importation of cereals, but still the specter of famine stalked everywhere. The poor just didn't have the money with which to buy. Even the political picture took a turn for the worse.

General Joaquin Crespo, a protégé of Guzmán, had "inherited" the Presidency in April of 1884. Unaware of his ineptness as an administrator, he found the job of President much to his liking. With Guzmán off in his beloved Paris where he chose to live as Minister Plenipotentiary, Crespo laid plans to prolong his power. He began steam-rollering through congress a new Constitution which would lengthen the presidential term from two to four years.

In the Andes, and especially in San Cristóbal—the perpetual sore spot in the side of Venezuela—there were heard deep rumblings of discontent which threatened to break out in revolt at any moment.

CHAPTER TWO

Cipriano Castro, Fighting Lawyer

To understand, judge, and account for Juan Vicente Gómez, we must understand, or at least visualize the Venezuela of his day. Though the country had thrown off the Spanish yoke and assumed the status of a republic, it was not a republic in the true sense of the word. When Gómez took to himself the reins of government in 1908, this so-called republic was an infant—a stunted, sickly infant—incapable of administering to its own needs and showing little likelihood of growing out of its swaddling clothes. Politically inexperienced, emotionally unstable, its people were ignorant of their rights. They had already shown themselves easily persuaded to surrender their prerogatives to the politicians in power. They had yet to learn how to convert chaos into order and knew nothing of the art of self-government, that necessary background for any healthy growth as a nation. The era of darkness, almost medieval, bred confusion and spawned in crime and corruption legions of bellicose warlords and avaricious politicians. Scoundrels all of them, most of them were weaklings as well. Those who had climbed to power asserted that they had seen the light of liberty and progress. Yet they ruled not as public-spirited leaders but as conquerors who exploited the country to their own ends and maintained its people in a state of peonage.

Gómez was of this same stamp. He was a dictator and a tyrant rather than a patriot. His personal ambition matched that of any man. Yet it could be said of him that he was the nation's first administrator to achieve some semblance of order and prosperity, and to win for his country a measure of world respect instead of scorn. He was gifted with that rare temperament which made him capable of rising to far greater heights than had any of his predecessors. Time and

17

again during the last decade of his rule he struggled to throw off the stigma of despotism and attain the stature of a patriot, but prevailing circumstances were always against him. It was inevitable that his administration would be marred by the suppression, the intimidation, and the violence he must have required in order to maintain his power.

Surpassing former rulers by a wide margin in sagacity, acumen, and cunning, Gómez amassed a huge personal fortune through his public office. The political customs of his time were still very lax and were but a carry-over from the licentious periods dating back to Spanish rule when crime and corruption were widely practiced in order to cheat the Crown. The country, moreover, was almost continually in a state of political turmoil, never quite able to get its bearings on the road to democracy because it was constantly beset by devastating civil wars. The heartfelt and confused aspiration of the poor and well-to-do (there was no great wealth in the country) was the establishment of peace and order so that the country could grow in greatness and be as distinguished in peace as it had been in war under Bolívar. The humble members of the proletariat longed for steady, remunerative work but, instead, the unhappy lot of the males was the certain prospect of being conscripted and carried off to a bloody war which would, ostensibly, be fought on their behalf.

The masses lived in miserable hovels, some working on coffee or sugar plantations, others working their barren farms. Once off to the wars, their families would be left in want with no institutions to look after them, not even a school for their children. As if these afflictions were not enough, the belligerents—guerrillas, insurrectionists, and government troops—would purloin their meager possessions, the few ears of corn from the barren soil, the milk goat, the two pigs, the half-dozen hens; even the burro would be carried off. Not even the peace-loving and hard-working hacienda owner would be spared; his land would be ravaged and oftentimes his buildings burned to the ground while his sons fought and perished in still another far-off conflict. Most of these long-suffering people considered war a natural phenomenon, like hurricanes and earthquakes.

The new race that was being fused out of the mixture of Spaniard, Indian, and Negro, showed elements of weakness which retarded national progress and the stability of government. The uneducated *mestizo* masses were handicapped by a constant resentment, and were wholly lacking in restraint and the art of self-government. Impulsive and confused by vague reasoning, their insubordinate spirit refused to yield to the unification of a national party and the attainment of common aims. Divided by strong personal ambitions, the small existing parties were the casual personal followings of individual leaders rather than nation-wide organizations built around political philosophies.

The War of Independence had set the precedent for armed rebellion against tyranny. A characteristic feature of the Venezuelan psychology and political customs was that to join a revolutionary movement or to rise against the government was not considered at all dishonorable. Not dishonorable, that is to say, unless the conspirator was serving that government or used arms entrusted to him by the government for its defense. It appears that to be an enemy of the government was considered a stamp of honor. Often as not the revolutionary leader, or *caudillo* as he was called, commanded great prestige in his own bailiwick. He knew how to sway the masses with grandiloquent and hollow phrases. He knew how to win recruits from among the have-nots by arousing a desire for adventure and martial glory.

Many a *caudillo* was motivated by the sincere conviction that he was going to redeem the country when he exercised "the sacred right of insurrection." People were always hopefully awaiting the man who would bring about the miracles for which they all yearned—the end of civil warfare and the arrival of peace and political and social security. They looked eagerly toward their leader as the Messiah who would lead them from the bondage of tyranny and poverty. Though less than one in ten revolutions or "crusades" ended successfully, most of the men who attained the Presidency arrived there on the crest of armed revolt. From revolutions these men derived their strength and prestige, and once in power they learned quickly how to exploit both. In the process each evolved as a dictator in his own right, thus establishing the grounds for a new revolution. Venezuela's history, consequently, became a vicious cycle of armed rebellions.

The one *caudillo* to achieve some degree of peace, benign benevolence, and popularity was Antonio Guzmán, who laid seige to Caracas and overthrew the government in 1870, when Gómez was thirteen. Despite Guzmán's varied administrative talents, the improvements which characterized his government were infinitely less than the evils which followed. Practicing every form of graft imaginable and enriching himself and his retinue at the expense of the nation, his system of government contributed more than any other to the corruption of political customs in Venezuela. Yet such became the power and prestige of Antonio Guzmán during his long dictatorship, that few men dared to oppose him while he remained on Venezuelan soil.

It was during President Crespo's regime that the long-threatened revolt finally broke out. In January of 1885, the president of the state of Los Andes was forcibly ejected by the Conservatives. Simultaneously, there occurred an armed invasion by Venezuelan exiles from over the Colombian border. Thus came to an end fifteen years of peace, and there began another era of civil strife and revolutions. From now until 1900, insurrections would occur more or less frequently. In government offices, military jackets, heavy field boots and wide-brimmed campaign hats—once almost forgotten—replaced civilian dress. Persecutions, imprisonments, forced assessments and confiscations returned once again.

The border invasion, which was nothing more than a skirmish, was repelled, but from time to time the Conservatives made sporadic guerrilla attacks against government garrisons. What was apparent as the result of these far-flung forays was the total absence of systematic planning and a leader capable of assuming the supreme command. The Conservatives had in General Juan Bautista Araujo a *caudillo* wise in experience but very old in years. He barely had the stamina to spend an easy day in the saddle, much less the strength to lead a battle charge and swing a machete. The general had in effect retired from active campaigning but remained the titular head of the party. Acknowledging his drawbacks, General Araujo cast his expert eye about for a likely successor, and found him much sooner than he anticipated. The man he selected was a twenty-seven-year-old lawyer and ex-deputy to the National Congress by the name of Cipriano Castro.

As one of the disgruntled Conservative minority, Castro had stomped out of the legislative chamber in Caracas the year before muttering dark threats against Crespo and his henchmen. Back in his home town of Independencia, a short ride east from Gómez's farm, he had gone into private law practice but quickly tired of his humdrum existence and of the humble folk who shuffled in to consult him. He was consumed by an overpowering ambition that gnawed at him like a cancerous growth. Putting his glib tongue and flair for leadership to good use, he plunged headlong into revolutionary intrigue.

As friend, mentor, and companion-in-arms, it was Cipriano Castro who was destined to shape Gómez's future and unavoidably propel him into the role of dictator. Yet up to this period, neither man knew the other except by name. Gómez could not stomach dirty politics and the horrors of war that went on around him. Nor had he the time to keep abreast of current events. He was much too occupied in working the soil and in pursuing the girls in his leisure moments. So each man went on plodding his separate path, Gómez on his isolated farm, and Castro as a struggling lawyer whose livelihood from helping illiterates hurdle the red tape of bureaucracy was often halted by the armed clashes between the guerrilla Conservatives and the Liberal troops.

It was not until April of 1886 that Castro, now entrenched as one of the *caudillos* of the Conservatives, decided on a plan of action. Crespo had announced his decision to retire from public life, and congress, soon after, had elected Guzmán president for a fifth term. In acknowledging the honor in a cable from Paris, Guzmán explained that he would be detained for a few weeks due to preparations for the forthcoming marriage of his daughter Carlota to the French Duke, Charles de Morny.

Castro's decision was to strike in force before Guzmán arrived in Venezuela. In April he journeyed through the Andean towns to alert his followers and recruit new adherents. In May, General Araujo arranged a meeting in the high mountain city of Mérida between Castro and Colonel Colina, second in command of the city's garrison. The colonel, at odds with his superior, joined the movement and agreed to head the outbreak in the city. The students of the university were to take an active part. As for San Cristóbal, which was garrisoned by a strong hostile force, Castro deemed it prudent to move his operations as far away from that city as possible. The young *caudillo* had yet to undergo his baptism of fire and prove his mettle as a revolutionary leader.

Before dawn on June 8th, "Colonel" Castro's small revolutionary army took over Independencia after heavy fighting. Simultaneously, Colonel Colina's group in Mérida seized the barracks and gained control of the city, and another armed band under General Prato invaded Venezuela from Colombia. Castro's campaign met with one success after another; almost every town and village in the Táchira area fell under his growing army's onslaught. On June 23rd he was encamped in the village of Capacho Viejo when it was attacked by a superior government force.

Forewarned of the attackers' movements, General Prato had dispatched a battalion of guerrillas to attack their flank should Castro need assistance. Bypassing the main road, the guerrillas took to the hills and approached the group of houses known as La Mulera to ask for directions. It was Gómez himself who went out to meet the motley band, some on mule and horseback, others on foot, all of them laden down with war gear. Time and again during the past few days he had heard the valley reverberate with the sound of rifle fire. Now, it appeared, the war was drawing closer to his door. What, he wondered, did these sons of misfortune want of him?

The guerrilla captain addressed the *campesino* by name. Would Señor Gómez be so kind as to direct them so that they could reach Capacho Viejo unseen by hostile eyes? If the captain knew who he was, thought Gómez, then surely he knew that he was a neutral, that he had friends in both camps. The captain had asked a small favor of him, and it was not in his nature or upbringing to refuse. He smiled as he replied that he would be glad to oblige. Moreover, he would take the time to escort them personally.

If the captain wondered why such a strong specimen was not out fighting in a man's war, he said nothing. After Gómez buttoned on a clean white tunic, donned a sombrero and tucked his trousers into leather puttees, he mounted the sturdy mountain pony that a peon saddled for him. The good-bys to the womenfolk and children over, he led the way along a narrow path that skirted rock-strewn fields, and then on up the slopes to the treeless summits of the low Sierra de Capacho. As the caravan picked its way northward along the lonely, winding trail that led ever upward toward tawny brown and gray peaks that towered in the thin Andean sunshine, the grave *campesino* made small talk with the captain. He learned that the fighting had gone well for the Conservatives, that their military might had grown, and that in Colonel Castro they had found a man who took to the sword like a duck takes to water. Unfortunately, the young lawyer from Independencia was now on the defensive. Perhaps at this moment he and his worthies were fighting for their very lives. Dread the thought! But, God willing, they would arrive in time to route the enemy.

The declining sun had bathed the dun-colored slopes in a golden glow as the caravan descended the grade at an ever-quickening pace toward the rear of Capacho Viejo. The white and brown adobe houses of the village, nestled on the hillside, crowded down, row beneath row, to the winding road which led to Independencia and points east. As Gómez reined his horse aside to permit the soldiers to precede him, he could clearly hear the sounds of gunfire and could see dark figures darting about in the plaza.

What was it that drew Juan Vicente into the village? Was it the dark-eyed señorita he knew who lived at the head of the steep street? Or was it a new-found sadistic desire to witness the contest to the death between desperate mountaineers and government troops? A few moments later, Juan Vicente unhurriedly tethered his horse at a neat white house, paid his respects to the frightened young lady of the dwelling, and then moved on cautiously to watch the battle at closer range.

Below him, only a short block away, the battle ebbed and flowed around the village plaza whose stunted saplings gave meager refuge to the figures which crouched behind them. Suddenly there was a great surge from all quarters as the attackers and defenders rushed to meet each other on the trampled ground. No cowards these! Government red and blue mingled with homespun gray and brown. Flashing blades rent the air. Hoarse cries and the sharp rattle of small arms fire echoed long and loud from adobe walls.

Juan Vicente Gómez stood watching the bloody melee like a man transfixed. He saw a guerrilla officer wrest a rifle from a soldier and down him with it by a blow across the face. He saw the officer raise the rifle and fire point-blank at a charging enemy. In that instant he glimpsed the pale face framed in a jet black beard and the glint of gold stars on the campaign hat. It came to him in a flash that this was the famed Cipriano Castro, the fighting lawyer.

Again and again Castro, for the bearded figure was he, fired until his gun was empty. Then he flung it to the ground, grasped a machete from a dying man, and charged into the thick of the fight. Time and again a rifle was leveled at him, but the bullet failed to find its mark. Uninjured, imbued with rash courage, Castro swung his machete right and left, parried blows, and landed the blade home. First one man then another and another went down before his onslaught. Once Gómez lost sight of him among the struggling figures and feared him dead. But there he was again, filling the breach in still another quarter, still fighting like a man possessed.

Gómez watched fascinated, all his attention focused on this one man. There stirred in him a warm admiration for so brave a warrior. Never had he seen such a display of courage, such an utter disregard for death. He marveled that the man was still alive and uninjured. Certainly the good saints protected him. "From that moment," Gómez reminisced long afterward, "my admiration for Cipriano Castro was without bounds. I knew in my heart that here was a man of extraordinary skill and courage. It was as clear to me as the sun in heaven that this guerrilla would play a great role in our country's history."

Before the pitched battle in the plaza had finally ebbed and the last of the enemy troops had been put to flight, Juan Vicente had returned to the house of his *novia* of the moment. It was there that he heard the last distant shots die away in strange echoes, and felt the stillness of death settle upon Capacho Viejo. Another day, another battle was over. Where would it all lead to? When would it end? Among the swath of dead in the blood-drenched plaza lay the body of the guerrilla captain. Dead also was a good friend of the Gómez family, General Evaristo Jaime, commander of the attacking force.

It was when he had gone out into the gathering dusk to mount his horse that Gómez was apprized of his friend's death. So fate had caught up with him. He would have to find Castro and ask permission to bury his friend's body. As though in a distorted dream he rode through the shadows and scenes of death. In the government house on a corner of the plaza he was ushered into a whitewashed room lit by a kerosene lamp hanging from a crossbeam. He had removed his hat like any humble citizen, but it was with confidence and dignity that he confronted the guerrilla commander who leaned against a littered table.

Gómez had been told that Castro carried the blood of Motilone Indians—a formidable tribe which lived in complete isolation in the tangled jungles of western Zulia. The fact that no one in the Andes had the remotest idea of what a Motilone looked like permitted the allegation to pass uncontested. However, one glance at the high sweep of the forehead, the finely-chiseled nose and the thin sensuous mouth convinced Gómez that more Spanish blood coursed through Castro's veins than through his own. In contrast to Gómez's stocky frame, Castro was slender, though slightly shorter; his skin was white and he had the long delicate fingers of an aristocrat. Black smouldering eyes set off an elongated face framed by an imposing black mustache and a neatly-trimmed beard. Fingering his own straggly brown mustache, perhaps Gómez was conscious for the first time of his own physical shortcomings. In other ways too, Castro was everything Gómez was not. Whereas the farmer and cattleman spoke slowly and softly in keeping with his rustic simplicity, Castro's speech and mannerisms matched his sleek, urbane appearance. When he spoke, his articulation was close-clipped, intense, and every muscle of his face went into play. When he listened, his behavior was that of impatient courtesy. As a lawyer, Castro was known to betray at times a contempt for others in his dignity of manner, but his personality and intelligence were such that he commanded the admiration and respect of many public figures of his day.

"Yes, you can have him," he answered Gómez's request. "It will save us the trouble." And then impressed by the stranger's own magnetic personality he asked, "And what might your name be, señor?"

"Gómez, Juan Vicente Gómez." He paused for recognition.

"Ah, yes, I know of you." Castro nodded politely. "My pleasure, Señor Gómez."

"I have the farm La Mulera close by to San Antonio," Gómez continued. "It was there that your captain came to ask the way, and I rode with him and his men over the ridges. The fighting, I saw some of it from up the street. You were *magnifico*, truly *magnifico*."

"Indeed?" Castro smiled his pleasure, white teeth showing through his beard. "Please!" He indicated a chair with a rawhide bottom. "Perhaps you would consider becoming one of us, a supporter, I mean. You have not yet chosen sides I hear. We need men, good men." He looked at Gómez sharply, judging him to be a man who held tightly to his purse strings. "And we need money and guns. The war may be long but we are going to win." He pounded a fist into a palm. "We've got to win!"

Gómez appeared noncommittal, but he had already made up his mind. "I am just a simple farmer," he explained, choosing his words carefully. "My farm, my cattle keep me busy, but I will give the matter thought. I suppose I shall soon have to make up my mind, though living in Conservative territory, I don't have much choice." He smiled at the implication.

"Pues bien, perhaps we can talk about it again under more favorable circumstances. You will want to get on with burying your friend, and I am keeping you. Besides," here Castro nodded toward a group in the doorway, "I appear to have more visitors."

"Permit me." He led the way out through the narrow passageway, apparently looking for someone. To the sergeant-of-the-guard lounging against the massive main door he gave orders that two men be assigned to assist Señor Gómez with his grim task. Then he grasped Gómez's hand in a firm grip and said with a soft warmth in his voice, "God willing, we shall meet soon again." And then he was gone.

The corpse slung over the saddle by two bandoleered guerrillas, Gómez led his horse toward the crumbling wall of the cemetery, a borrowed lantern lighting the way. His burden finally consigned to God through the help of a harassed gravedigger and a sad-eyed *padre,* he mounted and set off toward the main road. By the light of the stars he wended his way slowly homeward, his thoughts tumbling over each other like a rushing mountain stream.

CHAPTER THREE

Conspiracy

When his troops occupied San Cristóbal two weeks later, Castro rode into the city as a general. It was while he was busy setting up a civil administration and taking on supplies that Gómez went to visit him at his headquarters. Warm expressions of friendship were exchanged, and Gómez handed over a sizeable sum in cash, asking no receipt in return. He expressed one concern: the war so far had been fought on friendly territory; the most difficult campaigning still lay ahead.

To which the impetuous fighter retorted: "If it's the last thing I ever do, I'm going to topple the Tiger (Crespo) from his perch."

Gómez counseled caution. *"Cuidado, compadre*—be sure of yourself before you leap. It would be bad enough to lose those costly arms, but your life . . . that is another thing."

At the head of his growing army, Castro headed north to do battle and conquer. From time to time news of his slow but steady progress through the Andean towns filtered through to Gómez at La Mulera. But then came the dreaded news of the arrival in Venezuela of Antonio Guzmán on August 27th. Still the cool, shrewd politician at fifty-seven, Guzmán personally took charge of the military situation. Troops were dispatched to the Andes by way of the sea and Lake Maracaibo. His major stratagem, however, was a long telegram to old General Araujo at his farm, summoning him to Caracas and calling him to account for the deeds of his protégé.

General Araujo rode after Castro, overtook him in the high mountain village of Timotes, and endeavored to restrain him. At first Castro was indignant, then sullen. He had gambled everything on this venture and to him his chances of success still looked good. Araujo finally showed him the telegram from Guzmán which held him re-

sponsible for peace in the Andes. And to clinch his argument he conveyed the bad news that four thousand troops were on the way by
sea to attack the rebel army in the rear.

Araujo's stand was decisive, and Castro turned south to disband
his forces and hide his guns with the hope that a better occasion would
arise.

In September, Guzmán formally accepted the Presidency, but
chose to live on his ostentatious estate in Antímano, where his ministers were required to report in their carriages daily to give an account of themselves or to attend cabinet sessions. During December
work continued feverishly on the railroad from Caracas to Antímano.
Guzmán inaugurated the railroad from Caracas to Petare, and widespread alarm was occasioned by the news from Guayana that the
British had encroached on Venezuelan soil; these were the salient
impressions of the end of 1886.

Still feeling in an expansive mood the following year, Guzmán
lifted the lid from political censorship of the press—an act which
he soon had cause to regret. Politics being a favorite Venezuelan preoccupation, the press in those days, when censorship permitted, took
a fierce delight in carrying on defamatory campaigns against the men
in power. In that, of course, there was nothing contrary to true democratic procedure. The same thing was being practiced in the so-called
democracies which the Venezuelans so heartily admired. But these
campaigns were carried on in Venezuela where racial conditions and
customs are very different and where defamatory propaganda often
led to insults, and from there to fatal encounters.

The Venezuelan *caballero* of the nineteenth century always went
armed, not from fear of bandits, but to be ready for any "personal
affair." In Venezuela, the preliminary formalities and the classic encounters of the duel were conveniently dispensed with. "Where the
steer is killed is the place to skin it," was a very common saying, used
in the sense that when an insult was received it should be avenged on
the spot without delay. To the sensitive Venezuelans the insult could
be any expression at all susceptible of disrespectful or sarcastic interpretation, although it was often necessary to stretch a point to find
an intentional offense. The duel was to the death, for at the first provoc-
ative words revolvers were pulled out. One of the two combatants,
and sometimes both, were killed or wounded. It would have seemed

Juan Vicente Gómez as he appeared in 1918.

ridiculous to them and unworthy of their manhood to exchange blows. Such affairs could be avoided only by treating each other with civility, consideration, and courtesy. That was the rule, since it was understood that otherwise an incident was being provoked, and acceptance was obligatory.

It being beneath his dignity to hunt down his tormentors with a gun when their attacks became too violent and embarrassing, Guzmán retaliated by throwing them into the Rotunda—Caracas' colonial prison. Throughout the country opposition papers were suppressed, among them the religious paper *El Ancora,* whose director, a priest, was banished from the country.

Guzmán's administration was, for the general good of the country, a dictatorship based on force. To maintain that force he disregarded one of the tenets of his party, i.e., that in a land of free peoples forced enlistment is unthinkable. During the entire period of his administration, forced enlistment was practiced openly, and it fell only on the poor and unprotected. It would be much the same with Gómez when he rose to power. A dictator relies on a strong army to maintain his position.

Guzmán's absolute dictatorship, his overbearing manner, and his accumulation of wealth by shady deals provoked several assassination plots against him. Eight sojourns abroad had begun to alienate him from his friends and followers. Perceiving public opinion growing against him, he turned over the Presidency to a protégé, General Hermógenes López, and departed for France with his family. Guzmán was never to see his homeland again.

During the last days of 1887 the British warship *Forward* arrived in La Guaira from Trinidad bearing an ultimatum to the Venezuelan government. Venezuela's conflict with the British dated back to 1835 and concerned the disputed boundary line between Venezuela and British Guiana. Only a few months previously Venezuela had severed diplomatic relations with Great Britain on the charge that the British had encroached on Venezuelan soil. Now the British were retaliating by demanding material satisfaction for the illegal imprisonment of several crew members by Venezuelan guerrillas four years before. Faced with a seven-day ultimatum to pay or the prospect of war, López's administration grudgingly made payment.

By 1888 it became apparent that President López was nothing

more than another ruthless dictator. From Trinidad, General Crespo wrote a scathing letter denouncing him as a tyrant. He declared that López was making a farce of Venezuela's institutions, he was sending his enemies into exile or imprisoning them in the Rotunda, and was even jailing members of congress so that he could fill their places with his own men. All of these charges were true. However, before this letter began to circulate clandestinely in Caracas, congress had elected the Federal Council, which in turn had chosen Doctor Rojas Paúl as the next president.

A stout, bearded fellow, habitually bubbling over with good cheer and affability, Rojas was every inch the politician he appeared to be. Of a certainty he was the chosen mouthpiece of his mentor, Guzmán, in whose shadow he had long followed, but he was not the disciplined henchman he had been taken for. Coached by long letters from Guzmán in Paris, Rojas replied with jovial assurances of his loyalty, but pointedly ignored his orders. With the President's power firmly in his hands, he meant to use it. To the consternation of his fellow Liberals, one of his first official acts was to release all political prisoners; to roars of rage from Paris, he authorized the re-entry on Venezuelan soil of several religious orders.

He permitted municipal elections for councilmen, despite the fact that many of these affairs culminated in miniature civil wars. Free elections, it had long been maintained, were the very foundation of the republic, but the spectacle often disillusioned many a righteous citizen. Throughout the campaigns each party intimidated its adversary, and, from name-calling popular demonstrations degenerated into bloody contests in the streets. It was a common sight for belligerent "generals" to appear at the polls, each with his squads of henchmen, all of them ready to do battle at the drop of a hat.

In Caracas' Central University, constitutional law was being taught from the book written by the Colombian, Florentino Gonzálo, who in his youth had been involved in the unsuccessful attempt on the life of Simón Bolívar. Even in his doddering old age, Gonzálo continued to labor under the belief that it was possible for the political system of the United States to function in Latin America. No one doubted it in Venezuela either, for no one knew the differences of temperament and psychology between the Latin and North American peoples.

In due course another fiery letter came from Trinidad, which was openly commented upon in the Caracas paper *El Siglo*. This time Crespo attacked Rojas. Said a contemporary of the now garrulous and unhappy exile: "It appears that the Tiger is stewing in his own bitterness."

In the Andes, Castro and Gómez read the editorial in *El Siglo* and merely shrugged. In South America, the fortunes of politics are fickle. He who is in power today may be out tomorrow.

To Castro, the time was not propitious to try another sortie. Rojas was much too popular with the public. Then too, he had received reports that Crespo planned to invade Venezuela and seize the government by force.

Backed by the large colony of Venezuelan exiles living in Trinidad, Crespo attempted to carry out such a plot, but after a series of mishaps was captured on the Caribbean by a Venezuelan gunboat. Imprisoned for a time in the Rotunda, he was exiled for a year by President Rojas.

As was to be expected, President Rojas, despite his failing health, followed in the way of his predecessors and sought to prolong his stay in power. He devised new reforms to the Constitution, including a longer presidential term of four years, and he sent his project in secret to the state legislatures just when they were ready to convene. As they were packed with men of Rojas' choosing there were almost no modifications—only the Andes put in a heedless protest.

In the Andes the political front was quiet; General Araujo still exerted his sobering influence and was hopefully mentioned as a presidential candidate. In Independencia, Cipriano Castro had resumed his practice of law; and at La Mulera, now a growing village, Juan Vicente Gómez labored long hours toward the accumulation of wealth.

It had become a ritual of Juan Vicente to spend a few hours each Sunday at Castro's home. They had become bosom friends, but theirs was not a friendship born of common interests. Rather, Castro, the politician, vented his hate of Crespo and Rojas while Gómez, the cattleman and farmer, listened in shocked silence. Eager ears took in Castro's eye-witness accounts of shady deals in the capital, the absolute control of congress by the man in power, the corruption of public officials, the graft of public funds, all the scandals which had passed from one regime to the next. As their friendship grew, Castro confided to Juan Vicente his hopes and fears and his plans for the future.

Castro's charming and cultured wife, doña Zoila, was likewise impressed by Gómez's strange but strong personality. When she interrupted the animated political discussions in the main *sala* to serve steaming cups of black Andean coffee, doña Zoila observed Gómez closely. She fervently hoped that his quiet and reserved nature would be a sobering influence over her husband's volatile and impetuous temperament. As was usual in matters concerning politics and war, doña Zoila was not consulted for her opinion. The woman's sphere was in the home as she very well knew, and she could only pray for the best.

But there was to be no curbing of the scheming and ambitious Castro. He craved action, and he diligently prepared himself for it. He continued to acquire contraband arms, smuggled over the Colombian border through the help of Gómez. Often as not these were rusty old carbines which had passed through many hands. Occasionally there turned up a few modern Winchesters and Mausers, which were highly prized. When one or two burro-loads of rifles and ammunition arrived during the dark hours of the night after a long trek over mountain trails, they were immediately unloaded and buried in the fields outside of Independencia.

Castro was smilingly confident that the hour of reckoning was drawing near. Already the popularity of Rojas was waning and the man himself was displaying weakness. Just a short period of watchful waiting until—perhaps a slip by Rojas, or a sign of help from some unexpected quarter. And then the thrust!

"But what of the Tiger?" queried the cautious Juan Vicente. "He's back on his hacienda in Guarico."

"Crespo?" Now the schemer was thoughtful. "Yes, he's the unknown factor. He and his Guarico cowboys. No telling what he'll do, but I'll have to take the chance."

"They say he's a good fighter," Gómez observed.

"And what a fighter! Did you ever read an account of his battles? No?" Dark eyes flashed. "Imagine crossing swords with the Tiger himself! That would be something to see! But I think I can beat him, Juan Vicente. I think I can beat him."

"Guarico is a long way off, more than half way to Caracas."

"So it is, but there is more than one route to get to Mecca! We don't go through Guarico, my friend. We bypass it. Oh, it won't be easy, I grant you. It will be a long, hard grind. But wait until you see Caracas! You'll forget the fight and sweat, and you'll forget these wretched mountains. Caracas! What a city! And what women!"

And so the suave, glib lawyer weaved his spell over the uncouth mountain peasant who worshiped at his feet. Juan Vicente Gómez was unable to help himself. He who was born to lead men, who had bowed to no man as his master, now permitted himself to become the servile disciple. He became engulfed in the whirlpool of intrigue. All too soon he would be sucked to the depths of despair by ill fortune and defeat, but by sheer stamina and will power he would emerge at the very top, safe, serene, and triumphant.

CHAPTER FOUR

Failure

Toward the end of 1889 it became apparent that President Rojas would be unable to serve longer than his two-year term. He was observed to be suffering weaknesses of health which his enemies attributed to his flings with a beautiful diva of an opera company then visiting Caracas. Although Rojas managed to appear in person with his annual message to congress in March of the following year, it was to announce his retirement from public office. Two weeks later his Minister of the Interior, Dr. Andueza Palacio, was inaugurated as President.

The news came as a surprise to Castro, and it placed him in a quandary. During his sojourn in the capital five years before, the high placed politician had taken him under his wing. They had gone out to stag parties together. They had imbibed the same brand of cognac. And they both had an eye for a well-turned ankle. Small wonder then that Castro threw scruples aside to dispatch a telegram to the new President expressing his congratulations and placing himself at his orders.

"What is he like?" Gómez wanted to know.

"Short, heavy, with the usual whiskers. Not much to look at, but a fine fellow."

Andueza Palacio may have lacked the personality and aggressiveness of either Guzmán or Rojas but his habits belied his mien of pious, country doctor. He dedicated his two years in office to a mundane life of pleasures and dissipation. With his retinue of followers and hangers-on he frequented the capital's brothels and gambling halls where he tossed gold pieces recklessly right and left. When one of his ministers cautioned the President that his conduct would surely

34

bring on a civil war, Andueza Palacio replied with calloused uncon-
cern: "I don't believe it, señor, not even the cocks know how to fight
in this country; you have to import them from Puerto Rico!"

The carefree President, however, had reckoned without General
Crespo, the fighting cowboy from the plains of Guarico.

Reforming the Constitution had come to be regarded by the country's presidents as a hereditary prerogative. Andueza Palacio had proceeded to institute his own reforms, putting special emphasis on the
clauses relating to the election of the President and the duration of
his term. Congress was to convene on February 20, 1892, upon
the expiration of his term, but when he found that he lacked the
necessary quorum to ratify his remodeled Constitution, Andueza
Palacio prevented that body from assembling.

When the twentieth of February passed and General Crespo
learned that the President had failed to relinquish his office to the
president of the Federal Council as stipulated by the Constitution, he
issued a proclamation of war. Here was a case of a "legal" revolution
against a revolutionary government. Yet Crespo was denouncing
Andueza Palacio for the same political crime he himself had attempted to commit six years before. The truth of the matter was that
Crespo's fortunes had ebbed considerably. Here was a heaven-sent
opportunity to recoup his losses. He was now the acknowledged leader
in both military and political circles. His ulterior motives would be
overshadowed by the ostensible design of fighting for a principle. So
in self-righteous anger the opportunist issued his manifesto of war
in his native state of Guarico, and adherents by the thousand rallied
to his standard.

The same charge can be made of Castro and Gómez, and history bears this out. Since his return from Caracas, Castro had acquired
a large personal following, and by 1892 we find him vying with General Araujo for the leadership of the Andean Conservatives. The
cantankerous old soldier was no match for this talented and energetic
young lawyer, whose dynamic personality dazzled the simple and impressionable mountain people. It was inevitable that Araujo, long
bound by a strict code of honor and ardent patriotism, came to the
parting of the ways with this overly ambitious and ruthless protégé.
Castro's decision to take to the field on the side of lawlessness and
despotism was the final straw.

"I've done it," Castro informed Gómez at a hastily arranged meeting. "I've just sent off a wire to Andueza Palacio offering my services. Crespo has risen in Guarico. It's now or never, Juan Vicente. I'm calling my men together and I am counting on you to go with us."

"To go where?" came the sharp retort.

"On to Caracas, where else? Don't you see? Most of the government troops will be on our side. Crespo will be on the defensive. How can we lose?"

"But what of Araujo? He's not for Andueza Palacio. He's against him."

"To the devil with Araujo! The Andes will follow me, not that broken down war horse!"

"And what makes you think the President will put you in charge here?"

"I know Andueza Palacio, and I think he knows me. With state governments collapsing all over the country, he'll be calling on all the men he can get. If only his reply will come through before Crespo cuts the wires . . ."

"And what would I get out of all this?" asked the sly Juan Vicente.

"Always the businessman, eh? Look! You sell your coffee, your steers. You clear maybe one hundred per cent profit. But this is something bigger. Much bigger. On this kind of a deal you can be sure of a thousand per cent on everything you put in. Maybe more. Don't worry. You'll be richly rewarded . . . and you can be sure that there will be a good-paying job to go with it."

"But I'm not a soldier," Gómez countered. "I've never slain a man in my life . . . I hope to God I never will. I've told you that I would back you with money, and that I will continue to do. But don't ask me to carry a gun and expect me to use it. Honestly, Cipriano, I can't do it."

"Well, then, let's put it this way. You are my closest friend. I'll need your advice, your moral support. I'll need someone who knows this terrain well. You are the one man who knows the entire mountain region like the palm of your hand. If anyone knows the untraveled mountain trails, the short cuts for a revolutionary army, it's you. Say you will do it. Say you will accompany me as my aide just to show us the way."

Juan Vicente resigned himself to his fate. "All right," he answered,

"I'll go along, but on one condition. I will serve as your guide, not as a fighter. And remember this, I make this decision only to please you."

It had taken considerable persuasion, for Gómez was rooted to his home and the soil and had no desire to seek new horizons. Besides, his woman was about to have another baby. But perhaps the promise of a high government post and its attendant potentialities for graft won him over. Gómez chose, then, not the safe sure path of the successful farmer and cattleman but the glorious and exciting life of a soldier and satellite of a scheming general, insecure though it might be and fraught with danger and perhaps death. So, at thirty-four, Gómez stood at the most important crossroads of his life. What actually prompted him—always conservative and cautious as he was —to decide such a gamble was worth the risk, will remain one of the enigmas of his life. "I never had the desire to be a soldier or politician," he wrote to Castro sixteen years later. "It was you who induced me to leave my hacienda and enter public life . . . my only guiding motive has been my great admiration and sincere affection for you."

With Castro appointed commander-in-chief of the Andean government forces by a now frightened and tottering President, the Conservatives split into two camps. The remaining group, spurred on by Araujo, who was outraged by Andueza Palacio's abuses in office, rose up in arms under Crespo's standard.

In March of 1892, Castro's ill-fated army trudged along the tortuous paths of the Andes in pursuit of the rebels, Juan Vicente Gómez behind the vanguard, the three gold stars of a colonel glistening on his wide-brimmed campaign hat. Flanking him on the march were his brother Juancho and his cousin Eustóquio Gómez, captains both. Toward the east, on the *llanos* of Guarico and Apure, General Crespo's formidable army already was sweeping north.

Stretching southward from Lake Valencia for over two hundred miles are the most remarkable plains in the world, the *llanos* of Venezuela. Neither prairie nor desert, they are intermediate between the two, depending on the seasons. There are no rolling prairies, no undulations, no sandhills or ridges, only flat, almost treeless plains covered with occasional clumps of chaparro trees, moriche palms, and tall prairie grass, which stretch from the Orinoco deltas to the spurs of the Andes. There are only two seasons, the wet and the dry. During the rainy season the *llanos* are a vast sea of green, waving grass. In some places the sandy soil is inundated for miles or it is dotted profusely with lagoons and criss-crossed with streams that pour into the many rivers which have become rushing torrents. Deer, half wild cattle, and herds of wild horses still roam the land as in the time of Bolívar. From the fringe of hills ferocious jaguars still stalk the land preying on the cattle. There are myriads of beautiful birds of many hued plumage, pigeons, quail, prairie chickens, and ducks. There are electric eels up to six feet in length which are powerful enough to stun and drown a horse. There are armadillos, turtles, poisonous snakes, and huge alligators. And in some of the rivers swim the fierce, flesh-eating *caribe,* a fish which will attack and devour the man or beast that inadvertently enters the water with a fresh scratch or open flesh wound.

Toward the end of the dry season in April the land has become parched. The streams, some of the rivers, and most of the lagoons have dried up. From a cloudless sky the unrelentless sun bakes the land with an oven-hot heat. The once pea-green grass is now withered and the color of the soil. Sometimes it is set on fire, leaving thousands of acres black with ash and soot. There are countless tracks leading to a muddy water-hole, around which are gathered exhausted, thirsty animals and birds. In this dry, silent world nature's pulse-beat throbs but faintly.

Here dwelt the *llanero*—the cowboy of the plains—who earned his livelihood from the cattle and wild horses. He was a coarse and primitive creature, accustomed to a rugged and sometimes harsh living. On foot he was humble and awkward. In the saddle he was arrogant and superb. It was the *llanero* who was the mainstay in Venezuela's War of Independence, the hero of many of its civil wars. Together with his horse, his prowess as a fighting machine was unequaled. He was a tough and indomitable fighter, afraid of nothing. To bed at eight and up at four in the morning (Crespo adhered to these hours even while President), he spent twelve hours a day in the saddle with nothing to sustain him but black coffee in the morning and a meal of beef and beans at night. If he became thirsty under the hot sun he drank from a stagnant pool; if he became hungry he took a bite from the strip of venison or beef he carried under his sweaty saddle. He could hunt without a gun, swing his *reata* with an unerring eye, and crack his fifteen-foot whip with a noise like thunder. He was an expert swimmer, as was his horse, and he knew how to fight off alligators while fording a raging stream. And he could fashion anything of leather, and fasten a house together with bush twine in place of nails. Though he ate without bread and was a stranger to vegetables, the *llanero* was a healthy, self-sufficient creature who loved the great outdoors and prized his horse above his woman. Given his sturdy, faithful pony, his blue and red woolen *cobija* rolled up on the saddle horn, his strip of beef under the saddle, and his chaw of home-grown tobacco, the *llanero* was ready and willing to go anywhere. This was the type of soldier that followed General Crespo on his march on Caracas.

Despite the bravery of the *llanero* and the Andino, the caliber of Castro's and Crespo's troops left much to be desired; to call them an "army" is to use the term loosely. Of the rank and file, roughly ninety per cent were illiterate and had never received even rudimentary military training. Many had yet to fire their first rifle. And as for arms, there were never enough of the smuggled magazine rifles to go around. Only one man in four was fortunate enough to receive this coveted weapon; the majority armed themselves with the machete— the tool of all work. Outside of one or two antiquated artillery pieces, they possessed almost no military equipment to speak of. The wearing apparel of the Andino was scanty and ill-suited for the rugged campaigning; most did not even possess shoes but wore *alpargatas,* fiber sandals common to the peasantry. Rations never varied; whether in camp or on the march, the fare was beans, rice, and plantains, augmented once a day with a chunk of beef from the herd of cattle which followed behind every army.

In both Castro's and Crespo's armies there were many self-styled "generals." "Colonels" were even more numerous. None of these officers had studied at any military academy. Few had seen regular army service. Most of them had assumed their titles solely because they had furnished their quota of "volunteer" troops to some campaign, putting themselves at the service of the government or of the revolution.

Contrary to the forced conscription method used by successive government regimes, enlistment in the revolutionary army was regarded as voluntary, and to a large degree this was so. The exceptions were the peons on the large haciendas who—as in the feudal system of old—lived the lives of vassals, sacrificing their private rights to the claims of their feudal lords, the *caudillos* or the self-styled generals. The regulations of the revolutionary army were strict; those involved in acts of rape, pillage, wanton destruction, insubordination, or desertion were summarily dealt with by execution on the spot. The revolutionary soldier received no pay, the incentive being the dubious prospect of a bonus payment and the laurels of victory.

Once again Cipriano Castro's military venture ended as a humiliating failure. In seven months his army progressed only as far as the lowlands of Trujillo. Andueza Palacio fled the country.

Crespo had swept all before him. At the head of his victorious army he rode into the capital on October 7. Ensconced in the presidential chair in the *Casa Amarilla* and surrounded by his generals, he dictated a proclamation declaring himself in power and naming his cabinet.

CHAPTER FIVE

Exile

One would think that his recent experience should have cured Gómez of all notions of a revolutionist's career, but such was not the case. More than once he had stood firmly and unafraid on the treacherous, rocky slopes of the Andes, the hills reverberating with the sound of shot and shell. His broad nostrils had inhaled the acrid smell of burning powder and the pungent odor of sweaty leather—and he had found himself. He was in his element now and he must stick to it.

Back home at La Mulera, Gómez faced grave problems. As with Castro, there was now a price on his head, and it would be but a matter of days before their properties were confiscated by Crespo's forces. He had much cause to be bitter, but strangely, his faith in Castro remained unshaken. "I still have confidence in you, *compadre*," he told him. "What happened was no fault of yours. Perhaps next time —if there should be a next time—we shall be able to strike quicker and harder." They shook hands on that and agreed to meet at a rendezvous over the border.

Sorrowfully, Juan Vicente prepared himself for exile. While the men of his clan scoured neighboring farms for burros, his peons packed the most precious possessions. What the clan would not be able to cart off they gave away or loaned to friends for safekeeping. Some day they would be back, but for now their homes must be stripped bare. Crespo's minions would find La Mulera a ghost village picked clean as a bone in a buzzard's nest. It was Juan Vicente's order that most of the women and children would have to walk. The men would carry heavy packs. Far too valuable to be used for human cargo, the horses and burros were loaded with everything portable—cooking pots and other gear, farming implements, chickens, food, and sacks of precious seeds. With armylike thoroughness the *cacique* of the clan strode up and down the line, checking here, discarding there. Astride one of the animals sat Gómez's mother, Hermenegilda. Beside her walked his woman Dionisia, cradling in her arms Gómez's son, Augusto Alí, born six months before. The goats and cattle were tethered one behind the other. The entire caravan was to travel over narrow mountain trails, by-passing the highway to avoid detection and capture.

The sun had reached its zenith when the exodus began. The caravan picked its way over the rock-strewn fields, skirted dense *quebradas* and clusters of challenging boulders. This was a land of stone. Everywhere, in field and valley, on every mountain slope, rocks lay more profusely and far larger in size than on any abandoned New England farm. Where the plowed fields ended and the first steep slope began, the path crossed a murmuring stream sparkling in the thin Andean sunshine. Juan Vicente knew this spot well. He had played and hunted here as a boy, had gathered watercress from the shallows and scooped minnows from the cold, clear pools. Blackberries still grew in profusion in the tangled underbrush. Sour oranges again lay rotting in the shaded nook where a tousled-haired youngster had dropped a seed many years before. Along the twisting path Juan Vicente and his brothers had often dragged saplings and brushwood for the family hearth. Now, trees were few and far between. Trees did not appear to thrive in this part of the country. Perhaps it was because those that had been cut down had not been replaced. Juan Vicente loved the earth and everything that grew. As he climbed the path, bent low under his load, his heart was not so cold that he did not occasionally look about him and take a last lingering look at a familiar landmark. It might be many years before he would see this place again, but he would be back. Yes, he would be back; of that he was certain.

Over the treeless ridges of the low Sierra de Capacho the caravan followed the lonely trail that had been worn smooth through the years by the feet of smugglers and exiles. The trek was not a difficult one, but it was long. As the crow flies, the distance from La Mulera to the spot in Colombia Gómez chose as a hideout is roughly eleven miles. Actually, the caravan covered almost twice this distance over twisting, winding paths.

Scouts had been sent on ahead to reconnoiter the route and prepare an encampment at a friendly smuggler's shack near the border. When the weary travelers arrived at the waiting campfire the tawny brown and gray peaks stood black against the luminous sky of night and the mountain cold had settled down like an icy poncho. After a pause and a stretch, their bellies full of hot gruel, the clan crossed the crest of the last mountain. Below them to the south they could see the few sputtering lights of San Antonio. At the foot of the slope flowed the Río Táchira which demarcated the frontier. Border patrols did not venture at night to this lonely spot. Led by guides who knew every foot of the river, the tribe and the animals forded the ice cold stream, dragged themselves up on the farther bank, and continued their trek for almost three hours more.

The *cacique* of the tribe was pleased with what he saw in the light of day—broad, rolling acres that stretched west to the high North Santander range, and north to the large border town of Cúcuta. Good cattle country this, and a safe haven too for all of his tribe. This he knew from the experiences of other exiles and from what he had observed on his many trips. He knew too that the cost of land and labor was low, much lower in fact than in his own country. Strapped to his waist, safe from prying eyes, he carried the bulk of his life's savings—gold *morocotas,* each worth four head of cattle at least. At the bank in Cúcuta he had a small sum on deposit. Also, there were credits due him for cattle shipped recently over the border. With all this and the tricks of his trade he would recoup his losses in this strange land where few questions were asked and few answers given.

With the stoical patience of their Indian blood, Gómez and his brothers began their lives anew. After considerable hunting and bargaining they obtained what they wanted—a hacienda not far from the cattle market of Cúcuta, yet close enough to the border to carry on illicit trade and maintain liaison with the underground. Its price was fifty thousand pesos. They named the place Buenos Aires. During the next seven years Gómez made enough from cattle, horses, and coffee to buy two more haciendas and still maintain a sizeable cash balance at the bank for emergencies.

In Caracas, General Crespo became known for his tolerance, which he demonstrated in 1893 by granting a general amnesty and restoring to the press its long lost freedom of expression. In May of

that year, the Constitutional Assembly convened and promulgated a
new Constitution. The President would be elected by direct and
national suffrage. His term of office would be four years. There would
be a Federal Council composed of a representative from every state.
The President of the Council would exercise the functions of Vice
President of the Republic. On March 5, 1894, General Crespo was
elected President for the four-year term ending in 1898.

In Colombia, Gómez and Castro, freed by Crespo's general
amnesty, debated on whether to seek repatriation. Gómez having
prospered, and finding his new surroundings much to his liking, decided to remain at Buenos Aires. Castro, somewhat embarrassed
—he had been living on his friend's bounty because he was unable
to practice law in Colombia—resolved to return to his wife and law
practice in Independencia.

Classed as a dangerous subverter, Castro's movements in Venezuela were kept under surveillance. When he received a command to
confer with the President in the capital, he had no choice but to go.
Crespo wanted to meet his most dangerous adversary face to face,
to feel him out as to his political plans. What he gathered from his
appraisal of the quick-tempered young lawyer did not please him.
When the interview was over and the door had closed behind Castro,
the President said to one of his aides: "We will have to watch that
man. He is going to cause a lot of trouble."

Castro had likewise arrived at an unhappy conclusion. Crespo
was a cleverer man than he had imagined. Reporting on the interview at a rendezvous with Gómez he told him, "The Tiger fits his
name perfectly. He's tougher than I thought. As long as he holds
the reins we had better not move."

Again it became a matter of watchful waiting. In due course
Gómez and Castro had the satisfaction of observing Crespo become
embroiled with a growing opposition and with foreign powers.

Strong opposition began to develop against Crespo, especially
after the scandal which followed the obtainment of a loan from
Germany. The loan, fifty million bolivars, was negotiated to finance
the construction of the Caracas-Valencia railroad. Instead, the greater
part of it found its way to the pockets of Crespo's subalterns. With
government services honeycombed for years with graft and corruption, Crespo's administration had inherited a tainted situation. In-

stead of eradicating the sources of these evils, Crespo nonchalantly permitted his office holders to abuse their authority as never before and to openly enrich themselves at the expense of the people. Even Crespo himself could not evade the accusing finger of suspicion. It was said that Miraflores Palace, which Crespo had registered as his private property, had been built with government funds and materials.

Early in 1895 the Guayana boundary issue again cropped up. Year after year Great Britain had pushed her way westward until her claims covered a territory of more than sixty thousand square miles. Her claims included valuable gold fields, the Isla de Patos in the Gulf of Paria, Barima Point at the entrance of the Orinoco River, and some four hundred miles of the river itself. All that either Great Britain or Venezuela possessed upon which to base their claims were some vague historical records and maps and nothing else. Great Britain fell heir to the rights formerly possessed by Holland. Venezuela obtained by conquest the lands formerly owned by Spain. The primary point at issue was to establish what were the possessions of Holland and Spain and, secondly, to define the demarcation line between them. Until British surveyors and explorers had arbitrarily set their landmarks—their operations being conveniently screened by the jungle—the greater part of the boundary between British Guiana and Venezuela had been nothing more than a hypothetical line drawn on paper. Venezuela had been content to let it go at that, assuming that as far as South America was concerned the era of British conquest was over, and that neither the British nor anyone else would be interested in colonizing an almost impenetrable, steaming jungle. The British, however, had made claims on the above territory, and now in 1895 President Crespo was informed that the authorities of British Guiana had established a police post on the Uruan River, which Venezuela had always regarded as well within Venezuelan territory.

True to form, Crespo ordered that the British officials be ejected, by force if necessary, and the disputed ground occupied. The mistake that his representatives made was to arrest the two British police officers, maltreat them generally, and keep them in confinement for several weeks under loathsome conditions. The half-dozen native constables were ordered away from the locality, the British flag was hauled down and the Venezuelan flag put up in its place. The British governor at Demerara made strong representations of the affair to his home government, which were repeated when the officers returned and issued a report of the occurrence and the hardships they had suffered. As diplomatic relations with Venezuela had been severed some time before, the British government requested an explanation of the affair through the German Minister in Caracas, who was in charge of British interests. Although Crespo's reply was vague and unsatisfactory, nothing more was heard from either side for several weeks. But the fire was only smouldering and soon burst into flame.

Through the German Minister, a note was delivered to Crespo's Foreign Minister in June informing him that Great Britain was preparing to demand a formal apology and indemnity for the Uruan River incident. Also, a strong hint was dropped that if both were not forthcoming, strong measures would be taken—an implication that Great Britain would resort to force to obtain satisfaction. President Crespo decided to lay the matter before the United States government, no doubt in the hope that the United States would invoke the Monroe Doctrine against Great Britain. Accordingly, Venezuela's version of the incident was explained to Grover Cleveland's Secretary of State Olney by the Venezuelan Minister in Washington.

From the very beginning, Great Britain was unconcerned about interference from the United States in the boundary dispute. The original intent of the Monroe Doctrine did not embrace such issues as a boundary dispute between two recognized sovereign states. Nevertheless, the United States had shamefully looked the other way when Great Britain had set up Belize (British Honduras) as a Crown Colony, and again allowed them to violate the Monroe Doctrine when they seized the Falkland Islands in 1834. But in 1895 the effects of the Civil War were over. The United States felt the intoxication of a new power, a new wealth due to its rapidly expanding industry. It could adopt a policy of iron-fist diplomacy.

In July and August, notes were exchanged between Mr. Olney and Lord Salisbury, the British Prime Minister. In a severe tone, which implied that Great Britain was deliberately encroaching on Venezuelan territory, the Secretary of State brusquely demanded that the boundary dispute be submitted to arbitration. How Queen Victoria must have fumed when the note was read to her. However, Lord Salisbury's reply was most temperate in tone. He pointed out that with the exception of a comparatively small area which Her Majesty's Government had repeatedly offered to submit to arbitration, the title of Great Britain to the territory claimed by the authorities of British Guiana was perfectly clear and conclusive.

This reply, of course, did not satisfy the United States government. In another note to Lord Salisbury, which was couched in even stronger terms, Mr. Olney stated: "The United States is practically sovereign on this continent, and its fiat is law upon the subjects to which it confines its interposition." Queen Victoria, however, refused to budge from her original position and through Lord Salisbury coolly replied that Great Britain refused to recede or to arbitrate.

Meanwhile, Germany and France had taken advantage of Venezuela's harassed situation to press some claims of their own. As their relations with Venezuela became more strained, Crespo requested their ministers to leave the country. Like everyone else in his administration, he was under the impression that the North Americans would back him up without question. He was convinced of this when an American squadron put in at La Guaira. The squadron visited the port at that time in accordance with a schedule already laid out for it in Washington some months previous, but Crespo and his ministers failed to take this into account. They believed that the squadron had been dispatched there to intimidate the British and to frighten the French and German men-of-war which were then expected in port to convey their dismissed ministers back to their own countries.

As to the British situation, there was very little change until December 18, on which day President Cleveland sent his now famous message to Congress which came close to causing an outbreak of hostilities between Great Britain and the United States. President Cleveland declared that unless Great Britain would agree to the demands of the United States administration concerning arbitration in connection with the Venezuelan question, the United States would resort to force to compel the evacuation of all such territory as a commission appointed by the United States authorities considered rightfully belonged to Venezuela. For some time the nation had been in a mood for war, and immediately after the President's message to Congress, the U. S. newspapers bristled with war talk.

Although Venezuela eventually paid off the claim of the two

British police officials, the Uruan River incident no longer held the center of interest in Caracas in view of the new controversy which had arisen. When the text of the Cleveland message was cabled to Caracas, printed copies were immediately posted in every section of the city and a résumé of the message was telegraphed to all state governments. The entire country immediately became the scene of the wildest enthusiasm. Meetings were held to applaud the stand taken by President Cleveland and to shower abuse on the British. In Caracas and other cities, boisterous processions tramped through the streets bearing placards inscribed with patriotic slogans and derogatory comments against *los ingleses*. Sensation-seeking politicians made impassioned speeches denouncing the British and whipping up their audiences into a patriotic frenzy. Throughout the country British merchants were boycotted, and in several localities their establishments were stoned.

While all these developments were taking place, President Crespo had assumed an air of austere reserve. Not once did he make any public utterances against the British, a rare stand compared with that of his predecessors. The Venezuelan papers, however, fairly bristled with bellicose editorials and bitter invective against the British and kept the people in a ferment by inciting them to demonstrate their patriotic feelings in every way possible. Recruiting centers were set up which would be ready to function in the event Great Britain made any hostile move, and while the project of an invasion of British Guiana was freely discussed, batteries were mounted on the hills of La Guaira to protect the harbor against attack from the sea.

During Carnival Week in February, 1896, the feeling of hostility against the British reached its height. Masquerade was the order of the day, but a new note was added in the capital. To the excited spectators lining the sidewalks and the more sedate householders peeking from behind the *rejas* of their windows, the center of attraction was not the colorful floats, the carriages of smiling señoritas, nor the handsome caballeros on prancing steeds; what drew the wildest applause and the most vociferous remarks was the spectacle of Venezuelan soldiers dragging through the main thoroughfares effigies of British soldiers and sailors.

On his hacienda in Colombia, Gómez had been keeping abreast of the news through the underground and the daily paper from San

Cristóbal. When he observed that Crespo failed to take any measures to bridle the press or the public in their attacks against the British, he was stirred to anger. "Crespo is no administrator," he told Castro at one of their meetings. "He's an incompetent fool."

Castro expressed surprise. "In what way?" he asked. Never had he seen his *compadre* so angry.

Gómez gave a snort of disgust. "Have you seen what went on in San Cristóbal? Have you read what went on in the streets of our capital? Just how degrading can a people get?"

"But what has that got to do with Crespo?"

"Stoning the British? Carrying on in the streets like wild Indians? Permitting soldiers on the government payroll to act like ruffians? Just this! If ever a son of mine carried on like that I'd brand his hide with a bull whip. I don't think Crespo has the brains of a gnat! If he had any sense he would have put a stop to this whole ridiculous business a long time ago. As it is, the whole nation has forgotten how to work. It is wasting its precious time and money shouting and writing millions of empty words against an imaginary enemy. And for what? Just because the British stuck their foot in our back door?"

"You overlook something," Castro replied with an air of a man who suddenly realizes he has met superior wisdom. "The British have always been our enemy. They have been trying to grab our land since long before you and I were born."

"So the papers claim. But it seems to me we have always treated them as an enemy, and they have reacted accordingly."

"But it's not only the British," countered Castro, who hated all foreigners. "It's the French and the Germans, too. They're out to exploit us. You know that. They've been wringing us dry for years. They are always demanding indemnities for one thing or another."

"And sometimes with reason! The trouble with us is, our Presidents have always refused to pay claims even when they are just. No wonder these countries get tough with us. We refuse to settle, we refuse to dicker, we tell them to go to the devil. Take this case of the Uruan River for instance. Both the British and we were in the wrong, but Crespo has refused to admit it. He just shuts his eyes and permits the matter to grow from an ant hill into a mountain of trouble. Now it's nation against nation, and all because some stupid patrol clapped two foreign trespassers into jail!"

"You can't rightly blame Crespo for other men's mistakes," came the rejoinder.

"Perhaps not, but he could have quickly settled the matter in some way or other. Do you know something? I've thought of this for a long time, and I can't help but think I am right. I don't think there is anything, anything at all, be it a stolen steer or the fate of a nation, that cannot be settled peacefully across a conference table. If ever you get to be President, Cipriano, I hope you will prove I am right."

Gómez had waxed mellow in expounding his wisdom, but his counsel had fallen on deaf ears. Whereas the Uruan River incident created a profound and lasting impression on the unschooled peasant, with Castro it was quite the contrary. It only increased his hatred of foreigners, which would lead to trouble in the future.

As all things must, the boundary dispute finally dragged to an end. From Washington, where a boundary commission appointed by President Cleveland held constant sittings, the issue passed to Paris where it was finally settled by an arbitration tribunal in 1899. Its decision awarded to Great Britain nearly all the sixty thousand square miles she claimed and gave to Venezuela only Barima Point and the gold fields. The verdict, however, served to settle the boundary question once and for all and paved the way for a renewal of diplomatic, if not friendly, relations between the two nations.

Crespo's growing antipathy toward politics included a strong aversion to foreign entanglements. The long-drawn-out affair of the boundary dispute only stimulated his desire to retire to private life. At the end of his term he quietly promoted the candidacy of his friend General Andrade. On February 20, 1898, President Crespo relinquished his office to the president of the Government Council. Congress convened the same day, dutifully went through the ritual of counting the votes—though the results were a foregone conclusion —and proclaimed General Ignacio Andrade President.

There was one presidential aspirant who did not take his defeat lying down. General José Hernández, at one time one of Crespo's stoutest allies, was the people's choice for President. Once the returns had been announced he began preparations for a rebellion. On the day of the inauguration ceremonies he issued a proclamation of war, declaring the election had been a fraud.

It was General Crespo who was appointed commander of the government troops which set out to hunt Hernández down. It was two months later in the mountainous region of the state of Cojedes that his scouts tracked the enemy to his hideout. Stalking his prey, Crespo shouted the call to attack. At the first volley, Crespo fell dead.

From more than one version of the story, the bullet which killed Crespo did not come from the enemy's side but from his own. No official investigation was made, and the matter was hushed up. President Andrade caused interest to be quickly shifted to Hernández by sending out another force after him. In the Andes, Castro's friend, Dr. Rangel Garbiras, headed a minor uprising in support of the rebel.

After a long chase and a minor skirmish Hernández was defeated and confined in the Rotunda. His captor, flushed with victory, started a revolution of his own, which was quickly subdued.

Upon the collapse of the Andean uprising, Castro and Gómez met in solemn conclave. Andrade's administration was fast approaching a crisis. For Castro it was the hour for decision.

"The time has come," he said gleefully.

Gómez nodded his agreement. "As you wish, *compadre*. But are you sure this time?"

"Quite sure. Andrade is a weakling. Already he is worrying about who is going to strike next. If what I hear is true, he is shaking in his boots. But I am going to make doubly sure. Tomorrow I leave for Caracas. I will look over the situation. I will line up some support. Andueza Palacio is back. We helped him. Now it's his turn to do something for us."

On horseback, Castro journeyed over mountains and plains to the capital. On every hand he was informed that Andrade not only failed to enjoy confidence and respect in official circles, but he was the object of scorn and ridicule as well. In the strong undercurrent of dissatisfaction and unrest that prevailed, Castro found stimulus in the support of several important men, including ex-President Dr. Andueza Palacio. The nucleus of a revolutionary committee was formed, and after several secret meetings, Castro departed.

Returning to the Andes in high spirits, Castro stopped off in the mountain towns and villages to form revolutionary committees. The commanders of three small town garrisons agreed to swing to his side once his revolution got under way. The committees in other localities were to sign up recruits and employ fifth column tactics in capturing the town's officials, communications, and hostile garrisons. Emphasis was placed on the capture of arms, which would be sorely needed.

On a dark night at an isolated hacienda in Colombia, two groups of revolutionary leaders and exiles met to join forces. One group was represented by Dr. Rangel Garbiras, the other by Cipriano Castro. Standing silent and watchful was Castro's right hand man, Juan Vicente Gómez.

It was agreed in principle that Dr. Rangel Garbiras would act as the political director of the movement. General Castro would direct all military operations. Gómez was forthwith appointed a general. The discussions, however, were handicapped from the start by constant bickerings from both sides and they could not agree on many details of the plan. The only agreement reached at the conference was that the group which could arm and attack first could count on the collaboration of the other group. Castro, naturally, accelerated his preparations and tentatively set the date of his revolution for the first week of December—the beginning of the dry season. There were unforeseen developments, however, and preparations dragged on for months.

It was on a day in May, two days before zero hour, that Castro and some twenty other officers were billeted at the Gómez hacienda. On the last day, May 23, Buenos Aires was the scene of feverish activity. Everything—guns, ammunition, and supplies—was checked and put in final readiness. Intelligence couriers continually came and went. Into General Castro's saddlebag was put away a manifesto written in the chief's own hand. The following day, if everything went well, it would be posted on Venezuelan soil, and it would proclaim to the world the reasons for Castro's actions.

CHAPTER SIX

The March to Glory

Three hours before dawn on the morning of May 24, 1899, the revolutionary band was ready to go. The peons of Buenos Aires had saddled the horses and loaded the pack animals. Kinsmen had given each other the *abrazo,* the formal hug, patting each other on the back. The head of the clan had embraced each member of his family down to the youngest, four month old Gonzalo. To brother Juancho, left in charge of the hacienda, had been given the parting words of instructions.

Gómez and the others mounted in the corral and formed ranks in front of the main house. To tearful farewells of *"Buena suerte!"* and *"Vaya con Dios!"* from the womenfolk the column moved off into the darkness, hooves beating a low, staccato thunder on the hard-packed soil.

Among the riders were Castro's brother Carmelo, Gómez's brother Aníbal, his son José Vicente and his cousin Eustóquio. Close behind Juan Vicente rode a squat, Colombian Indian. Eloy Tarazona was his name. At Buenos Aires he had served faithfully as a hard driving peon foreman. As bodyguard and hatchet man he was going to follow close on Gómez's heels for the rest of his master's life. Besides the few peons being taken along to do the cooking and menial chores, the group included five Colombian volunteers, a doctor, an engineer, and a chaplain. The military line-up: Castro, Commander-in-Chief; Gómez, Second in Command; General Garrido, Chief of Staff; General Méndez, Chief of Operations; and General Valbuena, Chief of Supplies. All told, there were forty officers. Once across the border they would be augmented by twenty more. *La Sesenta,* the Sixty, they

53

called themselves henceforth. Only two besides Castro had had any combat experience, but all of them were going to render a good account of themselves. Several were going to fall in battle.

Just before dawn the column forded the cold Río Táchira and in an isolated ravine on Venezuelan soil joined a waiting band of rebels. A half hour later the column entered the village of Los Capachos where a contingent of one hundred men with twenty rifles swelled the ranks of the revolutionists. Then on to the plaza of Independencia where the shrill notes of a bugle called the rebels and citizenry to watch the ceremony of General Castro posting his manifesto on the wall of the *Jefetura.*

Proclaimed Castro in his manifesto, which called the people to arms: "To take advantage of the popular desire for full autonomy for the States in order to consummate a dictatorship . . . is an unheard of procedure. Of course the autonomy of the States is a vital necessity and is desired by most Venezuelans . . . but the process should be fulfilled in a legal manner, without surprises nor excesses and above all without trampling on the Constitution and the laws in force."

Castro, his enemies claimed, had to find a mask with which to cover his true intentions and a platform to win public support. What more beautiful ideals could be found than those he chose to shout from the house tops—that he was going to defend the laws and the Constitution of the Republic and "to establish respect for the law, the sanctity of the home, private property, the practice of republican principles, political freedom, the tolerance of private opinions, and honesty in public office."

To much fanfare, replete with martial music and high-pressure salesmanship, some of the crowd lined up to enlist. With majestic seriousness, General Castro, jackbooted, spurred, and accoutered in field uniform, watched the proceedings and the forming of the nucleus of battalions which were to fight under such grandiose, historical names as Libertador, Junin, and Bolívar. By his side stood General Gómez, looking solemn and important in new khaki and shiny boots.

His attention absorbed, Castro did not see the two boys who stood waiting to catch his eye. Gómez nudged him. "*Mira,* some admirers to see you."

Castro favored the boys with an impatient glance. They were trying to look impressive by affecting a military bearing. The leader of the two, lanky but every bit as tall as Castro himself, thought he had the makings of a revolutionary soldier. He had, but Castro didn't think so at the time, nor did he see in this stripling the makings of a future President of the Republic.

"Perhaps you don't remember me, General." The youth spoke with the voice and assurance of manhood. "I am Eleazar López— López Contreras. My father was Colonel López who once fought against Guzmán. My friend here and I have read your manifesto and want to enlist."

Castro's impatience gave way to amusement. "And the recruiting officer wouldn't accept you, eh? How old are you?"

"Sixteen, General. So is my friend. We are old enough to fight. We heard . . ."

"Yes. Yes, I know. We need men, but we want experienced men. Sorry, boy, I'm afraid you are a little too young." The youth bit his lip in chagrin. "Disappointed, eh? Well, perhaps later we might be able to use you . . . and your friend, too . . . but we must await the outcome of some battles first. There's going to be some bloody fighting. See you some other time."

It was the next afternoon in the village of Palo Gordo that the report of a fight between two officers was brought to the attention of General Castro. A new recruit had closed in on the aggressor, succeeded in disarming him, and had marched him in to headquarters. For that the recruit deserved a citation, and Castro ordered that he be brought before him.

When he saw him, Castro's mouth fell open in surprise. It was young López. *"Caramba!* How did you get in my army?"

López managed a sheepish grin. "Well, I saw that I had to use my head, so I used it. I heard one of your men say that you preferred men who supplied their own animals, so I bought myself a burro They just signed me up, that's all."

"Hah! That's a good one! I think General Gómez will get a laugh out of this. You're a boy with brains and spirit. I like that. Well done. lad. So you are one of us now. Just keep on using that head of yours and you will get somewhere."

As Castro had foretold, the fighting was bloody. His force had passed the thousand mark now. He was ready to do battle on any sector. When his reconnaissance notified him that Andrade's General Velasco was marching toward San Cristóbal to aid in its defense, Castro's army sped in pursuit and hid in ambush on the jagged slopes of Tononó. Taken by surprise, Velasco's force was almost completely wiped out and the general himself was killed.

The next adversary was General Sarría, Commandant of the Frontier, whom Castro hunted down for almost a week. Their forces clashed at dusk at the crossroads village of Las Pilas. In one hour the battle was over, the revolutionists having won decisively. General Sarría, wounded, was taken prisoner with a large number of his troops. Also captured was a considerable amount of war booty.

Hardly had Castro's exhausted troops bivouacked for the night when a courier arrived with the news that General Santo Morales, having defeated Castro's forces in Mérida, was advancing south to find him. Leaving General Gómez in command of the forces in the San Cristóbal area, Castro headed north before dawn with the balance of his troops. At El Zumbador, on June 11, the two forces met in battle. Although outnumbered, Castro's army took and maintained the initiative. After four hours of hard fighting the enemy was completely routed.

As in almost every bloody battle of Venezuela's civil wars, there followed the gruesome task of disposing of the bodies. Very few of the fallen were selected for Christian burial. Only the generals and senior officers were buried in shallow graves. The bodies of the privates and junior officers were piled on great pyres of brushwood and consumed by flames. And from every direction vultures flocked to the ghastly scene, attracted by the stench of burning flesh. When the flames died out they snatched from among the ashes some bit of scorched flesh. When the fortunes of war did not permit decent burial or even the burning of the dead, the voracious vultures had the field to themselves. When they were finished devouring the bodies there was nothing left but scattered bones and remnants of tattered clothing. There were many such gruesome scenes which would well chill and sicken even a hardened old soldier.

Up to now Castro's campaign had been marked by speed, smashing surprise attacks, and decisive victories. Then suddenly there began a period of inactivity, indecision, and confusion which lasted almost six weeks and almost doomed Castro's revolution to failure.

Juan Vicente Gómez standing, Cipriano Castro seated. (Note revolver butt protruding from Castro's coat pocket.)

Bocono, a typical Andean town of coffee growers and small farmers.

*General Gómez as he appeared at the start of
Cipriano Castro's revolution, 1899.*

It started when Castro returned from El Zumbador and was stricken with a vague illness which kept him on his cot for over a week. It was not until June 23 that Castro made a half-hearted attack on San Cristóbal with twenty-five hundred men. He found that the enemy had taken to carefully prepared trenches. The following day he called off the attack, giving the excuse that only artillery could route the defenders. Artillery, it appears, was a weapon Castro did not possess.

Only once during the six weeks lull did Castro act like his old self. In an encounter with the enemy in the dead of night, he scaled a mountain with a company of men armed only with machetes. Falling on the sleeping enemy bivouacked on the summit, they hacked them to pieces. Only a handful escaped.

Although San Cristóbal remained the one stalemate of the revolution and was never taken by force of arms, new impetus was given the campaign by the capture of three villages during the last days of July. Castro's tactics were to leave the main highway and travel by night over rugged mountain trails to fall on the enemy by surprise. On the night of July 31, Generals Castro and Gómez conferred with their senior officers to map a new campaign. Although the fighting had been confined to a radius of only thirty-five miles since its start ten weeks before, Castro's army had grown enormously in size and was champing at the bit for greater conquests. The most dangerous opponent at the moment was General Fernández's army which had infiltrated through the mountain passes from Lake Maracaibo's port of Encontrados. Though backed by superior numbers and equipment, Fernández chose to sit and dawdle a safe ten miles out of Castro's reach. The new blueprint of attack was based on General Gómez's reasoning that Fernández, having repeatedly failed to take the initiative, would not make any serious attempt to attack them once they made a decisive breakout toward Caracas. The immediate objectives decided upon were the cities of Mérida and Trujillo. The line of march was northeast, and the success of the venture depended on by-passing Fernández's army and leaving it behind. In attempting it Castro could have said, as did Hernándo Cortés, "I have burned my ships behind me," and there would not have been any possible salvation for his men in case of a defeat. One can well imagine the boldness with which he had to fight; it is the most logical explanation for his later triumphs. Castro always spoke in terms of attack and victory, never of defense and defeat. Radiating cheerful optimism, it is no wonder that he inspired confidence and maintained such a high morale among his troops.

In Castro, Gómez had found the qualities he himself admired and strove to emulate—fearlessness and leadership, and a polish gained by education and experience. To Castro, Gómez was perhaps an awkward peasant, but he was a passionate soldier, utterly obedient, and physically courageous. In the precarious situations in which they often found themselves, Gómez's astonishing insight into human nature and his keen sense of military strategy stood them in good stead. Theirs was the ideal partnership in that they relied completely upon each other for the attainment and preservation of their objectives.

It was now the middle of the rainy season. Weighed down by weapons, cooking pots, and other gear, the men were often beset by thunderous showers and morasses of mud. To conserve strength, the army's march was slow, averaging twelve to fifteen miles a day. At dawn on the morning of August 6, an army group attacked and captured Tovar. In this engagement the insurgents lost a general and seventy men, but the royal highway to Mérida was now clear of sizeable enemy forces. On the 7th, the army arrived at Estanques, and on the 8th at San Juan. On the 9th, Gómez caught an occasional glimpse of the snow-capped peaks of Mount Humboldt and Bolívar, both over 15,000 feet above sea level. Trudging through coffee groves, with potato and wheat fields on the higher rocky slopes above them, the weary, grimy army skirted the fertile valley of Charua, covered with bananas, sugar cane, and cacao, and entered unchallenged the ancient city of Mérida. The government commander had abandoned the city with his troops the day before.

Founded in 1558, Mérida was three times the size of San Cristóbal. Not only was it the commercial center of the Venezuelan Andes, but it was the administrative and intellectual center as well. The University of Mérida, founded by the Jesuit Fathers (its location, 5,000 feet above sea level, was ideal because of its year-around pleasant climate), had been Venezuela's foremost seat of learning for close to three centuries. So seriously did the faculty regard their duties, they once taught for over a year without pay when President Guzmán annulled the university's autonomy and confiscated its properties. Guzmán's hatred for the university had not been without foundation, for its students, openly abetted by the clergy, had long distinguished themselves for their rebel activities.

In Mérida, as in Tovar and other large towns, Castro and Gómez were given demonstrations of friendship and loyalty, and the students of the university were among the foremost to swear their allegiance to the cause. The number of recruits were so numerous, that an additional battalion, the Tovar, was formed. General Valbuena, in charge of supplies, carefully paid out rock bottom prices for provisions which were brought forth in abundance. The army of the "Liberal Restoration"—as Castro called his revolution—was still traveling on a pay-as-you-go basis.

After a day and a half in Mérida the army marched on to the village of Tabay, ten miles distant. Despite the inclement weather and treacherous going—sometimes the sodden ground was transformed by the slightest pressure into a roaring landslide—the army made better time the next day, covering more than twenty miles of hairpin turns to reach the next village. Mucuchies, although founded three centuries before, consisted only of a few thatched huts whose inhabitants shivered in their *ruanas,* for the altitude was over 10,000 feet above sea level and the clouds hung low. Here the only crops grown on the rock strewn slopes were wheat and potatoes. Then the next day on to still greater and more rugged heights. The climb to the bleak and uninhabited *paramo*—that is, above the upper limits of cultivation—was through a heavy mist in which lay slippery crags and sudden sheer drops. The landscape had the aspect of an arctic tundra with evidence of former glaciation all about. Here grew patches of prickly mosses and hardy shrubs and a velvety-leaved *frailejón,* the white or cream-colored center leaves of which sat up on huge stocks to add the only bright note to an otherwise drab landscape.

The climbs and descents over this frosty, rocky terrain were ones of extreme hardship and the day did not pass without its casualties. Laboring up steep inclines under heavy loads, with inadequate clothing to protect them against the intense cold, the plight of the exhausted, the wounded, and the sick was pitiful. Hundreds dropped, too exhausted to go on, and the *padre,* himself too fatigued to dismount from his burro, performed the last rites over the dying who were left abandoned by the wayside.

As for Castro and Gómez, it was the slender Castro, sometimes riding, other times climbing the steep grades with his horse, all the while muttering curses through his beard, who had the worse time of it. It was Gómez, he of the sturdy legs, who had to wait on each ridge and summit for his chief to catch up, and to offer soothing words of encouragement. *"Caray!* It's tough going, eh, *compadre?"* he remarked at one point, glancing around him at the deplorable condition of the men. "But it could have been much worse, *por mi madre,* much worse. Has it occurred to you, *compadre,* that if Fernández had been smart, just a little smart, he would have been waiting here, hiding in the mist? He could have wiped us out, pouf, like that!"

"Don't even think of it," came back the sharp retort. "We're not yet over the top."

At the highest point of the *paramo*—over 13,000 feet—the tired army bivouacked for the night. Always curious, Gómez inspected a cairn of rocks which depicted the epic march of Simón Bolívar over virtually the same route eighty years before. A delicate man, Bolívar had performed feats of physical endurance. He marched an exhausted and starving force, dragging cannon and munitions from the steaming, flooded Venezuelan *llanos,* over these same cold and barren heights into Colombia. After a march of nearly a thousand miles and with only three days rest he had engaged and defeated the main Spanish army of twice his strength. To his credit were listed over two hundred bloody battles and the liberation of six countries from Spain.

As Gómez stood there with the cold, unfriendly mist swirling about his broad shoulders, deciphering the weather-beaten lettering and meditating on the past, he marveled anew at the exploits of Bolívar. Crossing the Andes under such conditions, he mused, deserved a more fitting monument. He vowed then and there that some day he would attend to it.

Descending the *paramo* over steep corkscrew paths, the bedraggled army camped the next night at the diminutive village of Chachopo, which was protected from the cold winds by tall, graceful willow and eucalyptus trees. Here were green vegetation, fresh food, and wood for fuel. The exhausted men were in the narrow valley of the Motatán River. Lying around their blazing camp fires they could hear from the black chasm below the sonorous roar of the stream as it made its swift, rocky descent toward Lake Maracaibo in the lowlands.

Rising early and fortifying themselves with hot, black coffee, the refreshened battalions descended eagerly into the warmer air. Hedge-hopping from one village to another and crossing and recrossing the shallow river time and again, they emerged from the ever-widening valley to enter the pleasant little city of Valera a day and a half later. Here again they marched unchallenged; the garrison had retreated to the north. Valera, a thriving "gateway-to-the-Andes" town, was on the last of the great mesas or alluvial terraces of the Andes.

After two days of rest and wenching and taking on of provisions, they were off over the sun-baked red hills and into the lowlands. Heat. Thirst. Heavy showers. Rear guard action with guerrillas who tried to make off with the cattle. Days of slow marching like a desert caravan through the arid wastes of Trujillo and Lara. There was no wild game. Just mesquite, cactus, and clumps of dividivi as far as the eye could see, and an occasional muddy stream whose water was unfit to drink. They paused in Carora, a sprawling town lying lazily in the sun, too sunken in lethargy to give a care for revolution. Rested, their bellies full, their thirst quenched, they took off again on the beaten trail. Gradually, the scenery changed. They passed patches of green sugar cane, trees, scattered farmhouses. They forded many streams. Then, on the afternoon of August 22, the army was brought to a halt by the Tocuyo River, which was swollen by heavy rains and full of floating debris.

The chiefs of staff held a consultation. Better to put the river behind them. They forded it with great difficulty. Nearby they came upon a large hacienda, and they appropriated it for the night. Despite the quiet, pastoral scene, Castro smelled danger in the air. The *hacendado* was much too co-operative. Trailed by Gómez, Castro inspected the grounds and deployed his men. The high command would spend the night in the main house; the arsenal and services were dispatched to the sugar mill close by; four battalions were sent to cover the trail to the river; others to cover the right and left flanks; one veteran battalion took to the dense underbrush on both sides of a low lying meadow which an enemy force would most likely cross in any attempted assault on the hacienda proper.

Into this artfully set trap walked a government force the following dawn. The boom from their artillery piece signaled the attack. It
also heralded the fire from the hidden battalion. Caught in a deadly
cross-fire, four hundred of the enemy fell. Two hundred more were
captured as were also numerous rifles, ammunition, and the artillery
piece.

With renewed enthusiasm, the army, now over two thousand
strong, kept circling the capital city of Barquisimeto and camped for
the night in Bobare, twelve miles to the north. They were seasoned,
hardened veterans now. Though weary, there was cause for rejoicing.
The revolution was half won. They were more than half way to
Caracas. In the plaza a soldier strummed a *cuatro* and strains of a
mountain ballad filled the air. There was talk of women and rum,
but no one seemed to have any money.

This gave young López, now a captain, food for thought. His
shoes were worn thin, his pockets were empty, and his burro had
long since been supplying transportation for the *padre*. Not one
centavo had he received for three months of hard campaigning. The
injustice of it all!

López did some inquiring. General Gómez was reputed to be the
richest man of them all. Why not go to him and ask for some money?
Taking along a brother officer for moral support, he found the General in his *pension* getting ready to bed down for the night.

Gómez was taken aback by the audacity of the youth. "You want
some pay? Pay for what? You know there's no pay in a revolutionary
army."

"Yes, sir. I know that, sir. That's what they told all the recruits.
But we are officers now. As officers, don't we rate anything at all?"

"*Mira,* López." Gómez's tone was kind but firm. "You want to
know the financial standing of a captain? I'll tell you. It's what he
had in his pocket when he joined this army."

"When I joined the army! Look, General. I did have some money.
Fifteen bolivars. But I spent that to get some decent meals in Valera
and to get my pants patched. My burro cost me forty bolivars, but
General Castro took it away from me to give to the *padre*. Now I've
got nothing. My pockets are clean."

"You don't expect the *padre* to walk all the way to Caracas, now
do you? Well, let me see." Gómez cogitated a moment, then fumbled

in his pocket and brought out a five bolivar piece. "Here, you can have this, but you will have to divide it between you."

And as he was closing the door behind López he added, "And be sure you don't tell anybody where you got that, *comprende?*"

During the days that followed, the revolutionary army moved with impressive speed due east toward Caracas. Crossing Yaracuy, Castro feinted north toward San Felipe, the capital, then shifted south toward Nirgua, which he captured after a two-hour pitched battle on September 8.

On September 12 the revolutionary army crossed the *Pica de la Mona* to enter the plains of Carabobo. Ahead lay the towns of Tocuyito and Valencia. Here, Castro realized, would be fought the decisive battles of the campaign. When he occupied Tocuyito the next day, Castro had no intention of remaining for long, as the town lacked any natural defenses. While the troops took a much needed rest the general staff burned the midnight oil poring over maps and listening to reports from their scouts who had been sent out at hourly intervals to learn the position and strength of the enemy The reports were not encouraging. General Fernández, who they thought had been left far behind, had just arrived at Valencia from the north. Instead of following them overland, he had embarked with his troops at Encontrados and had returned by sea to Puerto Cabello. Also at Valencia was an army under the Minister of War. All told, the enemy was estimated to be roughly four thousand strong, and they were encamped eight miles to the north.

Came the dawn, and with it a surprise attack on Castro's southern flank. Alerted as to his arrival in Tocuyito, the government troops had marched during the night and had set up their positions. From a hill three miles away, government guns began to pour a methodical fire of shells into the village.

Solemn, stern, and imperturbable, General Castro dictated his order of the day: "By your stamina and courage the Army of the Liberal Restoration has come far. The eyes of all Venezuela are upon you. Advance boldly, resolutely, and strike hard . . . and to-morrow Caracas will be ours."

Attack, always attack. The first wave of revolutionary troops were mowed down by rifle fire and grape-shot. Through field glasses, Castro and Gómez surveyed the battle line, searching for a weak spot. The artillery piece was wheeled into position and Castro dismounted to site the gun and fire at an enemy command post. A direct hit! Again the order to attack while Castro kept on siting and firing, trying to open a breach in the enemy line.

Together, Castro and Gómez made the rounds of their positions, watched while their troops charged in furious assaults. Hour after hour, as the sun climbed high in the heavens, the battle continued unabated. Though the toll in lives was heavy, Castro's tactics continued to be stubborn attack. Gradually, the tide of battle turned. First one, then other battalions, forced a wedge in the beleaguered enemy's lines. Yard by yard, on the various fronts, the government troops fell back.

At one point, when Castro attempted to cross a gully, his horse stumbled and fell throwing him to the ground. The cry went up that the Chief had been wounded, but Castro, cursing his luck, limped away with only a foot fracture. From a litter he continued to direct the battle. It fell to Gómez to make the rounds and report for orders.

On the enemy's side, matters went from bad to worse. Bitter rivalry in the high command, lack of aggressiveness, and faulty tactics began to spell defeat. Maneuvering in the high sugar cane of a plantation, two battalions met and clashed, each believing the other to be the enemy. Another force, sent to attack Castro's right flank, was fired upon by government artillery because of its failure to raise its flag. After these disasters, demoralization among the troops became so prevalent as to amount almost to chaos. Unable to hold his forces in check, the government commander ordered a general retreat.

After ten hours of bloody fighting, the battle of Tocuyito was over. Close to two thousand men had lost their lives. Among the dead was Gómez's brother Aníbal. Captain López had been wounded. It took two days for the last of the battered and exhausted army to tramp the eight miles to Valencia.

They found the state capital an abandoned city. The authorities and troops having been the first to flee, panic had spread and there had been a wild exodus toward the east. But the conquerors were not out for plunder. They wanted food and rest, and medical attention. Gradually, as the populace was prevailed upon to return, every spare room of the city was filled with the sick and wounded. Gómez, who had come down with a high fever, was billeted with Castro in the best room of the town's hotel.

Castro's line of action called for no respite. While one small force made an onslaught along the railroad that gave access to the sea, another swept eastward by rail to capture Guacara, a mere seventy-five miles from Caracas.

When it became apparent that the "Restoration Movement" would emerge victorious, there was a rush to jump on Castro's bandwagon. But mundane and politically wise Castro was no man's fool. From the motley droves of callers which began to descend on him, he could distinguish between the sincere well-wishers, the obscure bureaucrats out to make political hay, the shrewd, calculating seekers of patronage and graft, and the scheming politicians of chameleon hue. To all of them, Castro was graciously polite, but while he flashed a smile at them through his beard he mentally catalogued his callers for future reference.

In Caracas, President Andrade, already envisaging defeat, desperately sought a solution to stem the revolutionary avalanche, but not one general among his staff would volunteer for the ticklish job. The best that Andrade could hope to accomplish would be an expensive compromise with Castro. Toward that end he delegated his Minister of Finance, Manuel Matos, to confer with Castro at Valencia, and a safe-conduct was arranged for the trip.

Ushered into the hotel room, the minister found the rebel chieftain prostrate on a cot, his foot in a cast. Perceiving a sleeping figure on another cot, Matos hesitated. "Who is that?" he whispered.

"Juan Vicente Gómez. He's sick. Sit down and talk. Juan Vicente is almost a brother to me."

Matos, a glib, jaunty spellbinder, talked. He mentioned his ride through the streets from the station and of seeing the debilitated revolutionary troops. Hungry, haggard specimens of manhood, they appeared as if they would gladly forfeit all their hard-earned gains for a few hot meals and a bed. He tried hard to convince Castro that his revolution had been only half won, that Tocuyito had been only a sample of the cruel punishment his small army would have to suffer for the last grueling miles to Caracas. With Gómez incapacitated and himself nearly so, and only a handful of capable officers left on their feet, he argued that Castro was not in a strategic position to bargain. Thousands of the republic's fine young manhood had already lost their lives in a reckless, hopeless gamble. And for what? Perhaps because Castro aspired to power . . . or was it because Castro was at odds with President Andrade's administration which had failed to provide an equitable representation for the Andes?

"Let us assume," said Matos, "that it is the latter reason. Now then, President Andrade—in fact all of us—want to put an end to all this appalling bloodshed. The President feels inclined to overlook all the tragedy and evil that has happened up to now . . . if you will but surrender your arms. His terms are generous—a guarantee of immunity from arrest and confiscation of properties for you and all your men, and, if you so desire it, a place in the administration for yourself. No one, in your position, could expect to receive a more magnanimous treatment."

The speech fell on deaf ears. The most that Matos could get out of his visit was Castro's word that he would confer at another meeting. He did not know that Castro's colleagues in the capital were working behind the scenes to soften the enemy.

During the month that followed, while Gómez still lingered with fever and Castro's foot healed, negotiations dragged on relentlessly. One by one, Andrade's supporters deserted him until he faced the realization that it would be but a matter of days or hours before his administration would collapse about him. On October 19 he packed his bags and fled the capital.

The President having abandoned his office, the president of the Government Council, General Rodriguez, automatically became vested with presidential authority, and he so advised General Castro by telegram. But Rodriguez was Castro's man, and the conqueror, in his congratulatory telegram, requested the privilege of releasing the political prisoners from the Rotúnda. The same day, a mission was sent to Valencia, which paved the way for General Castro's triumphal entry into Caracas on October 22.

As the exultant revolutionary soldiers marched into the city from the station, one of them unslung his cornet, another his *cuatro*. As they started to play, hoarse voices filled the air. Once again, as in 1892, the streets of the capital reverberated to the strains of the national anthem:

". . . Glory to the brave people
Who were unshackled
By a law respecting liberty and honor! . . ."

On the morning of October 23, 1899, a solemn ceremony was celebrated in the *Casa Amarilla*. General Rodriguez relinquished his authority as Provisional President. General Castro named his cabinet and proclaimed his government. His program emphasized "new men, new ideals, and new procedures."

Then the self-proclaimed President went to the balcony to address the valiant soldiers of the Restoration Army lined up for review in front of the palace.

"This is your achievement," Castro shouted, using the familiar *tu*. "You should be proud of it . . . and alert to guard it so that you may remain worthy of the high honor you have won in history."

It was not until November 2 that Juan Vicente Gómez, recovered from his illness, beheld the fabulous capital for the first time.

CHAPTER SEVEN

Castro Holds the Reins

In the tradition of shrewd revolutionists, Cipriano Castro had made advantageous alliances to achieve his ends. As a smart politician in a land where the government can rise and fall all within a fortnight, he made no personal promises that he did not intend to keep. Castro had made his bargains and he lived up to them; for one, friend and foe alike shared in the distribution of patronage. General Hernández, for example, was released from the Rotunda to become the Minister of Development; Andueza Palacio, Castro's friend and ex-President, was named Minister of Foreign Affairs; Dr. Clemente Urbaneja, former legal advisor to Andueza Palacio, Minister of Public Instruction; Dr. Castillo, independent Liberal, Minister of the Interior; General Pulido, whose planned invasion to help Castro never materialized, Minister of War and Marine; and Castro's man Tello Mendoza, Minister of Finance. General Luciano Mendoza, who had collaborated effectively in the peace negotiations, was named Commander of the Army, and General Sarría, one of Andueza Palacio's former ministers, was named Governor of the Federal District. There were not many new faces here to be sure, but given time Castro would weed out the undesirables and replace them with his own men such as Gómez, Garrido, and others. Castro did not have long to wait.

Four days after President Castro named his cabinet, General Hernández withdrew as Minister of Development and was replaced by Villegas Pulido. Hernández would give no reason for his resignation, but Castro had good reasons to suspect that the volatile general harbored designs for another revolution. It was no great surprise to Castro, therefore, when on the following evening while attending a stage performance at the Municipal Theater with his entourage, General Hernández made a bold attempt to capture him. But Castro had not been caught unawares. Hernández and his band were pursued through the streets of the capital, but the wily general disappeared in the vicinity of the neighboring town of El Valle. From there he slipped through the states of Aragua and Guarico to Cojedes, where he was captured five months later by a government expeditionary force. President Castro had the ungrateful and belligerent general put back into his old cell in the Rotunda.

When General Gómez arrived in Caracas on November 2, he immediately conferred with Castro in the Miraflores Palace. Gómez was now forty-two. As right-hand man to the President, he was entitled to a recompense for services rendered and a reward befitting his station. Somewhat taken aback by the feminine pulchritude to be found in the capital, Gómez expressed a preference to remain there rather than be named to a berth in the Andes. "Take it easy for awhile," Castro told him. "Find a house, get settled and I'll see about lining up a job for you." If Gómez had had at least a primary school education he might have been slated for the post of Minister of Finance, which would have given him and Castro easy access to the national treasury. His natural bent was business, and since the time he had put on his first pair of shoes he had displayed a lively interest in figures; however, these were not of the kind which could readily be put into the national budget. Through Tello Mendoza, however, Castro was free to dip into the treasury at his leisure. What he found there, or rather what he failed to find, caused him to gnash his teeth in rage. He found the country saddled with weighty foreign debts and the government's cash balance at the Commercial Bank at its lowest ebb in twelve years.

Castro summoned General Manuel Matos to an interview. A Valencia banker, Matos had been Minister of Finance under Crespo and Andrade, and together with Guzmán and Henry L. Boulton had been one of the three principal shareholders of the prosperous Commercial Bank. Because of exorbitant rates charged the government for handling its funds during the Guzmán regime, this institution had consistently earned more than the Venezuelan government itself. General Matos arranged through the Bank of Venezuela for a government loan of one million bolivars, against which Castro immediately began to make heavy withdrawals. One of his first acts was to repay Gómez and Andueza Palacio for the monies they had put out. What he took for himself remained a deep secret. Another heavy strain on the government's bank account was the "victory bonus" which was paid to the rank and file of the revolutionary army.[6]

The week following Gómez's arrival in Caracas, Castro received word that the port of Puerto Cabello, holding out to the last, had refused to capitulate. Andrade's General Antonio Paredes had declared that he would rather fight. President Castro sent a force under Julio Sarría and Ramón Guerra to take the city, and appointed Gómez to Sarría's post as governor of the Federal District. Puerto Cabello was captured after a hard fight of thirteen hours, and General Paredes was taken prisoner to Caracas. He was imprisoned for a spell in the fortress of San Carlos at the entrance to Lake Maracaibo. When he started a revolution several years later in the east, Castro is reported to have issued secret instructions that he not be taken alive. So when Paredes, beaten in battle, surrendered of his own accord, he met his execution on board a gunboat in the Orinoco.

On January 1, 1900, General M. Velasco, in his capacity as Chief of the Corps of Aide-de-Camps at Miraflores Palace, and complying with orders from Castro, appointed Captain Eleazar López Contreras as an aide-de-camp to the President. But the strange behavior of this boy and his lack of experience and distaste for the job embroiled young López in numerous difficulties. Though the lad was considerably mature for his sixteen years and had been obedient and courageous on the battlefield, he had not as yet been tempered by wisdom and tact to travel in upper social and military echelons.

One morning in March, Captain López drew the fire of President Castro which resulted in the banishment of the youth from the palace. The occasion was a conference that the chief of state was holding with his generals Ramón Guerra, Luciano Mendoza, and Francisco Batalla, which López tactlessly interrupted to announce the arrival of an important looking (and unbeknownst to López—an

---

[6] Early in 1874 it came to light that General José Ignacio Pulido had received from the Guzmán dictatorship, as payment for his services during Guzmán's revolution of 1870, ninety-two leagues of land (over four hundred thousand acres), plus bonds worth sixty thousand dollars.

ousted) bureaucrat from the provinces. Forgetting the infirmity which kept him confined to a wheelchair, Castro rose up with clenched fists and let out a bellow which sent López scurrying out of the room like a whipped cur with its tail between its legs. For the rest of the morning Castro vented his anger on everyone within earshot but by mid-afternoon he had calmed down sufficiently to summon López and talk to him in a moderately low tone. "I've arranged a transfer for you," he told him. "A field assignment. I think you would like that better. Here's the order. Give it to General Olivares and he will find a place for you under his command."

In his new assignment in the battalion Junin quartered in San Mauricio, Captain López narrowly missed being present at the capture of General Hernández. His superior, General José Dávila, being named to head the expeditionary force against Hernández in the state of Cojedes, had included him among the men to accompany him. At the last minute, however, López was forced to remain behind to undergo another operation on his battle wound. Upon his return from the campaign after having fought and captured Hernández at Tierra Negra, General Dávila was so exultant over his feat, that the ambitious López solicited and obtained the appointment of chief of the battalion Restaurador, and with it a promotion to colonel. Evidently this lad of sixteen had a way with his superiors! Colonel López was based at Guacara near Valencia and had under his command several garrisons which were strung out from Lake Valencia to the sea. He was kept busy ferreting out and locking up insurgents who had taken up arms in favor of General Hernández and nationalism.

In Caracas—General Gómez having been packed off to the Andes as Military Chief of Táchira—exuberant, luxury loving Castro became the favorite topic of gossip. Although he had sent for doña Zoila to assume her rightful position as First Lady, and had installed her in "Villa Zoila," a sumptuous mansion, the President began to set up numerous love nests. His extravagant indulgence in women, fine food, and liquors kept his Minister of Finance hard pressed to keep him in funds. When the banks refused to grant his government any further loans, President Castro wrote an urgent appeal to General Matos.

Replied Matos from his beach residence in Macuto: "Six years

of fiscal disorder, two more of incessant war, coffee prices declining
in consumer markets, many haciendas abandoned as a consequence,
sugar plantations crushed by the decline in the price of sugar, work
interrupted throughout the country because of war, lack of confidence
on the part of investors, and the interest on public debts unpaid for,
have, after producing serious confusion in the country, wiped out
Venezuela's credit abroad . . . and the disastrous consequence of
all these antecedents have reduced commerce, investors, and those
individuals who exist by their professions or other means, to penury.
From them no financial help can be expected due to their tight
economic situation." As a friend and as a man wise in the ways of
business and politics, General Matos then advised the President
to change his cabinet to men more compatible with Venezuela's
need. Only in this way, he said, could confidence be restored and
Venezuela be set once more on her normal course toward peace
and prosperity.

The outcome of this letter was the Rotunda for General Matos
as well as for the officials of the leading banks, and the prominent
merchants and industrialists who had refused to extend loans or
advance credits to the government. Castro didn't limit himself to
this outrage; pretending that these prisoners were to be transferred
from Caracas to the fortress at Puerto Cabello or the one at San
Carlos, he subjected them to the humiliation of being marched through
the streets of Caracas in single file between two lines of soldiers from
the Rotunda to the railroad station. Once there, they turned around
and marched back to the Rotunda in the same way. When they were
released several weeks later, outraged General Matos declared that
he would not live in Venezuela while it remained under Castro's rule.
He did what many others had done before him. He packed up and
went to Trinidad where he joined a group of other Venezuelan discontents.

Eventually President Castro was forced to concede that there was
some wisdom in General Matos' advice. On August 1 he named a new
cabinet. Out went Drs. Audueza Palacio, Urbaneja, and the others,
to be replaced by new men. Only Ramón Tello Mendoza remained
as Minister of Finance. Two days later Castro decreed the reduction
in the number of states to fifteen.

On September 14, to commemorate the first anniversary of the battle of Tocuyito, President Castro visited the battlefield where so many of Venezuela's sons had perished. Numerous battalions had come from near and far to render honor for the occasion, and to the waving of flags and the blare of trumpets they marched across the field past the official reviewing stand. When General Francisco Alcántara saw Colonel López pass by proudly leading his battalion, he turned to the President and exclaimed: "Why—if it isn't López Contreras! And a colonel at that! Isn't he rather young to head a battalion?"

Replied Castro: "López Contreras and Sarmiento were the youngest officers in my outfit, General, but they were also among the most outstanding officers of the entire campaign. I wish I had more like them."

But General Alcántara's chance remark gave Castro food for thought. Of course López was too young to be a colonel. General Dávila should have known better than to have placed a beardless youngster in charge of a seasoned battalion. Not long afterward, Colonel López found himself transferred to another battalion as second in command but with no change in rank. When he found out that the orders had emanated from Castro, who had let drop the remark, "López is too much of a boy to play first violin," López was filled with bitter resentment. But he remained devoted to soldiering nonetheless and resolved, despite his fast declining esteem for his commander-in-chief, to comply fully with his duties as a soldier.

During the night of October 29, 1900, Caracas suffered a minor earthquake which toppled walls and killed scores of people. Mindful of the death of countless thousands who had perished like trapped rats during the terrible earthquake in Caracas in 1812, President Castro shed his dignity at the first tremors and ran to the palace balcony and jumped off. He was picked up from the street unconscious. While he was confined to his bed with severe contusions, wild rumors circulated about his delicate state of health. As Castro had not yet named a legal successor to the presidency, there were insistent attempts by his favorites to be elected, but Castro soon recovered and left his bed.

During his convalescence Castro had his fill of fawning, scheming men who pretended to be his friends. Far from being exemplary and sagacious individuals bent on serving their country to the best of their ability, the majority of the politicians of the oligarchy in power were the prototypes of their ambitious predecessors. But Castro, the man who had set up such high ideals, the man who had been ostensibly motivated by the sincere conviction that he was going to redeem his country, had reneged on his promises to the nation and had fallen into the same evil ways of his contemporaries. From the time of the Matos affair Castro had been branded as a ruthless tyrant. When he decided to ignore the Constitution and have another drafted to assure his re-election, the foulest epithets were heaped upon his head. Nonetheless, he managed, through chicanery and coercion, to make his legislators toe the line.

On March 26, 1901, congress convened and passed a new Constitution which provided, among other things, that the term of office of the President would be lengthened to six years. The present administration would be considered provisional until February 20, 1902, on which date the Constitution would go into effect. In plain words, this piece of legislation simply meant that one year hence "provisional" President Castro could count on becoming the legally elected President for a six-year term. It was an old trick that had been practiced by Guzmán and other revolutionists who had grasped power. And it had always worked.

When Cipriano Castro recalled General Gómez from the Andes to become his First Vice President he, unknowingly to himself, was summoning his own nemesis. Five years were to elapse before he would recognize his peril, but then it would be too late to mend his ways and atone for his political sins.

When Gómez returned to Caracas he brought with him his mother, his woman Dionisia Bello, and their children. The splendid establishment into which Dionisia Bello moved in Paraíso was a far cry from the dirt-floored, adobe house at La Mulera. Gómez's mother, Hermenegilda, a humble, God-fearing woman now past sixty-five, balked at living in the whirling hubbub of the city. She preferred the simple country life. So her son packed her off to a house at Macuto, a small beach resort near La Guaira.

Such a considerate son! He visited the old lady regularly, saw to it that she was amply provided with servants and money. Nothing to worry about, just time on her hands. Too much time. "A garden, *mamita!* That's what you need, a lovely garden! You will have the prettiest in Macuto. You'll see!"

So solicitous for his mother's welfare, that son of hers. Yes, he truly loved her, and *mamita* knew it. "He's a fine son, my Juan Vicente," she would say to visitors. But if they only knew how often that old lady prayed on her knees in church for the salvation of Juan Vicente's soul.

Faithful, plodding Gómez, always the obedient and unostentatious servant, remained constantly at the President's beck and call, unmindful of his bursts of temper, his shouted peremptory orders. Solemn and imperturbable Gómez was without a doubt one of Castro's staunchest friends. Although no pillar of strict respectability himself, Gómez was not—on the surface at least—of the same ilk as Castro and his intimates. He was a man of sober habits and apparently honorable intentions and no coercion was ever needed to make him do his duty. His rivals alleged that it was because of the money he had put up that Castro had chosen him as his successor, but the truth of the matter was that Castro, as well as many other public officials, recognized Gómez's sterling qualities. Cipriano Castro was never one to bestow praise, being an imperious and relentless taskmaster, yet he often referred to Juan Vicente Gómez as "the personification of the perfect public servant." In his maudlin moments with a group of drinking companions, Castro would sometimes grasp Gómez (a teetotaler) affectionately by the shoulders and say with sincere conviction, "Ah! My good friend Juan Vicente! . . . What would I do without you! . . ."

CHAPTER EIGHT

Triumphs on the Field

It was inevitable that Castro's enemies would hold him to account for his misdeeds and broken promises to his country and that there would be attempts to depose him. The threat to Castro, his oligarchy, and the national peace did not take long to be converted into action.

Since October of 1899, that is to say, simultaneously with the triumph of Castro's revolution, the Republic of Colombia had been inflamed by civil war. Whether out of personal sympathy or for deeper reasons is not known, but Castro made the mistake of openly showing his partiality toward the Liberal revolutionists and their leader, General Rafael Uribe Uribe. Not only were the Colombian invasion groups permitted to organize on Venezuelan soil but the rebels received aid in the form of arms and ammunition. More than that, Castro went so far as to officially recognize the consuls named by the revolutionists for the Venezuelan cities of Maracaibo and San Antonio de Táchira. In May of 1900, the revolutionists were roundly beaten at Palonegro, Colombia, and although they sustained themselves in other engagements with varied success, the following year General Uribe and many of his followers were obliged to seek sanctuary in Venezuela.

When General Uribe began organizing a new revolutionary invasion, openly abetted by the Venezuelan authorities, the Colombian government finally took reprisals. It was surprising they did not declare war on Venezuela, but it could very well have been because the country had been debilitated by the long fight against the rebels. For that matter, neither was Venezuela in a favorable position to wage a war.

At first, the Colombian government merely offered asylum in Colombia to those of Castro's enemies who conspired to wage war against him. The leader of these exiles was Dr. Carlos Rangel Garbiras, who had become estranged from Castro and had turned against him. Then, in retaliation for the overt acts of Castro and his government, the Colombian government furnished not only arms to Dr. Rangel and his fellow exiles but an army of more than four thousand Colombians as well. With this sizable force Dr. Rangel crossed the border into Venezuela in July of 1901.

With neither side stopping at scruples, it became a case of "even Stephen." The Venezuelans rallied their forces in the Andes and at their head they placed General Uribe and his band of Colombian exiles. It was an utterly ridiculous situation and, as was to be expected, considerable confusion resulted, what with Venezuelans and Colombians battling their own countrymen, and the armies of two nations fighting an undeclared war—all on the one battlefield.

Dr. Rangel's army managed to penetrate into Venezuela almost as far as San Cristóbal before the Venezuelans were able to stop them. After a bloody three-day pitched battle in which many of the exiles of both countries killed each other off, the Colombians were pushed back over the border. As there weren't many exiles left to cause either Venezuela or Colombia much concern, the incident, fortunately, did not grow into more serious proportions and was soon dropped discreetly.

Meanwhile, many of Venezuela's discontents either were leaving the country or were withdrawing into the interior. And most of them kept in touch with each other so that if an opportunity arose they could start an uprising. During 1901 these revolutionary elements—which included partisans of every political creed—began to form into a solid, tightly-knit block which, counting the rank and file who followed their leadership, numbered somewhere between eight and ten thousand men.

The man who emerged as the leader of these potential rebels was General Manuel Matos, the Valencia banker, who issued his orders from Port of Spain, Trinidad. General Matos had had no military experience whatsoever (his title was honorary) and the reason he was so willingly accepted as the leader of the coming revolution was because he was a very wealthy man and through his banking connections abroad could count on additional funds for the purchase of arms.

Through government channels President Castro got wind of what was going on and who some of the leaders were. And he had every reason to feel uneasy when it was whispered there might even be an attempt on his life. During the past few years there had been a wave of political assassinations throughout the world. The Queen of Korea had been assassinated six years before, followed by the Empress Elizabeth of Austria-Hungary in 1898, then Humbert, King of Italy, in 1900, and just about this time, on September 6 to be exact, President William McKinley was shot by an anarchist in Buffalo, New York. The world was still embroiled in a series of armed conflicts. The Boxer insurrection in China, the Italian-Ethiopian, the Turkish-Greek, the Spanish-American, and the Philippine-American wars had only recently come to an end. With the South African war now drawing the headlines, the world was not much interested in the internal affairs of a small, backward South American republic. In South America, it was noticed, revolutions followed one another as often as the seasons; eventually—so the comment went—the barbarians would succeed in killing each other off.

For President Castro, the matter now resolved itself into the problem of finding out when and where the rebels were going to strike. Toward the end of the year there prevailed throughout the country a strong rumor that the revolution—which it was said would be a big one—would take place some time in December. The President took precautionary measures to insure that only loyal troops be stationed at the various *cuartels* along the various railroad lines and in the towns along the coast.

On December 12, Colonel López, who had been transferred the month before to head the garrison at the port of Tucacas in the state of Falcón, received an urgent telegram from the President. It was similar in contents to dozens of others sent to army commanders and state governments throughout the country. In it President Castro confirmed the rumor that a revolution was expected to break out any time after December 20. In the event of a breakdown in communications between Caracas and Tucacas, López was to contact General Pacheco at Barquisimeto.

The coming rebellion was going to further the rise of another promising soldier—Juan Vicente Gómez. Military tactics was a science, but to Gómez, the art of maneuvering troops came as naturally as a duck takes to water. Castro chose Gómez as the most capable man to head the government forces, appointed him commander of the Center, backed him up with his best generals, and sent him out to wipe out the rebels. Gómez's enemies denied, as they did of his other talents, that he possessed any military skill, but Gómez soon silenced his critics. He left Caracas on December 21 fully confident in the ascendency of his own star, and when he came back, on February 26 of the following year, he was the mighty hero of seven triumphant battles.

Gómez transported his men by rail to San Mateo, headed south through the state of Aragua, and the following day at Villa de Cura met and defeated General Luciano Mendoza. Mendoza fell back to La Puerta, the gateway to the *llanos,* where Gómez defeated him again the following day. When Mendoza retreated into the *llanos* Gómez pursued him and on Christmas Day defeated him for the third time, this time decisively. Mendoza and a few officers fled on horseback to the hills of the *Sierra de Carabobo.*

Farther north, General Antonio Fernández, who with General Bautista Ferrer had lost the battle of Tocuyito, was vainly trying to establish contact with General Mendoza. Gómez met and defeated him near La Puerta on December 30. Six days later he defeated General Jesús Arvelo near the same place. Leaving some troops to watch for Mendoza should he leave the hills, General Gómez crossed into the state of Cojedes to ferret out the old veteran General Loreto Lima. Lima, it will be remembered, was the general who had switched from the side of the government to that of Castro after the battle of Tocuyito. Gómez's army came upon his forces at Tinaco on February 7, routed them and took the general prisoner. Turning north through Carabobo, Gómez encountered by chance a revolutionary force under General Barráez at Bejuma, which he also fought and defeated. With the region apparently pacified, except for the raiding of distant haciendas by small guerrilla bands, Gómez returned to Caracas a hero.

Except for the short haul by rail to San Mateo, Gómez's army had covered hundreds of miles on foot and had penetrated many miles into the *llanos* in pursuit of the enemy. Forced marches and

surprise attacks had been the keynote of his success. He had fought
and won seven battles in three different states but had been absent
from the capital for only sixty-six days. In a crude sense, Gómez
could be called the first master of the *Blitzkrieg* of the twentieth
century, yet years were still to pass before the world was to learn the
real meaning in warfare of the word "mechanized." For one who had
never before taken to the field on his own, Gómez's feat had been
truly remarkable. And Castro frankly acknowledged his debt and
gratitude.

Declared one, Emilio Guerrero, in frank admiration: "Known for
his honesty and hard work, Juan Vicente Gómez is now eminent for
his valor and loyalty."

And G. Maldonado: "Loyal without a stain."

Whatever doubts there had been about Gómez's ability as a
leader, his prowess as a soldier, and his loyalty to Castro were for
the moment completely dispelled.

General Matos, meanwhile, had not been inactive. About the
middle of December of 1901, a mysterious steamer arrived from
Europe and dropped anchor off Port of Spain, Trinidad. The name
painted on its stern was *Banrigh,* and it flew the British flag. From
bow to stern the *Banrigh* bristled with naval cannon, and lashed to
its decks were field pieces destined for Venezuela's revolutionary war.
Below decks were hundreds of cases of rifles, ammunition, and shells.
The *Banrigh* was General Matos' contribution to Venezuela's revolution.

Under cover of darkness, General Matos and the other Venezuelan
exiles in Trinidad boarded the *Banrigh.* The next morning as she
bore west along the coast of Venezuela the vessel was flying the
yellow, blue, and red colors of Venezuela, and the freshly painted
name that appeared on its stern was *Libertador.*

From the time it appeared off the Venezuelan coast—Castro's
government charged—the *Banrigh,* or rather the *Libertador* as the
revolutionists now called her, carried on a program of insidious warfare. The vessel discharged Venezuelan revolutionists, arms, and ammunition on Venezuelan soil; it patrolled the Venezuelan coast, gradually changing into a machine of wanton destruction and barbarism;
it captured the government gunboat *Crespo;* it bombarded the peaceful Venezuelan cities of Güiria, Juan Griego, Porlamar, Carupano,

and Cumarebo; it leveled poor fishermen's villages to the ground; and it caused a great loss in innocent human lives.

By executive decree, dated December 30, 1901, which cited the precepts of international law, President Castro declared this ship a "pirate vessel."

Twenty days after he returned to Caracas, General Gómez was again ordered to take to the field. The "Liberative Revolution"—as it was called—was far from over. On March 17, 1902, General Gómez left at the head of a new expedition, this time toward the state of Falcón, where Generals Riera, Montilla, Peñalosa and others had the government forces which were garrisoning the state, stalemated. After a hard battle, Gómez defeated Generals Gregorio Segundo Riera and Peñalosa at Urucure. After a march through Coriano territory, mopping up revolutionary bands along the way, Gómez returned to Coro and on April 27 embarked at La Vela for La Guaira.

On March 1, Colonel López had been transferred back to his old post at Puerto Cabello as second in command of the battalion Carabobo. With Gómez busy fighting the rebels in Coro, guerrilla bands became very active, pillaging and killing over a wide area. Colonel López was with the troops sent out from Puerto Cabello to subdue them, and he saw action in several engagements.

Arriving at La Guaira on April 29, Gómez was handed his orders from President Castro. Supplied at last with arms from the *Banrigh,* Generals Domingo Monagas, Nicholas Rolando, and Zoilo Vidal had raised the flag of rebellion in the east. General Gómez was to provision his vessels, take on additional troops and arms and proceed to Cumaná immediately to do battle with these dangerous rebels.

Even as Gómez sailed from La Guaira the following day, without having visited Caracas, the rebels were marching through the states of Monagas and Sucre, sweeping everything before them. Gómez disembarked on the coast and attacked the rebel-held port of Cumaná. General Vidal and most of his men, however, safely withdrew toward the east and joined General Rolando at Carúpano. At this point General Velutini, who knew the eastern terrain, arrived with additional troops to join Gómez. The government army now marched on Carúpano.

In the Battle of Carúpano on May 6, Gómez suffered his first battle wound—a bullet in the thigh—which forced him to withdraw from the fight. Leaving orders that the campaign continue, Gómez returned reluctantly to Caracas to have the bullet removed. In later years this wound became increasingly troublesome and he required the aid of a cane. In Caracas, Gómez was attended by Dr. Rafael Requena who was captivated at once by the general's winning personality. Thus began a long and steadfast friendship. Several years later, after Gómez had grasped the reins of government in a bloodless coup of his own, Dr. Requena became his Secretary General, a position equal in rank to that of a cabinet minister.

With Gómez incapacitated and the campaign in the east not going too well, the President himself took to the field. On July 5 he issued a proclamation to this effect, adding that Juan Vicente Gómez, as First Vice President, would be left in charge of the government. To the whispers of friends and advisers that Gómez was not to be trusted, Castro retorted angrily that this fine soldier who had just shed his blood in defense of his government was humble, efficient, and entirely trustworthy.

Castro embarked on July 5 for the eastern front. On the same day, his forces in the east were completely routed at Aragua de Barcelona. Castro learned the bad news when he touched shore a few days later. He returned at once to Caracas.

At this juncture, the military situation for Castro began to assume alarming proportions. General Gómez had left the state of Falcón apparently pacified, yet General Riera, whom he had defeated at the battle of Urucure, had been able to reorganize his forces and was again on the warpath. On the sand dunes between La Vela and Coro, Riera met and defeated General Colmenares Pacheco who had just disembarked at La Vela with government troops. Two days later, the revolutionary chief attacked Coro, the capital of the state, which was defended by Generals Ayala, Second Vice President of the Republic, and Tellería, president of the state. The attack on the city was fierce. The defenders resisted stubbornly, then fell back until the fighting was carried on in the streets and from house to house. Finally, their ammunition exhausted, Generals Ayala and Tellería were taken prisoner with most of their officers. Few escaped. When the shooting ceased, a multitude of bodies lay prone in the streets.

What happened at Coro occurred in many towns and villages throughout the country. Everywhere, civil war cut short lives and ruined property. In the *llanos,* the Andes, and the central and eastern parts of the republic, in fact everywhere, blood flowed in torrents. There was hardly a Venezuelan family that did not cherish the memory of a relative who had perished in this or in other civil wars.

As humane as he was valorous, Riera liberated the majority of his prisoners. He left a small force in Coro under the command of one of his generals, and he himself marched to the central part of the republic with his victorious army.

Victorious at Aragua de Barcelona, General Rolando also was headed toward *el centro.* Day by day Castro's government was losing territory, troops and authority, while the Liberative Revolution was gaining in prestige and adherents. To Castro's high command the picture now became clear. The conquering revolutionary armies meant to unite in the center of the republic and converge on the capital. Soon, Castro would have to fight the big decisive battle which would undoubtedly decide the fate of his regime.

Outwardly, Castro was not one bit concerned. He held one more trump card. He was expecting prodigious reinforcements—troops from Táchira under General Cárdenas, from Mérida under General Linares, and from Trujillo under General Leopoldo Baptista. These forces eventually united in Lara with those of Dr. Gonzales Pacheco. This sizable army marched on to Tinaquillo in Cojedes where it met and fought the western revolutionary army on September 8. The result was indecisive.

Meanwhile, Castro had stationed troops between Ocumare del Tuy and La Victoria so that he could easily concentrate at either extremity, no matter in which direction the enemy marched. He sent a detachment into Cojedes to engage the enemy, but it was defeated at Flores and Mal Paso. Learning that the enemy's main forces were advancing through Guarico toward Villa de Cura, Castro decided to wait for them at La Victoria. Leopoldo Baptista was left to guard the approaches to Caracas, and González Pacheco the town of Los Teques eighteen miles south of the capital.

In Villa de Cura, which the revolutionists took almost without firing a shot, an impressive array of military talent sat down to a council of war. The chief of staff, old Domingo Monagas—an octo-

genarian who had to be assisted to mount his horse—had died in
Chaguaramas on the march toward *el centro*. His place was taken by
General Rolando, experienced head of the eastern rebels. There was
General Crespo Torres, brother of the late General Joaquin Crespo,
who had assumed the leadership of the revolutionists in the *llanos*. As
for General Luciano Mendoza—who had once voiced his aspirations
to the presidency to Dr. Guillermo Tell Villegas—his fame as a
soldier dated back forty years to the Federal Revolution. The other
generals, all of them tough, seasoned veterans were: Gregorio Riera,
Juan Pablo Peñalosa, Amábile Solagnie, Rafael Montilla, Zoilo Vidal,
Gregorio Cedeño, Lorenzo Guevara, J. M. Hernández Ron, and
Dr. J. M. Ortega Martínez. General Manuel Matos, as commander-
in-chief, presided.

It was agreed, first, to combine the various armies under the
above commanders into one invincible juggernaut rather than battle
separately, and secondly, to establish the principal strategic objective and overwhelm it. By some, this objective was believed to be
Caracas, and by others, the main army of General Castro at La
Victoria. General Matos advised advancing toward Caracas by way
of Tuy. General Mendoza insisted that they attack Castro at La
Victoria. Mendoza's counsel prevailed, for he was more experienced.

In theory, the revolutionary plan of attack was sound and capable of fulfillment, but putting it into execution was another thing.
Enveloped in an aura of exultation over the prospect of an easy
victory, there arose among the commanders an intense rivalry which
doomed the project to failure. From the very first hour of combat
there developed a disintegration of unity in the revolutionary command and a lack of co-ordination in the deployment of its troops.
Undoubtedly the revolutionary command possessed capable if not
brilliant tacticians but, due to the keen rivalry among these ambitious generals, none of them intended to expend his forces or exhaust
his ammunition, reasoning that in the moment of triumph the general strongest in troops and armament would be in the best position
to dictate terms.

During the night of October 11, a strong detachment of revolutionary troops marched on Los Teques to menace the capital and at
the same time attempt to cut the railroad between Caracas and La
Victoria. The next morning the revolutionary army, fourteen thou-

and strong, marched toward La Victoria where Castro was entrenched with only six thousand men.

Fanning out to surround La Victoria on three sides, the rebels
attacked. General Guevara tried to take the ridge of El Calvario
while General Vidal opened fire in an assault against the well-de-
fended railroad station on the heights of Los Teques. Division after
division tried to dislodge the government troops but the defenders
held firm, using to good advantage a battery of Krupp "8" guns.

Fighting continued furiously all during the night and through
the next day, with President Castro personally directing the battle.
On the morning of the 13th Castro dispatched an urgent telegram
to General Gómez in Caracas. He was to bring more munitions and
as many men as he could immediately. For lack of munitions, Castro
had had to tighten his advance line by ordering the withdrawal of
some of his advance positions.

On the same afternoon, the expected train pulled in to La Victoria station. On it were Generals Gómez and Baptista with a thousand men and a carload of munitions. They were met with a fusillade
of bullets from the enemy.

General Baptista was named chief of the right line under General Gómez. General Bautista Ferrer, as chief of staff, commanded
the center line until General Castro could take over. Castro remained
the night and all day of the 14th at the foot of El Cuji hill until the
danger of losing El Calvario was past.

Generals Matos, Mendoza, and Rolando were in the center of
the revolutionary line. Starting on the 14th they initiated a series of
attacks, which they intensified from the 15th to the 17th. General
Castro, still the aggressive optimist, counter-attacked just as often,
until he had used up most of his reserves.

On the morning of the 18th the situation looked precarious for
Castro's army due to the excessive consumption of munitions. General Castro ordered General Olivares to fall back toward La Victoria.
His intention—if forced to give up the fight—was to open a path to
Las Colonias and continue on to Ocumare where the government
squadron lay at anchor. The government troops in *el centro* would
spread out and fight a guerrilla warfare while Castro would embark
with some officers for Maracaibo. With the five thousand rifles and
one million rounds of ammunition stored in San Carlos fortress and

with other armament available from the Andes, he would organize
a new army and return to *el centro*. He resolved on releasing General Hernández and the other recalcitrant generals imprisoned in
San Carlos as well as another group held in the fortress of Puerto
Cabello. That city, which was well provisioned, would figure as the
main base of operations. Castro hoped to arrive at some agreement
with General Hernández, supply him with armament and vessels to
disembark at La Vela to engage the enemy, thus gaining time so
that he could organize an Andean army.

This plan did not have to be executed, as on the afternoon of
October 18 a trainload of munitions arrived at La Victoria station
which made it possible to regain the abandoned positions and renew the offensive all along the line. The enemy began to give ground.

By now, wearied by battle and uncertain as to specific plan of
attack, Castro turned over active command to General Gómez. As
calmly as if he were planning a junket into the hills, Gómez pored
over his map and issued his orders. On dark nights his forces feinted
at the enemy entrenched in the hills. Then suddenly during the night
of October 21 his army attacked in a furious assault and captured the
enemy-held heights of Pipe and El Copey. Its left line destroyed and
its right thrown back to Cuesta de las Mulas, the revolutionists' center
had to fall back.

Thus began a general retreat of the revolutionary army, though
in good order and with full equipment. Though still superior in numbers, the rebels retreated at forced march toward Cagua with the
government troops hot in pursuit. At Cagua the revolutionary chieftains parted, each heading toward home with his followers—Rolando
and Zoilo Vidal to the east, Crespo Torres to the south, and Matos,
Solagnie, and Riera toward the west.

With the ten day battle of La Victoria fought and won, the threat
to General Castro's regime was over, temporarily, at least.

Back in Caracas, Castro, sure of his man now, wrote him a letter
saying: "I salute General Juan Vicente Gómez and congratulate him
upon the triumph of La Victoria, for the glories are legitimately his.'

But other major battles were still in the offing—Barquisimeto, La
Vela, Mata Palo, and Ciudad Bolívar. And Gómez would receive
still other congratulatory messages, and the memory of them would
make him purr delightedly for years to come.

CHAPTER NINE

Heavy Hangs the Crown

Settling down to the affairs of state, President Castro soon became embroiled in new difficulties. The *Banrigh* incident had touched off a chain of events which Castro was powerless to halt. Rather than leave well enough alone he had kept harping on the affair until the British minister delivered a note to the Venezuelan government. While admitting that the *Banrigh* was of British registry, the British government categorically denied any complicity in the piratical acts of the vessel. General Matos himself substantiated this statement by publicly declaring that neither Great Britain nor any other foreign power had contributed or aided in the arming of the steamer. Castro, however, pounced on the admission of British registry to demand of the British an explanation for the hostile acts of the ship. As this was not obtained, on March 13 Venezuela formally protested to the British government against the conduct of the *Banrigh*, reserving the right to demand compensation for the damages and injuries caused. The protest was renewed on April 6 when it became known that the vessel had put in at Port of Spain and the British authorities there had made no attempt to impound it or start an inquiry.

The reply that the British government gave to these just demands was the presentation of the old claims of British subjects for damages suffered during the last civil wars. Whereupon the German and Italian governments thought the time opportune to present their claims also.

To say that Castro was angry at this turn of events is putting it mildly. He was furious. Some of the foreign indemnity claims against the government—not to mention the enormous unpaid loans—dated back more than forty years and they were still piling up after each

civil war. Except for the settlement of a few individual claims, pas
administrations had either refused outright to make payment or ha
adroitly side-stepped the issue and left it to their successors. Th
debts of his unscrupulous predecessors heaped upon his unwillin
shoulders, Castro argued that it was unjust that his administration b
expected to pay for the sins of the past. Just as Andueza Palacio
Rojas Paul, and the others had done before him, he procrastinated, h
dodged, he denied the validity of these claims, declaring them ex
orbitant and outright frauds, and he placed every legal obstacle tha
his lawyers could devise in the path of an equitable settlement. True
he had set up an "Examination Committee" to review these claim
after "certain documentary proof" was presented. But the require
ments were stiff, and with "Venezuela for the Venezuelans" being th
popular maxim, Venezuelan witnesses would not furnish the neces
sary sworn testimony for foreigners. Only a handful of claimants—
principally the powerful German commercial chains—received settle
ments, and these were for only a fraction of the original demands
Great Britain, Germany, and Italy insisted that the claims of thei
nationals be settled as presented and without further delay. To th
Venezuelan government these claims were inadmissible, and wer
flatly rejected.

Castro's attitude in this matter was identical to that of Guzmá
thirty years before, when the Foreign Office had delivered notes t
the ministries of Germany, Great Britain, Denmark, Italy, Spain
France, and the United States in answer to indemnity claims (coverin
the looting and destruction of commercial establishments, etc.) o
their nationals. Totalling almost six million dollars, the claims wer
denied in their entirety and the foreign diplomats were regarde
as insolent in presenting them.

Declared Guzmán in a vehement outburst after United State
President Ulysses S. Grant had informed Congress of the state c
affairs with the fiery little South American Republic:[7] ". . . Th
claim of Mr. Quirke is another robbery which the Republic will nc
tolerate. General Grant can say what he wants to . . . the Nort
American Congress can decide what it wishes . . . and Mr. Willia

---

[7] In his wrath, Guzmán had written President Grant a personal letter. Whil
it could be called dignified in tone, it had labeled these claims "a monstrou
fraud."

Pile (U.S. legal representative) can keep on asking for the payment of a million and more pesos for claims that in their origin amount to no more than 80,000 . . . but I will not agree to any other solution than that arrived at within this country and through due process of law compatible with the administration of justice and the honor of my Government. The gist of any discussion I may have with these diplomats will be: 'Bring on your cannons and start shooting against Venezuela . . . because I won't stand for any more of this diplomatic robbery.' The words of General Grant in his message to Congress do not detract from our right nor my resolution to prevent anyone from sacking the country . . ."

The first foreign government claim presented to Castro's government was made by the German minister in April of 1900—less than six months after Castro had assumed power. It involved not only damages to property, but injuries and loss of life to German nationals during the recent revolutions. Also claimed was payment of the loan of 1896 to build a railroad, and reimbursement for the construction by the Germans of the Caracas abattoir.

It has been said that there was evidence to show that both Great Britain and Germany had consulted with the United States government to explore its attitude with regard to the application of the Monroe Doctrine in case of a belligerent demonstration on their part on the South American continent. The United States was said to have replied that it had no reasons to side with a government which reneged on its promises (meaning Venezuela) and that its sole preoccupation was the violation of territorial rights. Great Britain and Germany then induced Italy to join a united front against Venezuela.

President Castro wrote to the German minister that Venezuela was trying to amortize her debts; she was paying cash for government passages (movement of troops) on the Gran Ferrocarril de Venezuela; she had already made token payments on the settlements with the German commercial houses of Beckmann & Cia., Romer & Baasch, and Marcus & Cia.; and other claims, those of Steinvorth & Cia., Breuer, Moller & Cia., A. Ermen & Cia., and Van Dissel & Cia., were nearing settlement. But as far as the other claims were concerned, Germany would have to wait until the Examination Committee—created almost two years before—had reviewed and studied all the demands. It was the same old story of vague promises and delays.

This became a trying period for Castro—already a tired and unhappy man given to nervous outbursts and fits of sulking. He became supersensitive to the subject of foreigners and their claims. Sometimes he would explode in a rage, pounding the table and shouting: "Robbers! Thieves! Try to take advantage of a small defenseless nation, will they! Well, not one bolivar will they get! . . ."

Matters reached a sorry pass. Castro assumed an attitude of open disdain toward the claimant nations. He ignored rigid protocols and was "not in" when their ministers called. When the French minister made one of his periodic trips to La Guaira to wine and dine in the French fashion on a French liner which was visiting the port, orders were given not to permit him to disembark. He had to remain aboard for the return trip to France and an outraged French government issued an indignant protest. Other ministers were "detained" on various pretexts, and when the news reached their home governments the ministers were recalled. One after the other, diplomatic relation were severed with Great Britain, Germany, France, Belgium, Holland Italy, and the United States.

On December 7, 1902, the ministers of Great Britain and Germany delivered an ultimatum to the Venezuelan government requesting the immediate payment in full of those claims which were many year past due. Two days later the Venezuelan government replied that i would give satisfaction to all claims "after all of them had been care fully reviewed and studied and the country was financially able to mak payments." However, the notes could not be delivered. The Britis and German ministers had closed their legations and had boarde their respective cruisers anchored off La Guaira. These vessels the began to execute coercive maneuvers, using threats to force the crew of the Venezuelan gunboats *Ossun, Margarita, General Crespo,* an *Totumo* to abandon their craft, then sinking all but the *Totumo*.

Through all this, Gómez remained in the background, quiet, un assuming and inconspicuous. Inwardly envious of Castro and hi power, he abhorred his gruff and imperious ways, but outwardly he wa all smiles and "bravos" for Castro's every move. Those days ingraine in Gómez a healthy respect for the superior power of the *musius*—a the Venezuelans call all foreigners—and it can be said of him that h relations with foreign powers were always most cordial. Perhaps it was then that he deemed himself worthy to fill Castro's shoes, but he was smart enough to realize that he had first to learn all the tricks of his nefarious vocation.

Gómez learned fast and well. Yet he was in no hurry to usurp the power. Perhaps Castro would overreach himself, commit one more *faux pas* that would be his undoing, or perhaps succumb to the inevitable reckoning of his vice-ridden way of life. But Castro had a charmed life, and the twists of circumstances of this turbulent period won him the popular support he so sorely needed.

In a vibrating proclamation, President Castro informed the nation of the abuses committed by the foreign vessels: "The insolent project of the foreigner," he said, "has profaned the sacred soil of the Fatherland . . . Transgression of the national sovereignty has been perpetrated. In shameful collusion, vessels of the German and British armadas have fired on three Venezuelan craft . . ."

Public opinion, now thoroughly aroused, responded with alacrity to the President's appeal for their moral support. Almost five thousand volunteers crowded government offices of the capital to pledge themselves in the event of a call to arms should foreigners invade Venezuelan soil. It was the spirit of 1896 all over again. Even General Hernández, who had been released from San Carlos fortress, issued a proclamation to his followers throughout the country to lay down their arms and collaborate with Castro during the present crisis.

When Castro was informed that British, German, and Italian cruisers were reconnoitering off the Venezuelan coast, he ordered the transfer of all army units stationed in Caracas to La Guaira and vicinity to prevent any attempted landing. To this effect, General Bautista Ferrer assumed command of fifteen hundred troops spread out between El Vigia and Rio Grande. Each hostile warship was kept under constant surveillance and reports were dispatched by mounted courier to Ferrer at his headquarters in Maiquetía.

Throughout the country resentment against foreigners was transformed into demonstrations against them and their properties. But by the time the President admonished the citizenry to be calm and the authorities actually took steps to prevent violence, it was too late. At the docks of Puerto Cabello a frenzied mob seized and overran a British cargo vessel, the *Topace*. After the crew was marched off to

the *calabozo* for the sole crime of being British, the vessel was sacked
and its flag pulled down, trampled underfoot, and torn to shreds.

One of the crew had managed to hoist a flag of distress, and the
news of the *Topace*'s mishap was flashed to the British cruiser
Caribidis at La Guaira. The outcome was an ultimatum from the
British for an apology and redress under the threat of bombardment
of *El Libertador* fortress at Puerto Cabello. Cocky and defiant, President Castro refused to comply with the British demands on the grounds
that such a submission would be too humiliating to a proud and
peaceful nation. Although the British sailors from the *Topace* had
been released, the *Caribidis,* accompanied by the German heavy
cruiser *Vineta,* steamed toward Puerto Cabello to carry out the threat.

When the first shell from the *Caribidis* hit the fortress, Puerto
Cabello was thrown into a panic. From the first, Castro had misled the
military and civil authorities into believing that the matter was being
settled amicably. He purposely failed to mention anything about the
threat to the fortress. At the boom of the first shell, the populace and
military alike mistakenly thought the city was under bombardment
and they fled in panic. Many homes and business establishments were
left wide open. Fear had no respect for station. Despite his fame as a
fearless soldier, General Secundino Torres—to quote a bystander—
was seen to "fly by with the speed of a deer, more than two blocks
ahead of his soldiers!"

Being a fortress in name only, having been converted many years
before into a penitentiary, *El Libertador* was unable to reply to the
attack. Two boatloads of British sailors were landed and they made
off with some images and furniture from the prison chapel.

Fort Solano nearby boasted only two old bronze cannon. At the
moment of the first shelling these were loaded with powder and
wadding to celebrate the anticipated "amicable settlement." Hoping
to frighten off the British, Colonel Antenor Ugueto, the fort's commander, let go with the harmless charge. A few seconds later the
Vineta replied with a broadside that crippled both guns. In the wild
dash for safety a soldier fell down a flight of stone steps and cut himself. This was the only casualty of the whole "comical affair"—as one
restrained historian expressed it. The Caracas press, however, played
it up as a pitched battle in which "the shore batteries repelled the attack of the foreign fleets with valor."

From merely coercive, however, the foreign retaliation became openly aggressive. The foreign powers—Germany, Great Britain, and Italy—blockaded the Venezuelan coast from La Vela to Barcelona. All coastal traffic ground to a halt. Only the United States government refused to permit its vessels to be halted by the blockade.

On January 17, 1903, the *Panther,* a thousand-ton German gunboat of seven guns, hove to in the Gulf of Venezuela. Within range of its guns lay San Carlos fortress, which guards the narrow channel to Lake Maracaibo. Neither San Carlos nor its garrison had ever been put to the test. The fortress had been built almost a century and a half before to repel the attack of pirates, after Maracaibo had been sacked in 1662 by William Jackson, and again in 1669 by Henry Morgan. On this sunny, cloudless day the fortress was going to undergo its first test. Without warning, the *Panther* began firing salvo after salvo on the gray mass of stone and concrete.

To the Venezuelans, the design of the Germans [8] was all too clear. They wanted to cross the bar, steam the thirty miles down the lake to Maracaibo and loot the city. General Jorge Bello, the commandant of San Carlos, bravely met the challenge. He let loose with everything he had—two antiquated cannon, which sprang out of their emplacement at every recoil. To the surprise of everyone, the Venezuelans scored a direct hit. The *Panther* withdrew to Curacao with several dead and wounded, but reappeared on the 21st. This time she was accompanied by the *Vineta* and the British cruiser *Falke*. The bombardment was repeated, and again the fortress' guns replied with valor and good luck. This time the attackers withdrew for good.

Suffering twenty-four dead and wounded, the Venezuelans claimed that the foreign warships had poured more than sixteen hundred shells into the fortress and the village which nestles in its rear. A church and almost one hundred houses, most of them shacks, were destroyed and many families were rendered homeless.

General Bello became the hero of the day; President Castro wired his congratulations; and the headlines screamed: THE CAPTURE

---

[8] A few days earlier, the officers of the *Panther* had attended a dinner and dance given in their honor by the German Consul in Maracaibo, Edward von Jess. It was later charged that the consul had briefed the captain of the *Panther* on the forthcoming assault.

OF MARACAIBO PREVENTED BY THE HEROIC RESISTANCE OF SAN
CARLOS FORTRESS.

The news of these attacks aroused a wave of sympathy throughout the Americas. The United States decided it was now time to intervene. President Theodore Roosevelt, the vigorous exponent of iron-
fist diplomacy, informed the German Kaiser and the other powers
that any further aggression in the Americas would mean war.

A famous Roosevelt episode in connection with the incident concerns the arrival at the White House of the German ambassador to
receive the ultimatum. Roosevelt told him bluntly that he would give
the Kaiser forty-eight hours to remove his warships from Venezuelan
waters.

Twelve hours later, the German ambassador returned to say: "His
Imperial Majesty does not believe that forty-eight hours are sufficient
to permit the withdrawal of these vessels."

Roosevelt bellowed at him, "You haven't got forty-eight hours,
sir, you have only thirty-six hours left. You can tell the Kaiser that
if his warships are not removed by that time, I shall order the
Atlantic squadron to remove them!"

When the deadline arrived, not a foreign warship remained off
the Venezuelan coast.

It followed that through the energetic intervention of President
Roosevelt, the blockading powers agreed to submit to international
tribunals the claims they were upholding by force. It was proved that
some were unjust and others were greatly exaggerated. Other countries having nationals with pecuniary claims also agreed to submit
these to similar tribunals. The procedure was prescribed in the so-
called Washington Protocols, and the outcome was that the Venezuelan government agreed to pay 70,000,000 bolivars over a period
of twenty years.

To do Cipriano Castro and his administration justice, once those
arrangements had been made, he carried them out faithfully during
the entire period that he was President. There could not be much
doubt, however, that it was the wise counsel of Juan Vicente Gómez
that prevailed on Castro to do so.

CHAPTER TEN

The Humble Servant

With the blockade over and the prospect of war dispelled, the country anxiously looked toward peace. But it was a peace that was still out of reach and it would still have to be fought for with blood and sweat.

Of Castro's enemies, only General Hernández had been patriotic enough to call a halt to active revolt while his country was threatened by those who would attack her sovereignty. The blockade had prevented the government from utilizing its fleet to reinforce and supply its troops and to carry on its operations. On the other hand, the rebels, while lacking marine transportation, had better land facilities, and they feverishly prepared to renew their offensive.

In March, 1903, a revolutionary force advanced on Caracas by way of Petare but was repelled by General Ferrer. When President Castro's intelligence informed him that Generals Rolando and Ortega Martínez were expecting to receive a huge supply of munitions at Barlovento, he ordered General Gómez with fifteen hundred men to Higuerote. Gómez embarked at La Guaira on April 8, taking along his cousin Eustóquio Gómez (now a colonel) and Colonel López.

While General Gómez achieved some minor successes in the four days of battles in the state of Miranda (from April 11 to 14), they could not be called decisive victories. The revolutionists, however, had been pushed back toward the west, and Gómez resolved to return to La Guaira to prepare for a western offensive.

Gómez's expedition to the west began during the first days of May. Trying to disembark at Tucacas, his naval force was met with heavy fire from the rebel garrison. Colonels López and Felix Galavis, who both knew the land well, suggested landing some troops farther along and entering the village through the cemetery in the rear. Gómez acted on this suggestion and Tucacas was captured.

Once again General Gómez resorted to speed and surprise. Taking a circuitous route to the southwest, the army set out for Barquisimeto on a forced march. The only opposition along the way was a guerrilla attack at San Felipe and another at Urachiche, where Gómez suffered a few casualties in personnel and beasts of burden. He arrived to the east of Barquisimeto at dusk. At precisely the same time, the rebels reached the western outskirts of the city.

Founded in 1552, Barquisimeto, the capital of Lara, is on a semi-arid plateau surrounded by low, eroded, reddish hills. Barquisimeto, or in its older form, "Barisiquimeto," means "ash-colored water" in the language of the Indian tribe which lived on the spot centuries ago. Today, its Río Turbio, once called "ash-colored water," is generally dry, except for the hours of heavy rainfall when it is impossible to cross it. Waterless, the city still relies on rain-pools to provide the precious liquid all the year round.

Just a few kilometers east of the city is the little village of Santa Rosa. Here, in the whitewashed adobe houses and adjacent fields, the government army encamped. After shaking the dust of the road from their garments, Gómez and his staff immediately pored over maps of the vicinity. Scouts were sent out to learn the lay of the land and to make contact with the city garrison. He wasted no time, that man Gómez. He realized that there was a big battle to be fought, in all probability the decisive battle of the campaign. And every minute was precious.

More than one of his devoted followers has referred to Gómez as "another Bolívar." Actually, he was the exact antithesis of the famed military commander. Both were great generals—but there the similarity ended. Bolívar was impulsive, impatient, controversial, and highly emotional. Gómez was methodical, tolerant, cool, and soft-spoken. Both men achieved fame on the battlefield, as well as elsewhere, but there was no similarity in their methods.

It was after he had lost a battle in Barquisimeto on November 10, 1813, that Simón Bolívar is said to have remarked, "To contemplate a sunset at Barquisimeto is worth losing a battle." The Liberator had been watching the victorious breakthrough of his cavalry from a hill in what is today the very center of the city. Suddenly a confusing bugle call caused his soldiers to retreat in disorder, and the battle was lost to the Royal Spanish troops led by Ceballos.

Gómez read every book he could find on the life of his idol, Bolívar. That hot, dreary night in May, when in silent contemplation he finally faced toward the historic city, he relived history. He could see the dark, slender figure of the Liberator astride his valiant charger, watching from a red, eroded hill, his troops go forth to meet the enemy. He could hear the bugle call to charge, and the now familiar din of battle. He could smell the acrid smoke of powder and feel the tenseness and anxiety of the man in command. Then one small blunder, and the tide of battle had turned. Had Bolívar actually commented on the sunset as was said of him? Of course not! Not after hundreds of his countrymen had given their lives on that field of battle.

Somewhere out there under the dark, parched earth of Barquisimeto those fallen soldiers lay. Tomorrow, after the sun had set, others would be put to rest beside them. Now they were living, breathing men, snoring in their *chinchorros,* dreaming not of history, but of horrors and death.

The commander-in-chief had laid his plans well. By midnight, when he retired, he knew the position of every enemy corps, every strategic hilltop, every water-hole. So silent and swift had been the march toward Santa Rosa, the enemy had learned of his arrival only now. Gómez surmised, correctly, that there must be great consternation in the enemy camp.

Following Gómez's blueprint of attack, his generals deployed their troops during the last hours of darkness. The attack began at dawn, May 22, on the northern outskirts of the city. By 8 P.M., fourteen hours later, the battle had died down to sporadic firing. The contestants were weary and hungry, but neither side would yield an inch. The battle had reached a stalemate.

At his headquarters in Santa Rosa, Gómez was his usual cool, complacent self. At intervals a nondescript, unshaven peasant in mufti appeared at the entrance, whispered the proper password and was ushered into the presence of the chief. These would be scouts, reporting the latest intelligence of enemy movements.

Against one wall of General Headquarters sat a row of junior
officers, awaiting special orders. One of them, watching every movement of his chief and catching his every word, was Colonel López.

"You—there!" said Gómez, after hearing the message of a
courier. López half rose from his chair, but Gómez motioned to a
captain beside him. The man sprang to attention. "General Velasco
wants twenty thousand rounds of ammunition. Send him half that
amount. And mind you, use only two burros!"

A few minutes past eight, another courier was ushered in. He
saluted smartly. "Lieutenant Romero, my General, reporting for
General González Pacheco on the northern sector."

"And what does he want?" As if the chief didn't know.

"Twenty thousand rounds, my General . . . and one hundred
men."

"So! And why the reinforcements? Isn't the battle going well?"

"General González says we are holding strong, but he is planning
a strong offensive to start at dawn."

"MM-mm-mm, *muy interesante!* . . . but you can tell our friend
González that tomorrow, the 23rd of May, will be a great day. He
won't need those reinforcements and munitions . . . *because the
enemy will retreat tonight!*"

Gómez was right. The enemy retreated at three o'clock in the
morning. Gómez didn't hear about it, however, until he awoke four
hours later. By then it was too late to catch up with them.

It was an incredible prediction. Perhaps it was just another example of the extraordinary acumen of this strange and remarkable
man. At any rate, it has remained one of the many enigmas of his
life. How could this uneducated and virtually inexperienced rustic
foretell an absolute victory within a matter of hours when even his
best generals did not know which way the tide of battle was running?
There was no one among those who surrounded him who could answer that question, and no one dared to ask. Suffice to say that his
men regarded their leader with awe, and his fame spread far and
wide. One by one his enemies learned to their sorrow that in any contest of wits, Juan Vicente Gómez was a deadly adversary.

With the battle of Mata Palo a few days later, revolutionary resistance in the west was definitely crushed, and Generals Matos and
Riera fled to Curacao.

The third and last expedition of General Gómez was to Ciudad Bolívar where General Rolando was still a menace to law and order. This was a seaborne invasion that wended its way east along the coast past the farthermost tip of Venezuela, through the Gulf of Paria past Trinidad, then up the mighty Orinoco—Venezuela's "Father of Waters." For a landlubber who had never seen the sea until he was forty-five, the journey must have been a stirring experience for Gómez.

The Torbes River below San Cristóbal was a mere trickle compared with the Orinoco. Over one thousand miles in length, it is, in importance, the first river of Venezuela, the third of South America, and the ninth of the entire world. Originating in Brazil, it is fed by 36 monstrous tributaries and over 2,000 streams and rivulets, and its widest mouth (there are 17 of them) at San Rafael de Barrancas is 14 miles wide. In those days the great river was the home of the *manati* (sea cow), that browsed on the weeds, grasses, and other algae of the river, swimming lazily and lightly; the caiman —the alligator of South America; and vast numbers of turtles weighing up to 75 pounds, which supplied the Indians with meat, eggs, and edible oil.[9]

The Orinoco was first seen by Christopher Columbus on his third voyage in 1498, and was discovered by Vicente Yañez in 1500, but the first European to navigate it was Diego de Ordaz in 1532. During the two centuries of exploration that followed, many expeditions traveled its swift-flowing waters, some bent on filibustering, others on dominating the rich, wild territory. To the adventurers searching for easy wealth, the Indians dropped hints of the fable of El Dorado. Spaniards, Frenchmen, Dutchmen, Englishmen, all searched anxiously for the resplendent city, the city of the *cúspides* of gold, on the shore of a fabulous lake. As the Indians all pointed south toward the heart of the jungle, the Europeans hacked their way through the tangled underbrush, delirious with greed. But, like Walter Raleigh and his son—the latter was killed fighting his way up the river in

[9] In the jungle lives a red monkey called the *araguato*. Because of its great resemblance to man, long ago it gave rise to the popular belief that cannibal Indians inhabited Venezuela. What were actually *araguatos* roasting on a spit for the Indians' evening meal, were reported by horrified explorers to be murdered children.

search of the golden city—the adventurers found nothing but hostile Indians, strange animals and birds, and fevers of the jungle.

When José Solano returned to Spain in 1762 with the scientific expedition that had traveled the Orinoco and the territory of Guayana he gave King Charles III a glowing account of the luxuriant vegetation, praising "the fragrant, colorful flowers, the sweetness of the fruits." The Crown had been unable to maintain a governorship in the territory because its fort, Santo Tomás, some six leagues below the Caroni had been reduced to desolate ruins by the attacks of Raleigh and other marauding adventurers. Solano urged that Santo Tomá be moved to a more strategic location, and he suggested a cragged hill at a narrow part of the Orinoco where a fortified city could be built. Acting on Solano's recommendation, the King commanded that the fort be moved, and 1764 saw the founding of what was called Angostura (meaning narrow), which name was later changed to Ciudad Bolívar.

Under Manuel Centurión and succeeding Spanish governors Ciudad Bolívar grew and prospered, and before a century had passed foreign vessels were plying the Orinoco loaded with tropical fruits heron feathers,[10] skins, hides, and woods. Still to be discovered or exploited in the region were vast untapped riches: forests of valuable timber, wild rubber, medicinal barks and herbs, the asphalt deposit of Pedernales, the iron mines of San Félix—where the rich ore is 75 per cent pure iron—the gold mines of El Callao and the diamond in the Caroni River.

In 1818 Angostura became the provisional residence of the revolutionary forces in their fight against the Royalists. It was there on January 1, 1819, that the Congress of Angostura signed its memoria constitution and elected Simón Bolívar the first President of the new born republic.

With the discovery of gold in El Callao in the southern state of Bolívar in 1864, Ciudad Bolívar became the jumping off place for frenzied prospectors, many of whom never returned from the jungle The gold fever became so great, some European governments had to issue warnings to adventure-seeking nationals who were intent on forsaking the humdrum existence of their staid city jobs for the peril

---

[10] Which later commanded a price of five hundred dollars a pound.

of the unknown. Ciudad Bolívar became the Mecca for prospectors, adventurers, artisans (mostly German), goldsmiths, jewelers, tradesmen, and missionaries. Ships from all parts of the world crowded its wharves, and an American company, the American Steam Navigation Company, secured a government contract to ply the upper Orinoco and the Apure Rivers, making the trip once a month. Labor became scarce, American gold coins plentiful, and the city acquired fame for its two foremost products—cigars and gold *cochano* jewelry.

On July 11, 1903, General Gómez's squadron of three ships, *Restaurador, Zamora,* and *Bolívar,* under the command of Venezuela's "admiral," General Román Delgado Chalbaud, entered the Orinoco. Two days later troops were disgorged at Santa Ana, and they proceeded along the shore to surround Ciudad Bolívar by land while the squadron covered the city from the river.

In the number of troops, both sides had about three thousand men, but the defenders were entrenched in a more strategic position. As it was clear to both sides that the coming battle would be a bloody one, General Gómez was disposed to listen to the propositions made to him to avoid unnecessary bloodshed. While the American warship, *Bancroft,* and the French warship, *Jouffrey,* steamed up the river and stood by to protect their nationals, Bishop Sendrea, as well as the foreign consular corps in the city offered their good offices to effect a compromise. General Rolando requested guarantees for those who would surrender. General Gómez demanded unconditional surrender with no promises whatsoever of protection for General Ramón Farreras, who had made Ciudad Bolívar a revolutionary citadel.

When negotiations ended in a deadlock, Gómez ordered an all-out attack on the city at dawn on July 19th. After fifty hours of fierce fighting the enemy surrendered. Taken with General Rolando were fifty-four generals and the entire revolutionary army.

For General Gómez and the regime he represented it was a momentous occasion; the last revolutionary stronghold in Venezuela had fallen, and in no small measure the feat had been accomplished because of the superior prowess of one man.

Well did Juan Vicente Gómez realize that he had become the man of the hour when he sent off the following pithy telegram to President Castro: "On the 21st of December, 1901, I left the capital with a group of valiants to render into submission Luciano Mendoza, the first traitor to revolt against the institutions of the republic. Today, after fifty hours of bloody fighting, I have the honor to put this town —the last bastion of the rebellion—at your disposition. I congratulate you on the consolidation of peace in Venezuela. Details will follow."

To which Castro replied saying, among other things: "The man who since December 21, 1901, has been fighting with such great success for the salvation of the republic, of its institutions, of its chief and the great and sacred interests of the *Causa Liberal Restauradora*, could do no less, by his bravery and daring, than wipe out with one thunderous blow the bastion of the most iniquitous, infamous, and criminal revolution ever recorded in the historical annals of the civilized nations of the world." He ended congratulating again "the most humble, and at the same time the greatest of all the servants of the *Causa Liberal Restauradora.*"

On July 24th, the main plaza of Ciudad Bolívar echoed to loquacious speeches and the strains of the national anthem. A proclamation signed by General Gómez was read to the citizenry and the vanquished army: "Today, the 24th of July, the anniversary of the birth of the Father of our Country, I urge you to offer to his memory as a meritorious tribute the solemn pledge to declare ended the era of our civil discord."

The message was neatly phrased, but we know the words could not have stemmed from the limited vocabulary of Juan Vicente Gómez. Someone had written it for him. But he had been astute enough to take advantage of a propitious date to play on the public's sympathies and patriotism.

As for the defeated revolutionary chieftains, solemn pledges were neither expected nor demanded; in compliance with Castro's orders, they were all put behind bars, and to make doubly sure they would long remember why they were put there, irons of sixty pounds weight were riveted to each man's ankles. Among the prisoners these irons were referred to mockingly as *restauradores*.

The cells of the Rotunda and the fortress of Puerto Cabello became so filled with these obdurate and recalcitrant *caudillos* that many of them were shipped out in the dark hold of an old reconverted tug, *El Zumbador,* to San Carlos, where they were packed like sardines in small damp cells. Among those taken from Ciudad Bolívar to San

Carlos were Generals Farrera, Rolando, Vázques, Sánchez, Echenique, and Ducharme. Castro even went so far as to order the arrest and imprisonment in San Carlos of General Farrera's uncle and father, the latter a harmless old gentleman of over eighty years of age. Neither of these old men could stand for long the hardships and maltreatment by the prison wardens. General Farrera saw both his father and uncle carried out dead within a year.

To while away the long hours of heat, hunger, and thirst, some of the prisoners of San Carlos took English lessons from General Pedro Ducharme, an accomplished linguist. The first phrases they learned were "I am hungry," "I am thirsty" and "These irons hurt." Indeed they must have.

General Ducharme's brothers, Alejandro and Horacio, fared considerably better than he. Alejandro fled to exile in Trinidad, while Horacio, pretending to be a drunken English sailor, walked brazenly through the streets of La Guaira, all the while munching bananas like any *musiú* from the north. He escaped aboard a foreign freighter.

Some months later, while Castro's wife, doña Zoila, was visiting in Maracaibo, she got wind of the cruelties that General Jorge Bello was inflicting on his prisoners. She paid San Carlos a visit. Distressed at what she saw, she insisted that the irons be removed from the prisoners' legs, and she refused to leave until her demand had been complied with. But no sooner had this kind and sympathetic lady left the fortress than General Bello's blacksmith again set to work.

About this time, President Castro drastically curtailed military expenditures. The national armies were disbanded and many garrisons reduced to skeleton forces. Thanks to the prowess of General Gómez, there probably wouldn't be any more revolutions to cope with, as all the revolutionary *caudillos* were either in exile or under strong lock and key. When General Ferrer was ordered back to Caracas it was his painful duty to inform Colonel López and his fellow officers that with the disbandment of his battalion they were retired from duty. Said one of the officers, voicing López's speculation about the future: "Well, then, the war's over, but how are we going to live?"

But there was no stopping the aggressive and ambitious López. In the *Casa Amarilla* he talked himself into the appointment of second-in-command of *El Libertador* fortress. He remained in that hell hole over three years and advanced to the governorship of the penitentiary. It was a post that few men would relish, but for this military-minded young man of twenty, it was a stepping stone to greater things.

The arrival of Colonel López at the *Casa Amarilla* in search of a job and his encounter there with President Castro had not been very pleasant. In his *Páginas para la Historia de Venezuela* López relates that President Castro, without waiting for his salute, asked him in a gruff tone: "How many battles did you have between Barquisimeto and El Tocuyo?" To which López replied respectfully that only General Ferrer, who was fully informed of the army's operations could answer that question. Whereupon, in front of the many persons present, the President turned his back on the young colonel and ignored him completely.

From the events of the past few months, three salient manifestations became evident: the opposition *caudillos* of every party and faction had been obliterated, civil war had been dissipated in Venezuela —to all appearances for good, and the figure of General Juan Vicente Gómez had emerged as the man of the future. With the victory of the Ciudad Bolívar campaign, parties of every color became relegated to oblivion. That Cipriano Castro desired the elimination of all opposition parties was made clear in his reply to a letter from Dr. Luis Razetti, in which he said: "It cannot be said that political parties are essentially necessary to the life of nations, no matter what degree of culture they may have attained. No. This is an argument inspired by bad faith; this is a sarcasm of the diabolical sowers of discord. There are no more rational parties than the two which have been combating the emergence of new ideas in the strife of the centuries. But when the fight has been ended by the definite triumph of the right, when the shadows of political error have been dissipated, when liberty has extended its beautiful wings in the heavens of a country, there is not, nor can there ever be, more than one party—that of national unity."

With the country pacified, President Castro had to initiate the labor of reconstruction and administration. After five years of civil war, the nation was in a lamentable state of ruin. The accumulated debts of the past fifty years, which had provoked serious conflicts with foreign powers, had been solved only provisionally. Faced with the prospect of tackling these Herculean tasks, this inept statesman, though a brave warrior on the fields of battle, was further handicapped from the start by his clique of fawning, ambitious intrigants who exploited to the limit his vanity, sensuality, and intemperance. These scheming cohorts of Castro planted suspicion everywhere, and the consequences for many an innocent victim were ostracism, prison, or even death.

Castro, the champion, having arrived at the pinnacle, promptly cast off those who had fought to place him there. Suspicious and ungrateful by nature, he even went so far as to persecute some of his former comrades-in-arms and confiscate their properties. His gruff and imperious ways, of which his slight to López was an example, cost him still more friends. In his role as President of the Republic he was so pompous and conceited as to envision himself a superior being empowered with unlimited authority. Evidence of this was the telegram he once sent to the president of the state of Carabobo, which began: "In my dual role as Chief of the Church and of the State . . ." This "Napoleonic buffoon in comic opera," as José Rafael Pocaterra called him, banished priests from the country, while the Archbishop of Caracas was perforce obliged to intone a *Te Deum* Mass for his health and well-being.

While most Venezuelans were struggling in the perennial thralls of poverty, misery, and military despotism, frock-coated ruffians, wearing celluloid collars and packing pearl-handled Smith and Wessons, gaily wallowed in the graft and corruption of public office. With Castro and his colleagues setting up a system of absolute freedom for irresponsible and even criminal behavior, it was only to be expected that Gómez, the political novice, early became steeped in the rich venal tradition of perverted statesmanship and maladministration.

Throughout the land school children and an intimidated press sang the praises of "The Hero of May," an appellative that warmed the cockles of Castro's heart. As the first presidents of Venezuela had been heroes of the War of Independence, succeeding presidents harbored pretensions of being heroes also, and there followed a succession of self-styled "Heroes" of May, June, and so on. Later, Juan Vicente Gómez would become the "Hero of December"—which gave rise to the caustic comment: "With no more months left, future presidents will have to resort to the signs of the zodiac!"

In his secluded niche of Vice-President of the Republic, with no command over anyone nor authority over anything, Gómez appeared distant and unimportant. He appeared to conduct himself with more modesty than was expected of him, displaying attachment and loyalty to Castro, unpretentiousness and innocence, and even feigning weaknesses and ailments which were belied by his powerful physical frame. Although he had grown stout at forty-six, he had never been more virile.

It was to Gómez that the malcontents and others alienated by Castro brought their complaints and woes. His door was always open to them. When they left, such visitors took with them the impression that Gómez not only sympathized deeply with them, but that he was their warm friend as well. Yet this wily peasant had not committed himself in any way!

Himself taciturn, Gómez was unsurpassed at the art of patiently listening to others. This was one of his qualities that seemed to indicate a lack of egotism. He kept his innermost thoughts to himself. It was on a rare occasion that he shared a confidence or impression with a friend or close associate. He possessed (like his modern counterpart, Stalin) in a high degree the gift for silence, and in this respect he was unique in a country where everybody talked far too much.

Silently and subtly Gómez laid the ground work for his great plan. One by one his friends and relatives occupied places in the government, minor ones most of them, but they formed the nucleus of an organic structure that would one day greet the light of day as a multi-armed octopus with Gómez as its head. All things come to him who waits. And Gómez was patient, very patient. He was grateful too, grateful to Castro for having taught him the full meaning of power, and the wealth and pleasures it brought to him who held it. On the surface he always presented the thin veneer of humble obedience, the unassuming and hard working public servant. But inside, said his enemies, he was dishonest to his fingertips, rotten to the core.

To fashionable Caracas society, which had first regarded Gómez as an uncouth little upstart hardly fit to shine their shoes, he now appeared in a new light. This man, they said, was as different from Castro as day was from night. He was not the thieving carouser Castro was; he attended to his duties faithfully and was always the sedate figure of sobriety. Nor did he flaunt a harem of women openly and shamelessly. True, Gómez invariably retired with an ever-changing paramour, but they benignly conceded him his one pleasure. Didn't most every Venezuelan of means possess his discreet little mistress? Of course! Of course! It was just that these *affaires d'amour* were never discussed at state dinners or in private drawing rooms. They were tolerated silently as a matter of natural course and were acknowledged only by knowing winks.

There was no doubt that Gómez often presented a ridiculous figure at public functions, for he certainly was no man of manners. He detested these affairs. For him it was torture to escort a lady by the arm or go through a stiffly formal state dinner. He preferred the casual comfort of his khaki tunic and the down-to-earth conversation of cattle men. He knew his limitations and tried to appear as unostentatious as possible. To many simple and impressionable citizens he was a knight errant, who would some day rid the government of malfeasance and corruption. To the few confrères who really knew him, however, he was but a "Knight of the Bedchamber," who chuckled quietly up his sleeve at the ease of his clever deception.

CHAPTER ELEVEN

Suspicion and Intrigue

And every city or house divided against itself shall not stand.
—MATTHEW, XII. 25

By spring of 1906, the followers of Castro and Gómez were on the verge of splitting into two hostile camps. A bureaucrat was now no longer regarded as merely a member of the government but rather as a follower of either Gómez or Castro. Try as he did to frustrate the designs of his enemies and his own ambitious friends, Gómez found himself being drawn inextricably away from the intimate companionship of his *compadre*. No longer did Castro grasp him affectionately by the shoulders and say, "Ah! My good friend Juan Vicente!" Now cynical and morose, Castro had begun to distrust him. Because he had the feeling of obscure happenings behind his back, Castro devised the farce of the "Proclamation." It was not so much a device with which to expose Gómez as it was to cause him to overstep himself.

On April 9, Castro suddenly announced his intention to leave the capital for a long rest. Unaware that he was being made the target for Castro's clever scheme, Gómez made no attempt to dissuade him, but submitted resignedly to the formalities of accepting the power as First Vice-President. Castro left the same day for his *quinta* in La Victoria.

On May 23, the seventh anniversary of the *Restauración Liberal*, the President issued his proclamation from La Victoria. It came as a stunning blow to Gómez as well as the general public. In it Castro affirmed that on April 9 he had "retired transitorily from power, solely and exclusively for the reason of acquiring a rest indispensable to my strength and spirit—which had been overtaxed." He repeated what he had said on that date, that if his retirement "which perhaps can be temporary, has contributed to the union and fraternity of all Venezuelans for the complete aggrandizement of the homeland, it will be acceptable to me to remain in this retreat." He added that his decision had moved "certain public elements" to remonstrate in various ways that he return to the presidency as soon as possible; that "the valve of these manifestations had been closed" and that they had provoked tendencies which he considered dangerous for the cause and for the country; that therefore he was resolved to retire from public life and would await the convening of congress so as to present his formal resignation." Castro terminated, plagiarizing the last proclamation of the Liberator: "My last wishes, today, are for the greatness of my homeland, for the happiness of all Venezuelans in the bosom of union and fraternity."

If Gómez actually harbored pretensions to the presidency as Castro thought he did, he would accept the President's retirement without further ado and would exert powerful pressure on members of congress to assure his own election. Castro would hear about it immediately and he would return to the capital to accuse him face to face. But Gómez was much too clever to be caught off guard. He now recognized the trap for what it was and he adroitly side-stepped it.

The day after the proclamation was made public Castro was waiting impatiently to hear of his lieutenant's reaction when a courier arrived from the capital. The letter that was handed Castro caused him to raise his eyebrows. It was from General Gómez. The missive was so artfully conceived that it could only have been the handiwork of a skilled ghostwriter. The gist of it was that it had pained Gómez to read the proclamation as it appeared to indicate that he had not favored the acclaim accorded Castro; that he could not imagine who could have induced Castro to harbor such a distrust toward his person. He declared: "I never have had the desire to be a politician. It was you who induced me to leave my hacienda and enter public life, and on contracting the grave obligations that this decision has imposed on me, my only guiding motive has been my great admiration and sincere affection for you. May I be so happy that this assertion of my conscience as an honorable man merits your approval and that upon reading this you will say: it is true. I have the strongest conviction that it will be thus, and for this reason I am completely at ease." He added that he was convinced that remaining any longer at the head of the government would create greater difficulties, that he had accepted his assignment only to please his benefactor, that political fights were more distasteful to him than those on the battlefield, that for these reasons Castro should return to power as soon as possible; that he, Gómez, would continue to be his friend and would aid him in every way possible, that he wanted only to work in peace, and that, lastly, he asked for nothing but protection for his friends who were Castro's friends also. He ended by pleading that Castro return to Caracas to dispel the excitement that had been aroused.

The following day, May 25, Castro replied with a long-winded telegram in which he blamed unnamed conspirators for the friction between them. He affirmed that his confidence in Gómez remained unshaken and that he would not tolerate anyone's casting aspersions upon him—one of his best friends; that their friendship was as strong now as it was twenty years ago; *but,* while the air remained full of suspicions and intrigue, he would not resume the presidency.

The tone of this message stimulated Gómez to send off another telegram in which he insisted that Castro return. To this Castro replied that he would remain steadfast in his desire to resign; however, he proposed an alternative. Until congress could convene and consider his resignation, he would serve under Gómez as his Secretary General!

This was a tacit admission on the part of Castro that he was fully aware of his lieutenant's aspirations, and on the surface it indicated that he had no objections to subordinating himself to Gómez's ambitions. But he was only allowing Gómez more rope with which to hang himself. For Gómez it was a matter of simple deduction to arrive at the conclusion that Castro's suspicions of him were greater than he had imagined. His next move was to propose to Castro that they confer together in Los Teques. When a full day passed with no reply, Gómez wired Castro that if he did not return to the presidency at once, he would convoke congress to a special session, at which he would submit his resignation; that General Velutini, the Second Vice-President (who followed him in line of succession), being absent from the country, congress could then act as it saw fit.

The laconic reply to this telegram was a stinging rebuke: "Your telegram received. As you have not been able to arrive at an intelligent understanding with me—who was willing to accommodate you by offering myself as your secretary as a solution toward saving the republic, saving yourself, and saving me—you can follow the advice of your friends."

With each exchange of missives, relations between Castro and Gómez had become more strained and they had now reached the breaking point. Yet Gómez resolved to take one more step which would either ease the tension or precipitate a crisis. Without telling anyone, he set out to confront the fox in his own lair. Taking the Caracas express to La Victoria, he presented himself to Castro.

There never has been any doubt but that Gómez had a genuine affection for his *compadre,* and these and subsequent events seem to bear out the assertion that right up until the last, Gómez was somewhat reluctant to split with him. There could be no denying, however, that at one time or another, Gómez had made *compromisos* to betray Castro. Even before the battle of Ciudad Bolívar there was said to exist an *entente* between Gómez and numerous revolutionary elements. Yet when each opportunity to grasp the power presented itself, for some inexplicable reason Gómez would renege on his promises, and sometimes would throw himself at the feet of his *compadre* in abject humility. This occasion appeared to be one of those moments.

Gómez faced the haughty and sensitive Castro and said to him: "Do with me what you will, don Cipriano, but don't compel me to return to Caracas without your promise that you will return to assume your rightful position."

Castro was completely overwhelmed by this display of humble sincerity. In that brief moment all doubts as to his lieutenant's loyalty vanished, and he embraced him like a long lost friend. Gómez returned to Caracas with Castro's solemn promise that he would take over the reins of government on July 5—the anniversary of Venezuela's Declaration of Independence.

Meanwhile, there had been considerable maneuvering going on among the conspirators in the government to line up on one side or the other such of their colleagues as had remained on the sidelines. In the Revolution of '99, López had formed a warm friendship with Román Delgado Chalbaud and Eliseo Sarmiento. With their rise to the rank of general, these men had acquired considerable prestige.

In May of 1906 they took the colonel into their confidence and asked
him to join their block against Gómez. López refused outright to
go in with them, saying that notwithstanding his admiration and
respect for Castro, he had received kindnesses and demonstrations of
friendship on the part of Gómez, in whom he saw and appreciated
the best collaborator of the government. After another clandestine
meeting held in Puerto Cabello, at which several other important
figures were unsuccessful in winning López over, attempts were made
to discredit the young officer. When even his superior, General
Froilán Prato turned against him, López was maneuvered into resigning his position as governor of the penitentiary.

At the Ministry of War in Caracas, where López reported his
resignation as due to ill health, he received a summons from General Gómez to a private interview at the *Casa Amarilla*. Gómez had
an inkling of what was going on in Puerto Cabello and he asked
López to explain the true reasons for his resignation. The colonel told
him frankly that he had declined to enter into the political intrigues
of Puerto Cabello because, to him, General Castro would continue
to be the commander-in-chief, and General Gómez, second-in-command of the Cause.

Gómez took this statement to mean that López's first allegiance
was to Castro. Immediately he formed a distrust toward the young
man, dismissing him with the remark that he was not satisfied with his
explanation. To get at the bottom of the affair he arranged the assignment of a trusted aide to fill the post vacated by López.

No sooner had the colonel left Gómez's office than he received
another summons, this time to report to President Castro in La
Victoria. Castro had learned of the existence of a letter written by
General Sarmiento to General Delgado Chalbaud, which warned
that there were plans afoot to effect the release of General Solagnie
and other important political prisoners from the fortress at Puerto
Cabello. What was more significant, the same letter asked Delgado
Chalbaud to investigate the rumor that López had been the man
responsible for the freeing of General Entrena from the fortress.

What—Castro wanted to know—had the colonel to say to that?

It was easy enough to explain, said López with his usual aplomb.
General Entrena had shown signs of a mental lapse and had tried
to commit suicide by slashing himself with a piece of tin. López had

granted him a conditional release to have his wound attended to at the city hospital. That's all there was to it. If *el Presidente* would investigate, he would find that General Entrena was even now behind bars.

He certainly would investigate, Castro replied sarcastically. As for the colonel's remarks concerning the intrigues of Puerto Cabello and "the necessary alliance of the *Jefe* of the *Restauración* with his loyal friend General Gómez," Castro snorted through his beard in annoyance.

Having incurred Castro's displeasure, López was left to shift for himself until his case was cleared up. On July 5, Castro took over active command of the government. The wheels of justice having turned at a leisurely *Latino* pace, it was not until several weeks had gone by that López was informed his name was in the clear. To make amends, Castro offered him another chance as aide-de-camp. López demurred at this and asked, instead, permission to visit his mother whom he had not seen since he first left home. Castro told him to make the trip with his brother, Carmelo, who was due to leave within a day or so. On saying good-by he wished him luck and a speedy return.

Castro neglected, however, to provide the young man with funds for the trip; López arrived at his home in Independencia no better off financially than when he had left seven years before.

For some months it had been noticed that the President's health had not been good. He had begun to pay the fiddler for his excesses. Hardly two months after his return to Caracas, Castro, gravely ill, was hurried off to the shore resort of Macuto. His decline had come on so suddenly, there had not been time to officially designate Gómez to carry on in his absence. When it was whispered that *el Presidente* might die, rival factions jockeyed for position to grasp the reins of government. On one side there were the intimate friends of the sick President, on the other the friends of Gómez and their allies, the discontented. Also to be reckoned with was the group which surrounded the Second Vice-President, General Velutini. To add to the confusion, a rumor flew the rounds that General Alcántara was preparing to execute a military coup aided by the garrisons from La Victoria and Valencia.

The situation was an especially trying one for Gómez. Single-handedly he was trying to run the government and maintain order while warding off a swarm of conspirators. Furthermore, after he became aware that he was being spied on incessantly by Castro's agents, it was whispered that he did not sleep two nights in succession in the same bed. Fortunately, Castro recovered, but if he had died, Venezuela again might have become the scene of a bloody civil war.

When relatives sallied forth on rampageous orgies which shocked the capital, Gómez used menacing dissuasion to curb their base instincts. When his cousin Eustóquio committed a cold-blooded murder all Venezuela was shocked and waited expectantly to see what the Vice-President would do. Would he, or would he not interfere with the due process of law?

On the night of January 27, 1907, Eustóquio Gómez and two of his Andean cronies, both colonels, created such a disturbance in a Caracas saloon, that the proprietor had to call the police. Informed of the matter, Dr. Luis Mata Illas, governor of the Federal District went to the saloon and spoke to the group, telling them to go home Eustóquio, drunk and in a fit of passion, shot the governor dead.

When Eustóquio fled to the mountains of Miranda, a detective pocketed a warrant for his arrest and set out in hot pursuit. When the official tracked him down and faced him with drawn revolver the swaggering bully of the Gómez clan whimpered like a coward "Don't kill me!" he cried. "I give up! Don't kill me!" And he handed over his revolver, trembling, to the official. Eustóquio Gómez was taken under heavy guard to Caracas and was lodged in the Rotunda on the charge of murder. To the astonishment of everyone, the Vice President made no attempt to intervene. Gómez couldn't afford to jeopardize his political career by disillusioning his followers and the general public at this juncture. But once he attained power it will be seen that he resorted to highhanded tactics to secure Eustóquio's release.

Cautioned by Gómez to bide his time, Eustóquio quietly went through the procedure of a hearing, the passing of sentence, and the months' long wait in the Rotunda. There was no trial by jury (the Venezuelan judiciary being patterned after the Spanish system) and the case was heard and the sentence passed by Dr. Juan Abreu Judge of the First Instance. The sentence was for fifteen years.

According to the penal codes promulgated by Gómez in 1915 and

1926—the latter of which are still in force—the penalty for murder is from 12 to 18 years imprisonment. For the killing of one's spouse, forebears, descendants, or the President of the Republic, the penalty is higher—from 16 to 20 years. Twice during the history of the republic the death penalty for murder or political crimes had been written into law. Twice it had been repealed, the last time by President Juan C. Falcón in 1863.

When General Antonio Paredes was taken prisoner in one of the revolutionary battles of 1903, Castro had ordered him shot, but had not the courage to make the fact public for fear of censure. Instead of following the example of Guzmán, who had General Matias Salazar, a troublesome *caudillo,* court martialed and publicly shot by a firing squad, Castro tried to make it appear that Paredes had been killed while attempting to escape. When the people of Venezuela learned the true facts, Castro was discredited.

By 1908, Castro had become a chronic invalid. When the doctors advised that he go to Europe for an operation by specialists, Gómez, the faithful family friend, convinced Castro through his wife that not only his life but the future welfare of the country hung in the balance.

Juan Vicente, the faithful family friend and *compadre* of old! Now Castro was going to display his trust in him by leaving him in full charge. Was it blind trust or were there misgivings? Suffice to say that doña Zoila's opinion carried some weight in the matter. Her fondness for Juan Vicente had mellowed through the years and her confidence in his loyalty to Cipriano had never wavered. How Juan Vicente had nursed and pampered that confidence! Never did he forget a birthday or an anniversary. His own *quinta* being situated nearby, he made it a point to visit *Villa Zoila* almost daily, sometimes to report to Castro in his sick room, on other occasions merely to pay his respects to the lady of the house.

For some months during 1908, Castro had been secretly negotiating for the purchase of a small warship in Germany through the Venezuelan chargé d'affaires in Berlin. Why Castro resorted to secrecy to spend upwards of one and a half million bolivars of the nation's money for the procurement of such a vessel has never been divulged. When the matter became generally known, even Gómez was unable to fathom his motives. It developed that either through

the naïveté of doña Zoila or through spies that he maintained in the
Castro household, Gómez learned that when Castro definitely decided to voyage abroad, he sent a cable canceling the purchase
Gómez mentioned the matter to a group of close friends, among
whom was Bernabé Planas, at that time Chief of Protocol in the
Foreign Ministry. Chatting on a certain occasion with José de Jesú
Paúl, the Foreign Minister, about current matters, Planas innocently
brought up the subject, assuming that the Foreign Minister was cog
nizant of the details. Paúl, however, knew nothing of the transaction
as it had been handled behind his back. He reported to the Presiden
what he had learned from Planas, and Castro, angered, ordered him
to question his informant as to how he had learned his secret and
through whom. Trapped though he was, Planas realized he had to
shield Gómez at any cost, even to the extent of sacrificing himself
So he refused to reveal the source of his information. When his de
cision was relayed to Castro, the President ordered his discharge
Those who were in on the secret arrived at the same conclusion; the
bon-vivant was going to divert the purchase money—which was al
ready banked abroad—to finance a pleasant sojourn in Europe.

Castro need not have worried about funds for his trip. Gómez
not only arranged everything for the journey, but he helped doña
Zoila amass a sizable fortune in gold and saw to it that a "grateful
nation" paid for the letter of credit, for one million French francs
which was handed to Castro.

On the afternoon of November 24, 1908, a small quiet gathering
stood on the dock at La Guaira alongside the French liner *Guade
loupe*. Provisional President Juan Vicente Gómez and a group of
officials and their families, as well as members of the diplomatic
corps, had come to see Cipriano Castro and his señora off for Europe

Castro had given positive orders that General Gómez be obeyed
in everything, "no matter what happened." Here was proof, if proo
was needed, that Castro still trusted his lieutenant implicitly. Yet
it was said that Castro had left his bosom friend surrounded by a
ring of his own collaborators, both in the civil administration and in
the army. They had been instructed, so it was said, to watch Gómez
closely and at the first symptoms of reaction to send a cable to the
ailing chief.

As the *Guadeloupe* cast off, Castro shouted from the rail, flash ing a toothy smile through his beard: *"No os digo adiós, sino hasta luégo"*—"I'm not saying good-by but—see you later."

When the *Guadeloupe* arrived at the eastern port of Carúpano the following morning, Castro dispatched the following telegram to Gómez: "Have just arrived at this bit of earth of my beloved homeland from where I say my last good-bye to all Venezuelans. We have had a wonderful voyage. A very fine ship. No seasickness as yet. Sea tranquil as a lake. A good omen . . . Your friend embraces you . . . Cipriano Castro."

After an uneventful voyage, Castro disembarked in France, continuing straight on to Germany by train. He arrived in Berlin on December 15.

Cipriano Castro had left Venezuela with Gómez's staunch assurances that pending his return he would be rendered detailed accounts of his *compadre's* stewardship. But Castro would be betrayed by his friend of twenty-two years' standing, and like many another disillusioned victim of Venezuela's usurpers of power, he was to die in lonely exile without ever seeing his homeland again.

CHAPTER TWELVE

The Bloodless Coup

One morning late in November of 1908 there appeared a brief notice in the *New York Times* to the effect that one, Cipriano Castro, President of Venezuela, had embarked for Europe aboard the French liner *Guadeloupe*. It caused considerable excitement and speculation among the Venezuelan exiles living in New York. The very same night, a group of them met to discuss the possibilities of forming a coalition with Gómez to depose Castro. Among those present were General Nicholás Rolando who had been released from San Carlos and banished into exile two years before, General Arístides Tellería, former Minister of Development under Castro in 1905 and a voluntary exile, and Oscar Larrazábal, member of the revolutionary junta led by General José Hernández, who was then in Curacao.

Neither Tellería nor Larrazábal were fully convinced that Gómez would turn reactionist, but they thought the time ripe to sound out his views, and Larrazábal so advised General Hernández by cable. Hernández, in his reply, authorized Larrazábal to proceed with a "feeler," preferably a letter to be delivered personally to Gómez, and the stipulated basis for the joining of forces was to be a change in the system of government, with full constitutional liberties for all.

While Tellería joined Hernández in Curacao to await developments, his emissary, Dr. Domingo B. Castillo, continued on to Venezuela with two letters, one for Gómez and one for his Secretary General, Dr. Leopoldo Baptista. Delivery was effected on December 9.

For five days Gómez deliberated on the matter, undecided as to his course of action. More than one version has it that Gómez had the sincere intention of safeguarding the interests of his *compadre* until he returned. But on the other hand there were several weighty factors which gave credence to the belief that Gómez would one day depose his benefactor. Gómez was a natural born revolutionist in the true Latin tradition. If he had not hitched his wagon to Cipriano Castro's star he would have joined up with someone else, or even started a revolution of his own once his prestige had grown to sufficient proportions.

As President, Castro had become, perhaps inevitably, the target of widespread and vicious attacks. He was regarded as a tyrant—though perhaps a mild one at that—but then the tyrants were, of course, the men in power who did not please those who desired to take their places. As men go, Gómez was as vain and ambitious as any, and there could be no denying that, notwithstanding his sincere friendship and admiration for Castro, he envisioned himself a better president. A good many of his fellow citizens were inclined to feel likewise, but there were some who felt a deep-seated suspicion of him. Both Gómez's nature and his varied talents and pursuits had been studies in subtle contradiction. He was a poised, intelligent man with a gift for gaining authority, and so far he had not abused this gift. He was a cattle trader with the intellect of a learned judge or great statesman, a public servant with a deep desire for obscurity, who drove himself with a kind of quiet intensity. He was a farmer who loved a battle of wits and the excitement of combat. And he was a simple rustic with an enormous devotion to his country. In keeping with his mystic character he was quiet and reserved, seldom if ever given to eloquent speeches, gay repartee, or frank revelations of his feelings—in fact, he was quite the opposite in this respect from Guzmán, who once said at a banquet in Puerto Cabello during the early days of his rise to fame: "General Falcón's inspirations are orders for me. I am but a blind instrument which obeys his will. If he had told me to steal, I would have stolen; if he had told me to commit arson, I would have committed arson; if he had told me to kill, I would have killed."

Time and again Juan Vicente Gómez had sworn his devoted fidelity to his bosom friend, but with Castro many miles away, Venezuela's conspirators deemed the time propitious and Gómez vulnerable to the idea of deposing the absent President. Much against his will Gómez became the central figure of the gigantic plot, and was swept away like a wisp of straw in the strong revolutionary winds.

But first there occurred a new international crisis which lent itself beautifully to the conspirators' plans.

Venezuela, it seemed, would barely pull itself out of one great crisis before it would slide back into another. This time the trouble was with Holland. It had its beginnings in July, when Castro was informed of the contents of a letter published in a Dutch magazine. The letter had originally been written by the Dutch Minister in Caracas, J. H. de Reús, to a Dutch commercial house, and it spoke in derogatory terms of the Venezuelan President. Castro's vitriolic remarks concerning de Reús were not recorded, but it naturally followed that that gentleman was handed his passport by the Venezuelan Foreign Minister and informed that he was *persona non grata* in Venezuela.

On July 25, the Dutch cruiser *Gelderland,* which had been dispatched from Curacao to pick up de Reús, arrived in Venezuelan territorial waters, first at Puerto Cabello, then at La Guaira. In neither port did she comply with the Venezuelan navigation laws concerning foreign warships giving the proper salute on entering and leaving a Venezuelan port. This considerably irked the Venezuelan authorities. On the 26th, the *Gelderland* steamed out of La Guaira with de Reús aboard. On the same day, demonstrations were held in front of the Venezuelan consulate in Willemstad, Curacao. Then, starting on December 1 and ending on December 12—when she appeared off La Guaira as if to taunt the authorities of that defenseless town—the *Gelderland* interfered with coastal shipping and carried out minor acts of piracy by capturing and boarding several Venezuelan sailboats.

The news of the *Gelderland*'s hostile maneuver off La Guaira began to circulate through Caracas the following morning, a Sunday. It was at this juncture that both Castro's and Gómez's adherents pounced on this delicate situation to achieve their individual ends— Castro's men to embarrass Gómez and cause him to commit a *faux pas,* and Gómez's men to impel him by force of circumstances and whipped-up public fervor to renounce his absent chief.

As on many another occasion in Venezuela's history, the university students were made the "front" in the farce that followed. Using as a pretext "the aggressive acts of the Dutch," a group of students obtained permission from Baptista, the Secretary General, to circulate handbills inviting the people of Caracas to a public demonstration against the Dutch to be held that same Sunday afternoon in the Plaza Bolívar. Before the day was out, some of the most prominent men in the capital had become involved in the affair—among them Generals Pulido and Sarría, Juan Pietri, José Paúl and Bernabé Planas, as well as many others who remained hidden behind the scenes pulling the strings.

When one of the leaders of the demonstration asked a group of Gómez's aides the pointed question whether General Gómez would be at the *Casa Amarilla* "during the critical period," Juan Pietri let drop the remark that *as General Gómez had not yet declared himself against Castro,* he would remain at his home, but if he heard of any shooting or if his presence were required, he would immediately go to the *Casa Amarilla.*

The demonstration started off innocently and quietly enough. A band played patriotic airs. There were fireworks, and following that, the speeches. As the minutes ticked by the assemblage swelled until it overflowed into the streets. When the more audacious orators used the word "reactionist" in alluding to their President, the crowd applauded. It was on Castro that the blame fell for the strained relations with Holland and other nations.

A glib spellbinder by the name of Elías Toro was scheduled to deliver the *pièce de résistance* in front of the balconies of the *Casa Amarilla,* and there the crowd proceeded, hoping that Gómez would show himself. From that time forward, the public became accustomed to waiting for General Gómez for indeterminate periods and to seeing him appear when he was least expected.

As speakers harangued the impatient crowd and whipped it up into an ugly mood, there were heard piercing calls to arms and action. This was all that was needed to set these impassioned citizens off on a wild rampage. They were in a fighting mood. They wanted to destroy. Suddenly, the milling mob poured in a shouting wave toward the nearest objective—the offices and plant of the newspaper *El Constitucional* on the corner of *el Conde.* They found the establishment closed tight, so they satisfied themselves by firing shots into the doors and windows. From inside, the employees replied with their own revolvers. In this affray one of the demonstrators fell dead. The "reaction" had received its baptism of blood.

By the time the bookstore "Cosmos" owned by Gumersindo Rivas, a Castro man, and the drugstore of the Dutchman Thielen, son-in-law of Tello Mendoza, were broken into and sacked, Gómez was in his victoria and on his way into town. Passing the wrecked "Cosmos" he muttered his displeasure at the way things were going. When the rioters glimpsed his carriage they greeted him with cries of *"Viva* Gómez!" and hastened to points of vantage in front of the *Casa Amarilla.* Gómez entered the building and appeared within a few minutes on one of the balconies with José Paúl, Juan Pietri, and a few others.

The shadows of late afternoon were falling fast, and the steep, rounded slopes of the Avila Mountains lay bathed in hues of dappled green and brownish-purple when Elías Toro began his explosive speech. He touched only lightly on the Dutch issue; his speech was a passionate tirade against the absent President and his clique.

Thoroughly ill at ease, Gómez listened in silence throughout the long attack against his chief. When it was over he made no attempt to defend his old friend. The truth of the matter was that Gómez was totally unprepared and incapable of handling this situation, which had been instigated by his scheming friends.

During a long moment of weighty silence the crowd waited expectantly for the Provisional President to speak. Perspiring profusely, Gómez fidgeted, then started to leave the balcony.

Seeing this unusual opportunity for profitable action slipping away, Juan Pietri grasped the general by the arm and pulled him back. With Gómez by his side he faced the sea of faces and bellowed: "Death to Castro!"

From the crowd there echoed a mighty roar. "D-e-a-t-h t-o C-a-s-t-r-o!"

"Viva Gómez!" bellowed Pietri.

"V-i-v-a G-ó-m-e-z!" thundered the multitude.

Assuredly, agitators had been planted among the people, but this acclaim accorded Gómez was spontaneous and genuine.

Leopoldo Baptista, another opportunist, gestured to Gómez. "Speak, General, speak! The people want you to say something!"

Juan Vicente Gómez realized only too well the sore dilemma he was in. Behind him were standing several of Castro's loyal ministers, and they would undoubtedly convey to their master the lurid details of that momentous event. As for the public, for the moment Gómez was assured of its enthusiastic support. At a word from him most of Caracas would probably swing over to his side. But Gómez was a very thorough man, given to sound reasoning and split-second timing, and his natural instinct rebelled at being propelled into a hasty maneuver that might prove his undoing. To the men who surrounded him the moment was a golden opportunity that might not be repeated, but to Gómez, who had not yet fully consolidated his position, it was not as propitious as at first glance it appeared. In those few fleeting seconds Gómez resolved—perhaps wisely—to back out of the delicate position into which he had been maneuvered. Unfortunately, he did not do so with good grace, for the simple reason that he was struck with stagefright! Instead of saying a few words to pacify the multitude, Gómez stood frozen to the spot while rivulets of perspiration streamed down his face. For another long, drawn-out moment he returned the silent stares of the upturned expectant faces, then he turned and rushed from the balcony. It was José Paúl, the Foreign Minister, who spoke a few words to the people in the name of Gómez.

The aftermath of this episode was the arrest of Juan Pietri and Bernabé Planas on orders from Gómez, who felt he owed it to Castro to take some reprisals. José Paúl was instructed to send a cable to the President, informing him of what had occurred and adding that the instigators had been taken into custody.

After the balcony scene and the issuance of orders for the arrest of Pietri and Planas, Gómez fled to the quiet of his *quinta* in the suburb of *el Paraíso*. It was there that Leopoldo Baptista was hastily summoned by the conspirators an hour or so later when they found out that General Gómez intended to renege on his agreement with them.

Nodding a greeting to Tarazona, Gómez's grim and omnipotent bodyguard, Baptista came upon Gómez pacing up and down. He had removed his coat and opened his collar, but he was still perspiring freely and his shirt was completely soaked.

"Come in," Colonel Félix Galavis said to Baptista. "Look at General Gómez! We're lost! He says he is not going through with it!"

Suave, cultured Baptista tried to remonstrate with his chief, but in vain. *"No, señor!"* the exasperated man cried vehemently. "I cannot go through with it. I won't do what you want me to do with don Cipriano! I am going to tell him everything!"

Such is the chronicled record of that historic scene. That night behind the locked doors of *Bella Vista* heavy pressure was brought to bear on the tired and confused peasant from the Andes, until finally he gave in. When the conspirators picked up their hats and coats and departed into the night, they had all agreed on a concrete plan of action and had exacted from Gómez his word of honor that he would fulfill his end of the bargain. And that he did.

The following morning, perhaps an hour or so before Caracas usually reported to work, Gómez was already at his desk. With him was José Paúl who had been roused from his bed before dawn. As Paúl was only now let in on the plot, it would seem he had switched over to the side of Gómez during the past few days, yet Gómez entrusted to him a delicate mission.

As diplomatic relations with the United States had been severed six months before due to the intransigent attitude of Castro, Paúl was instructed to solicit the good offices of the Brazilian Minister to send a cable to Washington requesting that American warships be sent to Venezuela "to forestall any incidents." Conscience-stricken by his Judas role, Gómez was mortally afraid that Castro was aware of his plans and would attempt a landing on the Venezuelan coast. Propelled by fear he had the audacity to request the aid of a United States naval squadron to protect his *coup d'état!*

That same morning, the Brazilian Minister, *Señor* don Luis de Lorena Ferreira, sent the following cable to the Brazilian Embassy in Washington: *"Reaction against General Castro initiated stop Foreign Minister requested me today to ask that it be made clear to the American Government President Gómez's willingness to satisfactorily end all international questions stop The presence of American warships at La Guaira would be convenient to prevent incidents stop Am repeating this communication to other legations."*

What was even more astonishing, the United States government was favorably inclined to recognize the new regime before it had actually outlined its foreign policy! In his communication dated December 21—just two days after the new regime came into being—

Elihu Root, Secretary of State, declared: ". . . *It is understood that the object of the important communication made by the Venezuelan Administration to the Government of the United States through the representative of Brazil in Caracas is to indicate the intention of the new Administration to revoke the policy that was followed by President Castro and which led to the instructions sent to Mr. Sleeper on June 13, 1908, by which the Legation of the United States in Caracas was ordered closed and the chargé d'affaires withdrawn."*

A squadron composed of the battleships *North Carolina* and *Maine* and the cruiser *Dolphin* was immediately ordered to La Guaira. On board the *North Carolina* was William I. Buchanan, the High Commissioner appointed by the Secretary of State to deal with the new Venezuelan government.

Unapprised of the purpose of the visit, the good citizens of La Guaira were thrown into a panic by the appearance of the American squadron and the roar of its guns fired in the traditional salute. Having developed a painful allergy to foreign warships, the Venezuelans raised a storm of protest, especially in congress. Although it was tacitly acknowledged that General Gómez had been the perpetrator of the whole affair, no one dared to mention his name. Yet someone had to be sacrificed to appease the clamoring public. The most likely scapegoat at the moment appeared to be José Paúl, who had already been replaced as Foreign Minister. Paúl was relegated to political oblivion, and he retired to his *quinta* where he remained to brood the ingratitude of Gómez and the injustice heaped upon him by his fellow bureaucrats.

Gómez's coup was consummated on Saturday morning, December 19, but an unusual development occurred the day before which precipitated his act of treachery. While Gómez was waiting patiently in his office to hear of Washington's response to the Brazilian Minister's cable, an aide burst in with startling news. Word had just come in from an agent in Trinidad that he had learned of the existence of a cable supposedly sent by Castro to the Venezuelan consul in Port of Spain. The message was tantamount to an order to assassinate Gómez!

Legend has it that on hearing this alarming news, Gómez's frozen countenance blanched and lost its mask of immobility. The muscles and nerves of his face twitched. He swallowed hard once or twice. For a moment he actually appeared incapable of speech. "What did it say?" he finally asked.

"It said: *'To kill a snake you strike at the head.'* "

Gómez slowly repeated the words out loud as if to get their full import. "I just can't believe that of don Cipriano," he said softly. He glanced from face to face but met only polite stares. Suddenly his voice became grim as he addressed Baptista. "Leopoldo! I want you to get that cable for me. I don't care how you get it—but get it!"

Efforts to obtain the cable or even a facsimile proved unavailing. The Venezuelan consul in Trinidad was questioned and denied ever having seen such a cable. Sir Vincent Corbett, the British Minister in Caracas, was asked to use his good offices to obtain a copy, but he subsequently replied that the authorities in Trinidad had met with no success.

To Gómez—assuming that he really believed Castro had sent such a cable—the symbolic message was a cue, and a very obvious one at that. For the past few days he had been under heavy tension, fearing that Castro would surely take some sort of reprisal, but he did not know from what quarter it would come. In a way, it was a relief to know in what manner retaliation might take form. At last Castro had tipped his hand. Now he felt perfectly free to act, free to throw every last Castro adherent into prison on the charge of conspiring against his life. And what a relief it was to be free of the grim bearded figure that hovered behind him by day like an avenging phantom and haunted his dreams by night. His last ties of friendship with Cipriano Castro now severed, they were to be irreconcilable enemies. So be it. From this day forward, Juan Vicente Gómez would never again be troubled by pangs of conscience.

During the late hours of that unforgettable day, Caracas was the scene of mysterious activity. Gómez's victoria—escorted by a carriage full of trustworthy military aides—clattered over the cobblestones of the narrow streets to many a secret tryst. There were whispered consultations, stern issuance of orders, and when Gómez bedded down for the night in the home of a friend—for he dared not sleep at *Bella Vista*—every Gomecista knew the part he was to play on the morrow.

Early the next morning General Gómez drew up at *Bella Vista* with Baptista and his aides. At the entrance a group of small-time bureaucrats and office seekers had been waiting to snatch an interview, expecting the master of the house to emerge at any moment. But like a cold unfriendly wind, Gómez and his retinue stalked by the astonished group and into the house, where they sat down to a hot breakfast. Then quickly out again, into the carriages and off to the *cuartel Maméy*, the one barracks he was not sure of. Gómez was fully aware that its commandant, General Eliseo Sarmiento, one of the youngest veterans of the '99 campaign, had been one of those who had tried to turn López against him. But Sarmiento was shrewd enough to comprehend on which side his bread was buttered. He saluted smartly and, upon request, swore his allegiance to the new commander-in-chief.

That little matter settled, the party proceeded to the *Casa Amarilla,* where it arrived at 8 A.M. Colonel Galavis, a trusted Andean henchman, was on special duty at the entrance with an honor guard of picked men. No one was permitted in or out of the building without a special pass.

In the upstairs rooms loitered a dozen or so loyal henchmen, keeping an eye on several of Castro's officials who had been summoned to hear their fate. Gómez came upon one of them, Pedro María Cárdenas, governor of the Federal District, in the corridor. As they confronted each other, the man could read his doom on Gómez's face. The quiet, unassuming and loyal public servant had shed his mask. Seething with hatred for everything that bore the imprint of Castro, he vented his wrath by pouring a string of vile epithets upon the unfortunate man's head. Then, "Arrest this traitor!" he snarled. "Take him away!"

Baptista raised his arm in protest. *"Por favor,* General!" he admonished him. "No insults, please!" Then to Cárdenas, "You are under arrest!"

Cárdenas had bristled at the insults but offered no resistance. They removed his revolver and two aides led him away. Going down the stairs, one of them, Colonel Américo Spinetti, gave Cárdenas a violent shove and he fell headlong down the steps.

Entering one of the rooms, Gómez came upon Dr. Rafael Garbiras Guzmán, Castro's Secretary General, who backed away nervously and stumbled against a chair. Guzmán had overheard what had taken place in the corridor. His forehead glistening with sweat, he reached for a handkerchief in his rear pocket. Instantly a dozen pistols were leveled at him. "Take him away," ordered the loyal public servant.

It was the same with all the others. The Rotunda became filled with the men who had chosen to side with Castro. Among the few who managed to elude the police squads sent to arrest them that day were Simón Bello, brother-in-law of Castro, and president of the state of Aragua, and Castro's brother don Celestino, vice-president of Táchira, who escaped over the Colombian border.

In Sabana Grande, Castro's sister, doña Laurencia, was stunned by the news of her brother's betrayal. Only a few days previously she had stoutly defended Gómez for his actions on the 13th, saying: "It was probably just a trick of Juan Vicente to discover certain things for Cipriano."

Gómez was harsh and even brutal on that climactic day. He lost his head many times and he gave contradictory orders. Sometimes he forgot the names of men he wanted arrested. Although the day was not a bit too warm he was perspiring freely and he constantly dabbed at his face and neck with a sodden handkerchief. Seated at his desk like a stern oriental potentate who was ordering the beheading of all of his viziers, he commanded sharply: "Also arrest that . . . that . . . what's his name? . . . that man of the telegraph . . . the one with the beard . . . no, the old one!"

To his lieutenants, the "old one" meant General Carlos Manuel Velásquez. But Velásquez was a Gomecista. The *Jefe* must be thinking of some other official in the telegraph.

"Are you referring to Bermúdez, General?" someone asked.

"That's the one! . . . Bermúdez. Arrest him!"

When an aide leaned over the banister to transmit the order to the officers below, he noticed the man they had just talked about standing there looking curiously at all the soldiers.

Several times during the morning Gómez paused to ask: "Any news yet of Casanova?" General Maxiano Casanova was the commandant of the *cuartel la Trinidad*, and he was one officer that he wanted apprehended at any cost. When he was informed that Casanova had been found standing quietly and alone on the corner of *la Torre* and had surrendered without protest, he breathed easier.

At one interval Gómez exclaimed suddenly: "I want you to

call the doctor . . . the doctor engineer . . . the friend of mine. What's his name? The doctor! . . ."

And he glanced from face to face until someone said: "Would it be Vargas, General?"

"That's it! . . . Vargas! I don't see him here. Tell him to come."

In the list of appointees that Gómez had drawn up the night before, he had slated Roberto Vargas to be his Minister of Public Works, and the next day he couldn't remember his name!

"I believe I know why Vargas couldn't come, General," someone offered. "His wife died last night. General Alcántara who just came in can tell you about it."

"Heh! Mm-mm . . . well, just the same he should have come. He had his orders! Go and tell him to come."

Inflexible, unyielding Gómez did not like to be crossed.

Twice during the day his aides tried to induce him to go to the balcony and say a few words to the crowd that was converging below in the Plaza Bolívar. But Gómez refused flatly. After his humiliating experience of December 13 no one would ever again be able to get him to face a crowd. *"Nada de manifestaciónes!"* "No manifestations!" he muttered, annoyed. And he repeated this phrase monotonously.

The cruel and unrelentless purge on that day of denouement had opened a revealing little window on the controversial personality of the peasant from the Andes. This quiet, gentle, and unassuming product of Indian blood had changed overnight into a cruel and ruthless man of iron at whose slightest command learned and intelligent men cringed and crawled. At last, at the age of fifty-one, this humble, crude, almost illiterate mystic character had come into his own. As he relaxed for a few moments in lordly grandeur, surrounded by his fawning lieutenants, after meting out his own peculiar form of justice, he probably mulled things over a bit. And in his own peculiar way he surely must have gloated with inward satisfaction over the gains that his deeds of the day had brought him.

On the morrow, Juan Vicente Gómez would awake as "The Hero of December." Later he would be called "The Founder of Peace," "The Rehabilitator," "Cavalier of the Order of Piana," "The Illustrious American," "The *Caudillo* of Peace and Work," "The Well Deserving." And so on *ad finem*.

CHAPTER THIRTEEN

"The Hero of December"

To Castro in Berlin Gómez sent a cable bluntly informing him that his exile had better be considered permanent "for reasons of health . . . and the general welfare of the republic." Castro was bitter but was not surprised. "I don't know what it was about him," he said afterward, "but I always had a premonition that some day he would betray me."

Of course Gómez's revolutionary regime bore not the slightest shred of legality. Like his predecessors, he bestowed on it some semblance of legality by calling it a "provisional period." Provisional state presidents were appointed but, whereas these had formerly totaled thirteen, they were increased to twenty—so as to create more patronage for Gómez's friends and relatives. A year or two hence, after his political machine became strongly consolidated, the peasant from the Andes could be assured of formal election to the Presidency for a four- or six-year term.

After the purge that Saturday, Leopoldo Baptista had dispatched from the *Casa Amarilla* the telegrams and circulars listing the appointments to the cabinet and other administrative posts. Gómez's most trusted men occupied the key positions: General Francisco Linares Alcántara, Minister of the Interior; General Régulo Olivares, Minister of War and Marine; Dr. Leopoldo Baptista, Secretary General; and Dr. Aquiles Iturbe, Governor of the Federal District. The portfolio of Foreign Minister was assigned to the capable Dr. Francisco González Guinán, exhumed from twenty years of political oblivion since the time of Rojas Paúl, under whom he had served in the same capacity. González Guinán hewed to no party line, nor did the rest of the appointees: Dr. Jesus Muñoz Tébar, Minister of Finance; Dr. Roberto Vargas, Public Works; and Dr. Samuel Darío Maldonado, Minister of Public Instruction. Although holdovers from the previous regime, the last three had long ago veered away from Castro's influence and favor.

On Monday a proclamation to the people announced the policy of the new administration—"The Rehabilitation"—devised and to be carried to a fruitful completion by their new President, Juan Vicente Gómez. In it the "Hero of December" blandly declared that everyone knew he had assumed power by virtue of legal succession; also, that the friends of Cipriano Castro had not only attempted to hinder his administration, but they had aided and abetted the conspiracy against his life; that on taking the action he did against them he had saved not only his life but the honor of the high position he occupied. Then he stated a premise. He had, he said, named a cabinet in which national public opinion was well represented. With this group of earnest collaborators he aspired to better the chaotic situation of the country and he expected the loyal co-operation of all political groups toward this end. He ended with a plea for the maintenance of public order "because the violence that follows rising passions is against the concepts of civilization; the best road for the nation to follow is that of modesty and ardent patriotism."

Cipriano Castro had left the republic in as bad a state as he had found it: relations broken with leading foreign nations, a mountain of debts (although in all fairness it must be said that he didn't increase them), the sources of wealth of the country strangled by taxes and monopolies, the under-privileged masses abused and neglected, and public opinion smothered by the rivalries and ambitions of the *políticos*. The treasury was burdened with the enormous sum of 210,307,000 bolivars in pressing obligations. The foreign debt and Washington Protocols alone amounted to 147,866,000 bolivars.

Said Gómez in his Message to Congress many years later, describing the state of affairs as he had found them in 1908 when he took over power: "Anxiety over these debts was increased by the instability of the situation at home and abroad, anarchy in the fiscal administration, an unbalanced budget, the decrease in our production, and the general stagnation of commerce and industry. Aided by Providence, and inspired by love for our country and by the sacred

debt of gratitude which all Venezuelans owe to the men who won
for us the right to be free, I began the necessary reforms; I made
order the rule in all branches of public administration; I restored
confidence; and I opened new channels for labor."

No matter how black his sins, Gómez's great achievements cannot
be denied nor the patriotism he must have harbored to attain them.
But though congress listened to his high-sounding phrases with all
due respect, the majority swallowed them with a grain of salt. Though
he possessed exceptional talents for diplomacy and organization, and
his self-claimed achievements to a great extent were true, in reality
Juan Vicente Gómez combined fine, lofty principles with under-
handed, despicable tactics which he cloaked in a dazzling mantle of
patriotism, glamour and dash. Seldom, during his long career as
Venezuela's ruler, did he veer away from the perverse path of the
traditional Venezuelan despot. As always, prevailing circumstances
were against him.

When Juan Vicente Gómez had the above message written to
be read to congress he knew that his days on this earth were numbered, and—astute visionary that he was—he was actually going on
record for posterity. He hoped that the evils of his reign would be
interred with his bones and the good would live on forever. Still the
egoist in his doddering old age, he continued to envision himself as
another Bolívar, or at least he fondly hoped that posterity would
venerate him as such.

From the first day that Gómez assumed power, it was his constant purpose to cancel the country's debts instead of contenting himself with paying the interest. So he saw to it that the interest was paid
punctually and the capital was slowly but steadily amortized. Eventually the debts arising from the judgments rendered by virtue of the
Washington Protocols were canceled and the others considerably reduced, a process which continued uninterruptedly even during the
great depression of the early nineteen thirties.

The immediate result of this compliance with his obligations won
for Gómez the recognition and respect of the foreign powers. Diplomatic relations with the United States and other nations were
promptly resumed and they remained—with one or two exceptions
—on a friendly basis until his death.

As always happened after these political upsets in the government, the political prisoners of the previous regime were freed and fresh contingents were locked up in their places. From the San Carlos fortress alone, over eighty released men took ship to Maracaibo where they celebrated with a rip-roaring party in the Hotel Zulia. From abroad, the exiles began to pour into Venezuela. Gómez considerately dispatched a vessel to bring back old Dr. Rangel Garbiras, Generals Rolando and Tellería and many others with whom he had made pacts. Several months later, he ordered congress to set aside a certain sum to repatriate those who had been summoned to collaborate in the new government but who had not the wherewithal to return home.

It has been said that when many of these expatriates—some of whom had been banished as long as nine years before—again beheld the Venezuelan shoreline and the green undulating hills of La Guaira, tears welled up in their eyes. Be it the hot sultry city of Maracaibo, dry dusty Barquisimeto, chilly Mérida, or cool beautiful Caracas, each lonely, heartsick exile was returning to his beloved homeland. As in all Latins, it is in the nature of the Venezuelan to wax poetic when he is roused to deep emotion—whether it be by a beautiful woman, a breathtaking landscape, or a joyous homecoming. A famous Venezuelan poet, Pérez Bonalde, returning to Caracas from a long and bitter exile, was so stirred by the sight of his native city he wrote a beautiful poem which put into words the feeling that was in his heart. Appropriately named "Return to the Homeland," it starts:

> *Caracas allí está . . . sus obscuras lomas*
> *Y sus bandas de tímidas palomas . . .*

Since then it has been recited aloud, with emphasis and deep feeling, by every returning *Caraqueño,* and as long as the city of Caracas shall stand this poem will live immortal for its people of both high and low estate.

Most of those returning exiles would naturally have been expected to regard Gómez as their unequivocal enemy for the simple reason that he had been a binding party to all of Castro's sins. But, strangely enough, this was not the case. In their eyes and also to the man in the street, Gómez's reputation was still above reproach—the purge being considered as a necessary evil. They wanted to believe the old adage that a new broom sweeps clean. But these good citizens had yet to live and learn. The disillusionment would come later. During the purge, the misfits and crime-soddened perverts had all been swept out—Gómez's relatives and close friends being the exceptions of course—and in their places were installed men of talent and experience. So, eagerly, hopefully, these men responded to the call for collaboration with the new administration. Some of the *caudillos* vanquished by Gómez in battle from the time of La Puerta to Ciudad Bolívar would soon occupy positions of importance. General Matos would be a minister, and Generals Rolando, Solagnie, Vidal and others, presidents of states.

The ovations given to the returning exiles by the citizens of Caracas were tremendous. As was to be expected, the university students were the most vociferous of the spectators. When irascible General Hernández arrived in the capital he received the greatest ovation of all. A throng met him at the railroad station and followed his coach to the Plaza Bolívar; when he went to pay his respects to the President, he was received with great ceremony.

By law, as well as in fact, the press again regained its freedom and with the presidential elections in the offing, the old political parties, waving their varicolored flags, emerged from the political graveyard with renewed vigor. Not since the early days of Guzmán's regime had Caracas known such happy times. Here at last was liberty of movement, freedom of the press, and the promise of free elections. And it took General Gómez to do it. *Viva* General Gómez!

In the Palace of Miraflores, situated a few blocks west of the Plaza Bolívar, President Gómez sat in solemn splendor like an oriental potentate. Acknowledging the acclaim with polite platitudes, he occasionally bestowed upon his happy subjects a wry smile in the manner of an engrossed parent who has just given an annoying offspring some small bagatelle to keep him quiet. It was a wonderful world of make-believe, far too wonderful to last.

Then slowly, so slowly that the change was barely perceptible at first, the collaborators of the new regime began to see this man Gómez in his true form. The denouement actually began early the following year during the course of a lavish political banquet, but the first blow struck was delivered so subtly and with such split-second timing that the recipients failed to realize they had been hit.

During one of several short triumphal tours by rail to neighboring towns and villages, the President and his party of several dozen persons were fêted at "La Providencia," the hacienda of General Raimundo Fonseca in Aragua. The gathering was a conglomeration of every class and group. Some were die-hard *caudillos,* veterans of many revolutions, now big-wigs in the government; others were political hacks of the old classic parties who were trying hard to appear under new colors; the rest were distinguished hacienda owners or up and coming aggressive *políticos.*

The host, his wit gracious and his stories mellow, did right by his honored guest by getting up at the banquet table and telling what a great fellow Juan Vicente was. The honeyed praise met with warm applause and a toast was drunk to the President. When General Tosta García raised his glass to toast "the great Liberal Party," Gómez interrupted him. *"Por favor!"* said he with disarming casualness, "Suppose—instead—you offer your toast to Unity and the Homeland."

García hesitated but a second. "To Unity and the Homeland!" he echoed, again raising his glass.

That's all there was to it, but that simple utterance set up another milestone in the turbulent history of Venezuela. It signified on the part of the chief of state the repudiation of all party influence in the new government and it pronounced the obituary of all political parties throughout the republic. In Táchira, Dr. Ezequiel Vivas coined the phrase *"Gómez Unico,"* which was to become the popular appellation for the sole political creed that flourished for the next twenty-seven years. Later, Gómez forbade the press even to comment on matters relating to political parties, and all mention of same was deleted from school textbooks. To the vanishing generation the subject gradually became a forgotten segment of Venezuela's history; to the younger generation it was an unknown entity.

Declared Pedro M. Arcaya, one-time Minister of the Interior and Minister to Washington under Gómez, in condoning this suppression of political liberties: "His (Gómez) extraordinary good judgment made him understand what men of letters and learning had not been able to discern in spite of the misfortunes of the country; that political excitement necessarily brought on civil war. From the very first he made it clear that he would not sponsor any party, and he summarized his program in simple terms: Union, Peace, Work. General Gómez rightly saw as causes of undesirable disorder not only the tendency to preserve or resurrect former parties, but also every-thing which might make burning questions out of matters which should be considered calmly and quietly."

There have been many such arguments pro and con, but whether they extolled or disparaged, the clear fact remains that in stifling all forms of political expression, Gómez was deliberately flouting the Constitution of the Republic and the democratic form of government for which it stood. One by one he was to wrest from the humble proletariat the very prerogatives for which they had fought so long and so hard. When he ignored the Constitution in 1909 and had another drafted (which went into effect in April, 1910, the existing administration, meanwhile, being considered provisional) to suit his ends, Gómez claimed he was following the sacrosanct legality of his high office. Though he had his tenure of office reduced to four years, he nullified this patriotic gesture by inserting another amendment which in effect permitted his re-election without limit. There was another amendment which delegated to the President of the Republic "for the time being" the authority to appoint the state presidents—a very handy clause which permitted that sanctimonious official to assign his relatives and friends to highly remunerative posts. "For the time being," it should be added, actually turned out to be twenty-seven years. Still another amendment was the one which did away forever with the system of electing the President by direct ballot; henceforth, the election of the President would be a function of the National Congress. "In this way," adds Pedro Arcaya lamely, "there was no need for the obstreperous electoral campaigns which so in-flamed men's minds, as was the case in 1897."

Though most of the members of congress were motivated by patriotism and honest intentions when they passed this Constitution —believing Gómez to be the true fulfillment of the nation's need for a great leader—they soon enough found cause to regret what they had done and to admit that they had been roundly tricked. Through artful device on the part of Gómez, the National Congress became in effect a hall of puppets which responded to the pressure of cajolery, bribery, and intimidation by performing faithfully the master's will.

Juan Vicente Gómez believed in a myth: the legality—the holy, intangible legality of his regime. And in his good time he set himself up as a despot.

CHAPTER FOURTEEN

The Rehabilitation

Practical and efficient administrator that he was, Gómez set about immediately putting his government house in order. He reorganized the nation's financial structure, established credits, started paying off debts, and, most important of all, brought in increased revenues. The national budget for 1909 rose to an all-time high of fifty million bolivars, an increase of almost fifty per cent over that for 1888.

His undeniable personality, as well as his instinctive repulsion for the so-called Venezuelan aristocracy, and his liking for the farmers and working men of the field, won for Gómez some small measure of devotion of this working class. Theirs was a natural kinship that stemmed from the soil. Gómez thrilled at the sight and touch of nature's handiwork, the fields of waving wheat and corn, the herds of healthy, fat cattle. Conversely, it pained him to see the land barren and idle—a condition brought on by the havoc of civil war. Whenever he visited the battle-scarred scenes of his early victories, he remembered, not the exhilaration of victory, the resounding trumpets, the triumphant reveilles, or the thunderous cheers, but the inert dead lying in pools of blood, the cries of the wounded, all the wanton destruction of man and nature. A few years before his death he declared in a public document that whenever he walked over the fields and heard so many sorrowful echoes it seemed to him that from the blood-soaked soil of Venezuela rose the accusing voice which was first heard when Cain killed Abel. Seeing the fertile soil of his country abandoned and unproductive because its sons were too busy fighting among themselves to attend to its cultivation, it also seemed to him the very land bemoaned its sterility.

With the winning of the peace it pleased him to see Venezuela's sons at last working the soil. To create employment and stimulate production, he had congress repeal the export tax on national products. He saw to it, too, that the government began exploiting some of its natural resources: the coal beds in Anzoategui, the iron ore in the hills of the Territorio Delta Amacuro, and the copper deposits in Yaracuy, which had last been exploited by the Spaniards.

When Gómez took over the government, the capital was rife with crime and corruption, its streets scenes of armed robbery, unbridled gambling, and drunken carousals. He was confronted with an intolerable situation which he felt he had to eliminate, and eliminate it he did with the ability, common sense and severity which were his characteristics. However, when the governor of the Federal District attempted to enforce the ban against gambling within his jurisdiction, the ordinance which was received with thanksgiving by the people caused friction between Gómez and his friends. To save face with his cronies, the President blandly declared that Dr. Carlos León, the new provisional governor, had issued the ordinance without first consulting him. Outraged at the prospect of being made the scapegoat, León resigned in protest, and gambling was resumed. Later, gambling was actually outlawed, but only to the extent that no one but a member of the Gómez clan or official clique could profit by it. Every city and town had its gambling hall run by Gomecistas, but Caracas and Maracaibo were recognized as the private preserves of four of Gómez's sons. Back in 1872, when it came into being, the Caracas lottery operated as a private company. For Gómez's sons it remained as such. Both the Caracas and Maracaibo lotteries were rich bonanzas from which they extracted millions.

On June 27, 1910, the President signed the *Ley Enseñanza Antialcohólica*—a law which required that a course in temperance be given in all national schools as well as in army barracks, prisons, penitentiaries, and aboard vessels of war. Being an abstainer from alcoholic beverages, it was his fond hope that some day he would be able to impose prohibition on the country, but in this he was never successful.

At the Pan American Congress gathered at Santiago, Chile, in 1923, one of the Venezuelan delegates, after making the inevitable eulogy of the "Hero of December," broached the subject of prohibition. Referring to "the necessity of saving the peoples of America from the vice of alcoholism," he invited the other delegates to adopt a resolution recommending the establishment of a prohibition law in their respective countries. To the other delegates, occupied as they were with such serious projects as immigration, international commerce, and labor legislation the proposal by the Venezuelans was regarded as impertinent, and it provoked a wave of laughter in the Assembly.

The United Press, in a spirit of diligence rather than humor, picked up this bit of news and wired it throughout the continent. One of the official Caracas dailies, on quoting it, added the wistful note: "*El Benemerito* (the Well Deserving) General Gómez, with his paternal wisdom, is inclined toward temperance in the social customs of our country." Yet how incongruous is this widely-publicized trait of the Well Deserving with the actual facts; on the one hand he sanctimoniously preached temperance and restraint, and on the other he countenanced his sons engaging in the gambling and liquor business, by which means the people were exploited, debased, and subjugated to his tyranny. It all smacks of hypocrisy to the extreme! And one cannot overlook an additional fact which all Venezuela was aware of—that this supposedly benign, paternal ruler indulged in promiscuous sexual relations to such excess that he was regarded as an ogre. But more of that later.

In 1908 not a single road worthy of the name existed. The only road which had been opened in the nineteenth century went from La Guaira to Valencia by way of Caracas. Actually, it was generally impassable, due to the rains and lack of repairs. Back in 1877, when he was asked to recondition it, President Linares Alcántara was said to have replied: "I have two good engineers who can take care of that job—Brother Sun, whose rays will dry the mud, and Brother Burro, whose hooves will harden it!"

Up until the time of Gómez, such was the general attitude of practically all of Venezuela's presidents—personal welfare was always paramount, and the country be damned. As for the public works of Guzmán, these were limited to Caracas and its vicinity so that the "Illustrious American" could revel in the homage of the capital and bask in the glory of his fame. While Gómez's first preoccupation was with himself and his family, he did, to a minor extent, hearken to the call of duty. His view in such matters could be summed up as: "Help yourself, *amigos,* but don't be too greedy; we must leave something to appease the public!"

Gómez recognized the need for roads, but at the start of his administration there were almost no revenues, only vagrants and criminals; so the roads he could not build for lack of revenues he built with vagrants and criminals. In this way, to quote one of the faithful, Gómez made two useful things: roads and men. If, in the process of being made into men some of the victims were broken or died, the loss was shrugged off as insignificant. Others were found, somehow, somewhere, to take their places. This system had a terrifying influence on the criminal element of the country, for during the twenty-seven years it was practiced, crime—with the exception of "legalized crime" in the name of the government—became almost nonexistent.

The system also had its evils. In the first place, the task of cutting the first roads across the Andes was not assigned to competent engineers but to the most bellicose generals of the army. As can be imagined, these men had no conception of what was required in the way of planning and carrying out the work. Yet they were eager to try, especially when it was intimated that any funds left over from their allotment of funds could revert to their own pockets. If one wonders why Gómez lapsed from his usual thoroughness and employed such men instead of qualified engineers to build his back-country roads, this is easily explained. Because the army had been reduced to a skeleton force, this astute ruler used the road projects as a means to keep the *caudillos* remuneratively employed and out of mischief.

As in the Rotunda and other Venezuelan penitentiaries and prisons, prisoners in the road gangs were given sustenance to the amount of three-quarters of a bolivar daily—about twenty-five cents. To be more explicit, that was the amount allotted for each man, but more often as not the generals in charge let the mess out on contract for a lower figure, and pocketed the difference. Naturally, the contractor expected to make his profit, too. So the food, if it could be called such, was more fit for animal consumption than it was for humans. Working conditions were even worse. Men were chained in squads, they slaved from dawn to dusk, and were driven by hard-bitten officers who wielded bull whips on the laggards.

Surveyors and transits were unknown—the route being planned by map. Drainage was overlooked, and breast walls, buttresses, and culverts—a must in mountain roads—were casually dispensed with for the sake of speed. Let the streams cross where they wish and the earth cave in where it will, epitomized the popular philosophy. Each general was apportioned a stretch of road to work and he was expected, with a reasonable tolerance for errors, to join up with a fellow officer at a set point and on the same elevation. But each bungling general went his own merry way following the path of least resistance, and the junctions did not always take place as planned. The result, the Trans-Andean Highway, as that narrow ribbon of mountain road to Colombia is called today, wends its way crazily through precipitous mountains with its attendant dangers of hair-breadth turns, sharp precipices, and sudden landslides, to challenge the nerves and strength of the weary traveler.

It has been said that no less than five generals were assigned the job of building the first concrete road between Caracas and La Guaira. It turned out to be thirty-six kilometers long, although as the crow flies the distance is only ten. After its completion in 1914, the road became known as the "spaghetti road," because of its hairpin turns and convolutions. To the tourist and native alike, it is both one of the wonders and terrors of the country; wonderful, because it offers beautiful scenic views, and terrifying because its 395 curves and many sudden sheer drops keep the nervous traveler constantly on the edge of his seat.

The year 1909 appeared to mark the beginning of a new era for Venezuela. During this period of startling changes, crime and economic chaos quickly dissipated to be replaced by cheerful optimism and bustling, peaceful activity. The creation of new industrial and agricultural enterprises provided gainful employment for all, and everyone was expected to pitch in and do his share and thus build up the prestige and power of the nation. Even Colonel López tried to adjust himself to the new order of things. When the colonel called on *el Presidente* to pay his respects and give assurances of his loyalty, he was given a cordial reception. López hankered for an army assignment, but he was informed that with the army pared to the bone it would be better that he remain for the time being in his present line of work—as a commandant of the *Resguardo*—which entailed customs vigilance and prevention of smuggling at provincial border towns. When López tired of that indolent occupation after a couple of years, he became administrator of the government salt works at Salinas de Araya.

Industrious and practical man that he was, Gómez loathed idlers and political parasites and he allowed no special privileges. When the university students attempted to create disorders in the streets, he declared with all seriousness: "The Treasury pays so that they may study. If they do not want to study they will have to work . . . because there is nothing more prejudicial to a country than vagrancy." For passing this remark, Gómez became the target for the students' penned barbs and childish pranks.

"We have to open that road," "We have to work," "We have to produce," were the expressions which Gómez constantly employed to spur work and production. His primitive patriotism and the pride of being the commander-in-chief made him pronounce those desires, and to his subordinates, his wishes were orders. Gómez was a natural born leader and, endowed as he was with the necessary sagacity and temperament, he became an able administrator of public affairs, capable of leading the nation a long way on the road to greatness. Gradually, his government attuned itself to his way of thinking and adjusted itself to the local environment and national needs. Although Juan Vicente Gómez made all the top decisions, his principal collaborators were experts in their field, and the fruits of their endeavors—whether in business, finance, or law—redounded to the welfare of the nation.

Early in his regime, his lawyers convinced Gómez that most of the laws of Venezuela were antiquated and ill-suited to the requirements of a growing democratic republic, being patterned as they were after the colonial laws of Spain. Past presidents had seen fit to change only the law on minerals, as gold, diamonds, natural asphalt, and then petroleum became substantial sources of government revenue. The laws passed by Gómez were devised to conform to the growing and ever-changing needs of the nation, and it is noteworthy to mention here that many of them—some with only minor modifications—are still in force today. The first petroleum laws—there were seven of them during the Gómez Administration, as technical and practical knowledge was gradually acquired with the growth of the petroleum industry—were excellent examples of progressive government legislation, and they ably demonstrated the skill of the high calibered lawyers Gómez employed in his government. To the legal staffs of the foreign oil companies, who certainly knew their business, these men were looked upon as "pretty smart fellows."

In 1927, Gómez repealed the old patent law of 1882 and substituted a new one, which is still in force. Under this law a patent is obtainable for either five or ten years but is subject to revocation after one or two years, depending on which stipulations are chosen, if the invention has not been developed and made available to the public by that time.

Another of Gómez's laws still in force is the Penal Code, which was promulgated in 1915 and subsequently modified in 1926. So thorough and air-tight is this piece of legal legislation, it could well serve as a perfect model for other Latin American republics to follow. Unfortunately, the sad fact must be told that seldom, if ever, did Gómez and many officials of his government adhere to the spirit and letter of the law. The Penal Code clearly defines what constitutes a crime against the state and its citizens, and it sets forth the penalty to be meted out therefor. Yet, Gómez, his relatives, friends, and administrators flagrantly violated every law in the book with absolute impunity. This is said without any exaggeration, though in all fairness it must be added that a few of Gómez's children did lead upright, orderly lives, if one can overlook the fact that they did so because of the generous bounty of their begetter. On the other hand, if a humble member of the proletariat so much as offended a member of the Gómez clan or a government official, he was cast into a dungeon, his possessions were confiscated, and his women, if pretty enough, were taken into concubinage by coarse minions of the law. For slander, disrespect, or attempted assassination of the Federal Exeutive the penalty was almost doubled, but in actual practice—so it was said—the penalty was slow death by torture.

Though Gómez's law clearly states that any person held by the authorities can be released after twenty-four hours on a writ of *habeas corpus* if there is no concrete evidence against him, during the Gómez regime thousands upon thousands of unfortunates languished in jails and dungeons for months and even years without the slightest shred of legal evidence to hold them. These victims were not taken into custody by means of a formal warrant for their arrest, they were—to apply the correct term used by the Venezuelans themselves—kidnaped by force. To forestall any legal action—not that the services of a lawyer would have done any good, because it never did —the prisoner was held incommunicado for the duration of his incarceration. The length of his imprisonment depended entirely on the benevolence of *el Presidente,* the charitableness of his jailers, and the state of the prisoner's health. Even if his family did learn of his whereabouts there wasn't a lawyer in the country who would accept the case of a political prisoner, even though the word "political" covered a broad range of sins.

Once during the early days of his regime, Gómez summoned Marcial Padrón, the warden of the Rotunda, and said to him, "I want you to give fifty lashes to every political prisoner I send to the Rotunda." Noting the look of repugnance on the official's face, Gómez added angrily, "What's the matter? Don't you know how to do it? If you don't, I will show you how!"

A few days later, Padrón found a pretext to resign.

Such was the cynical travesty of justice in Venezuela during the regime of Juan Vicente Gómez, "The Hero of December," "The Well Deserving."

Despite all his high-sounding propaganda to the contrary, Gómez did almost nothing to better the lot of the common working man and his children. With the exception of the "Confederation of Workers and Artisans of the Federal District," workers' unions were not permitted. The "Confederation," by the way, was in reality a social organization whose president was a loyal Gomecista. Twice during Gómez's regime articles appeared in the press advocating unionization of workers, and in both instances the author was thrown into the Rotunda.

Although Gómez signed in 1928 the *Ley de Banco Obrero* which decreed the construction by the government of housing projects to alleviate the critical housing problems of workers, no action was ever taken to put the law into effect. It was always "Tomorrow we will do this" and "Tomorrow we will do that," or "The most pressing problems must come first." Venezuela became, in effect, the land of *mañana.* It was not until 1941, six years after the dictator's death, that a new law was passed and an appropriation of 13,200,000 bolivars obtained, that the *Banco Obrero* actively engaged in building homes for workers.

Education was another farce and a stain on the controversial character of "The Hero of December." At the time of his death, over 85 per cent of the population was illiterate. The reason was painfully apparent. There were very few schools. Only the larger cities boasted secondary schools; the hundreds of towns and villages did without. The only primary schools Gómez provided (primary schooling ends with the sixth grade) were a few two- or three-room decrepit buildings confiscated from his enemies, which his partisans had rejected as unfit for their own use. A half-dozen rough benches on a dirt floor, and a sandaled and generally unschooled *maestra* before a tiny blackboard—expounding the parallel greatness of Simón Bolívar and Juan Vicente Gómez—bore the somewhat dubious title of a "federal school." Education of the masses, therefore, was almost completely neglected. To Gómez's mind, the children should be taught only to love and fear him and to revere the memory of Simón Bolívar.

But what happened to the law which Guzmán signed in 1870 which decreed that the revenue from the sale of fiscal stamps would pay for the cost of primary education? Many Venezuelans have asked that question. It appears that a good many years previously this law was shelved and forgotten, although the sale of fiscal stamps continued and the revenue was diverted to other purposes. For a good many years—that is until revenues from the petroleum industry and the income tax (1943) came into the picture—receipts from the sale of fiscal stamps and sealed paper ranked fourth as a source of government income; import duties and taxes from cigarettes and liquors preceded it in that order. Of the 86,053,970 bolivars reportedly earned [11] by Gómez's government during the fiscal year ending June 30, 1910, about 15 per cent, or 12,900,000 bolivars, was derived from the sale of fiscal stamps. Obviously, this was too small a sum to provide adequate school facilities for a population of about 2,400,000 spread out over an area as large as Texas and Minnesota

[11] No one will ever know how many unreported millions went into the pockets of the rank and file of office-holders.

combined. Nevertheless, very little of this money was used for the purpose for which it was intended.

One of the most commendable acts of Gómez's career was the creation of the Academy of Political and Social Science in 1915. Comprised of the foremost Venezuelan intellectuals of his time (there are thirty honorary memberships open to foreign savants), they were given by Gómez the responsibility for drafting the nation's laws. Modified by a new law in 1924, the decree now reads in part: "The prime purpose of the Academy shall be: to co-operate toward the progress and betterment of Venezuelan legislation through the medium of conferences to be held by that body, also through the medium of studies of such subjects as may be determined; to draft and revise projects of codes and other laws of a general character which the Federal Executive may deem it convenient to submit to its study, with the object in view of presenting them in due course to the legislative bodies; to draft and revise projects of laws of a local character which the executive of any state may deem it convenient to submit to its study, with the object in view of presenting them in due course to the state legislature; and to form a library in which shall figure the best works on political and social science of national and foreign authors, and the universal legislation of all cultured nations."

For all his forthright speech and dignified bearing, the peasant from the Andes stood in awe of eminent jurists and brilliant men of letters. One of the latter was Dr. González Guinán, who induced the President in 1910 to have the government underwrite the cost of publishing his voluminous *Historia Contemporánea de Venezuela*. Shortly after the third volume came out, Gómez used to say as an eulogy to the author, with sincere conviction in his voice but with a mischievous gleam in his heavy-lidded eyes: "This Doctor González Guinán is very intelligent. He has written three volumes . . . as thick as this . . . !" And of the fourth volume he was finishing: "It's a thick one too!"

With the fall into disgrace of Gonzáles Guinán in 1912, the work was suspended, but the rest of the books began to appear about ten years later.

If a stranger had chanced to come upon General Gómez as he emerged from Miraflores Palace, trailing hovering aides like gulls behind a tug, he would have mistaken him for a rich *hacendado* rather than the President of the Republic. There were no outward indications of a Don Juan in this man, no rakish elegance of dress or Adonis charm of figure, no suggestion in the face or bearing that this was the republic's most renowned soldier and leader of men. His clothes were of good quality but were somber in tone, as was his cravat. And, what was unusual for the tropics, he always wore gloves. It was a mania with him. He changed them as often as two and three times a day. They were not worn to hide a deformity or skin disease, as the general public thought. It was just that he detested clasping clammy hands and touching anything that had been handled by others. His words, his gestures, his features, the coarse drooping mustaches, the small heavy-lidded eyes, all bespoke rustic simplicity and a mediocre intelligence. A superficial appraisal of him would have evoked the comment: "A kind man," or "A good and simple man, but dull."

But where to look for a telltale sign that would denote what people whispered was a deep ingrown streak of cruelty? Perhaps in his voice. But no. His voice matched his personality. It was the soft drawl of the *mestizo* farmer. He spouted the quaint homespun philosophy of a man who had long lived close to the soil. He talked in simple sentences, using his hands to emphasize a point, and he sometimes repeated a pithy phrase two or three times so there would be no mistake of his having said it. He knew few verbs, and some of these he could not conjugate correctly. No one dared to correct him. His conversations were short and they invariably ended with an emphatic *"Sí, señor!"* or *"Pues, cómo le parece . . . ?"*—"Well, what do you think?"

And the invariable answer, said in chorus, would be: "You are perfectly right, General."

Two psychological traits of this man were distrust and impenetrability. In a way, they were assets in that they served as a fence of security around the "Sphinx of La Mulera"—as his intimates dubbed him. With them he dominated everyone—his most intimate friends, his loyal counselors, and even those who were bound to him by kinship. In essence he trusted no one, so he would not divulge his plans to anyone. He kept even members of his cabinet in a state of constant expectation, and sometimes consternation. It wasn't rare for a minister, who had remained the night with him after a hearty supper and a cordial parley, to awake to find himself deposed. Not even his favorites knew when he left on one of his short sudden trips, and when he returned. Many men of great intuitive talent have tried to fathom his thoughts, but they all failed, some of them with hard disappointments because they never knew when the *Jefe* was in a good or bad humor. In his own strange blend of Christian religion and primitive superstition, Juan Vicente Gómez was a baffling enigma which never could be solved.

To the man on the street it became a riddle as to how this low-born, unschooled man could solve the nation's problems and make weighty decisions on which the welfare and the very life of the republic hung in the balance. "Surely," voiced the curious, "there must be someone who inspires *el Presidente*. It isn't possible for him alone to solve all the problems of the country."

To which the most servile of *el Presidente*'s lackeys would exclaim in mock astonishment, "Don't you know that the *Jefe* is a great statesman?" But the cynical, remembering the distinguished intellectuals who always surrounded *el Presidente,* would smile incredulously.

Later, after the scandals involving Eustóquio Gómez and an obscure bureaucrat by the name of Eleuterio García became aired in the press, the veil of mystery surrounding Gómez's source of inspiration was lifted. The man to whom General Gómez most often gave ear was an aged Colombian who was known diversely as Dr. José Rosario García and Dr. Gris. Dr. Gris, by which name he became more familiarly known, appears to have been a man of vague antecedents and undefined status in the administration and the community; in fact, everything about him was shrouded in an aura of mystery. All that the administration, Caracas society, and the public knew about him was that he was a Colombian. One obscure legend has it that he was related in some way to Gómez, but no one could say for sure. Those who were in daily contact with both men were of the opinion that the intimate relationship that existed between them dated back to the old days when Gómez was a cattleman in the Andes. But where "Doctor" Gris obtained his doctorate and in what branch of science has remained a mystery. But, doctor of medicine, engineering, law, or dentistry, all doors were open to him, and though he possessed no official title, Dr. Gris frequented Miraflores Palace and the inner sanctum at will.

CHAPTER FIFTEEN

The Villain Unmasked

The closing months of 1909 marked the beginning of a series of startling events which climaxed the complete denouement of the "Hero of December." It was as if the man himself had deliberately set off a packet of giant Chinese firecrackers, so tremendous were the repercussions, so grave were the charges which followed one another in rapid sequence.

The martyrdom of General Zoilo Vidal, a man of high principles and steadfast courage, was the first of many outrages which shocked the entire country. Being a soldier, Vidal had been willing to fight for his principles, but the war he and other revolutionary leaders had waged against Castro had ended disastrously. For his integrity and herosim he had distinguished himself not only among the leaders of the revolution, but among all Venezuelans as well. Such was his popular prestige in the capital and in eastern Venezuela, Gómez came to look upon him with envy and distrust. Because of his fame, Gómez was perforce obliged to find a place for him in his provisional government, and he appointed him to the position of president of the state of Sucre. After Vidal took office, Gómez began to systematically take over the most lucrative of Castro's monopolies and rackets in Sucre and to ease his relatives and friends into various positions in the state government. Astounded at this turn of events, Vidal voiced his protest in a series of denunciatory letters to the President, which culminated in his being summoned to Caracas.

In the Miraflores Palace he told Gómez to his face what he thought of the whole rotten business. He had sided with him, he told him, because he had firmly believed that he and Castro had not been cut out of the same cloth. He had never dreamed that Juan Vicente

149

would follow the same crooked road of corrupt politics as had Castro . . . but now he had seen enough . . . he could stand no more . . . he was resigning then and there. And he strode out of the office in disgust.

During this entire tirade Gómez had sat silent and immobile. Neither by word nor sign did the "Sphinx of La Mulera" reveal his reaction to this outpouring of censure and abuse. But no sooner had the door closed behind the stalwart defender of honest government than the "Sphinx of La Mulera" came to life. As calmly as if he were ordering his carriage, Gómez told Baptista to issue an order for Vidal's arrest. When he reached his quarters, Vidal was seized by the police and taken to the Rotunda. Later he was transferred to the fortress at Puerto Cabello.

Caracas and the entire country were stunned by the news. General Vidal's wife journeyed to the capital to plead for the liberty of her husband, but she could not gain admittance to the Palace of Miraflores. When Gómez left to spend the week end at Macuto, she followed him there and managed to break through the heavy cordon of men who surrounded him. "Please listen to me, General Gómez!" she pleaded, blocking his path. "I have come to beg for the release of my husband, General Vidal . . ."

For a few fleeting seconds General Gómez gazed unmoved into the beseeching eyes of the distraught woman. Then he spoke, but his words did not express the compassion that Señora Vidal had hoped to hear. "Get on with you," he said coldly, "and let us pass." And he signaled to his aides to remove the lady from his sight.

General Zoilo Vidal spent eleven years in the fortress of Puerto Cabello. For all of those eleven years he lived in solitary confinement with heavy irons on his legs. He suffered the torment of the *verga*,[12] the lash of the whip, the foul food, all the humiliations that his jailers could heap upon him, but he took his punishment unflinchingly and never complained. One night the prisoners in the criminal section of the penitentiary rebelled against the head warden. Invited to join the revolt, Vidal chose to remain in his cell. When Gómez heard of it, he believed that Vidal had been subdued at last, so he sent one of

[12]A leather-covered swagger stick made of the penis of the bull, once very popular with the army officers and cattle men. Since the death of Gómez, its use has died out.

his sons to offer him freedom if he would accept a place in the government. Vidal, still as obstinate as ever, turned down the offer.

In 1921, when it was reported that Vidal's health had been dangerously weakened by dysentery and that his mind had become affected, Gómez ordered him released. The ovation accorded the old general when he stopped in Valencia on his way to Caracas was tremendous. Never, during the long years of Gómez's rule, did anyone ever see greater crowds and more spontaneous expressions of popular homage than were paid to this tired old hero. It was while he was taking his first walk through the streets of Caracas after a long convalescence that the old soldier cracked up. He never reached home. Gómez's men, who had been following him, carried him off to the insane asylum in Catia. Released several months later, Vidal was taken by his wife to the cooler climate of Los Teques to recuperate. Once again the secret police carried him off, and although his wife swore he was sane, they kept him locked up in the insane asylum at Caracas. He died there in 1930—"from slow poisoning," said his wife, but she was unable to obtain custody of his body to prove it.

The aspects of the Eustóquio Gómez scandal were somewhat similar but more far-reaching in scope. One day, Dr. Juan José Abreu, Judge of the *Primera Instancia,* received a note from the President suggesting that he re-open the case of Eustóquio Gómez and review the evidence. It had been Dr. Abreu who had sentenced Eustóquio, a cousin of Gómez's, for the murder of the governor of Caracas. Weighing the clear-cut evidence, Abreu had seen his duty and had complied with it. There had been no startling repercussions at the time, nor had he feared any. And now this note asking him to re-open the case.

Surely, wrote Gómez, now that the excitement and cry for blood had died down, the good judge would find that Eustóquio had been innocently convicted. But the good judge didn't think so, and he flatly refused to reverse or even commute the sentence. Lightning struck then, and swiftly. The judge and the secretary of his court were unceremoniously hustled off to the Rotunda.

But Gómez, now recognized as the unmitigated rogue that he was, didn't stop there. He had to add a little ironic touch that made everyone catch his breath and wonder what would happen next.

One day, General Linares Alcántara, Minister of the Interior and one-time President, received at his office a very insolent telegram. It bore the name of one Evaristo Prato, *Jefe* of the fortress of San Carlos. Enraged at the impudence of the man, the minister made inquiries concerning him in the Ministry of War. Prato, he was told, had received his appointment on direct orders from General Gómez. Still in the heat of anger, Alcántara went to see the President with the intention of asking for Prato's discharge. He showed Gómez the telegram, but the "Sphinx of La Mulera" appeared to be in a non-responsive mood. "Take it up with Dr. Baptista here," he said tartly, and he went back to perusing his papers, indicating that the interview had ended.

Baptista followed the minister out into the anteroom and closed the door behind him. They faced each other and Alcántara wondered at the wry smile on Baptista's face. "Don't you know who Evaristo Prato is?" Baptista asked him.

"No, I don't," replied the befuddled minister.

"Well . . . Evaristo Prato is actually Eustóquio Gómez!"

"Eustóquio Gómez? How can that be?" exclaimed the minister, astounded. "Eustóquio is a prisoner in the Rotunda for the murder of Dr. Mata Illas."

"He *was* in the Rotunda!" Baptista corrected him. "General Gómez ordered General Olivares, Minister of War, to appoint him *Jefe* of San Carlos under the name of Evaristo Prato. When the appointment appeared in the official gazette, he was released from the Rotunda and sent to San Carlos without anyone knowing about it."

Alcántara refused to believe his ears. He had to go to the Rotunda to find out for himself if what he heard was the truth.

Marcial Padrón was still warden of the prison at the time. "Yes, it's so," he told him. "Some of his relatives came and took him away in a carriage. I had to let him go when they handed me an order signed by General Gómez himself . . . What else could I do? . . . Disobey *el Presidente* and end up in one of these cells myself? . . . Not I! . . . Say—is it true that they made Eustóquio *Jefe* of San Carlos?"

But the disillusioned minister had rushed off. Back home he brooded over the disgrace of being associated with a scoundrel. Letting a murderer go scot free was a disreputable act in itself, but putting a murderous brute in charge of Gómez's helpless victims, with the prerogative to torture and kill, was too much! Several times that day Alcántara found himself on the verge of writing his resignation. Later on he was to regret not having done so.

The news of this skulduggery on the part of Gómez leaked out, as such things will. It raced through the capital like wildfire. The press, shocked into a sense of shame that such an ignominious deed could have been perpetrated by "The Hero of December," openly commented on the case and decried the miscarriage of justice. But "The Hero of December" remained silent, Eustóquio Gómez carried on as the commandant of San Carlos fortress, and Dr. Mata Illas remained in his grave unavenged.

Hardly had the ink of the newspaper editorials on the Eustóquio Gómez case dried than another scandal broke. During an investigation of graft in the Municipal Council of Caracas, Eleuterio García, a nephew by marriage to Dr. Gris, was required to take the stand in his own defense. An arrogant and obnoxious youth, who had made the most of his uncle's powerful influence, García scornfully refuted the charges as ridiculous, yet against him there appeared a minor government employee by the name of Enrique Chaumer, who gave damaging testimony. Incensed, García resolved to get even. Early the next morning he set out in a carriage and came upon his enemy near Las Carmelitas, leading his little daughter by the hand to school. García jumped from the carriage and from a newspaper, which carried the story of the preceding day's proceedings, he pulled a revolver and shot Chaumer to death. Assuming an air of impudent bravado, García permitted himself to be taken into custody, but brazenly boasted that he would not remain long behind bars.

In airing this cold-blooded crime, the Caracas press archly wondered if the strong influences behind García wouldn't pull a few strings to release him; and two newswriters, Arévalo González and Manuel Flores Cabrera, recklessly demanded, but with tongue in cheek, the maximum penalty. Surprisingly, Gómez took no reprisals, but he was only biding his time. Later, he would clamp down hard on the freedom of the press.

As for the outcome of the "trial"—if it may be called that—it was one of the vilest mockeries of justice ever perpetrated in the Venezuelan courts. A court *ad hoc* declared Eleuterio García "acquitted of homicide," and he swaggered out of jail a free man to occupy another government job under an assumed name in Puerto Cabello.

One may wonder—even at this early stage of his regime, which already revealed with startling clarity the real man Gómez—why the country's leading political figures tolerated such despicable conduct in their chief-of-state. By now Gómez had dropped all use of pretense. His power already solidified, he was smothering one by one all civil liberties, using the flimsy pretext that the Venezuelan people wrongfully abused them. Some red-blooded Venezuelan patriots, like Abreu, Vidal, and Hernández courageously rebelled, while others like Generals Peñaloza, Olivares, and Tellería, and later, Alcántara, Drs. Leopoldo Baptista and Martín Requena and many more fled into exile. But there were many others, some of them eminent personages and learned scholars, who remained behind to bolster Gómez's regime by their luminous presence and subservient obedience to his wishes. Their loyalty to Gómez, it has so often been asserted, was not motivated by sentiments of patriotism or bonds of undying friendship; one has only to observe at close hand the vast wealth some of these men or their descendants possess today to deduce the reason why. The "pork barrel," as it is known today, certainly has its Latin counterpart, but the Venezuelan *políticos* of those days—if one can judge by the stagnant and colonial condition of the country's provinces —must have embraced it for all it was worth. Gómez was astute enough to abhor the use of intimidation in trying to win the support and loyalty of his collaborators. But when even bribery and intimidation failed, he resorted to violence only as a means to an end—never as an instrument for sadistic pleasure.

Perhaps the principal reason for Gómez's success, and the secret of his long rule, was his ability to win the loyalty of his colleagues. He possessed an extraordinary talent for judging men. *"Conozco a los hombres,"* "I know men," he once confided to a subordinate. He believed that every man has his price; when inviting an initiate to climb on the gravy train he always intimated that the ride would be a long and profitable one. Though he and his family kept the lion' share of the take, Gómez gave generously and spontaneously, thus keeping his political family well fed and content. In that roseate atmosphere of brotherly love, it was—to quote one former political bigwig—"a pleasure to do business with him."

There were a few instances, however, when Gómez had his awkward moments, which could be attributed either to maladroitness in the use of his tongue, or to miscalculation in his judgment of a man. He lacked subtlety in his methods. He just couldn't realize that to suddenly thrust a wad of money into a man's hand without first employing artifice to pave the way would be an affront to the average man's pride and honesty. Such an instance occurred one day when Gómez was conversing genially with General Hernández in Miraflores. He was striving to win over the general as a partisan and as a friend, and with apparent success. During a lull in the conversation Gómez drew out of a drawer of his desk a packet of negotiable bonds. Thumbing casually through them so that Hernández could not fail to see what they were, he extended them with a toothy smile. Hernández, a glazed look of indifference on his face, budged not an inch. To which Gómez countered in his own crude way: "Take them, General, take them . . . *They belonged to don Cipriano!* . . . Later on I will give you more . . . !"

According to his own version of the story, General Hernández didn't accept the bonds, and because he remained at odds with Gómez, we can assume that he spoke the truth.

A somewhat similar but amusing episode occurred which involved one of Gómez's old cronies, a *caudillo,* who had accompanied him on the memorial march from the Andes. Shortly after his arrival in Caracas, this *caudillo*—who must remain unnamed—summoned his concubine, called Rosa from the Andes, set up housekeeping with her, and started raising a family. Years later, when Gómez named him to his cabinet, the *caudillo* decided to discard his simple mountain woman for one who could better conform to his new social status. After considerable search he found one who responded to his courting. She was cultured and attractive, came from a fine family, and brought a promise of a dowry. Once the date was agreed upon, the *caudillo* approached General Gómez with the intention of asking him to be best man.

Hardly had the man gotten the words out of his mouth that he intended to marry, than Gómez, surprised and pleased, exclaimed: "Well, at last! I'm glad to see you do right by Rosa. Now all your children will be legitimate! Your Rosa is a fine girl and she has been a good and faithful mate."

At this point the *caudillo* started to change color; Rosa had been packed off to the Andes. "We should," continued Gómez, "remember those who have been with us from our humble beginnings and who have remained loyal through our trials and hardships. Do you know something? . . . I think Rosa should be rewarded. She should have a dowry, a handsome dowry . . . and I think I shall be the one to give it to her." Here Gómez called in his secretary and told him that the deed for an estate he had recently taken over in Guarico should be made out in Rosa's name. He was also to see to it that Rosa received 20,000 bolivars in cash. "That will be my wedding present to the bride," the *Jefe* said, beaming. "And you can count on my being best man."

Dazed beyond coherent thought, the *caudillo* mumbled his thanks and stumbled out of the room. Cursing himself for all kinds of a fool, he began to figure how he could extricate himself from the dilemma he had gotten himself into. To go back and try to explain would mean losing face with the *Jefe*. No—there remained only one thing to do. He would send Rosa a telegram to return at once to Caracas. Now that she had become a woman of means he would marry her. And perhaps, he thought wistfully, his attractive fiancé of the *alta sociedad* might deign to become only his mistress.

According to *salon* gossip, that was the way it turned out.

CHAPTER SIXTEEN

Father and Lover

If ever a President of the Republic felt ill at ease living in Miraflores, it was Juan Vicente Gómez. To him, the enormous edifice that Crespo had so lavishly built, with its ornate furniture, flamboyant pantings, and retinue of servants and lackeys was a palace better suited to the taste of a king than to that of a peasant. As much as he frowned on the aristocrats as a class, Gómez detested their high style of living even more. Small, simply-furnished *Bella Vista* had set off as nothing else could the sharp contrast in personalities and mode of living of the rustic backwoods cattleman and the urbane luxury-loving Castro, whose palatial *Villa Zoila* had been a pretentious display of his exotic vanity. Since his arrival in Caracas, Gómez had acquired the habit of living alone. Spurning the prosaic pleasures of what one may call a normal life, he had relegated doña Dionisia and their children to a separate establishment while he gallivanted around as he pleased. He demanded the absolute freedom of a bachelor and refused to be encumbered by the petty annoyances of a houseful of children and the watchful jealous eye of a woman. In this, doña Dionisia pleased him by declining to be anything but what nature had intended her to be.

There is one phase in the lives of men of state that is not always pleasing to investigate—their amorous transgressions. By all the standards of ethics and morals of civilized peoples, the province of sex is tacitly regarded as an inviolable part of private life. Sexual behavior may disclose an eccentricity in the habits of a man, but beyond that it cannot tell us much more. Experience has shown, with all due respect to Freud, that it is a pretty risky presumption to judge the morals of a man on the basis of his erotic impulses. Gen-

erally, in the biographies of men of state, such delicate matters are
seldom mentioned, and when they are, it is because they outshine
other facets in a man's life. It is impossible to overlook the part that
sex played in the life of Gómez, because it was sex that predominated
over everything else in his life—his honor and self-respect, his love
of country, and his faith in God.

For an occidental dictator of the twentieth century, the love life
of Juan Vicente Gómez was phenomenal. There can be no denying
that. But unlike a certain few of his most intimate colleagues, Gómez
was not a pervert. As to be expected, it was not these colleagues who
were the topics of delectable gossip—it was the man in the limelight—
Juan Vicente Gómez. The more conspicuously great the individual,
the greater the incentive to slander him, for the interest is com
mensurate with the eminence of the person slandered. Gómez's
enemies painted him to be a terrifying ogre, and many Venezuelan
believed it. True, Gómez was endowed with a greater sexual urge than
most men, but his sexual relations with women were perfectly normal.
He craved sex-fulfillment. He could no more resist a pretty girl than
he could resist food, when hungry.

Whatever his private life may have been, however lurid, how
ever romantic, Juan Vicente Gómez bore himself with aplomb and
dignity. To him, sex was not a topic for lewd jokes or barroom
discussions; therefore the subject was banned in his presence. His
love affairs were carried on with the greatest of secrecy and he never
permitted himself to be seen publicly in the company of his paramours.
He maintained no equivalent of the Harding administration's "House
of Mystery," with its midnight champagne suppers and boisterous
girlie parties. Not once was he so indiscreet as to have a woman
conducted surreptitiously to his quarters in Venezuela's "White
House." To him, Miraflores typified the "home" of the nation. It
must be protected from any slander or any shadow of scandal. It
must be, like Caesar's wife, above suspicion. Speculation has sug
gested that all this reticence and secrecy was because of a sense of
shame, but there is no worthy evidence to substantiate this, and
knowledge of Gómez's character contradicts it. Many public men,
many great men, have had their careers utterly ruined by indiscre
tions. That the public career of Juan Vicente Gómez had not been
wholeheartedly devoted to upbuilding the dignity and honor of the

country was common gossip. Doña Dionisia knew it, a great many Venezuelans knew it. And Gómez was aware that they knew. He simply had the good sense and self-control to keep his love affairs from encroaching on his public life—a remarkable achievement, considering that his multiple affairs followed one upon the other.

No one, probably not even Gómez himself, could say with any certainty how many hundreds of mistresses he had had in his lifetime. Lithesome Indian maidens, winsome Latin beauties, blondes, redheads, brunettes, French, Dutch, Spanish, and German, he had them all. Some of his affairs had been as fleeting as the tropical night. Others lasted longer, perhaps because the girls were dazzled by his wealth and position and aimed to please. One foreign girl, a redhead known to an intimate few as *La Rojita,* was a favorite for almost three years. Then, later, there was Carmen, a striking Latin beauty, the daughter of General Ramirez. She too lasted for close to three years. It was said that General Ramirez had threatened to kill Gómez, but fortunately for him he had been persuaded to go to his estates in Carabobo to forget.

While these affairs were going on, Gómez was maintaining doña Dionisia and her children in a sumptuous establishment in fashionable El Paraiso, which he visited about once each week. However, sexual relations with Dionisia had become a memory of the past, for she had grown too old for him. There is no firsthand knowledge of Dionisia's having gone into any jealous tantrums. She had lived with her lover long enough to be utterly resigned to his whims and fancies, especially where women were concerned. And although she had fervently hoped for marriage and had cherished the thought of occupying the social throne of the nation, to be the First Lady of the Land, she settled down resignedly to enjoy with pride and satisfaction the children of their union.

The only women who ever wielded any influence over Gómez were his mother and his eldest sister Indalecia. After the death of his mother in Macuto in 1916, it was Indalecia, a spinster throughout her life, who took an active interest in her brother's career. Her homes in Caracas and Maracay often served as meeting places for her brother and his friends.

What was so extraordinary about this man Gómez was the number of love nests he maintained simultaneously. If he had been a

Mohammedan living in Turkey during the days of the fabulous
sultans, he probably would have possessed the greatest harem of his
time; so great was his passion for virgins, so great was his liking for
variety.

Scattered about Caracas, and later in Maracay where he chose
to live, Gómez sometimes maintained upward of a dozen mistresses.
When he tired of a girl, he simply paid her off. If she had means of
her own, he sent her a parting gift. But if she had not, and if the
stopping of his maintenance meant hardship, he gave her a sum of
money and the deed of the house in which she lived.

This story is told of one of Gómez's love affairs.

"I have come for the señorita!" said an officer to the girl's father.
"General Gómez desires to see her!"

"*Dios mío!*" exclaimed the hapless man. "Why did he have to
choose *my* daughter!" But to the girl he said hopelessly, "You had
better go, *mi querida* . . . I am helpless to interfere."

The girl, beautiful, an aristocrat and spirited, confronted Gómez.
And she defied him. Finally he opened a drawer of his desk and
withdrew two papers. He handed them to her. "Take your choice,"
he said, and he sat back with a wry smile while he drank in her
fresh virgin beauty.

One was the deed to a furnished house in El Paraiso. The other
was a warrant for her father's arrest.

"She loves him now," say the people of Caracas. "*Dios!* What a
devil that man is!"

Perhaps that story is not altogether true. Stories have a way of
changing when they are passed on by evil-wishers. But it is probably
true in essence. Gómez obtained his girls in many ways. Sometimes
he spotted a likely candidate at a fiesta, at a ball, at the theater, or
even at the bull fights. One of his henchmen, a specialist in such
assignments, would track her down. Twenty-four hours later, the
conquest would be history. He also used procurers, and it has been
said that a few desperate families voluntarily offered to sacrifice a
pretty daughter so that Gómez would release the breadwinner of the
family from prison. It is not known, however, whether Gómez ever
deliberately stooped to take such unfair advantage.

On the other hand, many of the minor administrators of the
government were known to be utterly ruthless in their methods. To

those prisoners who passed through the Rotunda or the prison at Puerto Cabello during the early years of the Gómez regime, the story of General Alcántara was well known. A widower, seventy-four years of age, Alcántara had been living on the *llanos* with two young daughters, both of whom were sought after by the *Jefe civil* of the village. Although this man had a wife in the Andes, Alcántara eventually found himself obliged to "give" him one of his daughters to avoid trouble. One day the old man left for a neighboring town to buy some supplies. The *Jefe civil*, knowing of the trip, telegraphed Caracas that he was headed there because he was involved in a revolutionary plot. From Caracas an order was telegraphed to the other town to arrest Alcántara. He was not permitted to return to say good-by to his daughters or even to send them a message. Thrown first into the Rotunda, then later into the fortress at Puerto Cabello, General Alcántara died there several years later, bemoaning his children's fate.

Because such crimes generally occurred only in the lower echelons of the administration, there is good reason to believe that the case of General Alcántara never reached the ears of the chief of state. If it had, he would most certainly have taken stern measures. There have been but few tyrants in modern history who have so persistently upheld social formalities as this dictator. Though he appeared to be blind to the sexual crimes of an intimate few, Gómez would not tolerate the seduction or rape of young girls by any other man. Whenever reports of such a crime reached his ears, he would sternly order that the man involved be made the proposition that he choose between marriage and a pair of heavy irons. Naturally, the man always chose the former. This asperity of Gómez was carried even to his own sons. It is said that he once imprisoned one of his sons in a cell for some time due to his illicit relations with an actress.

Both in private and public life, Gómez once expostulated to a subordinate, ethics is all important in conducting sexual relations. One must conduct oneself with the utmost decorum. One must not betray children. One must remember the sanctity of the home. One must remember that he is a Venezuelan citizen and as such must uphold the honor and time-honored traditions of this glorious nation. Such high moral standards coming from the country's leader, who seldom practiced what he preached—installing himself as he did on a plane above public censure! The King can do no wrong!

In matters of sex there is no typical Mr. or Mrs. Venezuela, for their sexual mores are stratified, each layer largely determined by educational background and economic status. On the lowest level, more often than not the man and woman, living together and bringing up a family of half-a-dozen children, are not married. Nor is any social degradation attached to this form of concubinage, which is partly due to the fact that the fees charged by the priests for a marriage ceremony are unduly heavy, often prohibitive.

In 1529, Bishop Zamárraga, in a letter to Charles V, mentioned the large number of Spanish vagabonds drifting about the country with two or three Indian mistresses, living off the bounty of the natives. The friars, too, wrote Nuño de Guzmán who was President of the Audencia, to the same monarch, were loose in their relations with native women. At first the Crown encouraged mating with Indian women as a means of breeding loyal subjects and Christianizing the natives, and although some Spaniards formally married these dusky women, fornication and indiscriminate concubinage continued unbridled through the centuries.

Having long ago failed to impress on the peasant class a standard of morality similar to that prevailing in most other countries, the Venezuelan clergy today finds itself unable to cope with the practice of "free love" and it has made no serious efforts to change the practice of past generations.

Though one cannot condone the fact that Gómez was unduly promiscuous in his sex habits, it is remembered that he lived in an age of moral laxness. The male is polygamous by nature, and especially is this so of the Latin. Many of Gómez's friends, some of them respectable pillars of society, maintained mistresses. Others who could not afford such a luxury sought their extra-marital pleasures where they could find them.

As Hitler had his Eva Braun and Mussolini had his Clara Petacci, so too did this dictator have his *femme fatale*—Dolores Amelia, a pretty, dark-eyed girl who for almost three decades rode the crest of his fame and fortune. Gómez was forty-nine when he first saw and desired her. She was fifteen, the only daughter of Dr. J. M. Nuñez de Cáceres, a Maracaibero then living in Caracas. Dr. Nuñez was eighty-four at the time, and he had a long and distinguished career behind him. A bibliophile and prodigious writer, he had authored the *History of Venezuela,* a voluminous work of sixteen volumes. He was also a poet, illustrator, accomplished linguist, and world traveler. In his younger days he had acquired the sobriquet of "The Walking Library" because he could recite from memory whole chapters and verses from well-known works written in six different languages. In his old age the loss of his daughter came as a hard blow. A true gentleman of the old school, he refused the favors offered him and retired in bitter solitude to brood his loss and grieve over the disgrace.

Dolores Amelia could not be called a beauty by any means, nor was she a scheming adventuress, but she possessed charm and intelligence and found favor in Gómez's eyes. She bore him eight children.[13] She saw *La Rojita,* Carmen Ramirez, and a host of other minor favorites come and go. She never lived more than a block away from her lover, and she was at his bedside (the only mistress accorded that privilege) when he died. After his death, Dolores Amelia suffered the ignominy of wild flight and exile, and on the streets of Madrid she was called vile names and was pelted with rotten tomatoes. Today she lives in Maracay, secluded and alone, her children scattered over half the globe.

As to the precise number of children fathered by Gómez, that remains in the realm of mystery. The most conservative guess has placed the number close to one hundred, the most imaginative at two hundred. One member of an old Caracas family, who was in an advantageous position to make his own observations of such matters, has ventured to place the figure at one hundred and fifty. And this, he added hastily, was a conservative figure! When one considers that in the Mohammedan world it is not at all unusual for a man to beget one hundred and fifty children, and that the actuating motive of Gómez's entire life had been a consuming passion to mate and propagate, it is as easy to believe one figure as another.

What rights has a mistress of any man in Venezuela, someone has asked. And what rights has an illegitimate child? None whatsoever. Although there appears to be little social stigma attached to illegitimacy in Venezuela, children born out of wedlock cannot come

[13] Juan Vicente, Florencio, Belen, Rosa Amelia, Hermenegilda, Cristina, Berta, and Juan.

into their father's inheritance unless they have been formally "recognized," that is, that the father has registered each child in turn with the civil authorities and has formally declared them eligible to bear his name and become his legal beneficiaries. The unmarried mother gets nothing, nor has she any recourse to legal action to compel the father to support her unrecognized children, should he choose to abandon her.

This woeful lack of legal protection for the unmarried, and especially impoverished, mother and her children, has, in recent years, presented the government with a growing problem it will have to solve sooner or later—Venezuela's abandoned children. A survey made by the *Consejo Venezolano del Niño,* a children's welfare agency operating under the Ministry of Justice, revealed that in 1951 there were 100,000 abandoned children in the country. Of these, 30,000 are wards of the state, being maintained in various institutions and foster homes. Because of the lack of funds and agencies to help them, the other 70,000 have been left to shift for themselves, to scavenge, beg, and steal and become pitiful problems to the police courts, who can only turn them loose again and again until they become lost to sight in the underworld. Almost all of these waifs have been reported as illegitimate, and each case history follows an identical pattern. The mother was a poor and ignorant *mestizo,* who had never heard of birth control, and rather expected the father of her child to abandon her. The man she passively gave herself to was irresponsible and self-centered, and cared not a whit about the outcome. Sometimes the culprit was a *"gran señor,"* married and the father of a legitimate family, who shrugged off all appeals for help, giving the implausible excuse that his abandoned offspring "harbored hypothetical pretensions" to being his recognized child.

It is difficult to believe such conduct of a *"gran señor,"* for by nature the typical Venezuelan is proud of his paternity and fond of his children. But one must reconcile oneself to the facts, and only hope that the future will see reforms in education, law, and custom.

Of the many children fathered by Gómez, those of Dionisia Bello and Dolores Amelia were the only ones he legally recognized. Gómez gave them a social calling card, so to speak, which gave them entry into the best Caracas homes. They attended the most exclusive schools, married into the best families, and enjoyed the same social status as if they had been the fruit of legitimate marriages. But the other hundred and some odd offspring of Gómez's were confined to a social limbo, struggling along in minor government jobs or living on the bounty of their begetter, many of them usurping a name that was not legally theirs.

If only this dictator and his multitudinous broods could have lived in the days of the Borgias, when illegitimate children had legal and social prestige, sometimes even holding precedence over those born in holy wedlock. No social stigma was attached to illegitimacy during the days of the Borgias. Cesare Borgia was an illegitimate child, and so was his sister Lucretia. They enjoyed their rank and inheritance, unchallenged on the score of their birth. However tragic and lamentable it is that the innocent should suffer for a condition that was none of their contriving, but merely accidental consequences following the lust of their parents, civilization, in some respects, appears to have moved forward but little since the days of the Borgias.

The quality of his morals may be questioned, but no one doubted that Gómez was a first-rate father. He fairly doted on his children, and though he was severe with them, he was seldom harsh. Nothing was too good for his children, that is, the recognized ones. Whether it be a fine motor car, an elegant house, or a trip to Europe it was theirs for the asking. When a daughter married into an aristocratic family he considered it a social achievement, but he rather expected it. When a daughter chose, instead, to marry beneath her station, he demurred, but he did not prevent the marriage. He wanted, above all, to see his children happy.

One day he learned that one of his daughters had fallen in love with an illiterate peon on one of his haciendas. Summoning his wayward daughter to him, he chided her on her choice, but when he observed that she remained steadfast in her desire to marry the man, he agreed to the marriage. That the peon might possibly be a scheming scoundrel out after some of his money was beside the point. The important thing was that the girl was getting what she wanted. To make sure that what she would get would be something worthwhile, her father had the peon appointed a lieutenant colonel in the army and put through a vigorous course of training! After he had acquired some polish and the airs of a gentleman, he was appointed an aide-de-camp to his future father-in-law.

Never had this doting father been more generous in the matter of a dowry, and never, they say, has Maracay seen a more brilliant military wedding.

Of his sons he had high hopes. Speaking of them to a friend one day, he said to him, "That which happened between don Cipriano and myself happened because he did not have, as I have, sons who could assume the Presidency when the opportunity arose!"

He envisioned the republic as a monarchy, himself as its king, and he dreamed that his eldest son, José Vicente, would some day succeed him.

But he did not permit his paternity to dim his eyes. All his life he had risen at five in the morning and worked as hard as any peon all day. He was not the kind of a father who would tolerate a worthless son.

"You are an idler," he told one of his sons. "You have refused to be a soldier and an officer . . . so now you will go to the farm and work in the fields. And see that you work!"

One of his sons was caught demanding a rake-off on the business that passed through his hands. "Everyone is doing it," protested the son in self-righteous anger. That was true. The division of spoils is a part of the business of being a Latin-American dictator, and Juan Vicente Gómez was a dictator in the true Latin tradition. Through his scores of diversified interests he was amassing millions of bolivars annually, but to smother discontent and bolster his security he did not let too much of it stick to his fingers. He was no fool.

"They have my permission," was the laconic reply. "You have been stealing without permission. You had better go to the farm until you change your ways."

When aggressive and ambitious José Vicente displayed more than an ordinary interest in his father's private affairs and the running of the government, his father said to him: "No doubt you would like to take my place, eh? José Vicente—you have been a stupid fool. If you had been the kind of a man who could take my place, no one would have known anything about it until after I was dead. But it will be a good many years yet before I will permit even you to take my place."

No, Juan Vicente Gómez was no fool.

CHAPTER SEVENTEEN

Maracay

The year was 1910. Snug and secure in its mountain girdled valley, Caracas had changed but little during the past few decades. Its population had only recently crept past the 100,000 mark. It was still the little town of spacious patio houses, of old colonial palaces, in whose musty nooks and cloisters the shades of cloaked viceroys and sword-bedecked grandees seemed still to linger. Its iron-grilled windows and massive spike-studded doors, which had opened to the knocking of two centuries, gave it the romance and air of antiquity of a Spanish city of long ago.

It was a Caracas of quaint customs and delicious vagaries. Though most houses and shops were properly numbered, they could be located only by naming the corners between which they stood.[14] Every corner had its own peculiar and often odd name, a name that arose out of the mists of past ages, and was often related to objects, incidents, and individuals who had long since passed into oblivion. The corner El Conde, for example, referred to a wealthy Spanish nobleman who once lived there in a white marble mansion; The Nuns referred to the monastery that once fronted on the Plaza Bolívar. Then there was Heart of Jesus, The Rosary, and The Green Cross. The Avocado probably referred to a grand old tree long since reduced to ashes, and Pepe Aleman and The Deaf One to notorious characters, perhaps cut-throats or smugglers. But only the ghosts of long dead ancestors could explain such chilling names as Vulture, Misery, and The Dead One.

In those days, householders were held responsible for sweeping

[14] This is one tradition of old colonial days which still survives, and is likely to survive as long as the people of Caracas continue to love tradition.

the streets and removing grass from between the cobblestones, which had been worn smooth from three centuries of use. As of old, flowering *señoritas* hovered behind the *rejas* of their windows, looking coy and dreaming of romance. In the late afternoons, youths of the best families, unconfined by walls or customs, showed off their manliness by parading past on horseback, the clop-clop of their horses' hooves lingering behind in a tantalizing echo.

It was still the languid age of the horse and carriage, and that long-suffering, patient animal, the burro, without which Caracas might have starved to death long ago. Like others of their ilk, the milkman and breadman made their rounds astride burros, the cans of milk and barrels of buns hanging on either side like saddlebags. Burros with the eyes of old philosophers were forever pattering along, loaded down with mysterious burdens or with produce and flowers from Los Teques, Petare, and outlying haciendas. Frock-coated gentlemen and their elegantly dressed ladies traveled by carriage. True, there were miniature street cars pulled by "one mule or two burros," but no one who aspired to be ranked among the *gente decente* ever rode in one.

In North America and Europe, the new-fangled contrivance called the automobile had already come into its own. *Caraqueños* ogled pictures of the latest Ford, Cadillac, and Pierce Arrow in their magazine *El Cojo Ilustrado,* and clucked their envy of the *musius* of the north. Reluctantly, the city fathers agreed that it might be time for an innovation—electrification of the street car system.

By 1910 Singer had become a household word and electricity had been accepted as a mysterious *fuerza* that gave forth light. Petroleum was a word known only to the dictionary and the Bureau of Mines.

One sunny morning during that year the good people of Caracas were startled out of their placid existence by a disturbing occurrence. The day had started off quietly enough, the streets resounding to the hum of normal commercial activity, the pedestrians rubbing elbows on the narrow sidewalks. Suddenly, in a congested part of the city there were heard a few scattered explosions, then a tumultuous gunfire. For a moment the citizenry stood frozen in their tracks.

Dios mío! A revolution! But who is fighting whom? And where is General Gómez?

A moment later, their curiosity was amply satisfied. With an unearthly roar, a black monster on wheels charged through the narrow streets like a wild bull on a rampage. Man and beast alike ran helter-skelter before it for the nearest doorway.

The automobile had come to Caracas!

Admittedly, the horseless carriage was a miracle that God had wrought. It was mechanically uncanny, and it was like nothing that had ever come to Venezuela before. As a vehicle it was hardworking and heroic, but it required these same qualities in the men who rode it. The rich young dandies of the capital met the challenge unflinchingly. What their elders muttered through their beards about the whole business is not recorded.

One oldster, however, recognized progress when he saw it. But Pius Shlageter was a Swiss, the owner of a prosperous lithographic shop on one of the side streets. He made a trip to Paris, and when he returned in 1911, he brought back not one car, but two, a Citröen and a Brasier. The Citröen he turned over to his shop—the first commercial establishment in Venezuela to use such a vehicle—while he used the Brasier to take his jittery family in uncertain splendor to the beach at Macuto. The Brasier was the fastest car in the capital at the time, and Pius Shlageter was regarded as a very daring man.

As for *el Presidente,* General Gómez, he flatly refused to ride in an automobile at first. Curious as always, he made a casual inspection of one, marveling at the gleaming metal and diamond-pleated leather seats. Listening to the roar of the engine, he suddenly wrinkled up his nose in displeasure and walked off. He had found the fumes of gasoline nauseating and the barks and growls unnerving. His only love was the horse, and for a long while he stubbornly held out for the comfort and dignity of the victoria and the smell of horseflesh.

Quiet was what he liked, preferably the quiet of the country, but he couldn't resign himself to giving up completely the little conveniences of the city. Less than a year after taking office he had made frequent visits to Maracay, some one hundred and eight kilometers west of Caracas, for purposes of personal business and relaxation. He saw nothing wrong in taking so much time off from his public duties. No doubt he assumed that it was a prerogative of his office. Castro

had done the same, spending weeks at a time at La Victoria. And
there was Guzmán, who spent several months of each year at
Antímano and Macuto. Each Venezuelan president had had his
favorite resort. Maracay had been the chosen spot of Páez and Crespo,
who found in the broad green acres of the quiet countryside a
panorama reminiscent of their native haciendas.

Having found in Maracay the peace and repose that he craved,
Gómez established his official residence there in 1910. Up to this
epoch Maracay had been a sleepy little town of whitewashed adobe
houses and a few more pretentious dwellings, some of which were
falling into decay. Though it had acquired fame through the years
for its excellent cheese, sleek fat cattle, and cock fights (all dear to
Gómez's heart), it was merely the typical nondescript little town often
encountered halfway between more important points. There was no
hotel, only a couple of vile *pensiones*. No hospital or clinic. No
public buildings worthy of the name, only a moldy town hall and
jail that had once been the elegant mansion of a Spanish grandee. A
few cubbyhole stores, a score or so of tidy *quintas* that set off in sharp
contrast the rows of run-down adobe shacks. Rutted and pitted
streets that were quagmires of mud during the rainy season. Toward
the south the streets led to open fertile fields, centuries-old haciendas
and placid Lake Valencia; toward the north, they died away in forest-
jungle, full of creeping, crawling things. Carrying on a languid commerce in cattle, cheese, and cotton, the wealth of the region was held
in the hands of a powerful few, while poverty and unemployment
were rife. Stagnant—that was the word for Maracay.

His habits and tastes being modestly middle-class, *el Presidente*
had chosen an unpretentious dwelling—a one-story rambling house
and servant annex fronting on the Plaza Girardot. It was in the huge,
carpeted front *sala* that *el Presidente* held his cabinet sessions and
affairs of state. Heavy velvet drapes hung at its windows, and on the
end wall above the chief executive's chair hung a life-size portrait of
Gómez himself. His office, next to the *sala*, was small in comparison.
For the last decade of his life it contained his desk and chair, and
three gilt chairs and a loveseat of Louis XVI period. Bordered with
Venezuelan inlaid woods, his desk was emblazoned with the Venezuelan coat of arms, as was his gold telephone, a gift from the
Caracas telephone company. In a corner stood a French bronze of

a blacksmith busy at his anvil. Its name, "Le Travail," bespoke the *Jefe*'s attitude toward life. His bedroom, adjoining, was quite simple— a brass bed, several chairs, a mahogany wardrobe (as in all Vene- zuelan homes, there were no closets) and chest-of-drawers, several religious pictures, and a hammock strung in a corner for daily relaxa- tion. In another corner stood a large safe around which grew the legend that it held millions in cash.

The high-ceilinged rooms opened onto a columned portico and a spacious patio, which was a bit of tropical garden riotous with frangipani, hibiscus, roses, palms, and potted plants. It was here that *el Presidente* liked to sit for a short spell in the evening and listen to the discourse of his learned friends, after which he would saunter off to one of his love-nests in the neighborhood.

In the golden glow of late afternoon while he sat in his wicker chair meditating upon matters of state or his far-flung cattle interests, he would gaze up at the azure sky, his glance flickering occasionally to the somber white steeple of the church *Santa Iglesia Parroquial,* whose long accusing shadow fell into his garden. Sometimes he would walk to the doorway of his house and drink in the verdant beauty of the tree-roofed plaza, with its shaded walks and ancient, backless rough-stone benches. But the instant a pixy-faced youngster shouted *"Allí está el General Gómez!"* to summon the curious, he would retreat inside.

Directly behind Gómez's house, on the Calle Santa Michelena, lived his daughter Servila and her husband Ignacio Andrade, son of ex-President General Ignacio Andrade. Across the street from this couple lived Dolores Amelia and her eight children. Around the corner were his stables. Within a stone's throw of his house lived his secretary and Eloy Tarazona, now a colonel and aide to the Presi- dent. Within a radius of several blocks lived his mistresses. No twen- tieth-century dictator could have asked for a cozier arrangement.

Maracay went through a surprising metamorphosis during those first few years. From a sun-baked, sleepy hamlet, it grew into a thriv- ing, substantial city. Hordes of *políticos* and job seekers descended upon it until it became necessary to set up dormitories and mess halls. Gómez's first concern was the streets, which were in a deplorable condition. "Pave them," he ordered. And they were paved. "Tear down those rows of ugly *casitas,*" he ordered. "There we will build *quintas,* strong substantial ones, for the officials of the government."

And the ugly shacks were torn down and in their place there rose large comfortable houses. But they were not all for the officials of the government. Built at government expense, they became, by some adroit juggling of books, the personal property of Gómez. To those officials and friends who could be induced to move from Caracas, they were offered rent free. To his numerous relatives and progeny, however, they were given outright as a gift.

In Macuto he had a fine house near the beach. There was another house in San Juan de los Morros. It was to this latter resort of hot sulphur springs that Gómez went when he felt tired and worn and wanted to indulge in the baths. However, it was in or around Maracay, where he was close to the soil and the army that he loved, that Gómez preferred to live. Even as Maracay started to grow under his benevolent patronage, Caracas remained the capital in name only. Congress often convened in a body to Maracay and even foreign ministers were perforce obliged to drive out if they wished to see him. Some, like Marshal Franchet D'Esperay, the French Minister, found it convenient to avail themselves of the splendid accommodations he put at their disposal. The French Minister's residence, especially, was an imposing one. Of white stucco, with Arabic mosaics, ornate furniture, and gaudy paintings, it was surrounded by a lovely garden and a blue-tiled fountain. Located on the backwoods road of Las Delicias, it may be identified still by the minister's name which appears above the portal.

In Paris, Marshal D'Esperay had heard hair-raising stories of Gómez and his regime. At the Quai D'Orsay he had read the file of confidential reports written by his predecessor and he had shuddered at the record of scandals, persecutions, imprisonments, and tortures. When he arrived in Venezuela in 1932 and was summoned to the presence of the dictator, he had fully expected to meet a gruff and imperious monster. Instead, he was quite taken in by the dictator's winning personality, his quiet and unassuming ways, his jovial good-fellowship. Surely, he thought, after several cordial interviews with Gómez, *Monsieur le President* is not at all like the man he was painted to be. Really, he's a jolly good fellow. Easy to get along with. A dictator, perhaps. Severe, *certainement,* but not cruel. Those stories —most of them anyway—must be a pack of lies. And as for his escapades with women . . . oh, la la! After all, Franchet D'Esperay was a Frenchman.

When the French Minister was proffered the splendid *quinta* in Las Delicias, he accepted with alacrity.

"Are your quarters comfortable?" *el Presidente* inquired solicitously. "Is everything to your liking? If there is anything you need, anything at all, just tell my secretary here and he will take care of it."

And after the French Minister had expressed concern because he had not heard from his wife for over two weeks, Gómez added in an offhand manner: "If you will be at home after seven tonight, you will receive an interesting 'phone call."

D'Esperay was curious, but Gómez would say no more.

Shortly after seven that evening the 'phone in the French Minister's *quinta* rang. The man servant who answered it came running.

"Marshal D'Esperay!" he called. "Come quickly! Paris is on the telephone! It is Madame D'Esperay!"

It need hardly be mentioned that after that evening Marshal D'Esperay became one of Gómez's most fervent boosters. It was the pleasant surprises such as this that won many of the foreign diplomats completely over. They partook of Gómez's hospitality in many ways, attended many a banquet and ball, many a *ternera a la llanera* —a succulent barbecue as prepared by the *llaneros*—at Gómez's big hacienda at Güigüe near Lake Valencia. On their wives, too, were bestowed numerous favors and sometimes gifts. The guile of this cunning peasant knew no bounds.

That these trifling machinations sometimes paid off handsomely there could be little doubt. While exiled Venezuelan writers were lambasting Gómez abroad for all they were worth, unobtrusive but outspoken Mrs. Preston MacGoodwin, wife of the United States Minister to Venezuela during the period 1914-1919, made a statement upon her return to the States which was loudly echoed in the American press. Said she in all sincerity: "President Gómez is a model governor and a gentleman."

For this remark the MacGoodwins were depicted by exiled Venezuelan writers as "lovers of Gómez" and were unmercifully lampooned. Mrs. MacGoodwin was accused of having been "bribed because she had accepted many presents from General Gómez," and her husband became the victim of vile slander. Unscrupulous writers

charged that the American Minister had been the silent partner in
a Venezuelan importing concern, and that through his diplomatic
connections he had imported goods into the country duty free, which
his partner sold at a fabulous profit!

Enormous sums were spent toward aggrandizing Maracay. During the height of the construction boom it was the custom to send on
Saturdays an open truck to the Banco de Venezuela in Caracas to
pick up the weekly payroll. On Saturdays the bank closed at midday
and as often as not the truck would arrive to find its doors closed.
Weary of being called from his home on such occasions to open the
bank and hand over the money, the manager one day decided to go
to the extreme to discourage these tardy arrivals. He gave orders that
each time the truck failed to arrive on time, the packages of money
were to be left on the sidewalk! If he cared to do so, the policeman
on the beat could keep his eye on them!

More than once during the following months, pedestrians passing the Banco de Venezuela on Saturday afternoons were treated to
a rare sight. Bundles of bills and bags of silver coins lay stacked
against the bank's doors like cordwood. Here, unguarded, lay a fortune for the taking!

That no *Caraqueño* in his right mind would dare to make off with
this half a million bolivars, the bank manager very well knew. During
the Gómez regime, organized crime was virtually nonexistent, the dark
dungeons and road gangs being a strong enough deterrent to discourage any sort of thievery. In Maracaibo, too, it was not an uncommon sight to see sandaled peons trundling shipments of newly-
minted money in wheelbarrows from the docks to the local bank—
without a police guard or even a supervisory escort!

Those were the days when homes could be left open while their
occupants went into town to shop, when belongings could be left in
open cars on the streets, and business houses had no use for safes!

That Gómez had only disdain for the capital of the republic was
quite well known. All his sympathies and efforts were dedicated
toward glorifying Maracay. One day, during the course of an inspection of the *Cuartel* Sucre in Maracay, an officer casually remarked that it would be nice to have a statue of General Antonio
José Sucre to embellish the barracks' grounds. To which Gómez re-

plied: "General Sucre, you say? . . . m-m-m-m . . . Why, of
course! *Bueno,* begin the pedestal—out there on the avenue would
be a good place—and tomorrow you will have your statue!" And
he took off in an air of mystery.

The officer shook his head in bewilderment. What was General
Gómez up to? Did he expect to pull the statute out of his hat? He
should know as well as anyone that the statue would have to be
ordered from Germany, that there would be endless negotiations,
that it would take many months to get it. No doubt *el Presidente*
wanted to have his little joke. Oh, well, he might as well forget about
it.

The next afternoon the officer refused to believe his ears when
his orderly informed him that a truck had just pulled in with a
statue. He had to go out and see for himself. Sure enough, it was
General Sucre.

"Where did this come from?" he asked the driver.

"From Ayacucho Park in Caracas!" the man answered sheepishly.
Then he shrugged. "What could we do? Orders are orders."

So, little by little—a statue, a park, a fine hotel—Maracay grew
and flourished. It became a second capital of sorts of the republic—
until one day. . . .

"*Anjá!* . . . I want congress to come to Maracay because I
have a proposition to make to it!"

The dictator's henchmen could guess easily enough what the
"proposition" would be, but they dared not smile because they were
all afraid of him.

A day or so later, a jampacked gathering tried to make itself comfortable around Gómez's patio. As *el Presidente* faced his congressmen, a respectful hush settled over the patio. Oh, how Gómez hated
to make a speech. He fidgeted, he fumbled with his cane, he cleared
his throat. Then in a few blunt words he told them. It was an unusual,
in fact, an audacious proposition that he had to make.

Inasmuch, he told them, as the President of the Republic and the
key men of the government had taken residence in Maracay, it was
his suggestion and strong recommendation that the distinguished
gentlemen present should *enact a law to transfer the capital of the
republic to Maracay.*

The legislators sat stunned. The gall of the man! They glanced at one another in consternation. What would he think up next?

One courageous figure took the floor. He was José Cárdenas. In a strident voice that showed a trace of anger he made a simple statement declaring himself opposed to such a move.

The next to stand up was Dr. Pedro Arcaya. If anyone would speedily concur with *el Presidente,* it would be Arcaya.

Pedro Arcaya, a noted bibliophile and an able linguist, was a lawyer who did not practice law. His maiden speech in the senate had been roundly applauded for its brilliance, but it had also shown the color of his feathers. In his reference to the President, he had said: "Venezuela, gentlemen, has twice produced a genius . . . in Simón Bolívar . . . and in Juan Vicente Gómez!"

This impressive eulogy of the peasant from the Andes was published in all the Venezuelan papers; the Associated Press wired the news throughout the world; the Venezuelan Academy made Arcaya *Miembro Correspondiente;* the College of Lawyers was filled with pride to receive the eminent jurist to its bosom; the Church was moved to send him a respectful message; and in a distant province a day of *fiesta* was declared for the absent illustrious son. As a staunch Gomecista who knew how to please, Pedro Arcaya was destined to go a long way up the political ladder. One morning, a couple of years hence, he would awake to find himself Minister of the Interior. Washington would come to know him as the Venezuelan Minister to the United States. And always he would be the suave and zealous propagandist, perhaps the best that Gómez ever had.

It was no wonder that when Dr. Pedro Arcaya stood up to speak, the gathering hung on his words. Even General Gómez, grasping the handle of his cane with clenched fists, sat forward in his chair expectantly. As usual, Arcaya spoke with fervent Latin eloquence, but his words were a terrible letdown for the commander-in-chief. In short, Arcaya firmly defended the historical capital from the point of view of history, legality, and economy.

By the time the next man stood up to speak, it was obvious that Gómez's absurd proposition was going down to a crushing defeat. Slouched back in his chair now, the dictator watched with drooping eyes those who spoke and those who remained silent. Not one man spoke in favor of Maracay. But neither by word or expression did Gómez give a sign of his chagrin.

After the meeting was over and the legislators were leaving, Gómez detained Dr. Antonio Alamo at the door.

"I observed, Doctor," he said to him, "that you remained silent during the meeting. Could you come to see me tomorrow afternoon, say at four, and let me know what you think? I would like very much to have your valued opinion."

"*Cómo no*, General. I would be pleased to. At four, then."

Promptly at four the next afternoon Dr. Alamo presented himself to the President and after the usual salute was invited to a chair.

"Now then," said General Gómez, getting straight away to the point. "What is *your* opinion?"

Dr. Alamo looked Gómez straight in the eye, but for a second he hesitated. He was not afraid of the dictator, but he knew he would not like what he had to say. "I am sorry to have to disappoint you, General," he said, "but I am in accord with the views of my colleagues. After all, General, Caracas is the birthplace of the Liberator. We must not permit ourselves to overlook that. It was there that the *Capitania General* was founded and the first authorities installed. It is a city extremely rich in old traditions . . . I am sure that by now you fully understand our sentiments in the matter."

Noting that Gómez appeared almost ready to take his defeat philosophically, Alamo pressed his point. "Furthermore, General, if the capital be moved to Maracay, you would have to construct many more luxurious *quintas* to house the diplomatic corps, the ministers, the members of congress, the visitors . . . and the hundreds of government employees. That would be a problem. Maracay would be transformed into a noisy, feverish city . . . and all the peace and charm that you like so much would disappear. . . ."

Gómez appeared pensive for a moment, then he said with obvious distaste: "And that fat woman . . . would she have to come and live out here?"

"You mean the———cultural attaché?"

"Yes, that's the woman."

"Why, certainly! She is a representative of a friendly country."

Gómez grimaced. "Cultural! Ugh! I think we'll leave things as they are. I can't stand that fat leech near me . . . !"

CHAPTER EIGHTEEN

Cousin Eustoquio and Friend Pimentel

Joseph Krämer, the German "Beast of Belsen," was still a boy in short pants when Eustóquio Gómez started his career as sadist and murderer. Aided by Colonel Isías Nieto, his old crony from the Andes, Eustóquio started off by padding his payroll and short-rationing the prisoners in the prison of San Carlos. Then behind the thick walls began tortures of the "special guests." When this palled, the pair diverted themselves by devising novel ways to administer the *coup de grâce*.

One prisoner, Dr. Leopoldo Maldonado, unable to stand any more tortures, tried to commit suicide by cutting his throat with a sardine can. When his cell-mates took the can away from him, he finished the job by tearing open his throat and severing his jugular vein with his fingers. Another victim of Eustóquio was Pedro Muñoz, who was beaten to death. Juan de Dios Jara, Carlos Gáfaro, Rosario García, Colonel Pedro Garbán, and many others whose names have been forgotten through the years, suffered lingering deaths.

Persons suspected of being involved in plots against Gómez were sent to San Carlos so that Eustóquio could inflict his special brand of tortures on them and wring forth confessions. Detailed reports of the methods used and the results of his work were sent directly to the President.

One day, a few months before he broke with Gómez and went into exile, Leopoldo Baptista read a batch of Eustóquio's reports to Gómez while they were boating on Lake Valencia. They dealt with a supposed plot in which doña Nieves Castro de Parra, Castro's sister, was said to be the principal conspirator.

178

From time to time as he read aloud some of the shocking details, Baptista glanced at his *Jefe* for some comment, but all that "The Well Deserving" had to say was *"Qué vagabundo!"*—"What a scoundrel!"

The soldiers of the garrison also suffered cruelties at the hands of Eustóquio. At midnight on October 6, 1910, San Carlos rose up in rebellion. Finding all the exits strongly guarded to prevent his escape, Eustóquio climbed a wall and jumped into the black waters of the channel. No one bothered to search for him; Eustóquio couldn't swim. By some irony of fate that sometimes favors the wicked, the tide that night was the lowest ever known at San Carlos. Eustóquio somehow managed to wade neck deep to shore and the safety of darkness among the sand dunes.

The prisoners, their cells opened by the guards, fled toward the barren wastes of the Goajira Peninsula and the Colombian border. Weighed down by heavy irons, most of them didn't make it. The soldiers of José García, president of the state of Zulia, caught up with them. Back to their cells they went to suffer added horrors.

General Luis de Pasquali took over as the new commandant of the fortress. His first act was to issue an order that these prisoners be struck two hundred blows with a stout stick. One of those who lived to tell the tale was Fernando Marques, who was approached by General Pasquali a few days later with the intention of finishing him off. Finding him in a weakened condition unable to move, the general said to him: "I have orders from General Gómez to kill you . . . but as I have sons, I am going to let God kill you."

Marquez, however, came from hardy stock and he refused to die. In 1927, on the occasion of an amnesty decreed by the benevolent "Hero of December," Marquez was among those freed from San Carlos. He had spent sixteen years in the prison, seven of them in solitary and all of them in irons. Nine months later, however, he was arrested by the famous spy Frías and confined to the Libertador prison in Puerto Cabello where he spent another seven years on short rations. Seriously ill, he was released in another general amnesty in December of 1934.

The case of Fernando Marquez is cited here because it appears to be the only case on record of a Venezuelan surviving so many years of prison tortures under the Gómez regime. The excruciating pain of the heavy irons, the loathsome food, the foul conditions prevalent in such prisons, the total absence of medical care, the cruel physical punishments meted out by the prison keepers, and the mental anguish that often developed into insanity, all took their heavy toll of death during the first few years of imprisonment. That only one man in five ever survived ten years of such hardships would be a fairly accurate guess; that Fernando Marquez could endure twenty-three years of such a life and live to give a rational account of his experiences in the Venezuelan courts of a later regime, attests to the extraordinary stamina of the man.

The ties of blood being very strong, Gómez ignored entirely the public censure that followed the rebellion in San Carlos. Eustóquio disappeared from the public scene, only to reappear a year later in San Cristóbal as brazen and arrogant as ever, followed by a retinue of coarse ruffians. His unsavory reputation had preceded him, and the townspeople endeavored to steer clear of this fierce-looking bearded figure of repugnant mien. Yet they were going to see a great deal of him for the next twelve years, for don Eustóquio Gómez (a general now) had been named to the post of president of the state of Táchira by His Excellency, the President of the Republic. To the long suffering people of the Andes the appointment came as a shock and a rank insult, but they dared not voice their displeasure for fear of terrible reprisals. But why this handsome reward for a worthless scoundrel whose hands were still red with the blood of his fellow countrymen? Had Juan Vicente Gómez no sense of shame, no feeling of responsibility toward his country and toward his own mountain people? Evidently not.

The Andes, forgotten by Gómez in his program of "Rehabilitation," were rumbling with discontent. Political refugees were continually fleeing across the border into Colombia, and the region appeared to be the most likely spot for a possible armed invasion into Venezuela. To Gómez's way of thinking, what Táchira needed was not just an able public administrator to carry on the affairs of the state, but a tough military commander who would protect the dictator's interests and have no compunctions about suppressing any disturbances. Tough, ruthless and presumably trustworthy, Eustóquio was as likely a candidate as any.

Yet, though the personal interests of the clan came first, Gómez could not quite forget his fondness and sense of duty toward the region of his birth. In a series of pep letters, he tried to inject into his hot-headed and indomitable cousin a spirit of enterprise, a feeling of comradeship for his fellow men, and a sense of responsibility in his position of trust. Said he to Eustóquio in one of his early missives:

". . . It is for us to safeguard the integrity of the name (Rehabilitation) of our Cause . . . and this we can achieve by forcing ourselves more and yet more in doing good at every opportunity . . . you on your part by promoting the progress of your state, uniting at all costs this great family (the various Andean groups) into a harmonious relationship, guiding its customs and behavior, and raising to the highest possible level the education of the inhabitants . . . so that tomorrow, when you leave office, you will leave in that land a vote of thanks for your administration and a religious respect for your name. Your friend embraces you. Juan Vicente."

It would seem that the dictator had his heart in the right place. That was Gómez—the same old study in complex contradictions; an angelic cherub of noble sentiments one moment, and a fiend incarnate the next.

In San Cristóbal, where he set himself up as a petty tyrant, Eustóquio ruled for twelve years with a hand of iron. As was to be expected, nothing in the way of praise can be said for his administration. Education of the inhabitants was sadly neglected, progress of sorts was accomplished through the building of dirt roads by road gangs composed of miscreants and enemies of the "Cause," and some semblance of harmony was achieved through brute force. When it came to guiding customs and behavior, Eustóquio carved a special niche for himself. Bored with the tedium of his job he whiled away more and more of his free hours at the pastime of seduction and rape. He took to sending minions out to scour the districts for pretty girls. When a girl would not come willingly, a sum of money was offered the parents for her purchase. When money and even intimidation failed, the girl was kidnaped.

Finally, the townspeople of San Cristóbal could stand Eustóquio Gómez and his methods no longer. One day in 1923, angry groups milled through the streets and converged on the square into an infuriated, threatening mob. There were flashes of cold steel and bold shouts of "Death to Eustóquio Gómez!"

Eustóquio Gómez had learned not to be caught off guard. A gang of bodyguards, armed to the teeth, always surrounded him. Squads of soldiers were constantly maintained in the *Palacio de la Presidencia* for just such an emergency. As the soldiers lined the building to ward off the shouting mob, Eustóquio, livid with rage, issued orders to the captain of the guard.

"Arrest the ringleaders!" he bellowed. "Wait! That won't be enough. Arrest twelve—an even dozen. I'm going to show those people something that they will never forget! Here is what you are to do. Get *garabatos* (meat hooks) and ropes . . . take those twelve troublemakers down the road outside of town . . . impale them and hang them up to the trees . . . !" [15]

The officer blanched. "But, General . . . !"

"You heard what I said. Get going! And be sure you leave them there for the buzzards!"

Not since the great earthquake of 1875 had San Cristóbal known such a catastrophe. Twelve human beings—fathers of families, brothers, sweethearts—were shackled and marched through the streets like a herd of cattle being led to slaughter. At the outskirts of the city their wailing loved ones were held in check by squads of soldiers while the funereal column continued on down the road and came to a halt at a stand of trees bordering a field of sugar cane. Shrieks of horror and pain. Brief struggles. Finally the dirty business was over with.

Along a stretch of road soldiers stood guard beside the swaying corpses, scanning the skies, waiting. An hour passed. Then another. In the west, the sun sank magnificently behind the blue and purple hills and the sky glowed with roseate hues.

Then suddenly one of the soldiers saw it. High up in the heavens, flying in a slow, lazy spiral—a black *zamuro*. In a moment there were two, then three, then dozens, spiraling, crossing and recrossing the heavens in determined flight, descending lower and lower.

At a command the soldiers formed ranks and marched with

[15] This was Eustóquio Gómez's favorite and most cruel method of execution. The victim was held prone on the ground with arms tied behind his back while the executioner jabbed a meat hook — tied to a length of rope — under his chin close to the throat. Then he was hoisted into a tree and left to die a lingering, painful death.

heavy steps toward the city. Once the captain turned to look back. Black forms with spreading wings were gliding into the deep shadows.

" . . . *so that tomorrow, when you leave office, you will leave in that land a vote of thanks for your administration and a religious respect for your name . . .*"

With a heavy heart Gómez recalled his cousin from the Andes. The blackhearted scoundrel had to sneak away from San Cristóbal in the dead of night. If the Andinos had caught him they would have torn him limb from limb. Eustóquio had betrayed the trust and confidence placed in him, and for this he was called to task. However, for the crime of mass murder there was no punishment, no redress. Only—*"Eustóquio, usted es un vagabundo!"*—"Eustóquio, you are a scoundrel!"

So the *vagabundo,* still smiling, went to live in Curacao for two years until things blew over.

There were other scoundrels, too, in the entourage of *el Presidente.* One of them, his best friend and constant companion, and godfather to his sons Juan Vicente and Florencio (by Dolores Amelia), was short, swarthy Antonio Pimentel. Pimentel was probably the only man who ever made Gómez roar with laughter, the only man outside of the clan ever permitted to embrace Gómez with the casual shoulder pat that is the common form of greeting in Venezuela. Like Gómez, he had made his start in cattle and farming. Through shrewd and shady deals he became a millionaire. He owned buildings in half a dozen cities, and extensive haciendas in almost as many states.

Pimentel had long coveted the vast haciendas of his friend Alberto Wallis in the state of Carabobo. These properties were known by the names of "Yagua," "El Toco," "Vigirima," and "San Diego," the latter made famous for the sweetest oranges in all of Venezuela. Wallis had invested close to four million bolivars in land and buildings. When he needed money in the early 1920's to install some improvements, Pimentel lent it to him, but when Wallis could not meet the note, it was said that Pimentel seized everything.

Immensely likeable, cordial to everyone, Pimentel had many friends who vouched for his kindness of heart, his hearty good-fellowship. Yet his consuming thirst for money and the tactics he employed to acquire it created numerous enmities. One day in 1914 a bomb exploded in his Caracas home. Fourteen-year-old José García, an errand boy for the neighborhood drug store, happened to be passing the house at the instant of the explosion, and he was struck with fragments of glass. Covered with blood and terribly frightened, the boy ran—right into the arms of a policeman. At the police station he was registered and questioned, then taken to a hospital where he was kept under guard. Four days later, his wounds not yet healed, the perplexed youngster was carried off to the Rotunda where he was subjected to hours of questioning. He knew nothing of the plot to assassinate Pimentel. So, when questioning failed, he was tortured, but all they could wring from him were protests of his innocence. To the hardened wardens of Gómez's prisons their victims were always guilty even if they sometimes could prove themselves innocent. José García was considered guilty solely on circumstantial evidence—he had been at the scene of the crime. So they shackled this fourteen-year-old boy with irons and left him to rot in the Rotunda for several years. Not once did Antonio Pimentel, he of the "kind heart," bestir himself to intercede for this friendless and innocent waif.

Pimentel was very fond—*muy aficionado,* as they say in Venezuela—of parties and dances. Perhaps it was through him that Gómez caught the fever for gay fiestas. Every Sunday evening there would be a dance in Maracay, or in whatever town Gómez happened to be visiting. It was a strict rule that dress be formal. No hard liquors. Only soft drinks. And no courtesans, only the belles of local society carefully chaperoned by their parents, who kept a sharp eye not only on Gómez but on Pimentel as well. The latter, slicked up in his best finery and reeking with cologne, but still looking every bit the Indian that he was, would head straight toward some pretty girl one-third his age. Sometimes the naïve creature would be unable to repel his crude approach and would dance with him—once. Sometimes she would be alert enough to glance toward a strict parent for the nod of approval. When it would not be forthcoming, Pimentel would murmur his regret and would try his luck elsewhere.

As for the old fox with the long mustachios now streaked with gray, he would sit on the sidelines drinking the whole scene in and enjoying every bit of it. If the young people failed through diffidence

The General, Dolores Amelia, and their eight children in Maracay, 1929. Left to right: Belen, son-in-law Roberto Santana, Rosa Amelia, Juan Vicente, Berta, Hermenegilda, Cristina, Florencio, and the youngest, Juan.

Gómez converted this modest home on the Plaza Girardot, Maracay, into the presidential residence in 1910. The policeman stands guard to prohibit all but official traffic.

The General at the birthday party of his little grandniece. The child's mother, behind Gómez to the right, is the daughter of General Colmenares Pacheco (seen behind her), who married Gómez's sister Emilia (far left). His sister Regina (far right) is next to General Rafael Velasco, governor of the Federal District.

Gómez boating with his children, their friends and parents on Lake Valencia. Florencio standing rear left, Cristina seated at her father's right, Belen in armchair, Juan (left) at his feet.

to take to the floor, Gómez would frown with impatience and strike the floor sharply with his cane. *"Qué bailan! Qué bailan!"*—"Dance! Dance!" he would command.

An American was once invited to one of these affairs by one of Gómez's sons. After gazing inquisitively at the dictator from a respectful distance for a time, he signaled young Gómez to his side.

"Do me a favor, will you?" he asked him. "I've got a handkerchief in my back pocket. Take it out for me."

"As you say . . . but what's the matter? Did you break your hand?"

The American forced a smile. "No—but every time I reach toward my pocket, those bodyguards behind your father reach for their guns!"

"Don't you dance, General?" another guest once asked Gómez, senior.

"Who, me?" snorted the peasant from the Andes. *"Caramba,* no! I'm too old for that sort of thing. Besides," and he patted his thigh, "there's that old battle wound you know—that's why I have to use this cane. Dancing, *señor,* was invented for the younger generation. It is only they who have the true grace and beauty." And his glance would wander away and alight on a flowering *señorita* twirling in the arms of a dashing cadet.

It was only during such rare moments as this that one could fathom for a fleeting second the old codger's mind.

The Sunday morning fiestas at the haciendas in the vicinity of Maracay were affairs of a different sort—cockfights, liquor, the succulent *ternera,* lively music, and a sprinkling of party girls who knew how to laugh appreciatively at vulgar jokes.

If the distance was not too great, Gómez would ride out on his handsome stallion, accompanied by his retinue. In the cool shade of a century-old tree *el Presidente* would rest and hold court, the guests approaching singly and in groups to pay him homage. Sometimes his proud host would parade for his critical inspection a prize bull recently acquired, and Gómez would grunt his verdict.

After they all had taken their fill of the abundant food and drink, Pimentel would stretch out beside his good friend and wax bold. They say that Pimentel had no fear whatever of Gómez. He took liberties that would have been disastrous for anyone else. And he dared to relate to *el Presidente* the latest jokes that were being circulated about him.

"Speaking of bulls," Pimentel would say in his most casual tone, "I just heard a new joke about you . . ."

"*Pues,* what is it?" Gómez would ask after a pause, his mustache twitching in his impatience. He was both receptive to a good laugh and fearful that the barb might be a sharp one.

"Well, it seems that some rich *hacendado* or other was informed by his foreman that the prize bull he had recently bought had turned out to be sterile. 'My God!' exclaimed the *hacendado*. 'To think of all the money that animal cost me! Lost! All lost!'

" 'I wouldn't say that, *señor*,' said the foreman. 'Why don't you take the bull to General Gómez. Now there's a man who ought to be able to fix it!' "

CHAPTER NINETEEN

Croesus of the Andes

For all his uncouth ways, Pimentel was as shrewd an Indian as they come, and Gómez had found out years ago that it was profitable to hearken to his advice. He was the only person beside Gómez's sister Indalecia and Dr. Gris whose frank opinion was solicited on weighty problems.

In the provisional administration which dated from August, 1909 to April, 1910, Pimentel had replaced Leopoldo Baptista as Gómez's Secretary General. Having shown a tendency to chafe under Gómez's despotic dictums, Baptista had been relegated to the Federal Council, where he found ample opportunity to air his grievances to the other nine members—Generals Rolando, Pulido, and Peñaloza among them.

On April 19, 1910, when Gómez was duly "elected" President for the period 1910-1914, Dr. González Guinán was named Secretary General, and Pimentel was advanced to the post of Minister of Finance. The latter appointment came as a surprise to everyone. What was Gómez up to? Pimentel hadn't performed any meritorious public service during his short term of office, nor did he possess the necessary qualifications to fill such a responsible position. That it was a close-knit partnership that would evolve to the financial profit of both, there could be little doubt.

During the years Castro was President, Gómez had been acquiring haciendas and grazing lands throughout the country and gradually expanding the cattle business in which he continued to maintain an absorbing interest. A few of these properties had been obtained through forced sales at ridiculously low prices, but most of them had

187

been secured through confiscation. Following the custom of his predecessors, Castro had confiscated the possessions of recalcitrant members of the previous regime, as well as those of his followers who were
purged during his nine years in office. A share in these went to his
compadre.

One of the first acts of every dictatorship had been to set up a
confidential bureau, whose activities were hush-hush and whose employees were, for practical purposes, maintained on the payroll of the
Ministry of Finance. In theory, the object of the confiscatory operations of the bureau was to provide a source of revenue to the government, despite the fact that confiscation of private property, whether
for treason or any other crime, was a flagrant violation of the Constitution. The duties of the bureau were ostensibly to keep the records
of all seizures, together with the reasons for which they were carried
out as decreed in the official gazette, to make appraisals and sales,
and to revert the proceeds to the treasury of the nation. In actual
practice the confiscations were seldom carried out in this way. By
successful revolutionists, from Páez to Castro, confiscations were
considered the spoils of war. It was standard procedure for the revolutionary leader to carry with him to the capital a list of his enemies
who were to be thrown into prison and whose properties were to be
confiscated. The very hour he entered the *Casa Amarilla* in triumph,
his agents would be rounding up the prisoners and checking their
material wealth. After reviewing the inventory of the seizures, the new
President—the same noble-spirited citizen who only recently had
vowed that he was "going to defend the Constitution of the Republic,
etc. etc."—would select the choicest plums for himself and distribute
the remainder among his deserving followers.

Many of the estates that were so freely handed out in these divi-
sions of the spoils were worth a considerable fortune. Almost all of
them more than defrayed the outlays made by their recipients in the
revolution. To cite a case in point, General José Ignacio Pulido (as
was mentioned previously) received as payment for his services during Guzmán's revolution of 1870, over four hundred thousand acres
of land, plus bonds worth about sixty thousand dollars.

Of all the usurpers of power in Venezuela, Guzmán was without
a doubt the most brazen disciple of this system. Although Gómez
patterned his behavior after that of the "Illustrious American," he

seldom went to the same extremes in this respect. After his success-ful revolution of 1870, for example, Guzmán was so unscrupulous as to not only confiscate the property of those who refused to recognize his dictatorship, but also he exacted from each of his adversaries a tribute of four thousand pesos (20,000 bolivars) "to help defray the cost of the revolution!"

It was during this turbulent period of imprisonments, confisca-tions, and forced assessments that Guzmán began to assert himself as a ruthless dictator. His policy of repression, taxation, and extortion ground the Venezuelans to the dust. One of his memos, dated April 18, 1872, which is identical in tone with the same type of order issued by Gómez, reads:

". . . Be very, very vigilant with the prisoners. I believe there are a few you can put at liberty—those who were arrested simply as a precautionary measure or who were involved in jokes and harm-less pranks—but release only those we can easily put our hands on again if it becomes necessary."

Another memo, written two years after he had occupied the Presidency, indicates that confiscations was a continual business. Dated May 6, 1872, it read in part:

"My confiscation orders have been carried out in such an original manner that I have not received even one cow, and all those which were supposed to be on the way to me have disappeared! What goes on here . . . ?"

Guzmán knew perfectly well what was going on. His agents were either diverting the cattle to their own haciendas or selling them and pocketing the proceeds. For that matter, the inventories they sub-mitted to the commander-in-chief were always falsified. Everyone ex-pected to get a share of the spoils, from the lowly peon who walked off with a burro or a piece of furniture, to the top agent himself, who simply marked down the number of cattle on the inventory of a given hacienda. Many of these agents accumulated sizable fortunes in these operations in the space of a few months.

After the upheaval of December 19, Gómez had reviewed with Baptista the list of those who had been purged. After he had scanned the list again and again to make sure that not an enemy had been overlooked, he ordered the properties of the landed gentry confiscated. No legal reason was given, because he had none. For himself he appropriated all of Castro's estates as well as his holdings in various business enterprises. Being a very wealthy man even before these seizures, Gómez could well afford to part with such a substantial gift as a hacienda as a wedding present to a crony's "Rosa" or a handful of bonds to win a new friend, as he tried to do with General Hernández.

Gómez's partnership with Antonio Pimentel in the "real estate business" dated back several years while Gómez was still serving as Castro's man "Friday." Knowing of the old cattle trader's mania for acquiring land, and comprehending his natural aversion to paying hard cash for something he could manage to get for nothing, Pimentel confided to him some of the tricks of his trade. The outcome was a co-ownership in a number of properties which were acquired under shady circumstances. Their most successful method of operation, and one which was carried on on a much larger scale after Gómez became President, was conducted somewhat as follows.

During the early days of their modest beginnings, Pimentel's sharp nose had learned of a way to ferret out valuable pieces of property that were illegally occupied. The country's many civil wars had brought about this state of affairs. In the bloody massacres of the nineteenth century, thousands of landowners and sometimes entire families lost their lives. Wherever the opportunity presented itself, guerrillas and other unscrupulous persons moved in on the properties of the deceased, duping the peon servants into believing they were the rightful owners. Any poor relation who appeared to claim his just due was driven off by intimidation or violence. Sometimes a false title was acquired through the connivance of a grafting civil clerk so that a valuable property could be sold. Most often, however, the usurper, like thousands of other ignorant and illiterate squatters before and since, believed that "possession is nine points of the law" and naïvely ignored the trifling and bothersome matter of a valid title. The fact that there was no such thing as a land or building tax permitted him to live on the land for years without molestation. Obviously, ownership of such occupied properties as these was suspended in a legal limbo, and to the descendants who "inherited" and tried to sell them in good faith, the denouement was bitter. Their only recourse was to rent out the property, trusting that the law wouldn't catch up with them, or resort to a fraudulent entry in the municipal records.

The civil registrar of records was morally bound to report any obvious or suspected cases of fraud so that the municipality could take steps to appropriate such lands. Often as not, however, this public servant was but a servile minion of some local *político,* whose task of finding fraudulent titles was done solely for the purpose of enriching his boss and not the municipality. The "boss" in most instances was either a fleshy, dark-skinned operator by the name of Antonio Pimentel, or a Gomecista. Judging from the high volume of real estate transactions that Gómez and Pimentel were involved in, the number of flaws found in municipal records must have been endless.

By degrees Gómez's long grasping arm gathered in haciendas, grazing lands, and sometimes entire villages in one state after another. No less than forty of the largest and richest haciendas in the country belonged to him. Some of them had been snatched from his political enemies, like the one in Guarico that had belonged to Dr. Roberto Vargas. A few were bought at forced sales, such as La Rubiera for example, which was wrested from the widow of Mier y Terán. The largest hacienda of them all, La Rubiera measured over 450,000 acres in size and lay in three states in the *llanos.*

La Candelaria, one of Gómez's ranches in the state of Apure, measured over 175,000 acres. At the time of his death it supported an estimated one hundred thousand head of wild horses and twenty thousand head of cattle on its lush pasturage.

Strangely enough, Gómez never went far afield to visit his newly-acquired properties. Some of them, like La Candelaria, he never set eyes on. He abhorred travel, but most important of all, he remained close to Maracay for reasons of safety. It was in this region—the states of Aragua and Carabobo—that he knew so well that many of his haciendas and cattle ranches lay. They extended in unbroken strings for many miles. In his *Memorias de un Venezolano de la Decadencia,* José Rafael Pocaterra relates that one day in 1918 he drove south from Maracay for three hours, but had to turn back without having reached the end of Gómez's holdings.

Yet, despite Gómez's enormous wealth in land, his longing for material possessions remained insatiable. Eight years later he was still scheming to add to his holdings. Perhaps the best illustration of one of his transactions in which the nation footed the bill and he reaped a handsome profit was the sale of a tract of idle land he owned in Caura in the state of Bolívar. In an act of congress, dated June 23, 1926, the sum of 17,000,000 bolivars was allocated for the purchase of this land from Gómez in the name of the nation "so that the well-deserving chief executive could have the wherewithal to purchase from his good friend Antonio Pimental some of his properties in Carabobo and Guarico."

What the slick cattle trader had done was to purchase several thousand acres of useless jungle land in far off Bolívar for 160,000 bolivars so that he could sell it to the nation for one hundred and six times the amount he paid for it! Congress justified this gouging of the nation by going on record as saying that "because of the patriotic [sic] motives of General Gómez, the nation will use the land to embark at some future date upon a vast colonization plan." And the business was quickly concluded lest someone ask what the nation was going to do with the other twenty million or more idle acres it already possessed.

Gómez could and did set his own price for whatever property took his fancy, but there have been a few known instances where the prospective seller acted quickly to make a present of the property to the dictator "in appreciation for having established peace in the country." These magnanimous gestures were nothing but a pretext so that the desperate owner could speak personally with *el Presidente* and plead for the freedom of some political prisoner. Despite all his defects, however, not even his enemies believed that Gómez ever resorted deliberately to the despicable practice of trafficking in human lives.

So that his enemies could not say that he robbed all widows and orphans, the genial peasant from the Andes astounded his aides one day early in 1913 by executing an unusual document. A few months previously he had been visited by *Misia* Jacinta Crespo, widow of the assassinated General Crespo, who offered in sale the Palace of Miraflores which she claimed had been built by her husband with his own funds. Although not in immediate want, she felt honor bound to settle an old claim against her husband. When he was President, Crespo had a military code drawn up by the Colombian General Vicente Sebastián Mestre for a stipulated fee of one hundred thousand bolivars. Crespo had reneged on the payment, and succeeding presidents had disallowed the claim in true Latin tradition. Gentle pressure on the part of the claimant had finally convinced *Misia* Crespo that she should pay off this debt.

"It is curious," said Gómez afterward, "that she should wait fourteen years to press her claim to ownership." Nevertheless, he was convinced of her sincerity. Then, too, he had been an avowed admirer of her late husband. The outcome was a cash payment of twenty thousand bolivars to *Misia* Jacinta Crespo and a written promise to comply with the following terms:

First, the portrait of General Joaquín Crespo would henceforth remain in its present location in the reception salon of the palace; second, the name of Jacinta Crespo which was wrought in mosaic in various places on the palace floors would be preserved; third, the Crespo family busts which stood in the palace gardens would be preserved; and fourth, payment of one hundred thousand bolivars would be made to General Mestre.

Gómez lived up to the first three provisions, but there is doubt about his compliance with the last. In all probability he found it an easy matter to settle this claim as he did all others—at a few centimos on the bolivar.

Slavery in Venezuela had been abolished by President Monagas in 1854, but during Gómez's regime the same state of servitude persisted as when the country was a Spanish colony. The emancipation of the slaves had hardly, if at all, bettered the situation of the peon class. Although he was no longer designated as such, the peon was still a slave, and he was exploited as though he were a beast of burden. The lot of the peon in the fields was the most unhappy of any Venezuelan working class. He was required to perform twelve hours of hard physical labor daily. His home was a mud hut, his bed the hard damp ground, and he and his family were plagued with miseries. His paltry recompense of thirty to forty bolivars per month (six to eight dollars) was paid out in chits or *fichas* which he was obliged to exchange in the hacienda owner's store for the few staple foods to keep his family alive. To the cold critical eye of the Gomecistas, these serfs represented only two legs to walk on and two arms to work. They were not given even a small plot of land with which to augment their starvation diet.

The peons on the haciendas and ranches of Gómez and Pimentel were whipped if a horse was lost, a cow died, or the harvest was below expectation. The hard-driving foremen ruthlessly committed every kind of iniquity. Rape and murder were common occurrences. The magnanimity of "The Well Deserving"—as Gómez liked to be called —never seemed to extend as far as the poverty-ridden and browbeaten peons in the fields. Yet it was the peon, the poor miserable peon with the sorrowful hungry look and the ragged clothes, who was the first to be forced to carry a rifle "to defend his country" against those who rose up to overthrow tyranny.

The profits from the haciendas during the days of Gómez were derived from the toil and sweat of this peon labor rather than from scientific methods. Up until 1936, the only plows, tractors, cultivators, and harvesting machinery in Venezuela were to be seen on the estates of Gómez, Pimentel, and a few other wealthy landowners. There was no agricultural department or college, The only veterinarians and agronomists were those who were brought into the country for the personal benefit of Gómez, his relatives, and a few close friends. On the other fifty-nine thousand haciendas and small farms, the primitive farming methods of the dark ages were still being followed.

Admittedly, power machinery isn't feasible on the average two-acre Venezuelan farm. Yet neither does the small Venezuelan farmer use draft animals. The *mestizo* farmer of today, when he plows at all, still uses the same wooden plow his great-grandfather used. He clears his land by burning, sticks his seeds in the ground with a pointed stick, then mutters a short prayer to the *Santísima Virgen* for a bountiful harvest. He knows that he is in for a dry season of six months and a wet season of the same period, so he never has to worry about when it is going to rain or when there will be a drought. The two seasons follow each other with almost perfect regularity.

Until 1925, when petroleum shipments climbed to first place, agriculture and livestock raising were the chief industries, with coffee, cacao, balata, tonka beans, beef, hides and rubber being the principal products of export. In 1937, declining agricultural production spurred Venezuela's first truly democratic government to an energetic program of agrarian reform, but the results were disappointing. Here was a country of less than 4,000,000 inhabitants living in an area of 325,170 square miles, with a climate and lands capable of producing abundant crops of cotton, wool, rice, sugar, coffee, tobacco, wheat, fruit, vegetables, and grasses which could maintain herds of cattle almost during the entire year, yet it continually had to import large quantities of food and textiles to feed and clothe its peoples.

While Gómez was alive he was blamed for all the ills of the country. Once he was dead another whipping boy had to be found. Because it had long been the prevailing opinion in Venezuela that the petroleum industry and agriculture were incompatible bed-fellows, the first was blamed by superficial judgment for the shortcomings of the second. The hue and cry went up among the farmers that agriculture and livestock raising had become losing propositions because the imperialistic oil companies had enticed vast numbers of farm workers to the oil fields by paying high wages. Besides, their operations were damaging agricultural lands. Yet, an analysis of the agricultural census of 1937 not only refuted these attacks, but revealed in startling clarity the sad plight of Venezuela's economic life.

Of the 172,630,350 acres that comprise the twenty states of the republic (omitting the federal district and the southern territories), only 8,491,081 were classified as cultivable land, and of this figure, 78.7 per cent was held by 4.4 per cent of the landowners. But what was more significant was that only one-fifth, or 1,750,669 acres, of this privately owned cultivable land was kept under cultivation. It is hard to believe, but true, that in this land of agricultural pursuits, *only one per cent of this entire national area was kept under cultivation.* With much of the land in the cooler regions being devoted to the growing of coffee, it was no wonder that the country was unable to feed itself.

And here was another significant point. On practically none of the land under cultivation did there happen to be any oil wells.

As to the influx of farm labor to the oil fields, this amounted to less than one per cent of the population, while it was estimated that 20 per cent, or 75 per cent of those gainfully employed, was engaged in agriculture and livestock raising.

So the enlightening fact came to light that of Venezuela's 59,000 and some odd farm owners, 2,600 owned almost 80 per cent of the country's agricultural wealth. But why, the question has been raised, did these owners cultivate only one-fifth of their holdings? In 1942, American agricultural experts, members of a U.S. Food Supply Mission, made a study of Venezuela's problems and pointedly replied to that question. While admitting the existence of great possibilities, they blamed the lag in agricultural production to antiquated farming methods, reluctance to invest in modern equipment and fertilizers, and the lack of transportation and irrigation facilities.

In his 1944 annual report to congress, the Minister of Agriculture made the following sorrowful admission. Said he:

"In Venezuela, capital is shy and its use expensive, for which reason capital has fled from the farms. It is evident that much of the backward condition of rural zones is attributable not so much to the distribution of the land itself, but rather to lack of capital and of technical knowledge. A vast concentration of funds on the activities of the land—which in itself is a guarantee to the farming industry—is something entirely unknown in the rural life of Venezuela. Perhaps this may come about with the increase in population, but it will also depend on transportation facilities reaching new and larger markets."

The landed gentry were an aristocratic group of "gentlemen farmers," many of whom took life easy, traveled extensively, and invested their money in securities that bore a high yield. Until the past few years, those who possessed a truly genuine interest in the good earth seldom strayed from their farms; consequently, they failed to keep up with the world trend in modern farming methods. With transportation in the backwoods regions limited to the horse and burro, they cheerfully remained in almost complete isolation, totally unconcerned about the rest of the world around them. From long habit they converted the proceeds of their sales into gold pieces of every available vintage, which they buried in a cowhide bag. A practice that originated in some ancient superstition, and which is still being followed, is to dig up these hoards of gold at periodic intervals "to air them in the sun."

In this land where there appeared to be shortages of everything else, cattle was in plentiful supply all the year around, and prices remained more or less constant. Ever since the time of the *Conquistadores* cattle raising has meant big business in Venezuela. The kings' armies and navies had to have their beef. Later, the revolutionary armies could not move without their herd of cattle following close behind. Then it was Europe and the whole Caribbean area that clamored for beef. Strategically situated as she was, and with a climate and lands favorable to such a project, Venezuela's cattle industry was already thriving when the first coffee beans were planted on the cool slopes of the Andes.

British business interests, with their usual sharp nose for profitable enterprises in the Americas, found the field far from crowded around the end of the last century, so they moved in. The Lancashire Investment and Trust Company, an English company, purchased from the Venezuelan government a tract of 780,000 acres of grazing land situated between the Cunaviche and Capanaparo rivers in the southern state of Apure. There they set up their operating company, the Lancashire Cattle Company, Ltd., and started raising cattle. During Castro's administration this company had acquired a government permit to establish an abattoir and refrigeration plant at Puerto Cabello. By the time Gómez became President, they had built up a profitable business supplying the local markets and exporting frozen meats and hides to Great Britain.

To the wily cattleman from Táchira, who by now had all but monopolized the country's cattle business, this was an unwelcome encroachment on his chosen enterprise. The refrigeration plant especially mortified him no end and made him deeply envious. It happened to be the first of its kind in all of Venezuela. Why hadn't he, who professed to know so much about the cattle business, thought of such a thing first? It rankled him that the *musiús* from the north, who were always so much more efficient in their methods, could outdo him at his own specialty. So he schemed to suppress their activities, by "legal" methods of course. When he became President, he began to put his plan into action.

Now Gómez had never been in Apure, but he had bought and sold cattle from this state many times during the old days in Táchira. He knew the land was good and the cattle it produced were among the best in the country. So he called in his land experts and they pored over a map of Venezuela.

"Who owns this land around here?" he asked, tracing with a gloved finger a large section south of the state capital, San Fernando de Apure.

"Antonio Velasco is the principal owner, General, but there are also two or three smaller owners. And right about here, although it doesn't appear on the map, there is a small communal village

which holds several thousand hectares. They have been established
there a good many years."

"*Pues,* it looks like they will have to move."

"Meaning, General . . . ?"

"Meaning that I want you to buy them out, all of them. If they
refuse to sell, you are to use the usual methods. And make sure you
buy right up to the boundary line of the English company. I am going
to do a little cattle raising there myself and I don't think those
Englishmen will dare to drive their cattle across my land!"

Intimidated by Gómez's agents, the large private owners sold out,
but the communal village proved a tougher nut to crack. Clinging
stubbornly to their land, the villagers had to be moved out by force.
In all, these properties came to forty square leagues, Gómez's second
largest single holding, and he called it *Hato de la Candelaria*—Candle-
mas Ranch.

The English, at first nonplused by this maneuver, simply drove
their cattle by a circuitous route to the west, and the matter stood
as it did before. Gómez, however, had another card up his sleeve.

To get their cattle to Puerto Cabello, the English company had to
drive their herds northward across three states—the *llanos* of Zamora
and Cojedes, and over the rough hilly trails of Carabobo to the
coast. This was done usually at the beginning and end of the rainy
season while the forage was green and lush and there was an abundance of water. There now remained only two possible angles that
would permit legal suppression of this company's operations without
giving rise to the charge that Gómez had deliberately set out to ruin
it. One was to prohibit the export of cattle—which he could not
very well do without cutting off the markets for Venezuelan exporters
—and the other was to dictate the passage of state laws which would
levy a state tariff on cattle entering one state from another. The
latter maneuver promised increased state revenues and the reduction
of federal grants, yet at the same time it would signify the end of
the free exchange of inter-state commerce and increased interference in the autonomy of the states. But Gómez's fiat was law, and
when the tariffs on cattle were established by the state legislatures,
the English company found its profits slipping away, while the herds
of *el Presidente* passed freely from state to state unhindered by

taxes. Caught in this squeeze play, many of Gómez's competitors for the local markets were faced with the alternative of curtailing their operations or selling their cattle to him at bargain prices. By such unscrupulous means Gómez became the indisputable king of the cattle business, the principal industry of Venezuela until the development of the oil fields.

To the surprise of Gómez and everyone else, the Lancashire Cattle Company, undaunted and uncomplaining, continued to ship their cattle through Puerto Cabello just as if nothing had happened. But a way was found to halt their exports, if not to put them out of business entirely.

The English company's cattle lost considerable weight on the long overland trek. With the English now working on a narrow margin of profit, it was essential that this lost weight be regained. It meant the difference between a profit or a loss. So they fattened up their cattle on rented lands just outside Puerto Cabello before leading them to the slaughter. What the crafty Andean peasant did was to buy up these lands in the name of one of his relatives, who was instructed not to rent them out. By this stratagem the export operations of the Lancashire Cattle Company finally ground to a halt, and their abattoir and refrigeration plant were closed down. Yet the English, with their characteristic dogged pertinacity, continued in business.

"*Caramba!* Don't those Englishmen know when they're licked?" Gómez commented, not without a trace of admiration in his voice. But he molested them no longer, and they eked out a meager living selling some cattle in Táchira and exporting the rest over the border into Colombia.

The Lancashire Cattle Company clung tenaciously to its land for years, always in the hope that Gómez would be deposed and a more tolerant man would take his place. They waited twenty-two years. After the death of the dictator in 1935, the company made a successful comeback, but increased taxes imposed by the revolutionary *junta* of Romulo Betancourt in 1945 and rising labor costs during the succeeding years finally forced them to throw in the sponge. In November, 1949, the parent company, the Lancashire Investment and Trust Company, sold its holdings—780,000 acres of land, buildings, 125 miles of fencing, and 8,000 head of cattle for 1,411,000 bolivars, or about $423,723. The buyer: the *Corporación Venezolana de Fomento,* a corporation both financed and managed by the government for the purpose of fostering national industries.

While the *criollo* or native cattle successfully withstood the ravaging effects of pests, parasites, and the oppressive heat of the tropics, its quality left much to be desired. Gómez frankly admitted the shortcomings of the native cattle, and he took steps to remedy this condition. But his motives were not at all patriotic as his idolizers believed. They were first and last purely selfish because Gómez did not trouble himself to establish cattle stations or veterinary service for other cattlemen. Whatever he did to improve the strain of the native cattle was done solely for his personal benefit and profit. Though he derived a great personal enjoyment in overseeing his cattle operations, his guiding motive was always personal gain. There is an excellent example of this in his absolute monopoly of the meat business in Caracas. *His was the only beef that was permitted to be sold in the capital!*

When the experts in animal husbandry that Gómez sent for arrived in the country, they were appalled at the little attention that had been given to either breeding or management. Dipping vats were unknown. So were the beef-producing grains and grasses familiar to all American cattlemen. The Venezuelan cattle were simply turned loose to forage all year around on the wild grasses of the *llanos.* In many sparsely populated areas they were—and still are—allowed to roam at will to scavenge on public and private lands, and they have been the cause of numerous accidents on the public highways.

In the hope of improving the beef-producing qualities of Gómez's cattle, the experts introduced several breeds of bulls from Argentina, the United States, and India. It was the sacred bull of India, the zebu, or Brahman, that gave the best results. By crossing this blood with the *criollo* stock a very hardy type of beef cattle of fair size was developed. But because the *criollo* cow has successfully fought every Venezuelan pest, she still remains the foundation of the cattle stock of Venezuela.

It was in Maracay that Gómez built for himself the finest abattoir and refrigeration plant in all of Venezuela. None but his own cattle were processed there, yet the construction was paid for with government funds, the materials were purloined from the warehouses of the Department of Public Works, and the greater part of the labor was done by conscripted soldiers.

There are no figures on Venezuela's cattle production, but it is known how much of it was controlled by Gómez. Cattlemen like to get together at times and exchange information, especially when a maverick plays havoc with their business. Men who were forced to sell at the muzzle of a gun were willing to talk. It was not difficult to figure out how many cattle cleared through Maracay. No less than 60 per cent of all the cattle raised in Venezuela passed through Gómez's hands; about 30 per cent of this came from his own ranches, the balance he acquired by purchase through gun-toting agents. Of the other 40 per cent, half belonged to state presidents, who supplied their local markets, and half belonged to private cattle raisers, who were forced to pay illegal local taxes at the source as well as the special tariff when crossing a state line.

It was much the same with coffee, cacao, tobacco, tonka beans, heron feathers, and rubber. Liquor taxes, salt, and matches constituted the most lucrative sources of government revenue; however, their control was vested in the sons of the President of the country, and an unknown portion was siphoned off into their pockets.

The gold mining industry, on the other hand, was permitted to carry on without interference. However, shipments of the precious metal once had to pass inspection at Maracay where the export tax was levied. It seems that the head of the clan wanted to know just how much gold Venezuela was exporting and he didn't want any sticky fingers getting into the tax money. Actually, all of the money did go into the national treasury, thereby enabling the government to publicize figures on production. Its figures were not accurate, however, as a great deal of smuggling went on. Rather than pay the 50 per cent tax, most of the twenty thousand individuals once engaged in hunting for gold in the southern tributaries to the Orinoco smuggled their gold across the border into Brazil. It would have been impossible to police that vast jungle area. Let those adventurers risk their own necks, reasoned officialdom. Let them pay eleven dollars for an emaciated chicken, two dollars for a package of cigarettes, one hundred and eighty dollars for a jug of rum. They went in by plane. Most of them would come out by plane, and officials reasoned that they could search them when they landed. Mother lodes? Rich bonanzas? Yes, quite a few. At bars in Ciudad Bolívar men bragged of having found them. These men didn't live much longer though. Jovial drinking companions saw to that.

Fabulous were some of the tales that filtered back from the jungle. Wide veins of the yellow stuff, only six feet down! *Dios!* If only one could get a power shovel in there! Those nuggets from the rivers! Some of them half as large as one's fist! And those naïve *mestizos* who followed the trail of the *pájaro minero,* the bird which sings only where there is gold!

To discourage smuggling and to attract foreign capital and technicians to Venezuela's undeveloped gold fields, Gómez reduced the export tariff on gold to 25 per cent. Two mining companies moved in—the New Gold Fields of Venezuela, Ltd., English, and the Compañía Francesa de La Mocupia, French. For over twenty-five years these companies together mined approximately 70 per cent of the total reported gold production, the value of which fluctuated from a peak of $10,000,000 annually to a low of about $4,000,000 in 1946, when both companies were forced to close down due to increased operating costs and the steady migration of its workers to the diamond fields. The mining of diamonds in Venezuela is a relatively new industry because, although the discoveries date from 1926 in the Caroni River and from 1931 in the Surukún River, it was not until 1936 that the diamond deposits really started to be exploited. Since then the production of diamonds has increased steadily.

Another precious commodity for which Venezuela once was famous was pearls. Gómez did not bother himself at all with the pearl fishing industry, perhaps because the individual returns were very small. He was content to impose a heavy tax on vessels, drags, and divers. Up until a few decades ago the industry employed as many as eight thousand persons, but heavy exploitation of the oyster beds and the loss of markets to the cheaper, cultured pearls of Japan relegated pearl fishing to a minor industry. Long ago, pearls from Margarita vied with emeralds and rubies for favor in the royal courts of Europe. For over a century in Venezuela, pearls were considered a more desirable medium of exchange than Spanish coinage. The pearls of Margarita inspired the famous Venezuelan artist, Tito Salas, to paint his "El Cuadro de las Perlas" which hangs today in the salon of the Bank of Venezuela. The story goes that a pretty Indian girl, Guaiqueri, daughter of a Margarita chieftain, accepted a gaudy porcelain plate in trade for her beautiful string of pearls, a string which was long enough to go around her neck three times and still reach her waist. Months later a Jewish trader sold the pearls in Amsterdam for a sum sufficient to equip and defray the cost of several expeditions to the New World. Salas' picture depicts the Jewish trader in the act of consummating the trade on the shore of Margarita.

Gómez had no particular fondness for the sea, but through confiscations he became involved in the shipping business. With the arrest in 1913 of General Román Delgado Chalbaud, who was involved in an abortive attempt to overthrow him, Gómez acquired the controlling interest in the *Compañía de Navegación Fluvial y Costanera,* of which Delgado Chalbaud was the president and principal stockholder. Through this company Gómez gradually gained control of all river and coastal trade. Not even in the distant region of Arauca could either a Venezuelan or a foreigner put in service even a small cargo launch. The local authorities, complying with "orders from the Boss," would crack down, because the "Boss" would not tolerate competition. Only his good friend General Leon Jurado, president of the state of Falcón, was permitted to participate in this monopoly. Jurado owned a shipyard in La Vela, and all coastal cargo destined for ports of Falcón were carried on his vessels. This privilege was a sort of added recompense to Jurado for serving as the "Boss's" "machete." Jurado repelled many revolutionary expeditions that attempted to land on the shores of Falcón.

The dictator's favorite method for gaining control or outright ownership of a business enterprise was to have one of his sons or relatives buy a small interest in the business, so that at the moment it started to prosper, the founders were forced out and their interests stolen. In this way he took away the electric power company of Valencia from Dr. Sales Perez. Supplying electric current to his fellow Venezuelans was a very lucrative business, as he found out, so he acquired a string of plants all the way from Maracay to Cumaná.

Unfortunately for many a hard-pressed businessman struggling to make a comfortable living, too many of Gómez's relatives, cronies, and local officials took up this nefarious practice of subtly seizing other people's property. Foreigners especially were harried repeatedly. If their business prospered and they refused to take in some local *político* or official as a partner, their license was revoked or they were framed on trumped up charges. The smart foreign businessman never started a new enterprise without first taking in a Venezuelan as a partner, preferably one who was well known in the community and whose integrity was unquestioned. It was in the Venezuelan's name that the business was registered and he was the nominal head of the firm. He was the one who handled all contacts with the customs and other officials, affixed and cancelled the multitudinous fiscal stamps and in general untangled all the red tape that might suddenly ensnare the unwary gringo.

Besides his vast undertakings in cattle, coffee, corn, and sugar and his ventures in other agricultural products and power plants, Gómez owned or controlled numerous other plants and factories. As the major stockholder he controlled the paper and glass factories in Maracay and a cigarette factory in Caracas. He owned outright three modern hotels, a frozen meat company in Puerto Cabello, a modern dairy, sugar refinery, and a cotton mill in Maracay. By-product industries sprang up and still more of his factories produced butter and cheese, lard, cooking oil, soap, candles, tanned leather, and textiles which sold at prices on a par with the expensive imported products. Not content with grinding his heel into the throat of a throttled and prostrate nation, Gómez had to put his hand into its pocket as well.

One cannot help but wonder how an unschooled super-brigand like Gómez could manage this vast industrial empire of his and still captain the Venezuelan ship of state. Though he had no puerile foibles to speak of, Gómez was by no means endowed with any super-human qualities. He did have, however, a vast store of cyclonic energy, a gritty common sense, and a shrewd insight into *mestizo* psychology. Actually, he ran his sprawling empire as he did his government, with the help of a crack team. Each man was a specialist in his own field. In selecting the administrators of his varied enterprises, Gómez evinced a knowledge of human nature that was almost uncanny. He admired intelligence and aggressiveness and mortally hated any man who would snatch a penny because the opportunity presented itself. He chose men who took great pride in their individual honesty—Luis Roncayolo, an official of the *Compañía Venezolana de Navegación,* and after Gómez's death president of the state of Zulia, was an excellent example—and his entire selection of men was based on this idea.

For all his seeming artlessness, Gómez had the adding-machine mind of a banker. He never forgot a figure. He knew the precise worth of each of his businesses, what portion of its construction cost had come out of his own pocket, and its record of earnings. Though he placed implicit faith in the honesty of his administrators, he had a pretty shrewd notion that among the underpaid rank and file there were some who had sticky fingers. He knew that he was being mulcted in a small way, but as his effort was to get an approximate result, he allowed latitude for bad bookkeeping. Serene and apparently well satisfied with his enormous returns, this Croesus of the Andes could afford to be tolerant now and then.

If one can believe the unbiased chronicles of Venezuela's historians, the country's presidents who were grasping and corrupt were legion. Gómez's predatory instincts, therefore, were by no means unique. Though Cipriano Castro had been the one to initiate his eager protégé in corrupt and vicious practices while in public office, it probably had been the extraordinary record of Guzmán that Gómez had set as his goal.

Perhaps no Venezuelan biographer has delved more deeply into Guzmán's record than has R. A. Rondon Marquiz in his *Guzmán Blanco, El Autocrata Civilizador.* Here in brief is what he says of the plundering incursions of the "Illustrious American" while he served as President of the Republic.

". . . G.B. was always involved in fraudulent and other kinds of money making transactions. When he was in exile in Curacao he made a deal with three friends who put up the money for arms. If the revolution turned out successfully, each would receive 15 per cent of all customs house receipts. For the thirty months that G.B. took his percentage, it is calculated that he received 4,800,000 bolivars. G.B. obtained numerous properties by confiscation or forced sale. These he sold to the government and others at their true worth. He demanded and received a commission of ten per cent on two government loans obtained from the British government. On the Spanish debt he bought credits cheaply and resold them after deducting his commission. On this deal he made 3,400,000 bolivars. He had a monopoly on the coastal trade, which was especially favored by the closing of the port of Maracaibo to Antilles commerce. He owned the major interest in a Caracas commercial firm which had a monopoly on wheat, a men's furnishing business and a carriage transport company, which received over 25,000 bolivars of government money yearly for carriage hire for himself. Together with Henry L. Boulton and General Manuel Matos he was a large stockholder in the Banco Comercial, which charged the government exorbitant rates for handling its account. Through this bank he also made enormous sums on the devaluation of the bolivar and on foreign exchange. His son-in-law, the French Duke Charles de Morny, received several lucrative government construction contracts. As a partner in a Caracas minting house, G.B. received 400,000 bolivars as his share of a 750,000 bolivar contract to mint nickel coins for the government. The coins were never put into circulation because they were short on nickel and were too small. In 1870 G.B. organized a personal honor guard called *Regimiento de la Guardia*. While in the field this body received regular army rations and while in Caracas it received 1,500 bolivars daily to purchase its own rations. On the occasion the honor guard was in the field for a period of 280 days, G.B. daily locked the ration money in his desk until he had accumulated for himself a total of 420,000 bolivars.

"When relations were severed with Holland, G.B. demanded of congress 2,500,000 bolivars for coastal defense. But he spent only 380,000 bolivars on two iron cannon, 2,000 Remington rifles and a trench at La Guaira which was strengthened with only a few hundred bags of sand and covered with coconut palms. The balance of 2,120,000 bolivars he pocketed. And one of his most despicable deals of all, which provoked a scandal and investigation in congress, was his acquisition of a hacienda which belonged to the Caracas University and was providing it with a steady income. Appraised at 2,000,000 bolivars, the hacienda Chuao had become famous for its cacao, much of which found its way into Marie Brizard's 'Creme de Cacao.' G.B. wanted the hacienda and he got it for 750,000 bolivars. Then he had the gall to blandly advise the trustees to invest this money in almost worthless government bonds."

There it is—fraud, defalcations, monopolies, exploitation of the masses, lies and deception—in fact the entire gamut of vile and contemptible tricks of a Latin-American dictator in full bloom. Is it any wonder then that Juan Vicente Gómez followed in the same wayward steps of his mentor Castro and that scoundrel Guzmán? Of course not. He just couldn't help himself. His path of behavior was too clearly laid out for him. Many Venezuelans say Gómez was the cruelest and most corrupt despot their country ever had. That he could be. But perhaps they speak of him with such vehemence because he ruled for such a long period. Perhaps his sins seem blacker because they are still fresh in people's minds. Gómez ruled the country for a total of twenty-seven years, compared with nine for Castro, and thirteen for Guzmán.

The acquisition of so many properties and enterprises raised many conjectures as to the dictator's wealth. A quiet investigation by an enterprising lawyer in 1927 disclosed that Gómez owned properties in every state of the union except Zamora. He still owned his old hacienda in Colombia. As he kept no bank accounts in Venezuela and no one knew how much money he had deposited in banks abroad, an estimate of his wealth could be based only on his material wealth within the country—farms, ranches, buildings, factories, and the like—which alone were valued at over 238,800,000 bolivars!

With the air of a tired conqueror Gómez once made the sage remark: "After all, every Venezuelan still has the same opportunities I had."

Coming from a peasant who had parlayed a few rifles and supplies into a national empire, this was pretty sound theorizing. All that a man had to do, evidently, was to start and of course win a revolution. But the exploited and oppressed man in the street could very well have voiced, if he dared, a withering retort of his own. Not one bolivar that swelled *el Presidente*'s coffers had come by honest toil. And as for the "opportunities" the benevolent *Presidente* spoke of, they were as unattainable as the stars. The iron-fisted vigilance of the *Jefe* saw to that.

CHAPTER TWENTY

Measures of Terrorism

On April 29, 1912, the cabinet resigned in a body at the request of the President. It was the second such upset in as many years. Even such supposedly strong figures as Gil Fortoul and Antonio Pimentel went out with the rest. This did not mean that friction had arisen between Pimentel and his good *amigo*. Gómez merely wanted to make a clean sweep of his cabinet and start afresh.

When quiet scholarly Dr. González Guinán had collected the letters of resignation and handed them over, Gómez said to him in a manner frozen with hauteur: *"Muy bien,* Doctor . . . and yours?"

González Guinán gazed at him in astonishment, but there was no expression on the *Jefe's* baked-clay face. "Why do unnecessary paper work, General," he replied, "when the same functionary remains. Besides, the Secretary General is not a member of the cabinet . . ."

"Isn't he?" challenged the dictator. But there was a menacing insinuation in his drawl when he added, "I think you had better put your letter with those of our other friends."

Thus did González Guinán fall with the rest. Once again the unfathomable "Sphinx of La Mulera" was going through one of his strange dark moods.

On May 17, a conspiracy to assassinate the President and seize the government was discovered. Involved were General Román Delgado Chalbaud, "Admiral" of the Fleet and director of the government shipyard at Puerto Cabello, his brother Miguel, and one hundred fifty-seven others. Delgado Chalbaud had pretended to be his friend right up until the last. When Gómez was convinced that he had figured as one of the leaders, he confronted him and called him a hypocrite and a traitor. All of them went to prison and Gómez wreaked his vengeance by appropriating for himself Chalbaud's stock in the *Compañía de Navegación Fluvial y Costanera*. Not content with this rich haul, he seized three haciendas belonging to Chalbaud by forcing his father-in-law to give them up.

In prison, Chalbaud fared almost as badly. His jailor was Duarte Cacique, who harbored bitter memories of his own days in prison under Cipriano Castro. Toward the end of 1907, when Chalbaud's wedding in Puerto Cabello was celebrated with a big fiesta, Cacique was a prisoner in the island fortress. From his cell he could hear the exploding fireworks and the strains of music which wafted over the water. His warped *mestizo* mind pictured images of a sumptuous banquet, flowing cheer, laughter, and pretty girls. And in his anger and resentment at his plight he made a vow. Said he: "I am going to make them pay . . . and *how* I am going to make them pay!" Then in 1913 the situation was somewhat reversed. Cacique was the jailer and the affluent navy man was the prisoner. Remembering that night six years before, Cacique singled Chalbaud out for special attention. At periodic intervals he cut off his food supply. After three or four days of hunger Chalbaud was ready to acquiesce to anything. Using this coercive method, Cacique had Chalbaud sign away sums of money which he collected from his wife. In all he collected something like fifty thousand bolivars.

During this period it was no longer merely a rumor that Gómez wanted to continue succeeding himself in office. The arrogance, the feeling on his part, in congress and among the people themselves, whom he patronized in the traditional manner of the demagogue, that he was a ruler entitled to privilege without question, was clearly evident. He consulted various members of the Government Council, feeling them out as to the possibility of securing re-election. He was politely but firmly told that re-election was not possible because it was prohibited by the very Constitution Gómez himself had signed in 1909. Somehow, an excuse had to be found to abolish the Council.

Dr. Pedro Arcaya, the eloquent lawyer, was the chosen instrument to accomplish this by means of the Franco-Venezuelan Protocol. At this juncture Arcaya was one of the substitutes of the Corte Federal y de Cesación, which position he resigned to become attorney general of the nation to put through the plan. This protocol was, in substance, an agreement to pay in gold the long pending French claims against Venezuela. Gómez had resolved to settle these claims once and for all, but he knew that he would meet with stubborn opposition in the council where the protocol had to first pass approval. Determined to find out which of its members were aligned against him, he had the protocol submitted to the council on May 1, but his adversaries, forewarned, failed to show up. Six days later, General José Ignacio Pulido, president of the council, announced to congress that the council had been unable to convene for lack of a quorum; congress, therefore, called the substitutes to convene, and they nominated Gil Fortoul as president of their body.

Though it had done little to strengthen his re-election aims, the "Protocol Affair," as it has since been called, served Gómez by revealing those who were opposed to him. Police were stationed at the home of each of these men. Some were caught and put into the Rotunda, while others, like Leopoldo Baptista, managed to evade the guards and flee the country. Gómez lived long enough to hear of their deaths one by one.

Then in July there began another wave of arrests and imprisonments, which was the aftermath of an editorial published by Arévalo González in his newspaper *El Pregonero*. For thirty years *El Pregonero* had lashed at tyranny and had defended free thought in Venezuela. Under each successive dictatorship the paper had been closed and its owner thrown into prison. In 1910, Arévalo González had campaigned against graft, specifically mentioning the monopoly of coastal transportation that was in the hands of "a few high government officials." Gómez sent an agent to offer him a sizable sum of money to desist from these attacks, but the newspaper man ejected him from his establishment and redoubled his attack in the next issue. On the day following publication, Gómez decreed the closure of *El Pregonero* and ordered the arrest of Arévalo González. After his release from the Rotunda about two years later, Arévalo González founded *Atenas,* an historical and literary magazine, and in 1913 reopened his newspaper.

Intoned the resolute voice of *El Pregonero* in its issue of July 11, 1913, which provoked *El Benemérito* to drastic action:

". . . We are going to exercise a right. We are going to do something more. We are going to comply with a duty. It is the right of suffrage. It is the citizen's right. In what way can we know if General Gómez is truly disposed to respect the right of suffrage if we don't even attempt to exercise it? Our desire is to offer General Gómez the opportunity to prove that he does not intend to imitate the conduct of his predecessors, but earnestly desires to restore to his compatriots the right of free citizens in full possession of Constitutional guarantees . . . because in this manner, and only in this manner, can peace be perpetuated and our beloved homeland be made happy and great . . . and although time has brought us bitter disillusions, never will we regret having complied with our duty nor of having refrained from thinking evil of General Gómez before having positive proof of abuses of the right of suffrage. Though one may be a foe of General Gómez, one cannot overlook certain unusual talents in him . . . because he could not have arrived at such a high position by having cleverly tricked a man as astute as Castro, nor have rid himself of so many political intriguers who aspired to dominate him, without these certain unusual talents . . . But what we need is a civilian president, one who is modest and without the presumptuousness of a *caudillo*. He should be, above all, a patriot, who will not put his private interests before the sacred interests of the homeland . . . Dr. Félix Montes is our candidate for the Presidency of the Republic for the constitutional period of 1914 to 1918 . . . a patriot, a man of letters and science, who does not aspire to be a militarist . . . but who could rely on the sword of General Gómez to enforce his authority and oppose any pretensions of Castro should he make any attempt to "restore" us for the second time . . ."

Unmindful of the livid scars of past imprisonments, Arévalo González had bestowed on the cowed populace of the capital a wholesome morsel of a forbidden prerogative—freedom of the press. *Caraqueños* shook their heads apprehensively when they read it.

The dictator's reaction to the editorial has not been chronicled. No doubt he recoiled in anger upon reading it. A despot does not concern himself with liberties of the citizenery. He is self-centered and truculent. Suffice to say that Gómez acted, and vigorously. Purportedly upon his orders, Arévalo González was arrested a few hours after his paper appeared on the streets. He was confined in a cell of the Rotunda with irons on his legs.

Incensed at this harsh treatment of his chief, Angel Garrido, a

sixty-five-year-old writer for *El Pregonero*, thought something should
be done about it. But what could an old man without influential
friends do? He sent off a telegram to the illustrious *Presidente*, decry-
ing the miscarriage of justice and pleading for his chief's release.
Surely, "The Well Deserving" would have some compassion.

The reply was an order to arrest Garrido. He was sent to the
fortress at Puerto Cabello where he was shackled with 60-pound irons.

No one protested this last arrest, yet "The Well Deserving," that
pillar of smug respectability, vented his wrath by ordering still more
arrests—Carlos Brandt, Dr. Eudoro López, and others.

Carlos Brandt, correspondent and agent for *El Pregonero* in
Puerto Cabello, was picked up on the street and taken to police
headquarters. He challenged the reason for his arrest. "Orders from
Maracay," they told him. Pondering over the matter years later,
Brandt could only vouchsafe the information that perhaps it had
been because of his friendship for Arévalo González or his failure
to "collaborate" with the dictator. A few months prior to his arrest,
General Rafael Velasco of the Puerto Cabello customs had pointedly
remarked to him that *El Benemérito* had commented on the absence
of his name on the endless adulatory columns appearing in other
papers. Brandt had assured his well-meaning friend that he would
comply with this requisite. He had not done so.

As they led him away to the fortress, Brandt asked permission to
notify his wife. He was told that was impossible because he was being
held incommunicado. He then requested permission to send a telegram to President Gómez. That too was impossible. It appears that
el Presidente had given strict orders that he was not to be annoyed
with matters concerning prisoners.

Meanwhile, Félix Montes had not been caught napping. Apprised
the same evening of his sponsor's arrest, he tied up a few belongings
and fled to the home of friends in a distant *barrio* of the city. The
next morning, finding him gone, the police posted a guard at his
home. For several weeks, while he made secretive preparations for
going abroad, Montes had to flee from hiding place to hiding place.
Disguised as a peon he escaped early one morning over the hills of
Caracas, picking his way over tortuous unused paths with the help of
a peon guide. That night the two slinking figures arrived at a lonely
stretch of beach at La Guaira. Before dawn Montes was at sea aboard

a small fishing sloop which carried him to the Dutch island of Bonaire. From there he went to Curacao where he lived for a time in the Venezuelan colony of exiles.

Montes passed twenty-two years in exile. Garrido was released from prison a broken, dying man. Arévalo González also was released, only to be thrown back into the Rotunda in 1921. Carlos Brandt, on the other hand, learned the wisdom of "collaboration." He emerged from the island fortress six months after entry and sailed to a consular post in Germany.

These events did not augur well for a presidential election. Montes had called the dictator's hand, and Gómez had revealed with nonchalant casualness that he was dealing with a stacked deck. He was playing the game his way, searching for some pretext, fabricating, wherever convenient, a tissue of lies so that he could stall off the election and maintain himself in power. He would compel the recalcitrants to bend to his indomitable will.

The country did not have long to wait for the final showdown.

On July 29, just eighteen days after the publication of the editorial, Gómez sent urgent telegrams to all state presidents, warning them to be on their guard. Castro was heading a revolution toward Venezuelan soil! Then on August 1 he signed in his laborious hand a decree which suspended constitutional rights.

Just where was Cipriano Castro? No one seemed to know. *El Presidente,* when asked, merely held a finger to his nose and looked wise. This so-called revolution of Castro was just a hoax, a bit of fantasy that had evolved in Gómez's head so that he could declare a state of emergency and postpone the election indefinitely. Actually, Castro never did risk the venture of stepping on Venezuelan soil, though he did, the following year, attempt to incite his partisans to rise in rebellion.

Gómez was astute enough to play his hoax down to the last card, with complete success. He never did things halfway. Seriously believing that a Castro invasion actually was in full swing, many of Castro's adherents fell into the trap and were captured.

Here in detail is how the talented peasant from the Andes played his master stroke.

On August 3, Caracas, and later the whole nation, was astounded to read the following proclamation issued by their President:

"The peace of the republic having been disturbed by General Cipriano Castro, I am taking to the field, and I am going to re-establish public order. I know that all *Jefes,* officers, and soldiers of the national army will comply with their duty. J. V. Gómez."

As head of the Government Council, Gil Fortoul accepted the reins of government as Acting President. Quiet, gentle Gil Fortoul. He could be trusted implicitly during the *Jefe's* absence. One more precaution. The governor of the Federal District (the son of General Ramón Guerra) was replaced with the dictator's own brother. Don Juancho—or don Juanchito, as everyone called him—was a simple rustic, less taciturn than his brother, plodding, colorless and circumspect. He was not exactly a political novice, having acquired some experience as the president of the state of Miranda. At least Juancho could be relied upon to keep an eye on things and report anything amiss.

The army that the commander-in-chief chose to lead was a ridiculous looking lot of military specimens. Raw recruits, most of them, they were outfitted in cast off, misfit uniforms. With nary a token lesson in the use of a rifle they set out in a daze to what they fully expected would be their slaughter.

To a flurry of fanfare, the army, some forty-five hundred strong, marched west out of Caracas, then trudged slowly through the mire of the country roads. It was the rainy season. General Félix Galavis, Inspector General of the Army, and his aide Colonel MacGil, a Chilean, each with a brace of pistols in his belt, galloped up and down the line wielding their sabers threateningly against those conscripts who strayed out of formation. In the vanguard of this serpentine column rode the commander-in-chief astride his white stallion. Looking resplendent in his immaculate uniform, plumed Prussian helmet, and shiny black boots, the sword of twenty-nine battles at his side, Gómez's mien was sometimes austere, sometimes debonair. The *Jefe* was on holiday parade.

It took this nondescript army three days to march from Caracas to Maracay. They encamped in the fields outside the town, and there they stayed. As the hours ticked off and nothing happened, the conscripts became restless. They burned with curiosity. Where was the enemy? What was the *Jefe* up to?

The scene shifted to the state of Falcón where *Jefe*'s "machete," General León Jurado, began manipulating the backstage props of this grandiose farce. Two of Jurado's lackeys went to Curacao where they spent several days conferring with General Simón Bello and other Castro adherents. The exiles were led to believe that Jurado had turned against Gómez and that they could count on Falcón to rise in rebellion.

With hope strong in their hearts and a prayer on their lips the victims of this despicable hoax disembarked at La Vela del Coro on the night of August 20. There were close to a hundred of them. Jurado's lieutenants met them on the quay and escorted them to a hotel in Coro where they all sat down to a solemn conclave. If Jurado's men had expected to meet Castro and Baptista, they were disappointed. Unbeknownst to the exiles, General Jurado and his soldiers, all armed to the teeth, surrounded the hotel in the darkness. At a signal they burst in, shouting that the exiles were all under arrest for conspiracy against the government. The exiles were too stupefied with amazement to offer any resistance.

Deep in the depths of despair and irately bitter for having been so roundly tricked, the prisoners were marched under a guard of over five hundred of Jurado's men to Gómez's encampment at Maracay. On August 28, Gomez advised Gil Fortoul by telegram that he was returning to the capital with his "victorious army." He arrived in Caracas four days later, more ruthlessly cruel than ever.

To those of his confrères who dared to voice their disapproval of such despicable methods, Gómez justified his action by saying he wanted to see if Cipriano Castro himself would disembark with the other conspirators. He knew better than anyone that Castro was not in Curacao. Actually, his spies dogged Castro's trail constantly. They followed him day and night, watched where he ate, with whom he talked, to whom he wrote letters. They reported all this to the *Jefe* in minute detail. Aware that he was being shadowed, Castro was hard pressed to elude these spies, and he fled from one Latin American country to another.

In January of 1914, barely five months after the Coro affair, agents intercepted a letter from Castro's brother Carmelo to Colonel López, at that time administrator of customs at Puerto Sucre. The

letter revealed the surprising news that Castro actually was planning
a revolution. Furthermore, the writer asserted, he had been authorized
by General Castro to invite López to participate in it.

The outcome was the immediate recall of the colonel to the
capital. The President having refused to grant him an audience, López
was given a severe dressing down by Secretary General Vivas. True to
form, the colonel didn't take the imputation lying down. Pointing out
in righteous anger that the contents of the letter clearly implied that
he could not have been in direct contact with Castro nor in league
with his partisans, he was insistent that his name be cleared.

After not a little reflection and investigation, López was reinstated
in the good graces of the *Jefe*. Yet, somehow, fate seemed capriciously
unkind. The post of *Jefe Civil* of Río Chico, the small sleepy town
in Miranda to which he was next assigned, was considered by the
colonel to be unworthy for a man who had redeemed himself from
a grave charge. Setting out with much misgivings, he favored Río
Chico with a disdainful inspection, but a few days later found him
back in Caracas pouring out his woes. As the ambitious colonel (he
was now turning thirty-one) had long since found out, tenacity of purpose quite often brought results. There just happened to be at that
opportune moment a promising opening in Ciudad Bolívar. Through
the efforts of his old and good friend General Galavis, López was
named commandant of the city's garrison. It was to be the turning
point of his military career. As he stepped from the steamer onto
the quay at Ciudad Bolívar, the city fathers who had come to welcome him had a difficult time recognizing the new commandant.
They had expected to meet a burly, weathered man in uniform. Instead, the pale and frail young man who greeted them was dressed
in mufti, and he carried, of all things, that symbol of passive resistance, an umbrella.

The year 1914 had started off with a grim and ominous warning.
Through his foreign minister, Gomez had declared that constitutional
rights would not be restored, nor would the newly conscripted army
be disbanded. Leopoldo Baptista and others, he affirmed, were not
only continuing their hostile attitude toward the "legitimate" government, but they were creating disturbances throughout the interior to
prolong armed rebellion in the country; therefore an election at this

General Gómez at the seaside resort of Macuto with his son José Vicente (right), the children of a friend, and (left) Dr. Adolfo Bueno, the physician who saved his life in 1921.

General John J. Pershing received by Gómez and his son José Vicente at Turiamo after General Pershing landed from the battleship U.S.S. Utah *in February, 1925. Gómez's other sons Florencio and Juan Vicente are in white suits and caps.*

time would be utterly out of the question. This, of course, was nothing but sheer balderdash, but it served to confuse the issue and to bolster the tottering "state of emergency."

From Curacao, on January 22, Baptista wrote Gómez a scathing letter. He not only refuted the charges but severely rebuked his former chief. Said he:

". . . I would like you to tell me what your reasons were for removing by flimsy pretexts more than half of the state presidents . . . for changing in June the government council which had been elected for four years . . . for persecuting in early July the only presidential candidate who has appeared, and imprisoning his supporters . . . for declaring the country in a state of war in August, when the only disturbances of public order occurred on the Colombian frontier, and only for a few brief days . . . for maintaining an exceptionally large army although no enemy has risen in arms . . . for suspending constitutional guarantees and filling the prisons with political prisoners . . . for prohibiting the carrying out of the legal elections at the time set forth by law . . . and lastly . . . why are you brutally violating today all the institutions which you solemnly swore to uphold, and once upheld?

"You, at the head of the nation, backed by the power conferred upon you by congress, should be the foremost servant of the republic and the most zealous defender of national peace. But far from complying with this sacred duty, you are performing the most disgraceful and iniquitous revolution ever registered in the annals of our history. Venezuela, which possesses every means to live legally in peace, which yearns for and desperately requires tranquillity for its development and well-being, which has maintained itself tranquilly in the hope that its institutions would be respected . . . you have launched on a terrifying and bloody adventure solely for petty and personal interests so that you could remain in power for a longer period than that stipulated by the Constitution. Would you carry on in this way if citizens could exercise their rights, if the states were legitimately governed, if the army—the guardian of our institutions—recognized its duties and endeavored to comply with them . . . ?"

None of these questions was ever answered. When letters such as this one were received by the dictator, they were invariably thrown into the waste basket. Conscious-stricken for having been associated with a tyrant, Baptista had assailed his former chief in the only manner he knew how, and he felt relieved for having done so.

During the early months of 1914 there were several minor disturbances in Guayana, in eastern Guarico, and on the frontier of Táchira and the dictator seized on these incidents as a pretext for maintaining the country in a state of war.

In April he intimidated congress into appointing him commander-in-chief of the national army with "unlimited powers," and congress passed a provisional statute to this effect. It was a job Gómez had usurped some time back, but this made it official. At the same time, Victorino Márquez Bustillos was appointed Provisional President and two other Gomecistas were appointed to the posts of First and Second Vice-President. It was all a put-up job so that the dictator could continue to enjoy to the full the pleasures of Maracay. But while on the surface Bustillos appeared to be governing the country, actually it was Gómez who phoned his orders to Bustillos through his secretary, General Vivas. When the Provisional President wrote to Gómez, which was almost daily, he signed his communications "your subordinate and friend."

In Trinidad, General José Hernández, the same man who had refused to seat himself at the same table with little Caesar, could restrain himself no longer. Hernández did not have the personality of an Andueza Palacios, nor the sword of a Crespo. As a result, his life was one long hard struggle of sterile sacrifices for his country. When he observed that Gómez was slowly but surely consolidating his power, he left Trinidad with General Dávila to join the Venezuelan rebels in Guayana. The British authorities, however, were alerted to the reasons for their trip, and they were obliged to return to Trinidad. From there the almost penniless Hernández went to Cuba where his subsistence was provided through the kind heart of a Cuban friend. Now old and infirm, but still conspiring against the Venezuelan dictator, he moved on to New York. He died there in 1921 at the age of sixty-eight. His funeral is said to have been as humble as his life.

Deprived of Hernández's leadership, the conspirators in Guayana, nevertheless, decided to revolt. Unfortunately, one of them turned traitor, and the entire lot were taken prisoner. Here is what happened to one hundred of these unfortunates. When they arrived in Caracas they were segregated into two groups of fifty. One group was put into the Rotunda. During the following seven years, only nine of the men managed to get out alive. The remaining forty-one died in their cells. The second group fared no better. Chained together like beasts, they slaved under the tropical sun, building roads near the seaport town of Guanta. At night they were packed into a small, bare customs building, which was already overcrowded with two hundred and fifty prisoners. Better death than this slow torture. Eighteen of them, unshackled for the night, tried to make a run for freedom. They were captured. Colonel Torres, the officer in charge of this makeshift prison, dutifully wired Maracay for instructions. The commander-in-chief, in his benevolent wisdom, would know just what to do. Back came the wired reply. "For the eighteen, 1,000 lashes each. For all the others, suitable punishment—100 to 500 lashes each."

For three days blood actually flowed in streams in the customs house yard. A guard later had the audacity to exhibit in Puerto Cabello a chunk of human flesh preserved in a jar of alcohol. He had picked it from the ground during the tortures. Not one of the eighteen men lived to receive the full thousand lashes. In all, almost fifty men were executed during those three bloody days.

For months Venezuela underwent a bloody reign of terror. Rumor had it that General Colmenares Pacheco, who long had vied with General Galavis for the *Jefe*'s favor, had at last joined the inner circle and had the ear of the dictator. A short Andean of jutting jaw and sadistic leanings, Pacheco had acquired a certain eminence by marrying the *Jefe*'s sister Emilia and serving as Secretary General (1910-1912). It was this man who advocated and put into practice in the Rotunda and on the Caracas police force the ritual of tortures to make men confess to real or imaginary plots and crimes. During his heyday the prisons were full to overflowing and men literally died like flies.

"Let me have him," he would tell his brother-in-law when they were discussing the case of a suspect. "I will make him sing. When I get through with him he will sing like a *turpial!*" And he would grimace his ugly features and twist his fist suggestively.

After a time, even the iron-clad stomach of Gómez revolted

against the tortures and assassinations. Pacheco had lost all sense of reason. He was wantonly blackening the good name of the *Jefe*. So Pacheco fell into disgrace and was swept aside.

The galaxy of satellites around Gómez revolved capriciously and erratically, perpetually losing old stars and gaining new ones. Another to fall was Colonel Américo Spinetti, the stalwart aide who had been his faithful shadow on that memorial day in December. Imprisoned in the Rotunda in May of 1914, it was not until four years later that his desperate wife managed to slip through the cordon of guards at Maracay and reach the inner sanctum. Her arms outstretched and tears coursing down her cheeks, she begged the liberty of her husband, invoking the name of Gómez's mother and his favorite children. The poignant scene would have moved the heart of any dictator. But not Gómez. There were times when this man of stone had no heart.

Stretching his legs out lazily and twiddling his thumbs, "The Well Deserving" was said to have replied: *"Lo siento, señora,* but I will have to consult General Gimón first. He is the only one who knows the details of the case."

And later to his staff he said, in a manner frozen with menace: "The next man among you who lets another one of these demanding women approach me will be put in irons! Do I make myself clear?"

Another year passed. Two. Three. Spinetti was unable to move from his cell. Weighed down with *grillos,* starved, racked with dysentery and tuberculosis, he died wallowing in his own excrement. After stripping the emaciated body of its stinking rags and bathing it, they rushed it to a clean bed in a local hospital. Then Spinetti's family was notified that he had died there! Identification of the body by his brother was almost impossible and was accomplished only after an examination of the teeth and the deformed fingers of one hand.

CHAPTER TWENTY-ONE

The War Years

By the time May, 1915, rolled around and the country's legislators, cowed and yielding, had expressed their willingness to toe the line, Bustillos, prodded by Gómez, called a special session of congress. The script for the hour-long session had been carefully prepared and rehearsed. The business at hand was to be the "free" election of a constitutional President. Yet the only candidate listed in the script was Juan Vicente Gómez—"The Well Deserving."

While the dictator lolled in carefree comfort on his estates in Maracay, Dr. Rafael Requena, his personal physician and president of congress, warmly extolled to the assembly the exalted virtues of the absent candidate. It was a speech that bordered upon rhapsody.

"The necessary man . . . the indispensable man for the present and the future . . . In him the very existence of the homeland is being perpetuated . . ."

When he had finished, the indispensable man's good and loyal *amigo* gazed upon the dutifully attentive assembly for a sign of hearty approval. But the reverberating applause for which he had hoped did not come. Only accusing silence.

The result was a foregone conclusion. Glumly the cast went through the motions of electing General Juan Vicente Gómez President of the Republic and commander-in-chief of the national army. Nary a note of dissension to mar the somber but very proper proceedings. The *Jefe* would be pleased!

When the official delegation trouped out to Maracay to convey the happy tidings, the President-elect, wearing his righteousness like a medal, greeted them in a matter-of-fact voice. Looking down with a kind of tolerant detachment on his subjects, he murmured, "It is very

221

gratifying. Very gratifying indeed. God willing, I will do my best."

This peasant with pretensions to omniscience thought of himself in a dramatic role. He bore himself with the aplomb and dignity of one convinced he was making a great contribution to his country.

That night, flowery speeches were made at balls in Caracas, Maracay, and Valencia. The health of *el Presidente* was toasted in champagne. It was the next day that Gómez sent his brief and insolent note to congress. Until he considered it "opportune and convenient," he advised that body, Dr. Márquez Bustillos would continue to occupy the presidential chair. Gómez continued to live in Maracay, but occasionally he made surprise trips to Caracas "to see how our friend Dr. Bustillos is getting along."

Riding high in the saddle and looking toward the future, Gómez felt that Crespo had lacked boldness when he had the tenure of office lengthened to four years. He saw to it that it was increased to seven years. Congress passed his new Constitution on June 13. Six days later it was signed by Bustillos and the cabinet. Its most important provisions were that the President would be elected henceforth by congress; the Federal Council, established by the previous Constitution, was eliminated; the constitutional period would last seven years, starting from April 19, 1915; and, what was most significant, *the President could succeed himself by re-election.*

Almost daily the corpulent figure of the *Jefe* could be seen mounted on a pure white stallion, watching with a critical eye his troops go through their paces. A strict disciplinarian, he tolerated no slackness and was always up at the crack of dawn ready to tackle the papers on his desk or ride out on the field. In this, the whole population of Maracay was forced to submit to his whimsy. As he liked music he had a large military band, which served not only for the beguilement of his idle hours, but also as an alarm clock. At 5 A.M. the band marched through the streets, blaring and booming the national anthem. *El Presidente* arose and so did the rest of the town—whether they liked to or not.

Though now a millionaire many times over, Gómez still followed most of the Spartan habits of his youth. Simple and unostentatious, he abstained from all frivolities and foolish expenditures. Since moving to Maracay he had discarded civilian dress for the uniform. In cut, his everyday khaki jacket was similar to the ones he wore as a *hacendado* back in the Andes. On his shoulders were the gold epaulettes of the *General en Jefe*. High shiny boots, a wide-brimmed Panama on informal occasions, gloves and cane completed his outfit.

The army was his pride and joy. He lived and breathed in a military atmosphere. Officers continually came and went, and he felt more at ease when talking with people if they were of the military. His sons José Vicente and Augusto Alí had high military rank, and "Papa Gómez" purred with pleasure when they visited him in uniform.

It had been Castro's aim to reorganize and modernize the army, but he had always procrastinated. All that he had done was to acquire several 15 mm. guns for coastal defense and construct a building destined for a military school. It remained for Gómez to inaugurate the school in 1911.

From the very beginning there surged serious discord and rivalry between the cadet officers enlisted in this institution and those who had won their rank on the field of battle. The latter officer reasoned that being a seasoned combat officer, he had reached the stage where he had no need for studies or the application of new combat tactics. He regarded the cadet officer, therefore, as being on an inferior plane. The cadet officer, on the other hand, even with only a few months training under the tutelage of first lieutenants, fairly burst his buttons lording it over his untutored confrère, whom he regarded with scorn. Later on, the cadet officers became involved in so many plots of rebellion, Gómez, in self-defense, had to close the school permanently.

From the time of independence until 1900, the manuals of instruction and battle tactics supplied to officers by the Venezuelan Ministry of War were printed in English. From 1900 on they were in French. Colonel López, who in 1915 had been transferred to Caracas, burned a considerable amount of midnight oil reading up on these text-books, and he tried to instill in his subordinates a similar desire for self-advancement.

In his *Páginas para la Historia Militar de Venezuela,* López recalls with bright good humor the occasion he came across an officer of his battalion reading a book while on duty. "What regulations are you reading?" he asked him.

"This isn't a book of regulations, my Colonel, it is a novel," the officer replied.

"Well, sir," remarked López caustically, "when you find yourself facing the enemy or in a tactical task, you will surely have to find the solution to your problems in the memory of some novel instead of a manual which might help you save your honor as an officer and perhaps the lives of the men under you."

Another day, when the second officer in command reported to his colonel that several dozen of his books had been stolen from the officers' library, López said to him, without flicking an eyelash: "Stolen, heh? Well, don't worry about it. I will get you some others. Here, take this." And he handed him a copy of the military work of Captain Bastein.

At mess a couple of days later the officer asked for another book, and López loaned him *The Art of Command.* When he finished it and asked for another, López led him to a storeroom. "Here are your books!" he told him. "I was the one who took them! Now that I think you are cured of reading such trash I will return them to you, provided you will promise to give them to your girl friend!"

In 1916, when Colonel López published a pamphlet entitled *Military Qualities of General Juan Vicente Gómez,* he was an intense and ascetic man of thirty-three. Punctilious to a fault, the umbrella now exemplified more than ever his cautious outlook on life. But while he lived zealously for the present, he kept an eye on the promising future. Hence the pamphlet, which made an instant hit with the *Jefe.* Reviewing the battles of 1901 to 1903 in simple but forceful prose, the budding author emphasized "the courage, character, and firm will of General Gómez, which greatly contributed to the success of his campaigns." However, he was smart enough not to portray the *Jefe* as too great a military genius. Comparing the prowess of Gómez with that of Castro, López depicted the two as being equally aggressive, but credited Gómez with being more attentive to minor details. "Despite his great capacity as a strategist, Castro did not always guess correctly when he lacked precise information regarding the theater of operations. When operating at a distance from the base of operations or in strange territory, the most cleverly thought out campaign can sometimes be doomed to failure through the oversight of one small detail."

It need hardly be mentioned that from then on, young López began to travel in upper social and military echelons. His future was assured. Gómez favored him with the accolade, "Now, there's a man with a good head on his shoulders!" Less than three years later, López, still a colonel, was appointed Director of War.

At the beginning of his administration Gómez had ordered several field pieces as well as a few thousand rifles. He still preferred, however, the antiquated Mauser. It took considerable persuasion on the part of López to convince him that it should be replaced with the modern rifle, which he demonstrated in target practice to be lighter and more accurate.

When Gómez beheld the first airplane to fly over Venezuelan soil in November, 1912, he stood open-mouthed with astonishment. Flying a 60-horse-powered biplane with a wooden fuselage, the French pilot, a Monsieur Bollánd, made an exhibition flight over the Caracas hippodrome, which served as Venezuela's first landing field. When Bollánd jokingly offered to take him up for a bird's-eye view of the capital, Gómez remarked, "I admire your courage, *señor,* but I prefer to keep my feet firmly on the ground." Three months later, Bollánd crashed to his death in a similar exhibition in Port of Spain, Trinidad.

During the following seven years not one airplane flew over Venezuela. In January of 1920, the Italian aviator, Cosme Renella, arrived with an Italian Fiat to make a bid for Venezuela's business. He performed acrobatics for the edification of the dictator, his entourage, and thousands of exicted *Caraqueños* who crowded into the hippodrome. When the Italian showered the crowd with flowers, one of Gómez's aides exclaimed, "Look, General—flowers! Flowers from heaven! How extraordinary!"

To which the General dryly observed, "Yes—but they could just as well have been bombs!"

Quick to perceive in the airplane a strong combat arm which could be very effective for the strafing of revolutionary troops, Gómez immediately set the wheels in motion to add an air arm to his army. He bought the Fiat from the Italian and contracted a French aviator to fly it. From organizational blueprints secured from Argentina, Venezuela's Military Aviation School was created by decree on April 17, 1920. Though the decree stipulated that the school would function under the immediate direction and inspection of the Ministry of War and Marine, it also provided—significantly—that the school would be located in Maracay so that it could be under the supreme command of the commander-in-chief of the army. The sum of 350,000 bolivars was to be assigned for the initial purchase of planes and equipment, and emphasis was to be placed on the training of machine gunners, pilots, and mechanics.

Oddly enough, Gómez never did buy another Italian plane, and it was not until 1938 that the first Italian aeronautical mission arrived in the country. From December 10, 1920 (when the aviation school opened) to 1933, the services of a French mission were employed exclusively, and the planes utilized were the French Farmans, Morannes, Breguets, and Caudrons. The Venezuelan government bought three American Curtis Hawks in 1932 but Gómez was disappointed in them; they could not fly non-stop to San Cristóbal and back as could some of the French planes. It was in 1933 that the French were replaced by the Germans, because Gómez took a fancy to a Fokker amphibian being demonstrated by the German, F. Von Fredemburgh.

It was not until World War II that the United States sent an air fleet and a staff of instructors to Maracay. Until that time, the only American airplane salesman to demonstrate his wares in Venezuela was a John McCook Knox, who represented the North American Aviation Company. Unfortunately, Knox crashed to his death with a Venezuelan officer on a demonstration flight in June, 1938.

There were no dearth, however, of American "good will" ambassadors who flew in by plane during the years when "first flights" were still front-page news. The first of these was Jimmy Angel, adventurer-extraordinary, who first arrived in Venezuela in 1922 after a flight around South America. Then came Charles Lindbergh on his good-will tour in 1928, and again in 1929 when he made a reconnaissance flight with Juan Trippe for Pan American Airways. Then in April, 1931—almost a year to the day when Pan American signed its first contract with the Venezuelan government—Will Rogers landed in Maracaibo during his fourteen-day jaunt over sixteen countries.

As to the regular army, in 1912, a German military mission arrived, which trained and spruced up a few crack regiments. These soldiers learned to do the goose-step and wear spiked helmets, and in time became a reasonable facsimile of a German army. Even the commander-in-chief, resplendent in a magnificent uniform and spiked helmet, his martial mustaches bristling upward as he sat astride his steed in review, bore a startling resemblance to the German Kaiser.

Through the solicitous attentions of von Prolius, the florid German Minister, and the talented officers of the mission, Gómez early became addicted to Germanomania. He set Kaiser Wilhelm up as his ideal of a man and a monarch, figuring, perhaps, that he was but a more highly-polished product out of the same mold as himself. "All that the Kaiser wished for," said Winston Churchill in later years, "was to feel like Napoleon, and be like him without having had to fight his battles . . . If you are the summit of a volcano, the least you can do is to smoke. So he smoked, a pillar of cloud by day and the gleam of fire by night, to all who gazed from afar."

To Venezuela's dictator, the fire and rumble of this mighty volcano was awe-inspiring indeed, and he did not hesitate to say so in admiring terms. When he expressed to von Prolius his high regard and admiration for Kaiser Wilhelm, he soon received from that obliging monarch a flattering letter signed in his own hand. Gómez treasured the letter all the rest of his life, though during the war years he had to keep it out of sight.

When it came, slowly and stealthily, World War I caught Gómez and his country in a profound dilemma. By 1914 Venezuela had a population of 2,500,000. When hostilities broke out, the country's foreign trade, and with it the government and national income, took a sudden dive. Starting in 1912, additional taxes had been imposed to provide extra funds for the dictator's growing military budget. For the fiscal year ending June 30, 1914, expenditures for the Ministry of War and Marine had far exceeded those of any other department. When Gómez was informed that as a direct consequence of the war, government income was dropping sharply below budgeted expenditures, he ordered a drastic curtailment of all government activities. His beloved army was the first to feel the ax. On September 1, barely a month after Germany had invaded France, telegrams were dispatched to all state garrisons ordering a reduction of forces by 25 per cent. The edict was a hard blow to the nation's strutting *caudillos,* and their vociferous protests carried all the way to Maracay itself. Yet the dictator, looking very solemn and austere during these troubled times, firmly stood his ground, and subsequent events proved that he had followed the soundest course.

It was Gómez's publicized theme that Venezuela had no justi-fication to become involved in the international conflict, and he resolutely deflected the internal currents which flowed toward inter-vention. From the beginning, his government made her neutrality plain and maintained it. But great pressure was brought to bear upon him from all sides to enter the war on the side of the Allies—by the foreign ministers, his cabinet and advisors, the public and press, and even the exiles abroad. The latter group made much of the fact that Venezuela had not declared war on Germany, and on that account began active intrigues. The stand taken by the foreign ministers, trained diplomats all, was that the issues involved were clear-cut and righteous, and they expostulated that to help their countries was the moral duty of Venezuela and all the other nations of the world. A mo-ment came when it was feared that several of these nations would break with the Venezuelan government. If that had happened, a revolution-ary movement surely would have broken out in the country, and then what remained of Gómez's whittled-down army would have found itself unable to cope with the forces which its enemies could have mustered.

It was at this juncture that the cabinet and Bustillos met with Gómez, and to a man tried to convince him that Venezuela should renounce her neutrality and declare war on Germany. Under this unsupportable pressure the average man would have succumbed. But not this man of large and warped talents. The precarious situation in which Gómez found himself engulfed was due largely to his own decision, and, buffeted by the fierce winds of public and bureaucratic opinion, he must have found the going hard indeed. Unmoving as the towering, frigid *Pico Bolívar,* this sagacious statesman who ran his government with dash and wisdom remained steadfast in his purpose. His uncanny coolness when faced with the task of stemming, single-handedly, a tidal wave of opposition showed that, whatever else he might be, he was a leader of titanic strength, though his leadership led inexorably to the spilling of blood and the imprisoning of men.

His hands straight at his sides, feet set wide apart like a general on the field of battle, the commander-in-chief faced his learned ministers with invincible determination. His eyes blazing with resolution, he is said to have replied to them: "The attitude which we have taken ac-cords with our rights and our dignity. Fear of the possible dangers which it might produce should not move us to change it . . . and I shall follow that course . . . even at the sacrifice of my life . . . for the concept of national sovereignty is the decisive factor in determining what is best for the country's domestic and international policies."

The *General en Jefe* had spoken; his decision was irrevocable.

A hidebound conservative, a friendly critic would have labeled him. His enemies, however, resorted to the most vicious method of attack—the spreading of malicious rumors. Obviously, it is well nigh impossible—many Venezuelan writers have tried and failed—to sift all the true stories of those war years from the hoary falsehoods. One significant fact, however, stands to the fore, and that is, while the sympathies of the Venezuelan people were strongly with the Allies, and especially with France, sufficient evidence has been uncovered to indicate that Gómez was pro-German.

On February 21, 1916, César Zumeta, Gómez's agent in New York, wrote his chief a long letter calling his attention to various aspects of the neutrality question. In his equally long reply the *Jefe* dispensed his erudite and decisive opinion, stressing "peace," "work," "harmony," and his abhorrence of "brute force," but between the lines could be read his sympathy for Germany.

It was whispered that Gómez had a huge fortune deposited in German banks and that he continued to buy marks even during the early stages of the war. His son Juan Vicente's hatred of France was well known, and it has been said on good authority that in 1915 he broached to his father the idea of establishing a German submarine base on the island of Margarita for the purpose of sinking French steamers. The government's mouthpiece, *El Neuvo Diario,* which had been publishing pro-German propaganda, forthwith proposed that Venezuela cede Margarita to Germany expressly for this purpose.

Although Venezuela had officially declared her neutrality, a German freighter, which had fled from the Dutch Antilles, anchored in a Venezuelan port for several days until Gómez, through the intervention of von Prolius, supplied the vessel with Venezuelan papers.

It was common talk that a Venezuelan vessel took on a cargo of American coal in a Venezuelan port and sailed to fuel armed German merchantmen on the high seas. It was also said that a German submarine lurked in Venezuelan waters alerting von Spee's squadron concerning the Allied men-of-war cruising the seas in search of it.

When the name of Eduardo López, a writer of pro-Allied sentiments, was mentioned to Leonard Borseaux, chargé d'affaires for Belgium in Caracas, as a candidate for the post of honorary consul, Borseaux inquired of the Venezuelan Ministry of Foreign Relations as to his fitness. He was informed that López was considered *persona non grata*. To say that a law-abiding citizen was an unacceptable person in his own country was of course ridiculous.

Under the heading "Sacrifice or Selfishness," Dr. Domínguez Acosta published an editorial in a special edition of *El Fonógrafo* of Caracas, in which he decried the government's neutral stand. He declared that it had been assumed under the pretext of economic reasons and he advocated that Venezuela align herself for idealistic reasons with other Latin American nations.

This editorial was reproduced throughout Venezuela and even abroad. Alarmed, von Prolius and several prominent German merchants protested to Gómez, and the outcome was the closing of *El Fonógrafo* and two other papers, and the imprisoning of their directors. Dr. Acosta died in the Rotunda four years later.

Undaunted by the fate of their colleagues, two other Venezuelan writers, Fermin Huizi and Rafael de la Cova, accepted employment to write for a newspaper founded by the British, French, and Italian colonies in Caracas. Barely had the first issue hit the streets than Gómez ordered the plant closed and all copies of the paper destroyed. Huizi was put into the Rotunda and Cova fled the country.

Summing it all up and discounting the rumors, one still arrives at the conclusion that Gómez's sentiments were pro-German.

In thoughtful, articulate phrases, the *Jefe,* in his paternal wisdom, continued to preach "peace," "work," and "harmony" and the solemn, downtrodden citizens went about their appointed tasks of producing and shipping more coffee, cacao, and cattle.

Flanked by his retinue and his bodyguard Tarazona, "The Well Deserving" often made surprise visits to the farmers in the fields, the site of a new construction project, or perhaps the docks at La Guaira. He now rode in one of the new-fangled automobiles, and his visits were heralded by the screaming sirens of a motorcycle escort. Stepping gingerly out of the leading car he would advance unostentatiously toward a group of surprised workmen. His broad smile never failed to put these lowly folk completely at their ease. Waving an arm expansively he would make neighborly small talk. "How is everything going, *señores?* Ah! *Qué bueno!* I am happy to hear it!" He would poke around for a few minutes, prodding and pointing with his cane, asking a question or two, then he would be gone as quickly as he had come. Even his enemies could not deny that Juan Vicente Gómez had a way with the common people, that his habitual good humor was contagious.

Despite all the grimness of the war years, Gomez still enjoyed a good laugh. In fact, his day was never complete unless he had been told a good joke or an interesting anecdote. During these rides of inspection he would often turn to his friend and physician, Dr. Requena, and say: *"Estoy fastidiado"*—"I'm bored. Tell me a funny story." Many were the times that poor, harassed Requena scurried about trying to replenish his fast dwindling stock of anecdotes.

One morning, a jocose sentence was found splashed in brilliant paint across the front of Miraflores Palace. When he heard about it, the *Jefe* did not find it funny. "He who sits in the presidential chair," it read, referring to Bustillos, "lives across the street. He who rules lives in Maracay!"

Noticeably absent from the streets of the capital during those hectic war years were the vociferous shouts of the university students, their cruel taunts against the government, and their chalked slogans and quips on the walls of public buildings. The university had been closed by presidential decree in 1912. "Those students are nothing but children," Gómez had snorted in disgust. "If they don't want to study, then they will have to work." It was not until July 23, 1923, eleven years later, that the university was permitted to reopen.

Because of the popular enthusiasm for the Allied cause, Gómez was apprehensive that many of the former students might offer their services at the foreign ministries. So he issued an edict forbidding any Venezuelan to enlist under a belligerent's flag. While the order proved effective as far as the nation's citizens within the country were concerned, two Venezuelans caught in Europe when the war broke out were swept into the bloody maelstrom. Ironically, they faced each other in the skies on opposite sides.

One, Camilo Ramirez-Rivas, a Caracas youth who had obtained

a pilot's certificate under the famous Louis Bleriot in 1912, was a first lieutenant in the French Military Academy of Saint Cyr. He enlisted and was assigned to the air corps. Two years later, Carlos Meyer Baldó, the offspring of a German-Venezuelan marriage, took to the skies as a fledgling flyer in one of the squadrons commanded by Baron Manfred von Richthofen, the German "Ace of Aces."

Both Venezuelans emerged from the war wounded and much decorated heroes. Ramirez-Rivas rose to the rank of lieutenant colonel in the French Foreign Legion and was assassinated by a Russian in Fez in 1935. Meyer returned to Venezuela in 1928 and was received by Gómez in Maracay with great ceremony. He served for a short term as an instructor in the Military Aviation School. Later, upon his return from a government-sponsored tour of U.S. military airfields, he was appointed a junior inspector in the Venezuelan army. Shortly after his death in a plane crash in Maracay in November, 1933, his grave was visited by a group of local notables and a delegation which had come all the way from Germany for this express purpose.

Intoned Herr von Birtner, head of the German mission, as he laid a wreath on the grave:

"The German Minister of Aviation, General Hermann Göring, has commissioned me to lay this wreath in token of his affection and friendship on the grave of the Venezuelan and German aviator, Lieutenant Carlos Meyer Baldó, who was, during the World War, his comrade in arms in the famous Richthofen squadron. With profound emotion, because close ties of friendship and blood unite us with the fallen one, I gratefully comply with this mission. I ask you gentlemen to join with me in bowing our heads before him who always complied with his duties as a soldier—who once responded bravely to the defense of his Fatherland, Germany, and who now has died in the service of his Homeland, Venezuela."

There was more to this simple ceremony than what met the eye. Several months before, the new Reichstag had conferred on Chancellor Adolf Hitler and his cabinet unlimited powers. Though the rest of the world was laughing at the rantings of this comic opera corporal, Gómez and his advisors thought they recognized the German goodwill tours and slick diplomatic exchanges for what they really were. Hitler was preparing the ground to bid for Venezuela's oil.

CHAPTER TWENTY-TWO

Prince of the Church

One prevailing fallacy regarding Juan Vicente Gómez is that he was an atheist. All that has been written of this man points to such a conclusion. Certainly, there can be no denying the multitude of facts that substantiate such reasoning: At one time or another he had broken each of the Ten Commandments, had openly flouted the laws and tenets of the Roman Catholic Church. All the entreaties of his women, all the urgings of the clergy could not make him attend mass or accept the sacraments of the confessional, communion, or marriage. He had imprisoned and banished priests; he drove thousands of Venezuelans to death; and throughout his rule of twenty-seven years his henchmen denied the last rites of the Church and the grace of Christian burial to those who were dying in his prisons. The sins of this man were many, and because of them Venezuela has assiduously and systematically expunged his name from all official histories and textbooks.

There was no reformation at the eleventh hour. Even during the last few days of his life, overwhelmed as he must have been with thoughts of life's swift pace and inexorable end, he stubbornly refused all spiritual counsel. He died without the last sacraments and without having atoned for his sins.

Actually, the religious belief of Juan Vicente Gómez, like other dictators before and since, was an incongruous mixture of Christianity and atheism. By spoken and written word he professed his belief in God with such oft-repeated phrases as "God willing," "God knows," or "With the help of God." True, he used these phrases much too often to have them taken seriously. Aware of his deeds, his people assumed he was shamming. It just couldn't be true that Gómez the tyrant believed there was a God. But he did believe.

It was not until late 1921, after he had recovered from a severe attack of uremia, that Gómez began to believe seriously in the Supreme Being. By then he had mellowed into a meditative old bachelor of sixty-four. He did not "get religion" in the sense that he performed religious duties faithfully. He remained always an abstainer from mass and the sacraments, but his intimates and his women and children began to notice an earnest religious feeling about him. He tipped his hat when passing a church, and he made his children do likewise. He treated members of the clergy with the respect that was their due. He reprimanded his children when they failed to attend mass. He himself could not attend, he said in answer to their innocent queries, because of the old battle wound which prevented him from kneeling or from standing for long periods.

In his old age he began to adorn his bare bedroom in the house on Plaza Girardot with religious pictures and images. As his family gave him more and still more (all blessed by the parish priest) his room became cluttered with them. To have seen the room, without knowing who the occupant was, one would have thought that here lived a religious fanatic. Yet though neither a fanatic nor a devout Catholic, Gómez obviously must have spent time in religious contemplation. He could hardly have done otherwise with all those holy images surrounding him. It was only in the morning, when the "Sphinx of La Mulera" was dressed and his door was open, that his servants could catch a glimpse of his inner being. He would take his cane from its nail on the wall by his pillow, tuck it under his arm, take a fresh pair of gloves from a drawer, then perform his daily ritual before stepping out. He would touch one of the images with an ungloved finger, cross himself, then say aloud—no matter who was within ear-shot—"In the name of God there is nothing evil." One phrase which he used often when with intimates was: "Life that God guards, no one can take away. God and my country guard me."

To the men around him, Gómez was an idol. This feeling ran to such extremes that his critics said he was surrounded by sycophants. Many of these men who served Gómez with a blind loyalty are alive today. They have no ax to grind, nothing to gain by admitting that they are still Gomecistas. They knew Gómez intimately, and they say that though he drove men to their death, he did not act from sheer cruelty or lust for power. They gave him the dubious credit of the sincere conviction that what he did served the interests of the country and that he alone interpreted those interests aright. Basically, they say, he was a good fellow, fond of children and animals. And he confessed to an abiding love of God. His children too, all of them, looked to him as a model of everything that is great and noble and virtuous in human life. They worshiped him, and to this day revere his memory.

As to his failure to contract marriage with Dolores Amelia, the woman who was his favorite concubine for twenty-nine years, he felt no shame. Until the very last he bore himself with the aplomb and dignity of one who felt he had fully earned the honor of being called "The Well Deserving." Whether he ever seriously considered marriage we will never know for sure. Dolores Amelia and her children say that he did. His dilemma, he is said to have told them, stemmed from the fact that he possessed two recognized families. To have married Dolores Amelia would have meant injuring the pride and prejudicing the interests of his children by Dionisia Bello. A plausible reason, but knowing the man's idiosyncrasies, it smacks of artifice to maintain his single status to the grave.

In a way, Gómez envisioned himself a Messiah of the twentieth century, marked for special favors and destined to rule over other mortals. But a Messiah should never marry. A man who is dedicated to all cannot be devoted to one. His was the divine right to worship his own God as he saw fit, to set up his own flexible laws in a way that seemed best for Gómez. He practiced a brand of religion all his own which he believed was superior to all others, but because of his *mestizo* blood and early environment, his religion was strongly blended with superstition and mysticism. He had a naïve belief in omens, lucky numbers, charms, and miracles. The figure "24" was of special significance to him. His birthday fell on the 24th, as did that of Simón Bolívar. The Revolution of '99 had started on the 24th. And Castro had left Venezuela on the 24th. He performed uncanny feats of character reading and divination which smacked of the supernatural. The simple-minded *mestizo* element attributed these talents to *brujería,* and in awe-struck admiration they labeled him *brujo.*

Brujería, as it is variously practiced in Venezuela, may either sink to the black depths of medieval sorcery or rise to the semi-respectable heights of modern quackery. Every Venezuelan town and village, from the cold and lofty mountains to the steaming, tropical coast, has its *brujo*—that strange admixture of good and evil, who promises, with hypnotic glance and commanding voice, so much for so little. His is a lucrative profession that he learned from his father, who in turn learned it from his father before him. From his vast storehouse of dubious knowledge he proffers both wise and foolish counsel and prescribes complex and fantastic treatments.[16] From his bulging pouch he dispenses amulets, elixirs, poisons, love-philters and magical remedies—some of the latter possessing truly remarkable curative powers. And all the while he mumbles meaningless incantations to the spirits, exhorting them to perform for his awed and trembling client. Business among the frustrated, the ailing, and the poor is always brisk. If he be denounced and halfheartedly prosecuted under the Law of Vagrancy and Corruption, the *brujo* serves his thirty-days' sentence and moves on nonchalantly to the next village. No amount of preaching and exposure on the part of the Church and state have been able to eradicate the *mestizo*'s ingrown belief in the power of black magic.

Though Gómez was without a doubt strong-willed and shrewd, he could not resist the magnetic attractions of the *brujos*. This cult of outlawed practitioners seemingly possessed rare gifts which transcended the power of ordinary mortals, performed awesome miracles, and communed with the spirits at will. As our *mestizo* peasant from the Andes profoundly believed in the miraculous and supernatural, he covertly countenanced the practice of *brujería* among his people. It has been said that as a young man he experimented with talismans and amulets, but as he rose in eminence and mingled more with devout Catholic intellectuals, he concealed his heathen instincts with Indian cunning. That he received all the promised benefits in bountiful

[16]A typical prescription: "Anoint the affected parts with milk of the quiripii tree while covering the head with the bloody hide of a red male monkey. On the stroke of midnight bathe the head with the blood of a domestic dove, taking a purge of the three salts mixed with the dung of a rabbit of foreign birth — same to be divided into two parts of three spoonfuls each, mixed with anti-phlegmatic elixir. Add to each dose a spoonful of juice of the sugar cane. The above doses are good for two consecutive days. After this, drink one each day in the order given, the contents of three flasks: the first, a potion of golden medal pills; the next, phosphorus wine; and the third, potential wine. During these days drink only boiled water and bathe in hot water."

measure goes without saying, though one wonders how much of his success he attributed to the power of these good-luck charms.

For a number of years and until his death, there hung above his bed in the house on Plaza Girardot a large picture of *La Virgen de Chiquinquirá* flanked by angels. It was of hand-tooled leather of exquisite workmanship, and was set in a massive, carved frame. The robes of *Nuestra Señora* were studded with pearls, emeralds, and semi-precious stones and below her was a crescent fashioned out of *cochano* gold. It was a gift from a priest, and Gómez treasured it highly.

La Virgen de Chiquinquirá, the faithful will have you know, made her miraculous apparition to a poor but devout *mestizo* washerwoman in the city of Maracaibo on November 18, 1749. Legend—and little else—relates that while scouring the shore of Lake Maracaibo for firewood, this washerwoman stumbled on a slab of wood, and she carried it home with her. As the good woman noticed that it bore the faint outlines of a crude painting she scrubbed and dried it and hung it up on a wall in her humble hut. A few days later, while grinding cacao beans in the lean-to which served as a kitchen, she heard the picture knocking against the wall. She paid no attention. The knocks were repeated. Still she paid no attention. When the knocks persisted, the woman, now thoroughly annoyed, decided to investigate. Great was her astonishment to see the weather-beaten piece of wood "illuminated," and where before there had been but faint outlines of a human figure, there now appeared the clear and unmistakable image of the Holy Mother herself. The woman ran to the street shouting, *"Milagro! Milagro!* A miracle has happened!" But the neighbors scoffed at her story and called her crazy. Why, Venezuela had not witnessed a miracle since 1651, when *La Virgen de Coromoto,*[17] with the infant *Cristo* in her arms, had deigned to appear and speak to a *cacique* of the Cospes tribe in a ravine close to the river Tucupido. No, they said, such things were not possible nowadays, for miracles no longer occurred. So the poor but devout washerwoman went to inform her curate, who listened attentively and did not scoff. Deeming it prudent to investigate, the *padre,* sure enough, found the weather-beaten piece of wood giving off an unearthly glow and he admitted that the crudely painted image could be none other than

[17] Now the patroness and protectress of Venezuela.

the Holy Mother. A miracle had been wrought here surely, and the *padre* devoutly made the sign of the Cross.

By now, the faithful and the curious were crowding into the little *casita* of the washerwoman, confirming that which at first they had disbelieved. It was decreed by the *padre* that the *iglesia parroquial* would be a more fitting abode for such a religious trophy, and a procession was formed to escort it there. Candles were lit and the procession started off, but they had gone hardly a block when the two fervent believers who had been granted the honor of carrying it, felt the precious thing suddenly wrenched from their grasp by an unknown force. To their horror, it fell in the dust, and they stooped quickly to retrieve it. The picture remained frozen to the ground as if under a tremendous weight and they could not budge it. Consternation reigned then, until the *padre* said with a trace of sadness in his voice, "Perhaps it may be that *La Virgen* does not wish to go to the *parroquial* but prefers, instead, to go to the Church of San Juan de Dios." So everyone faced in the opposite direction and an attempt was made once more to lift the precious burden. Lo and behold! It permitted itself to be lifted easily and carried off! Great was the rejoicing of the congregation as it wended its way slowly toward the Church of San Juan de Dios, where it arrived without further mishap.

And that is why *Nuestra Señora de Chiquinquirá*, as she has been named, is now the patroness and protectress of the state of Zulia, which observes November 18 as a religious holiday. The *Casita del Milagro* disappeared long ago. A tiny chapel marks the spot now, and that section of the city bears the name of "El Milagro." The church of San Juan de Dios has gone too, but that is because in the eighteenth century the governor of the province, Don Guillermo Tomás de Roa, ordered it replaced with a more imposing edifice at his own expense. Today, the holy picture of *Nuestra Señora de Chiquinquirá* can be seen in its glass-enclosed cubicle in the church which bears her name. For two centuries the lame, the halt, and the blind have prayed there regularly with never ending faith for one more miracle.

One cannot help but wonder if Juan Vicente Gómez truly believed in the miracle. Actually, the authenticity of the story has long been questioned, it being contended that it is based more on legend than on fact. Speaking of the mysteries of the story a few years ago, a priest of a Maracaibo parish said: "We know the date, the place, and the form of the miracle but, unfortunately, we do not know who was the artist of the primitive painting nor the name of the woman who found it." He said he had combed old archives and perused old papers without success. Then he quoted the parable wherein Jesus appeared before Thomas, who had doubted the miracle of the Resurrection, and said to him: "Thomas, because thou hast seen me, thou hast believed; blessed are they that have not seen, and yet have believed."

Though for many years Gómez harbored no strong love for the Church, he was never antagonistic toward it. He felt that the clergy should confine themselves to spiritual and religious matters rather than dabble in secular affairs and meddle in politics. In this, his trend of thought ran along the same lines as those of Guzmán, whose criticism of the Church was so vitriolic and his reforms against it so sweeping and harsh, there remained no further restrictions to impose once Gómez rose to power.

During Venezuela's colonial days, when her churches and convents were built as fortresses and were intended to serve as such, the priests and monks were expected, if necessary, to shoulder a rifle. During the War of Independence and subsequent revolutions, priests often took an active part in the fighting. There is even one case on record of a priest who was awarded the title of general and given command of a regiment. As the clergy grew in numbers and the wealth of the Church increased fabulously with it, it insidiously became an integral part of political control. Alarmed, government administrations sought by genial means to rid themselves of this encroachment in civil affairs, without much success. It fell to Guzmán to initiate a series of reforms which abolished or restricted the powers of the Church once and for always.

When the clergy of Valencia once conspired with the "Blues" against Guzmán, he is said to have remarked: "Those priests are always up to something. Now they have converted the church of Valencia into the general headquarters of the reactionary oligarchy of the West!"

Guzmán made donations to the Church because it was expected of his high position, yet he had a church in Caracas razed so that he could replace it with a theater. The theater was never built. He appropriated another church and converted it into the National Pantheon.

In Caracas, the Church exercised such a rigid control over the burial of the dead, arbitrarily deciding who could or could not be buried in the city cemetery, that Guzmán decreed the establishment of a separate burial ground so that the dead of any denomination could be buried there. Yet woe betide the dead of any faith if the cemetery rent was not paid promptly! As in all Latin American countries, long lists of corpses whose rent has run out are posted yearly at the gates, and unless it is paid by the end of the month the remains are dumped in the boneyard. Even beyond death the poor taxpayer is relentlessly exploited!

In 1872, Guzmán decreed the closing of the seminaries. For many years thereafter, aspirants to the priesthood had to go to seminaries abroad. In 1873, the payment of tithes to the Church was outlawed because they were considered "more than a donation and a voluntary act." To Guzmán, the priest was less often a shepherd than a wolf preying upon his flock. In 1874, tax exemptions for ecclesiastical institutions were discontinued. And in the same year Guzmán signed a decree abolishing all convents and parochial schools "because such institutions were administered under special laws not compatible with the national sovereignty." For years in Venezuela there had been a growing aversion against convents for the reason that insensate parents had their daughters secluded in them against their will as a means of correction or discipline. With the closing of the convents, their properties were confiscated and the nuns were forced to eke out a miserable existence on a scanty pension.

No action had to be taken against other religious orders for the reason that they had been either suppressed by law in 1837 or barred from entry into the country by another law passed in 1850 by President Monagas.

During Guzmán's regime a new civil code was promulgated which ended the legality of the church marriage and established the requirement of a civil ceremony. The code also stipulated that the Church could not perform ceremonies of baptism, marriage, or burial without first complying with the civil formalities, under pain of severe punishment. The civil authorities, thereby, became the guardians of registers covering births, baptisms, marriages, and deaths.

One law specifically prohibited priests from holding public office. And because there were so many dissensions between Guzmán and the prelates of the Church, he laid down the dictum to the Holy See through the Papal Nuncio that future appointments to the Caracas archbishopric and the various bishoprics would be subject to his approval and ratification by congress. This was tantamount to saying that he would select his own nominee, which, in fact, is just what he did, choosing from among the candidates proffered by the Papal Nuncio, the most humble and servile priest.

Thus did the Church, whose undisputed authority for centuries had affected virtually every phase of the life of the faithful, see its jealously guarded prerogatives wrested from its control one by one, and its time-honored rituals and traditions either abolished or reduced in significance and importance. Lest it provoke greater wrath upon its head, the Church had no other recourse than to reconcile itself with modern progress in order to live in peace with the dictatorial regime. The Papal Nuncio was, perforce, required to be a diplomat of sharp intellect and great political talent.

During one period of strained relations with the clergy, Guzmán proposed to congress the creation of a Venezuelan Church, independent of Rome, the priests to be elected by the parishioners, the bishops by the priests, and the archbishop by congress—"thus returning to the primitive church founded by Jesus and his disciples." As to be expected of a Catholic congress, its reception of this bit of radicalism was a cold one. The proposal was unanimously rejected.

As can be seen from the record, Guzmán was forever locked in mortal combat with the Church, but he emerged the victor in that he had taken the last aggressive steps necessary to complete the historic separation of Church and state. When Gómez assumed power, he found no thorny religious problems on his doorstep, no burning issues to provoke heated battles with the Church, because its influence had been relegated to the pulpit and affairs spiritual. The Church had accepted this situation reluctantly but with good grace, and rarely thereafter did a maverick priest dare raise his voice in the political arena.

Guzmán, then, had carried out the necessary reforms; it remained for Gómez merely to see that they were adhered to. The "Hero of

December," however, decided to make some changes of his own. It had been pointed out to him that there was a dearth of priests in the country because the great majority of aspirants to the priesthood could not afford to travel abroad to foreign seminaries. This situation, he admitted, would never do. It was his reasoning that idle minds and undisciplined behavior would breed discontent and incite rebellion. So he permitted the seminaries to reopen. This action, for one thing, would mark him as a good Christian, but what was more important, this astute ruler knew that strong doses of religion would dull the peasant's mind to his miseries. The Church and Gómez had two aims in common—submissiveness of the peasant to authority, and contentment with one's lot.

In the matter of education, Gómez realized that Venezuela's rickety school system was deplorably lacking in other essentials besides school buildings and the tools with which to work. Discipline in the schools was almost unheard of, perhaps because they were manned by young and poorly-trained teachers.[18] In the Central University, especially, rebellion against the professors was commonplace, rowdyism and violence frequent occurrences. Ever since its founding, the university had been a hotbed of intrigue and the source of many of the country's revolutionists. What the Venezuelan youth needed was sterner discipline and a heavy curriculum to keep his mind busy and away from things that would lead him into trouble. Dr. Gris, said to be a product of the Jesuit schools of Colombia, had a solution for this. He suggested that the Jesuits be permitted to open a school in Caracas. Once convinced, Gómez granted the Society of Jesus permission to enter Venezuela.

The subject of Jesuit-controlled schools had been a controversial issue in Venezuela for almost two centuries. In 1733, the governor of the then captaincy-general of Venezuela, Don Sebastián García de la Torre, had made the same proposition to the civic leaders and Catholic hierarchy of Caracas, but the overture had been met with rebuffs on both fronts. The Jesuits were too well known for their intrigue and lust for power. The colonists, particularly, refused to

[18]During the Gómez era, rural classes were taught by eighteen-year-old youths with only six years education. At present, six years of primary and four years of secondary schooling are sufficient to qualify for a teacher's post in a primary school.

permit the sandals of this order to enter their homes or influence their way of life. Was not the good governor aware, they expostulated, that the Jesuits expected all laymen to either bend the knee or bow the head in submission to their higher authority?

It was thirty-four years later that the Spanish monarch, King Charles III, expelled the Jesuits from his dominions, and six years after that that Pope Clement XIV abolished the entire Jesuit Order irrevocably from the Church and the world "for the peace of the Church." The Jesuits had overreached themselves.

In 1814, the pro-Jesuit Pope, Pius VII, re-established the society, and the Jesuits gradually rebuilt their power over the entire Church. Seven years later, Venezuelan independence achieved, the Jesuits began a systematic campaign to establish schools in the republic, but without success. By 1850, the law promulgated by Monagas specifically barred them from entering the country.

Gómez's actions were always sudden and secretive. When he broached his project to congress he rocked it to its heels, but that body had been paralyzed long ago into a state of impotent despair by his long string of successes. Gómez presented such a strong *prima facie* case in this instance, that congress agreed to do his bidding. Yet when he scrawled his signature in a childish hand on the concordat with the Church, the anti-Jesuit elements were not fully convinced. They suspected that *el Presidente* had not the slightest interest in religious contemplation. Why, then, would he, ultraconservative as he was known to be, wish to permit the hated Jesuits to gain a foothold on Venezuelan soil? But the peasant from the Andes, truculent and uneducated though he may have been, was shrewdly visionary enough to know what he was about.

Events did not prove him wrong. When the Jesuits opened their *Colegio San Ignacio* in Caracas in the early 'twenties, and later schools in other cities, Venezuelan society, accepting the inevitable in true Latin style, enrolled their sons without undue prodding. They never have had cause to regret it. In compliance with the terms of the treaty, the Jesuits have continued to confine themselves to their chosen task of teaching the primary and secondary grades, and the net result of their virtual control over the whole life and curriculum of the pupil is a more rational and sedate specimen of Venezuelan manhood.

In contrast with Guzmán's intransigent and intolerant attitude toward the Church, Gómez's policy was not so much one of "live and let live" as one of judicious expediency. Every liberal decree that he signed was conceived as a means to an end, *i.e.,* the stability and prosperity of his government and country, thereby insuring the preservation of his power. By the same token, every severe reform he ruthlessly enforced was undertaken for the same purpose.

In 1920, three years after the Red Revolution, Gómez wrote the following letter in his own hand to Dr. Márques Bustillos, who was still occupying the Presidency:

> *The Worker* of this city (Caracas), of which Sr. Candido de Armas is Editor and Publisher, carries subversive propaganda bearing on the working classes of these times, and in the issue of Friday the 19th of this month published an editorial under the heading "What is Bolshevism," which is the first of a series that in my opinion tends to undermine and corrupt the honorable sentiments of the peaceful and industrious Venezuelan people.
>
> Therefore I deem it expedient to ban said newspaper. As for its Editor, Sr. de Armas, deport him from the territory of the Republic if he be a foreigner; if the contrary, take him prisoner and pass him to the Rotunda. Also, it is expedient that you discreetly make known to the newspapers that they should abstain from printing cable news or press articles referring to Bolshevism, strikes and, in general, everything that could produce expectation and excitation in the popular masses or could channel them through those pernicious currents that are inundating the world with crime and barbarism.
>
> Cordially I salute you.
>
> Your friend
J. V. G.

This man was astute enough to recognize a menace when he saw it, and strong enough to stamp it out.

He vigorously suppressed Communism and labor unions because he realized they fed on the discontent of the have-nots. Their very existence, he maintained, would engender anarchy and lead to the inevitable overthrow of his regime. He called Communism a "plague"

—a favorite word of his to describe any evil which might jeopardize his sovereignty—and he referred to labor unions as "a tool of the devil." It was his concept that progress is poison as well as food and that personal liberty is the most foolish of all human hopes. Yet, despite his spells of extreme harshness, he did not complacently rely on superficial, forced, or patched-up agreements to achieve accord. As in his relations with the Church, he aspired to essential and more lasting harmony. His slogans "Peace," "Work," and "Harmony" were not quoted as idle gestures; they constituted a program that he heartily endorsed and diligently followed, and taken together they spelled prosperity and contentment—of a sort. That is what he strove for in his own peculiar way, not just for himself and his clan, but for the entire nation as well.

One is led to believe, then, that his relations with the Church were, in the main, most cordial. As a matter of course, he continued to exercise the presidential prerogative of appointing the bishops and archbishop. Naturally, the ambitious ones among the clergy curried his favor. They visited him often, showered him with blessings and when he fell ill they said masses in their churches for his health and well-being. Even the Archbishop himself was moved, when the President lay abed seriously ill with uremia during the summer and fall of 1921, to inquire solicitously concerning his condition and to prescribe a homely remedy. He wrote to Gómez's brother-in-law, General Antonio Cárdenas, who maintained a constant vigil at the patient's bedside:

> It grieves me deeply to hear that our beloved President has not shown much improvement since he was stricken with this malady. I have prayed daily to our All-Merciful Father that he may recover quickly.
>
> Years ago when I was but a humble priest stationed in outlying districts where there was no doctor, circumstances often required that I administer to the body as well as the soul of many of my poor parishioners. During the years I came to discover the remarkable curative properties of many of our indigenous medicinal plants and herbs. In ailments such as that suffered by the General, I always obtained positive results with the following treatment.
>
> Upon noting a pain in the bladder—which indisposition

is caused by considerable time having elapsed since the last urination—a hot water bag should be applied to the groin. After a few minutes remove the water bag and rub the groin with an extract of belladonna leaves. At the same time the afflicted one should drink a cup of brew of almond (three or four almonds are sufficient) and sapodilla seeds.

Whether *el Presidente* by-passed his doctors to try the Archbishop's remedy has not been divulged. Credit for saving his life was given to a young doctor, Adolfo Bueno, who was rewarded by the dictator with the appointment as his private secretary.

When Gómez was convalescing in Puerto Cabello, his son José Vicente dispatched telegrams to all state presidents notifying them that "the *Jefe* is out of danger and disposed to continue laboring for the happiness of the homeland." And in the church of Maracay, a *Te Deum* was sung in thanksgiving for the recovered health of the "Hero of peace and work."

From Rome, Pope Benedict XV had dispensed the Papal blessing on the peasant from the Andes, calling him "my favorite son." In 1916, through the intervention of Archbishop Carlo Pietropaoli, Papal Nuncio in Caracas, he had elevated him to a Prince of the Church, awarding him the decoration of Cavalier of the Order of Piana, a nobiliary title which cannot be obtained for little.

When he read of the award in the newspapers, Dr. Luciano Mendible, a lawyer who had been president of Guarico under Castro, wrote a ten-page letter to the Archbishop berating him for his action and denouncing Gómez and his tribe in no uncertain terms. The usual reprisal was not possible in this case because Dr. Mendible had written from Trinidad.

Gómez had no qualms about imprisoning a man of the cloth if he stepped out of line. He always took quick reprisals against any fearless priest who was too outspoken in his pulpit oratory concerning him or his numerous progeny. There was Bishop Salvador Montes de Oca, for example, who spoke against divorce and cited the dictator's son Gonzalo as a shameful example. He was expelled from the country. There was *Padre* Maldonado, of whom it was said that his parish was located in the Rotunda—he spent so much time there Of the four other priests thrown into the Rotunda, three of them died here. All of them suffered equally with the other prisoners the pangs of hunger, the miseries of cold nights and filthy cells, the tortures of the irons. None of them was permitted to say mass, hear confessions, or perform the last rites over the dying.

The first of the four arrested was *Padre* Tomás Monteverde, who went to prison in 1913 for having aided "enemies of the Cause" to flee the country. Eight years later, in thanksgiving for the remarkable recovery of the *Jefe,* he was one of a group granted amnesty. On Christmas Day, 1921, the irons were removed from his emaciated and pain-racked body. He took a bath—the first in eight years—was given a shave and haircut, and was told he could notify his relatives to send him clean clothing. On New Year's eve, still unsteady on his spindly legs, he walked to the street to meet the cheers of the populace. The next day, the customary New Year's Day reception was held in the *Salón Elíptico* of the federal palace. Doctor Márquez Bustillos, the Provisional President, read a speech which stressed the "progress, happiness, and liberty of the Venezuelan citizen" and lauded the program of the "Hero of 1908, who will continue his great work as Rehabilitator." Three months later, *Padre* Monteverde was laid away in his grave.

In 1914, *Padre* Luis Mendoza was arrested for having delivered a sermon against concubinage. He withstood the tortures of the Rotunda for eight years, only to succumb in his cell to a heart attack.

In 1915, *Padre* Evaristo Ramírez was confined to the Rotunda because his brother-in-law was an arch-enemy of the "Cause." Two years later he died in his cell after a sudden seizure. Someone had put arsenic in his coffee.

In 1917, *Padre* Régulo Fránquis was arrested on the beach at La Guaira at the precise moment he was embarking in a small boat to escape to Curacao. On him was found a letter addressed to the Pope, denouncing Gómez as unworthy of Papal honor. Appended to it was a long list of the dictator's crimes. A few months later the corpse of the priest was carried out of the Rotunda. He too had been poisoned with arsenic.

When Gómez's mother lay dying in Macuto in 1916, she called her wayward son to her side to plead for the release of the two priests, Mendoza and Monteverde. "My son," she said to him gravely, "it is the last thing that I ask of you. Let them go. Free the *padres!*"

Clasping and unclasping his hands in anguish, his eyes brimming
with tears, Juan Vicente answered, *"Sí, mamita, sí.* I will release them
right away."

The old lady died and was buried,[19] yet Gómez made no move
to release the priests. When, weeks later, his sister Indalecia re
minded him of his promise, he replied to her candidly, *"Pues mire, no*
I can't let them go. But at least *mamita* died with an illusion!"

Not a pretty record for a true son of the Church. Yet the sub
servient priests and the proud bishops and archbishop continue
to praise and pamper Juan Vicente Gómez and to invoke divin
blessings upon his head. And the Indian *mestizo* who had risen t
such dizzy heights that he could violate the laws of God and ma
with impunity continued unhindered and blessed on his sinful way

By an ironic twist of circumstances, a frequent companion o
Gómez's in his later years was a priest of warped talents—*Padr*
Carlos Borges by name—who liked to plow forbidden ground in th
Lord's vineyard. Like the monk Rasputin, this priest was obsessed b
sex. His second love was liquor. Following his ordainment at the ag
of twenty-six, his unholy conduct alienated him from the Churc
several times, but strange as it may seem, he was never de-frocked
Carlos Borges was a robust and exuberant man of great persona
charm, brilliant eloquence, and exceptional literary talent, which ex
plains, perhaps, why his conduct was condoned by both Gómez an
the local Roman Catholic hierarchy. In 1924, at the age of fifty-seven
he was appointed chaplain of the army at Maracay, a post he hel
until his death eight years later. While he may have been the one sou
note to the army's spit and polish, to the royal household he was th
indispensable jester of sparkling satire and brilliant wit. To boot, h
was a poetic genius of national renown, but like Byron, his pursu
of carnal pleasures often overshadowed the radiance of his works. Sai
one of Venezuela's contemporary poets of him, "He officiated no
only at the altar of Christ, but also at that of Bacchus and Venus—
symbolic enemies of Christianity . . . He was a priest by circum
stances and a man by vocation and nature."

The fourth of nine children, Borges was born in Caracas of piou

[19]As the funeral procession drove along the country road to the Caraca
cemetery, the hearse stirred up such a cloud of dust, Gómez shouted to h
chauffeur: "Get to the front! Let the dust fall on the others!"

and moderately well-to-do parents. So captivated were they by his talents, Carlos had his own way from early boyhood. He naturally gravitated toward law, and while studying at the Central University, spent his spare time writing obscene verse and carrying on torrid love affairs. His early works were publicly burned by the parish priest. It is said Borges became a priest because of unrequited love. The girl's family objected to him and sent the girl to school abroad. Trying to find solace in liquor, Borges became very ill. When he recovered he told his father he had decided to abandon worldly ways and wanted to study for the priesthood. When he left for the seminary, his best friend—who understood him better than anyone else—remonstrated in vain. "Remember, Carlos," he told him, "what you need are not chains but new horizons."

Nevertheless, Borges made good as a theological student, devoting himself wholeheartedly to the service of God. Ordained a priest in 1894, he said his first mass in the *Iglesia de Santa Teresa,* the church of his first communion. Because of his adeptness with the pen he was not assigned to a parish but was set to work writing for *La Religion,* the Caracas Catholic daily. During those first few years of writing, his behavior was almost saintly. Those years, he recalled later, were the happiest of his life. Then one day the *padre* confessed to a friend that he had committed a sacrilege. He had stooped to seduction of a pretty eighteen-year-old nun who had fallen in love with him.

After this fall from grace, Borges' love affairs followed one another without respite. To one of the girls, he proposed marriage. But there was a stipulation; they would have to travel abroad to be married. The girl replied that she preferred to love him as a priest without marriage. And so it continued. After sinking deeper and deeper into sin, Borges suddenly turned repentant, sinking his head in the dust of humility and praying for an impossible salvation. As a last resort he resolved to enter a religious order so that he could isolate himself from the world. He broached the subject to his superiors and they agreed. With another priest he journeyed to the United States, and while lodged at a Dominican monastery both fell ill of a mysterious malady. Only Borges survived, and he took the next boat for Cuba. A year later the wandering shepherd turned up in Mexico.

In 1901, after an absence of two years, *Padre* Borges returned to

Caracas, still the moral bankrupt. Although he managed to regain his position with *La Religion,* he began to write risqué verse for *El Constitucional* under the pseudonym of "Oscar Sutil." Growing bolder, he allowed some of his work to border on the obscene, and this touched off a scandal in the capital. Abashed by all the hubbub, the priest was compelled to declare in *La Religion* that unknown parties were having fun at his expense by signing his name to their work. But *Padre* Borges fooled no one, least of all the Catholic hierarchy. After a stormy session with Monseñor Salvaggioni, the Papal Nuncio, the erring priest was summarily dismissed with no stronger ecclesiastical censure than a stern reprimand.

It was during this period (1904-05) that *Padre* Borges began a warm friendship with Gómez and Cipriano Castro, both men being struck by his winning ways. At President Castro's request the priest officiated for the Church at the inauguration of public works and headed an inspection tour of the country at government expense. To procure some wealth "to throw at the feet of his beloved," Lola Consuelo, also a poet, he talked Castro into appointing him his private secretary. Soon thereafter he was able to present his lady love with a magnificent piano, which inspired him to dedicate a beautiful poem to her. Titled "Your Piano," it began:

> *Desnudo, negro, hermoso, brillante, lo contemplo*
> *en la artística sala como un Dios en su templo.*
> *Sobre menudas islas de cristal en la alfombra*
> *toca la inmuda tierra no más que con su sombra.*
> *Su escultural belleza de curvas femeninas,*
> *la desnudez venusta de sus formas endrinas,*
> *despiertan en mi alma profundas emociones;*
> *y reviviendo simbolos de muertas religiones*
> *el noble confidente de tus veladas finge,*
> *en su silencio augusto, el sueño de una esfinge.*

Wrote the *padre* of his dearly beloved in his *Cartas Liricas*: "From the time I beheld your beautiful eyes, heard your sweet voice and touched your charming hand, I felt that my heart had been infallibly pierced by an incurable love." Borges later declared that his love for Lola Consuelo was the greatest he had ever borne for any woman. To his disappointment there was no consummation of this love because Lola would not permit herself to forget that he was a priest. Yet love him she did. For her the *padre* stood ready to forsake the Church and his family; in fact, because of the continual conflict at home, he was obliged to give up his residence with his mother and sisters (his father had died) and move to a lonely, chilly room.

Borges held a higher regard for Castro than for Gómez. When the latter usurped the power, the priest publicly called him "a traitor," for which he was confined in the Rotunda for two years. What sustained him in prison were Lola's letters, which were smuggled in to him regularly and which clearly manifested her love and concern for him. He also found some consolation in the company of his friend Alfredo Arvelo Lairiva, a poet whose cell was nearby. When he emerged in April, 1912, shortly before his forty-fifth birthday, his beloved was in the final throes of tuberculosis. She died in his arms.

The death of Lola Consuelo transformed Carlos Borges into a humble repentant and he submitted himself to a rigid discipline of prayer and work. Assigned at last to a parish, that of *Sabana Grande,* he requested of the rector that he be delegated the menial task of ringing the church bells early in the morning.

The following year, homage was rendered to the poet-priest at the National Academy of Belle Artes by the reading to an enthralled audience of his poems "Your Piano" and "The Bath." His more notorious but equally brilliant works [20] were discreetly relegated to oblivion.

In 1914, Borges met *Monseñor* Aguedo Felipe Alvarado, Bishop of Barquisimeto, who had just returned from Rome. Although the Bishop knew of the priest's bad reputation, he was so impressed by his magnetism and talent that he offered to guide him along the righteous path. He suggested a transfer to his own diocese, to which the priest agreed. Abiding by an ecclesiastical edict, the penitent went through the mortifying procedure of having published in *La Religion* a public manifestation of his penance. In his declaration he said he had been unfaithful to his sacred vows and vocation, had failed in his duties and obligations as a priest, had completely abandoned himself to a worldly life, causing scandal and irreparable harm to the

---

[20] One of them was "The Confession," wherein a wayward beauty divulges in the confessional her sinful thoughts and sacrilegious love for her Father-confessor.

Church, and that he would go into seclusion for one year as penance. Borges had been very humble; in fact, some who read it thought he had even exaggerated his failings.

Under the watchful eye of the bishop, *Padre* Borges conducted himself with priestly punctilio for the next three years. At last the bishop saw fit to relax his vigilance, happy in the thought that the *Padre* had fully redeemed himself. By now Borges had become rector of the Church of the Immaculate Conception in Barquisimeto, he was preaching in the pulpit with Savonarola-like eloquence, and was composing only religious verse. In a letter to a friend in Caracas he wrote: "I am extremely busy, but am well in health, at peace with my God, and perfectly happy." Then, suddenly, the bishop's complacency was rudely dissipated.

While on a visit to Caracas to see his mother, the priest met a girl. Again it was love at first sight and again the *padre* plummeted from grace to new depths of degradation. The affair dragged on for almost two years until even the pious bishop gave up all hope of salvation for the soul of his capricious charge. In October of 1919 Borges embarked secretly and in layman's garb on a ship for New York, where he was to keep a rendezvous with the girl, who had preceded him. Upon his arrival he learned that she had met another man, had succumbed to his whirlwind courtship and had gone off to live a sedate married life in St. Louis. Embittered, the *padre* sat down in his hotel room and wrote her a tear-jerking letter of some twenty pages. A masterpiece of perfection, it produced the desired effect. The girl rushed back to New York, threw her arms around her lover and with tears in her eyes told him her marriage had been a mistake, that she loved only him. At fifty-two, Carlos Borges was still the dashing Romeo. The couple spent several weeks in the teeming metropolis enjoying their sinful bliss, until the *padre*'s money ran out. A friend had to come to their aid and pay their passage back to Venezuela.

To the country at large, the *padre*'s flamboyant career had long been the subject of delectable gossip. To Maracay, his record was an open book. Ever since his release from prison Borges' writings had been carefully scanned by government censors. Delightful pieces which might divert the *Jefe* were sent to his office to be read to him by Dr. Requena. At some choice tidbit Gómez would chuckle with pleasure and exclaim, *"Aaaaay! Qué hombre!"*—"What a man!"

When the statue of Simón Bolívar which the Venezuelan government was donating to the "sons of Washington" was about ready for unveiling in Central Park, New York, Gómez remembered a eulogy which the *padre* had once written on the Liberator. When he sent word that the government would like to use it for the ceremony, Borges demurred, but after some persuasion by his friends gave in. To President Harding, Secretary of State Hughes, and the dozen or so other dignitaries who were present at the unveiling ceremony on that sparkling spring day in 1921, the oration delivered by the Venezuelan ambassador was positively brilliant. Perhaps it was best that the author's name remained anonymous; to have mentioned it might have ruined everything.

Although the *padre* again had become the humble penitent since his return from his illicit honeymoon, his standing with the Church sank to a new ebb. There was talk that he would be ordered to abandon his ecclesiastical attire, but nothing came of it. Restless at having to reside at his mother's home because his superiors refused to assign him to a parish, Borges finally accepted the position of chaplain of the army at Maracay, which had been offered to him some months previously. Gómez welcomed the opportunity to observe the poet-priest at close hand and he looked forward with eager anticipation to being entertained by him. He was never disappointed.

Once established in Maracay, the new chaplain took to wearing a semi-military and ecclesiastical habit. Within easy reach he carried a revolver—just in case an irate parent of one of his loves should come upon him unawares. He became a heavy drinker and could seldom refuse the proffer of a glass.

In November of 1924 the chaplain approached Gómez for permission to attend the celebration of the first centennial of the battle of Ayacucho to be held in Peru the following month. The dictator denied the request.

"But why?" asked the *padre*. "The invitation comes from President Leguía himself!"

"Mira, Padre," expostulated the great one. "All South America may know of your fame as a poet. No doubt that is why Leguía has invited you. But it would be unwise to let you go . . . Despite your

great talents, *Padre,* you have no will power. Do you hear me? No will power at all. It would be unfortunate if you got involved in a drunken brawl . . . but it would be much worse if you took up with some lady of Peru! No—I forbid you to go!"

By royal command, the priest visited the presidential abode frequently and both Gómez and his entourage were held spellbound by his drollery and flow of sparkling poetry. His talent reached its sublime brilliance when he was inebriated. If Gómez happened to be present on such an occasion, ministers and generals would be kept waiting until the *padre's* ready wit had spent itself.

Once, at the dedication of a new army building, the *padre* was not on hand to give the expected blessing, and some soldiers were dispatched to look for him. They found him in a *botiquin* (a plebeian bar) shaking a reproving finger at some frightened peons. The *padre* had been drinking. "Repent!" he exhorted them, "for the day of judgment is at hand!"

Averse to all haste, he hiccuped his way languidly through the service, to the amusement of the many visitors and the embarrassment of his *Jefe,* who wouldn't talk to him for many days afterward. He had let Gómez down that time but he more than made up for it years later. In 1930, at the observance of the centenary of the death of Simón Bolívar at his birthplace in Caracas, he made a brilliant oration which, like Bolívar's birthplace, has been preserved for posterity.

R. A. Rondón Marquez, Venezuela's famed man of letters, relates an anecdote of Borges' last years. One Sunday morning he came upon the priest as he was leaving Gómez's home in the company of an army officer, a lawyer, a poet, and two ladies. After some chit-chat there arose an indiscreet question which touched on the subject of the confessional. Between seriousness and gallantry, *Padre* Borges replied in his own inimitable way, "I wish there were women confessors so that I could find for myself a beautiful one to whom I would confess every day!"

It was at barroom tables that *Padre* Borges scribbled such lewd masterpieces as "Clericales"—popularly known as "The Detailed Confessions of a Reprobate"—which has long delighted Venezuelan schoolboys. His soul-stirring "La Lampara Eclesiastica," however, is one of the gems of Venezuelan literature. That alone, if nothing else, will win him a niche among his country's literary immortals.

CHAPTER TWENTY-THREE

Exit Brother Juancho

One morning in 1918 a case of the dreaded *gripe español* turned up in La Guaira. Soon other cases were reported—in Caracas, Puerto Cabello, and Maracaibo. Before long an influenza epidemic of huge proportions was ravaging the greater part of the country. The death toll mounted into the hundreds.

At the first outbreak, Gómez shut himself up in his house on the Plaza Girardot. It was there that he received the appalling news that his son Alí (Augusto Alí) had been stricken with the scourge and lay dying. Only twenty-six, Alí was a beloved son, docile and *simpático,* yet his father refused to go and look upon him for fear of contracting the disease. Before the night was out, Alí was dead.

As they lay him away in the family vault in the cemetery of Maracay, the grief of his father was pitiful to behold. One would have thought he had lost an only child. After he had dabbed away his tears he turned, not to Dionisia Bello, the mother, but to his sister Indalecia, and said with deep emotion, "He slept next to me many a night . . . When I go . . . I want to sleep at his side. Remember that, Indalecia."

When another member of the family was stricken with the disease Gómez fled to the sulphur springs at San Juan de Los Morros. Friends hinted to him that if the epidemic was dreadful in the cities, how horrible it must be in the Rotunda where there were no doctors. "The Well Deserving" just looked at them with his heavy-lidded eyes and said nothing. Yet, under cover of darkness, as the cold night air from the hills gripped the dark, damp cells, his friend Dr. Requena took it upon himself to visit the prison. He went from cell to cell

handing out blankets (bed clothing was strictly prohibited), checking
the symptoms of the sick, and distributing medicines that he had
brought from his pharmacy on Plaza Girardot. He had a heart that
one. Perhaps it was because of his medications, or the thick, high walls,
that the Rotunda was spared; not one prisoner came down with the
disease.

Throughout the epidemic, José Vicente, the heir-presumptive, had
been working and sulking on his father's hacienda at Güigüe. Because
of the outrages he had committed in Caracas and the valleys of
Aragua, the moon-faced braggart was undergoing another "period of
correction."

To his father, "Vicentico" was the apple of his eye, but Gómez
steadfastly nourished the fond hope that, given time, his offspring
would bloom into a man. Time and again the doting father had
lavished costly gifts upon his oldest son—a hacienda of his own, a
mansion in the city, another in Maracay; he had given him positions
of trust and responsibility; and always Vicentico—shallow, irresponsible, and overly ambitious—had betrayed that trust. There were
hints, not conclusive by any means, that thirty-year-old Vicentico was
being groomed to succeed his father. Wherever the father went, the
son had followed, always at his elbow, always in uniform. Gradually,
as the son gained self-composure and confidence in meeting the
country's legislators and foreign diplomats, he had begun to affect the
pose and mannerisms of his parent. When he grew a bushy mustache
and took to wearing gloves, the resemblance between the two was
striking.

Those who knew the son intimately and those unfortunates who
had suffered outrages and even tortures at his hands lived in dread
of the day such a succession would become an accomplished fact.
Vicentico was a reckless, ruthless desperado who raced his car through
the streets without brakes, just as he raced through life without
brakes. His father had seen fit to force through his appointment as
Inspector General of the Army, much to the annoyance of Dr. Carlos
Jiménez Rebolledo, the Minister of War and Marine, who couldn't
tolerate misfits, much less a blustering wastrel. On the other hand,
López Contreras, still a colonel, was plodding along as commander of
a regiment of the Maracay garrison.

For several months Vicentico had vastly enjoyed his important position. But he had been tough and abusive to his subordinates, with a temper that even his father had found obnoxious. Exceeding his authority, he had outfitted the gunboat *Zamora* with a torture chamber so that he could wreak sadistic vengeance on his victims on the high seas without fear of their screams being overheard. Those who failed to survive the pleasures of the crown prince were thrown to the sharks. When Vicentico and his squad of henchmen took to snatching petty wrongdoers from the guardhouse and the very streets of the capital, the Minister of War had no other recourse but to report the matter tactfully to the generalissimo. Vicentico was packed off forthwith to the farm.

For his sins Vicentico was properly penitent and rueful, and when trouble brewed in Caracas in January of 1919, he convinced his parent that his services as a trouble-shooter and stern dispenser of justice were indispensable to the Cause.

In the San Carlos barracks the junior officers had hatched a plot to overthrow their command, to arm waiting adherents in the streets, and to seize the other barracks of the capital. The signal to revolt was to be a revolver shot at four o'clock in the morning. Somehow, news of the plot had leaked out. Five hours before the crucial moment, the ringleader, captain of artillery Luis Rafael Pimentel, and a dozen or so other men of the garrison were locked up in the barracks' guardroom. Failing to hear the signal, the smaller fry who had hidden on rooftops and in trees and doorways, vanished into the shadows.

The following afternoon while the roundup of prisoners continued throughout the city, Vicentico's flashy car, followed by two cars of henchmen bristling with machine guns, drew up to the *cuartel* San Carlos. Inspector General of the Army, José Vicente Gómez, was now issuing the orders.

Fourteen selected prisoners, including Captain Pimentel, were herded into cars and taken to the old home of Cipriano Castro. With the overthrow of Castro, *Villa Zoila* had reverted to the nation and was presently being used as a police "guest house." General Colmenares Pacheco, brother-in-law of Gómez and former governor of the federal district, had equipped the mansion with intricate torture devices which raised the calling of the state executioners to a fine art. His crowning achievement had been to make the third degree a ritual of perfection, but his zeal for murder and gum-shoe politics had culminated in his undoing. Vicentico had been his most eager pupil.

In the *Villa Zoila* General Vicentico personally took charge of the proceedings. He and his henchmen took Second Lieutenant Pedro Betancourt Grillet, the youngest prisoner, into one of the rooms and pointed out two ropes which were looped through a pulley in a ceiling beam and tied to a spike in the wall.

"Do you know what that is for?" Vicentico asked him.

"No, General, I don't."

"That's to make you sing, boy . . . unless you tell me now the names of those who were in with you on this plot. What do you say?"

"I don't know anything about the plot, General. I don't know any names."

"Oh, so you won't talk, eh? Well, this will make you talk. Do you know what I'm going to do with you, boy? I'm going to hang you up by your *cojónes* until you sing! You'll sing all right! You'll sing plenty!"

The youth paled. "I don't believe you would dishonor your family by committing a deed like that," he countered.

Vicentico sneered. "So you don't believe me, eh? Well, I'll show you . . . !"

He signaled to his aides. They stripped the victim of his clothes. They put his shirt over his head like a hood, gagging his mouth with the sleeves and tying them behind his head. One rope was tied around him under his arms. The other, a thick strong cord, was looped two or three times around his genitals. Then they raised him a few feet from the floor. Suddenly, without warning, the heavy rope was let loose. Betancourt sank to an oblique position with his head down, his body hanging by his genitals. In that brief instant he reached for the cord, but his index finger, caught in the loop, was severed as if it were a toothpick.

When he regained consciousness, Betancourt was lying on the floor and they were throwing water on him. The pain was excruciating. Above his groans he could hear the voice of Vicentico speaking to him. "How did you like that, boy? Are you going to sing now? . . . or do you want us to string you up again . . . ?"

Betancourt sang.

It was much the same with the others. When a man fainted from the pain, he was lowered to the floor and revived. If he still refused to "sing" what he knew, he was hung up again. Some, like Captain Pimentel, displayed heroic resistance. Pimentel was hung up nine times and still they were unable to wring from him any compromising information. So they put him away in the Libertador prison where he languished in irons for almost eight years. Others lasted for only one hanging. Each man had his limit of endurance. Two of them, Captain Miguel Parra Entrenera and Second Lieutenant José Agustín Badaracco, had their genitals torn from their bodies. When they fell to the floor, leaving their genitals hanging in the knot, they were picked up and dumped in a corner where they bled to death.

Hanging by the testicles was the most barbarous punishment ever inflicted on human beings in Gómez's prisons, but it was also the one that was used the least. The above is the only known instance where this type of torture was applied to such a large number of victims at one time. In his *La Epoca del Terror en el País de Gómez,* Carlos Brandt estimates that in the twenty-seven years of Gómez's rule, this form of torture was used on no more than thirty-six men.

Restored to high favor in the eyes of his father, Vicentico made a pretense of conducting himself as a model officer and a dutiful son. López Contreras recalls that in November, 1920, the generalissimo received in audience the Minister of War, General Vicentico, and himself (López had been appointed Director of War the previous year) to discuss the details of armament and equipment purchases which López had been commissioned to carry out abroad. It was observed that Vicentico's opinion as to how the six million bolivar allotment was to be spent carried as much weight with his father as that of his confrères. Surely the old man must have tried hard to believe that the black sheep had truly reformed and was attending to business.

Juan Vicente Gómez was getting along in years now. He was nearing sixty-three—which is looked upon as a ripe old age in Venezuela. His illness in 1921 struck the Gómez clan as a stark warning. There was no telling but that the next attack might be his last.

Vicentico had begun to lay his plans carefully so that when the moment of decision arrived he would be designated to take over. First of all, he discarded the mistress with whom he had been living openly and took himself a wife—one who would lend him the air of respectability he sorely needed. In 1920 he married Josefina Revenga,

a pretty and ambitious girl of good family. Next, he began to cultivate and align on his side as many partisans in his father's government as possible.

There remained but one fly in Vicentico's ointment—Gómez's
brother, General Juan Crisóstomo Gómez, governor of the federal
district. He was the one towering hurdle in the way to Vicentico's goal.
Vicentico envied him, despised him, hated him. And as far as Uncle
"Juancho" was concerned, the feeling was mutual.

Certainly Juancho, as he was familiarly called, had not the attributes of a ruthless opportunist; he was a simple rustic, plodding,
colorless and circumspect. But he was steady and reliable, and what
was more important, his brother trusted him implicitly. Gómez made
it tacitly understood that should he die suddenly, Juancho would become chieftain of the clan. Vicentico had yet to prove himself.

With the advent of the presidential election in 1922, Gómez
thought the time propitious to solidify the dynasty of his "house." If
Europe had its royal houses, why not have the House of Gómez in
Venezuela? So he had congress create the positions of first and second
vice-presidents of the republic. Then he proceeded to rig the elections.

On June 25 he himself was re-elected for the next seven-year term.
Márques Bustillos was to continue to occupy the presidential chair
provisionally. Juancho was elected First Vice-President, and Vicentico
Second Vice-President. In the event of death or absence of the
President, or other contingency, the First Vice-President would as-
sume power. Following him in the line of succession would come the
Second Vice-President. Thus was assured for the royal house of
Gómez the possession, enjoyment, and fruits of the vast inheritance
of Venezuela. Now that the line of succession had been clearly defined, Juan Vicente Gómez could die tranquilly.

Stunned by the audacity of the man, Venezuela wanted to shout
its disapproval to the whole world, but it dared not. Instead, the
citizenry protested in the only manner they could. They whispered
jokes among themselves. They called the triumvirate the "Unholy
Trinity." Two more daring patriots went into voluntary exile. Shamed
by such flagrant nepotism, José Ignacio Varela resigned his position of
consul in Puerto Rico, and Dr. Santos Dominici flung his appointment as Venezuelan Minister to Washington at the rostrum of the
dictator.

When Vicentico learned of his place in the set-up he was beside himself with rage, but his scheming mother, Dionisia Bello, counseled him to bide his time. Vicentico tried then, through subtle innuendos, to convince his father that Juancho was a blundering dunce. He was unsuccessful because the astute old man saw through his scheme.

When Gómez deigned to make one of his now infrequent visits to her home in Caracas, doña Dionisia—now a frustrated and vindictive woman—could not refrain from broaching the subject. She had always assumed that her son Vicentico would inherit the rights of succession. By what right, she clacked in shrill protest, did Uncle Juancho have preference over the prerogatives which rightfully belonged to Juan Vicente's own son?

Papa Gómez merely bestowed on her his noncommittal smile and told her to shut up.

For months quiet reigned over the country, but it was an ominous quiet, for currents of intrigue were running strong.

Márquez Bustillos continued to act as Gómez's servile figurehead, reporting daily to his *Jefe* by telephone. For lack of any duties to perform as First and Second Vice-Presidents, Juancho Gómez continued to serve as governor of the Federal District, and Vicentico as Inspector General of the Army.

Eustóquio Gómez, reappointed by his cousin to the presidency of Táchira, was still browbeating the Andeans, totally oblivious to the gathering storm in that quarter.

In Caracas, the subservient press was hewing faithfully to the line, printing a steady flow of flattering pieces about "The Well Deserving" and the prosperous state of the homeland. *Padre* Borges had resumed writing for *La Religion*. Undergoing another of his spells of repentance, the priest had disowned all of his obscene poems.

Even Arévalo González, the newspaper publisher, appeared to be minding his own business. Having been refused permission to publish his *El Pregonero* when he was released from prison, he had opened a side-street store. On the strength of his spotless reputation, he was doing a thriving business.

In far off Puerto Rico, a pathetic, unhappy exile puttered around in the garden of his modest cottage. Now old and cantankerous, Cipriano Castro had become the target of pranks of the neighborhood children, the object of curiosity to passing tourists. Only recently he had been arrested for firing his revolver over the heads of his tormentors.

Suddenly, the head of the house of Gómez fell gravely ill. It was another attack of uremia. Consternation reigned then. The two rival factions, one on the side of the son and the other on the side of the brother, jockeyed for position to grasp the power should the old man die. In the government offices of the capital the atmosphere was electric with excitement. Only a spark was needed to light the psychological tinder. Often, unable to tell who was a "Vicentista" or a "Juanchista," ambitious bureaucrats and bristling army brass alike eyed one another with dark suspicion.

One day an aide of General Vicentico's who had once served under López engaged the colonel in an apparently aimless conversation. He was sounding him out to find out just where he stood or would stand at the crucial moment. Vexed at the officer's crude approach, López said sharply, "Speak out, man! Don't beat around the bush! Just what is it you want to know?"

"Well . . . I was just wondering . . . Are you a Vicentista or a Juanchista . . . ?"

"I'm neither!" barked the colonel. "I'm a constitutionalist! . . . and anyone who thinks otherwise is an enemy of the government! You can tell that to whoever sent you!"

Colonel López thought the incident of sufficient importance to report it to Dr. Rebolledo, the Minister of War, a man of upright principles and also a constitutionalist.

"The situation *is* serious," the minister admitted. "It looks as if everyone around here is getting ready to jump at each other's throat. If General Gómez should die now, it is almost a certainty that blood will run in the streets. We must do everything in our power to prevent it. I suggest that you sound out General Alcántara (chief of the Caracas garrisons) and Colonel Sayago (Director of the Military Academy) to see where their sympathies lie. Should they, please God, be on the side of law and order, make sure that they will be prepared to maintain order in the city in case of trouble."

Colonel López carried out his assignment and reported back to the minister. "I have bad news to report, sir," he informed him. "They are in opposite camps. Alcántara is a Juanchista and Sayago is a Vicentista! What a situation!"

Almost the entire army, in fact every branch of the government, was enmeshed in this game of sinister intrigue. Had Gómez died during this restless period, all the hatreds, jealousies, and ambitions of a few petty men would have been unleashed without a doubt into a tempest of dire happenings. Quite possibly, the country would have become engulfed in a bloody civil war. Vicentista would have been pitted against Juanchista, *caudillo* against *caudillo*. And the unfortunate peons, wondering what it was all about, would have been forced to take up arms against their brethren. And for what? All because a depraved and vicious scoundrel lusted for the power and wealth of the dictator's chair.

But Juan Vicente Gómez did not die. Capricious fate ruled otherwise. After "The Well Deserving" had fully recovered, affairs resumed their normal, quiet course. To all appearances the undercurrent of intrigue slackened to an insignificant trickle. However, in the house of Dionisia Bello, a witch's plot was brewing.

Rankled by the injustice dealt her son, it occurred to Dionisia to indulge in a dangerous scheme of her own. Foolish woman that she was, she had confidence in her own mastery over political intrigue and she thought that she could outwit the peasant who had been her lover.

By no means could Dionisia be appraised as a stupid fool. It was said that she was a woman of some accomplishments, a capable conversationalist, and to a marked degree, intelligent. Yet, for all her female cunning, she could not foretell Gómez's reaction to her plan nor foresee the decrees of destiny. Because of one miscalculation in time, Dionisia's clever little comedy became converted into an eerie drama of pathos, tears, and blood which shook the country to its very foundations.

Dionisia's scheme was to make Juancho Gómez appear unworthy in the eyes of his brother so that he would be removed from office in disgrace. To achieve this illusion, nothing seemed simpler than to expose Juancho as the conspirator in a plot to assassinate his brother. With his uncle out of the way, Vicentico, her son, would then logically assume his rightful place in the line of succession.

To carry out her plan, Dionisia had need of an avaricious and brutal man. She found him in Juan Falero, a corporal of a Caracas garrison. In addition to these prime requisites, Falero had three murders to his credit. For money, he was willing to sell his soul. Delighted with her find, Dionisia rehearsed him in his part for eight days. Then with Latin *paciencia* she waited for the next visit of *el Presidente* to Caracas.

Miraflores—*Palacio del Presidente de la República*—at the end of Avenida Oeste, is situated only a few *cuadros* from the foothills of the *Sierra del Avila* and is set back in a narrow garden of palms and shade trees. Its high spacious rooms and shady porticos open on a formal patio with statues, a fountain, and flowerbeds.

In 1923, Juancho Gómez, a bachelor, lived in the palace alone. His retinue of servants—which included cooks, maids, chauffeurs, and gardeners among others—were maintained at government expense. He even had his own barber. When he came to town, Juan Vicente enjoyed these facilities also. Because his visits were always unexpected, his office and bedroom were tidied up daily.

The streets around the tree-shaded plaza in front of the palace were always closed to traffic. Access to the palace could be made only through a complicated process. The sentinels were scrupulously careful. They examined all passes with meticulous thoroughness and eyed strange visitors with suspicion. If *el Presidente* happened to be in residence, double precautions were taken. The soldiers in the corridor, at the gate, and on the street corners would be augmented by *la sagrada*—the sacred ones, the President's honor guard. After 10 P.M. no one could walk the street leading to the palace, and all through the night bands of horsemen would patrol the nearby streets. It would be utterly impossible for a stranger to get into the palace unobserved.

The *Jefe*'s visits were rare in those days. He visited the capital only to inaugurate congress, see his horses run in the Hippodrome (none of his twenty imported horses ever won a race), or enjoy a special performance put on in his honor by a traveling show too large to go to Maracay.

Sometime during the day of Friday, June 27, 1923, the wail of sirens of a motorcycle escort streaking through the streets of the capital heralded the approach of the presidential car. Staring thoughtfully through the bullet-proof transparency of polished windows, *el Presidente* sat back in the deep upholstery of his sleek black Lincoln as it whisked through the cleared streets.

In front of Miraflores the car glided to a noiseless halt. A flurry of attention from the lackeys. Salutes. A rattle of rifles as the soldiers presented arms. Beaming, "The Well Deserving" eased himself out and went inside.

El Presidente de la República was in residence.

What had brought Gómez to the city? To this day no one seems to know. His movements from Friday until early Saturday evening are clouded in mystery. It is known, however, that Gómez spent Saturday evening at the home of Dionisia. What they talked about also remained a secret.

This was the opportunity that Dionisia had been waiting for. How she must have struggled to conceal her tremblings and the pounding of her heart from the discerning gaze of the *Jefe*. Was Juan Vicente returning to Maracay tonight or . . . oh, *el palacio? Bueno.*

That was all she needed to know.

When Gómez returned to Miraflores it was a few minutes past 10:30. He went immediately to his office. At 11:30 Juancho returned from an evening at the theater and retired to his room.

It was not yet midnight when there came a knock on *el Presidente's* door.

"Adelante!"

It was one of the *sagrada*. "Your pardon, your Excellency, but Captain Leon of the palace guard requests an immediate audience."

Gómez frowned. "At this hour?"

"Yes, your Excellency. He says it is a matter of extreme urgency."

"Pues, let him come in."

Captain Leon entered, walked with military briskness to Gómez's desk and saluted smartly. His face was heavy with importance.

"Well?"

"It is not pleasant the news that I bring, my General. I have a man outside who says that he has been paid to kill you!"

Gómez sat unmoved. "Who are they who wish to take my life?"

The officer hesitated. He feared the generalissimo's displeasure. "Speak up!"

"Permit me to bring this man in, my General, so that you may interrogate him yourself," he countered.

Gómez was insistent. "Who is this person who has paid an assassin to kill me?" he repeated.

"This man . . . Corporal Falero . . . tells me that it was General Juancho, First Vice-President of the Republic, who paid him to kill you, your Excellency . . . !"

There was only a slight flicker behind the General's horn-rimmed spectacles. No movement. Not a word of surprise. He sat there immobile, looking straight ahead.

Then . . . *"Pues,* bring the man in."

Captain Leon went out. When he reappeared, it was to usher in the corporal.

Falero was a wiry little man, as brown as polished *caoba.* He stood there confidently, holding his cap in his hand, awaiting the *Jefe's* pleasure.

"Is this true, what you have told Captain Leon here?"

"By all the saints I swear it!"

"When were you supposed to kill me?"

"Tomorrow at one o'clock in the morning."

"Tomorrow, eh?" Gómez drew out his watch. It showed twelve o'clock. "I would have been left with but little time to live!"

Gómez observed Falero closely as he spoke. "How were you going to reach my room through the guard?"

"Miraflores Palace has a secret passageway that runs from the interior rooms to a ravine of the Avila!"

"Eh?" This time the little god did show surprise. Only three persons besides himself knew of the secret passageway. These were his brother Juancho, his son Vicentico, and his woman Dionisia. One of these three persons had revealed the secret to Falero.

Gómez was pensive for a moment. "How much was he going to pay you?"

"He gave me two thousand bolivars—with a promise of ten thousand more when the work was finished. And General Juancho told me that when he took over the presidency—which would be immediately—he would raise me to the rank of captain."

Gómez reached for a letterhead, took a pen from the desk, tested it, and scribbled an order on the treasury for ten thousand bolivars.

"Your first name, Corporal?"

"Juan, my General."

He continued scribbling. "Payable to bearer, Corporal Juan Falero." He signed his name with a flourish and handed the paper to Falero.

"You appear to be a loyal man, Corporal. Are you ready to prove the truth of your accusation?"

"Yes, my General."

"In any way I say?"

"Yes, my General."

"Bueno, pues, if my brother has paid you and given you the means to kill me . . . you are going to do just as he wished . . . at the hour and in the exact way that he told you . . . only . . . *instead of killing me, you are going to kill him!* Our rooms are next to each other. Do you understand . . . ?"

For a fleeting instant Falero's eyes reflected fear. He knew that at this moment his life hung by a slender thread. Then, just as quickly, his old confidence was restored. He answered calmly, *"Está bien,* my General."

The interview was ended. After Falero left, Captain Leon remained closeted with Gómez for several minutes. His parting instructions were: *"I want to find out if my suspicions are correct. Watch Falero. Watch him carefully. You know what to do . . ."*

Because of a miscalculation in time, Captain Leon failed to watch Falero and thus permitted a tragedy to happen. When Falero— referring to the time he was to have killed Gómez—said "Tomorrow at one o'clock in the morning," he meant Sunday morning. When he said this it was already midnight. The "tomorrow" had become "today." Gómez knew this and Leon should have known it also. But Leon did not have his wits about him. When he walked unconcernedly out of Miraflores upon finishing his tour of duty at 6 A.M., he was laboring under the mistaken impression that "tomorrow" meant Monday.

At exactly 7 A.M. a manservant carried a breakfast tray to Juancho's room. What he discovered there caused him to drop the tray and run screaming down the corridor. The First Vice-President of the Republic lay murdered in his bed. He had been stabbed three times, once through the heart. There were no telltale signs to indicate that there had been a struggle.

Within a matter of minutes the palace was in an uproar. The corridors echoed to shouts and the tramp of running feet. Every room, every nook and cranny was searched carefully. They found nothing.

Among the dozens of horror-stricken persons who viewed the body within the first hour were Gómez himself and several members of his family. No one dared to look upon the General for his face was horrible to behold. Time and again he moaned, "My poor brother! My poor brother!" His face was livid with rage and people shied from him.

"*Lo que Gómez sabe, no lo sabe ni Dios*": That what Gómez knows, not even God knows. That is what all of Venezuela said of Gómez while he ruled. And well might it be true. "The Sphinx of La Mulera" was a frigid, unfathomable enigma, a man with an intricate brain, yet seemingly a mortal without a soul.

For reasons known only to himself, Gómez led Venezuela and the world to believe that he had been the target of unknown assassins who had murdered his brother because of some outlandish blunder. To Leon he had said, "*I want to find out if my suspicions are correct.*" Quite obviously, Gómez *el brujo* had doubted Falero's story and in his own cunning way had set a trap for him. Leon had failed to watch the trap. For that he should be punished. Yet, rather than punish just Leon and Falero and admit the failure of his scheme, Gómez, crazed by grief and anger, sought to wreak his vengeance on others.

After special details of the *sagrada* had been dispatched to round up Leon and Falero, Gómez gave implicit orders to General Rafael Velasco, the Caracas chief of police, to "arrest and interrogate every person who possibly could have been implicated in the crime." All suspicious persons, all known enemies of the Cause who lived in the vicinity of Miraflores, were to be picked up and given the same treatment. How Velasco went about interrogating the suspects was to be his own affair, but the *Jefe* would not be satisfied until a full confession was forthcoming!

The first to be marched off to the Rotunda were the household servants and the palace guard. Not even the shift that had gone on duty at 6 A.M. were spared. Captain Isidro Barrientos of the day guard was taken to Gómez's office where he was tortured by Colonel Tarazona, the *Jefe*'s aide. But Barrientos did not confess. The hapless man had nothing to confess. After Tarazona had pommeled him until unconscious with his *verga*, Gómez said, "Take him away. Put him in prison. Don't do anything more to him."

They didn't have to; Barrientos died in the Rotunda.

By eight o'clock the news of Juancho's death already had circulated throughout the capital. By nightfall all Venezuela knew of the crime. Block by block the police dragnet was drawn tightly and relentlessly. To the accompaniment of kicks and blows, bewildered suspects were hauled off to the Rotunda and *Villa Zoila*. Gripped by panic, the citizenry withdrew indoors and closed and bolted its doors.

After the *Jefe* had grown weary of stomping and ranting through the rooms of Miraflores, he picked up his hat and set off on a pressing errand. He had a score to settle with Dionisia Bello. His visit was long. When he left, the servants found Dionisia in tears. That night she told her sons, Vicentico and Gonzalo, that she wished to embark as soon as possible for Europe. Until that time she would not sleep alone in her house. A son or daughter would have to sleep with her.

By sundown that Sunday, more than one hundred and fifty persons—ten of them women—had been crammed into the Rotunda. All through the night the cells of the prison echoed to the screams of the tortured. Residents of the *barrio* adjacent to the Rotunda were kept awake by the beat of drums and the shrill blast of a cornet. It was the *gari gari*, the music that accompanies the *pela*. The whips worked long and hard that night. Sometimes the music lasted more than an hour, other times only fifteen minutes. But always it began again and again until the light of day whitened the city of Caracas.

On Monday a fragment of news from the Rotunda flashed through the streets like wildfire. "They say that two women have been hung up by their breasts . . . how horrible!" Some refused to believe that even in his wrath, "The Well Deserving" would stoop to such brutal extremes.

The official bulletin issued to the press declared that the murderer had left no fingerprints. The Venezuelan Legation in Washington advanced the theory that the plot had been hatched by Venezuelan exiles residing in Cuba and the neighboring islands. Hours later the legation had to rectify this statement. The Venezuelan press screamed that no Venezuelan was capable of committing such a dastardly crime. It could only have been the work of a foreign hand! Congress called the deed "the most horrible crime in the history of the republic."

It was an impressive funeral. The Gómez clan attended en masse, as did the foreign diplomatic corps. Even Vicentico was there, dry-eyed but stern, trying to affect a grief he did not bear. If Gómez noticed the black, somber figure of Dionisia, sobbing quietly, he gave no sign.

El Presidente followed behind the hearse in his sleek limousine. Dr. Requena sat beside him. Staring through the windows with unseeing eyes, the *Jefe* mumbled over and over, "My poor brother!"

At the grave in the Caracas cemetery he shed tears unashamedly. He could never forgive himself for having done what he did. Later, for the benefit of the press and the public, he said with his usual aplomb, "They cannot frighten me with this. I will continue working for the welfare of the country!" He was born *político!*

And what of Leon and Falero? Monday's headlines, screaming "I WILL PUNISH THE CRIMINAL," were beamed directly at the missing culprits. On Monday Falero was picked up in Caracas and summarily liquidated. Of Leon there was not a trace. He had not returned to his home on Sunday, nor reported back to the palace for duty.

The task of capturing Leon was assigned personally by the *Jefe* to Colonel Cayama, a pugnacious underling who thirsted for glory like a Motilone brave. Tall and spare, of Negro and Indian forebears, Cayama was a man of varied talents. Imprisoned for a trivial offense when a raw army recruit, he won renown as a prison informer. For his deftness with the knife he won praise and promotion. Assigned to Gómez's hacienda *El Trompillo* as a lieutenant, he was put in charge of army recruit labor. A hard slave-driver, who often resorted to the whip and stocks as a means of chastisement, he soon won the admiration of the *Jefe*. Decidedly, Cayama might prove very useful. Promoted to the *sagrada,* he advanced, for services rendered, to the rank of colonel in command. As ferocious as a wolf and as devoted as a dog, Cayama had served the *Jefe* faithfully and well.

"Find that man," Gómez had told him. "Find him and punish him. If you don't . . . !"

Cayama knew what the hidden threat implied. He had to find Leon. His very life depended upon it. Night and day he sent out squads of the best police dogs of the *sagrada* and secret police. It became the greatest manhunt in the history of Venezuela.

Questioned by Cayama in the Rotunda, Leon's wife Rosenda

sobbed that she hadn't seen her husband since Saturday. They didn't torture her. Mere carelessness. Or perhaps Indian cunning.

Every road and path from Caracas was watched. The guards at the road *alcabalas* detained every suspicious traveler until he could clearly identify himself. At every port, passengers embarking for abroad had to pass the scrutiny of detectives. The search went on from one end of Venezuela to the other, to the borders of Colombia and to the jungles of British Guiana. Not a trace of the missing Leon could be found.

Cayama was convinced that Leon had not left Caracas. He organized searching parties to comb the city. Spies disguised as travelers, beggars, pedlers, thieves, penetrated into every possible hiding place. The homes of Leon's relatives and even those of his friends were ransacked from top to bottom. All of these unfortunates were taken to the Rotunda and tortured unmercifully, but to no avail. They knew nothing.

Cayama was up against a blank wall. The *Jefe* prodded him with a terse note. "What news of Leon?" Cayama racked his brain for a solution. Rosenda! Perhaps she knew something. So he went to the Rotunda. He resorted to artifice this time. Rosenda's mother had been a mulatto. The girl was still pretty. Cayama made love to her and tried to allay her fears. He was a widower, he told her. His wife had died four years ago leaving him with four children. How many children did she have? One? When they caught Leon, which would surely be soon, she would be left alone in the world. Perhaps they could marry.

He drew a check from his pocket. Look! Five thousand bolivars if she would disclose Leon's hiding place! Well, then, just a clue, one little clue that might lead to his capture. Nothing? Nothing at all . . . ?"

A complete fiasco! No, it couldn't be. Perhaps Rosenda's harrowing experience among the tortured and dying had fogged her brain. *"Mira,* Rosenda," he purred, "I am setting you free. Go home to the little one. Here, take this. Buy what you need. Tomorrow night I will visit you. Just a little social visit, you understand?" He was affable, even jocular in his guile. "Look your prettiest for me, eh?"

Torn between loyalty to her husband and a desire for security and happiness, Rosenda Leon waited in her *casita* with mixed feelings.

From behind the *rejas* of his window, a stooped *anciano* watched a car draw up to Captain Leon's house, discharge a passenger and drive off. It was Colonel Cayama. He straightened his jacket, set his cap at a jaunty angle and knocked. Rosenda admitted him.

The hours ticked by. Traffic thinned. Lights went out. Doors and shutters along the street were shut and barred. Tomorrow was a working day and all good *Caraqueños* retired early. The street was deserted now and almost in total darkness. Why, mused the old one, doesn't the *municipalidad* put in more street lamps?

The *anciano* sat in the dark, watching, waiting. Across the street, the shutters of the Leon house were closed, but chinks of light punctuated the darkness. Then, suddenly, blackness. From the church on the plaza came the sound of a bell pealing off the hour of midnight. The *anciano* sighed and reluctantly closed his shutters.

When Cayama emerged in the early hours of the morning there was a smile of triumph on his face. In the intimacy of her bed, Rosenda had revealed the information he sought. There had been another woman, she had said. No, she didn't know her name. Only her nickname, Tocha. Her husband had been fond of her before their marriage. She was a prostitute now, living perhaps in the *Barrio Caliente*. Rosenda suspected that her husband had been paying this *puta* clandestine visits.

In the poorer section of the capital lay the *Barrio Caliente*, a festering, cancerous growth in the side of the fair city. Putrid and corrupt, reeking of filth, rum, and cheap perfume, it was the haunt of hoodlums, footpads, pimps, and prostitutes. From countless bars presided over by squat Chinese *botiquineros*, jangling strains from decrepit pianolas rent the air. Here and there in their night-blooming glory were crowded gaming tables, groups of drunks making merry with painted women. Through it all flowed a discordant symphony of sounds and odors—the clink of glasses, the fumes of alcohol and *criollo* tobacco, the twang of a *cuatro* rendering a plaintive melody, the odors of sickening perfumes, the babble of strange tongues, the loud guffaws of men, and the shrill laughter of women.

Women, *mujeres de la vida alegre*, lounged in the flattering shadows of open doorways. Every infinite graduation in hue, from the Nordic blonde to the ebony Negress. French, German, Spanish, dusky *criollas*, white *criollas*. All smiled broadly. All beckoned suggestively in a language that was universal.

Around the *Barrio Caliente* Cayama flung a ring of cold steel. Slowly, stealthily, his men closed in. On a corner a Negro bootblack pricked up his ears and looked about him. Preying eyes. Glints of guns. The boy picked up his box and walked casually down a narrow street. One more block and he hurried to a door and knocked. The door creaked partially open to admit the passage of a frightened *criolla* face framed in unkempt hair. It was Tocha.

"*Ya viene la policia!*" the boy whispered.

"*Graçias,* Fiquin." The door closed and the bootblack returned to his vigil.

A murmur of voices, a rustle of garments from within. The door creaked open and Captain Leon stepped out. He was dressed in a cheap, ill-fitting suit and his hand grasped a revolver at his belt. Seven bullets—six for the first six men who opposed him, the last one for himself. That was the way he had decided to die. No tortures for him. Hah! Won't the old *brujo* be disappointed!

He crossed the street, reached the corner. Which way now? It was after eight o'clock. The streets were alive with people. He turned to the right, walked casually behind an old *mestizo,* meanwhile carefully scrutinizing every male figure on both sides of the street. He knew what to look for; the habits and mannerisms of the secret police were familiar to him. For that matter he knew many of these men by sight if not by name. It was well that the sidewalk was narrow and that people had to pass in single file; he had time to search each face before it reached him. Just two steps if need be, and he would be inside a shop or a woman's doorway.

Two-thirds of the way up the block something on the far corner caused him to stop and hug the wall. His back to the wall of a *botiquin,* a tall, well-dressed man was lighting a cigar. A secret service man.

Leon reversed his steps, then stopped in his tracks. Hurrying toward him from the corner he had just turned were two men. Police? Probably so. A second of indecision.

"*Adelante, señor!*" The voice came from the doorway at his very elbow. A *puta,* a fat, faded Pole with watery blue eyes gave him a smile of welcome.

"*Cómo no!*" Leon pushed past her into the small room, drew her in and closed the door.

A single, weak bulb burned in a tattered lamp by the bed. Magazine photographs covered one of the whitewashed walls. Remnants of a gaudy wardrobe hung on nails in a corner. There was a single rear window, shuttered for privacy. A stinking rat hole, but it was a refuge.

Leon stood there, eyeing the door apprehensively. There was something strange about this man. The woman studied his face, recognized the fear-glazed look of the hunted. Then she saw the gun stock protruding from his belt. "Get out of here! I don't want your business!"

She tried to push him toward the door but he held her off. "Quiet!" he hissed. "Just a few minutes and I'll go."

"No! Get out! Get out!" They struggled and he forced her to the bed.

The sound of many running feet in the street. Barked commands. The familiar thump of rifle stocks hitting the pavement. From the rear a clatter of tin cans as clumsy feet picked their way through the dark yard. Cayama was a good police dog. He would not finish the hunt until all the exits had been closed.

The crash of a rifle butt against a shutter. A scream from the frightened Pole. Shots in the night. Cayama's men swarmed through the window and the front door.

The pianolas had ground to a halt. Groups of the curious stood in the street talking in hushed tones, watching as the sullen Leon, his shoulder creased by a bullet, was led away. The body of the Pole, two bullets through her chest, was carted out and dumped into a truck.

The news spread rapidly through the capital—though the next day not one newspaper devoted even a line to the occurrence—that Captain Leon, Captain of the guard of Miraflores on the night of the murder of Juancho Gómez, had been captured in the *Barrio Caliente*. He had used a Polish prostitute as a human shield against Cayama's bullets.

In Maracay that same evening, Gómez smiled wanly as an urgent message was read to him. *"Assignment accomplished . . . Captain Leon captured and confined in the Rotunda . . . Details follow. Cayama."*

The following morning the grim details of the hunt were personally conveyed to Maracay by an officer of the *sagrada,* who found the *Jefe* tense and ill-humored. Tapping his fingers together, Gómez listened to the report in bored silence. At the point where the shooting began, he cut the officer short. "Did he try to commit suicide?"

"Yes, my General, he did, but one of the men grabbed his gun just in time."

"Did he make any admission of his guilt?"

The officer scanned the *mestizo* face but found only unassailable innocence. "No, my General. He denied all complicity in the crime. He said he fled because he knew he would be arrested and put in the Rotunda. By the way—Colonel Cayama plans to . . . ah, question him today. Are there any special instructions, my General?"

"No." Gómez frowned as he raised a hand. "I don't want to hear any more," he said with glacial firmness. "Cayama can conduct the investigation as he sees fit. And tell him that from now on I do not want this subject ever mentioned to me again."

Thus it was that the decision as to whether the unfortunate Leon lived or died was left to a blood-thirsty scoundrel who saw no other alternative but to apply the maximum penalty. Because Leon was subjected to torture to divulge his part in the crime and the names of his supposed accomplices, there is speculation that Cayama may have been apprized of the true facts. In all probability Cayama learned in the torture chamber what had actually happened that night in Miraflores, and he could not have failed to grasp the portentous significance of what he had gleaned. Lest Leon babble his dreadful secret to others, Cayama—so it is said—finished him off with a single shot from his revolver, then casually informed his fellow officers that Leon had died in his cell.

Neither Gómez nor Cayama knew what is known now—that Leon had given a full account of the night's happenings to Tocha, the prostitute, who in turn later confided in Fiquin the bootblack. It is due solely to the tireless probings of Gerardo Gallegos, a Caracas newspaper reporter, that the astounding story of how and why Juancho Gómez died has been pieced together.

As can be imagined, Dionisia Bello's fall into disfavor was hard and swift. Because she had mothered seven of the dictator's children and because he abhorred inflicting physical punishment on women, Gómez took no drastic reprisals against her. He merely banished her from his sight, and probably from Venezuela as well, for Dionisia was packed off to France. There she settled down in the spectral halls of a massive château to drink the bitter tea of a lonely old age.

As for the now bewildered Vicentico, he still dreamed of becoming the hereditary ruler of the Gómez empire, but tribulations began to assail him. Ironically enough, it was because of the strange quirk of circumstances that had caused Juancho's death that the unwitting Vicentico was depicted by all and sundry as the arch villain of the plot. "He did it who would profit by it," runs an old Roman axiom. Certainly, reasoned the man in the street, no one but Vicentico could have profited so much by his uncle's death. It followed that Vicentico became the object of scorn, the butt of jokes, and the despair of his father, who observed his conduct sink from bad to worse.

For all his pretentious paternalism, the mortified parent found himself inextricably drawn to a painful decision. Toward the end of 1928 he relieved his son of his duties as Inspector General of the Army and banished him from Venezuelan soil. Their last meeting together, in the Hotel Jardín in Maracay, was a stormy one, and it ended with Gómez ripping the epaulets from his son's shoulders. Gómez offered his friends and family no reason for his act, but servant gossip revealed that the son was involved in a poison plot against his father's life.

Vicentico took the verdict philosophically enough. "Well, I've made my millions," he bragged to a friend, "so now I might as well spend them! I think I'll go to Paris."

It was in Switzerland that Vicentico died in 1930, two months before his forty-second birthday. From tuberculosis, said his family. But rumor had it that Vicentico had been poisoned.

CHAPTER TWENTY-FOUR

Black Gold

In the boom town of Cabimas in the western oil fields, the passing of Juancho Gómez had been shrugged off as an insignificant loss. May the devil take him and the entire Gómez family as well! Under the blazing sun grim peons spat in the dust with vehemence. What had Juancho, or his exalted brother for that matter, ever done for Cabimas? Nothing. No concern, no compassion had they shown for the miserable wretches who lived amid the surrounding scrub and cacti in the same squalor and medieval darkness as had their primitive forebears. Even the town itself, in 1923, was still languishing in the eighteenth century. What its people had long begged for were schools, a hospital, paved streets, lighting, sewer and water systems. And what did the town receive out of the great benevolence of the dictator's heart? A bronze bust! Like other forsaken towns and villages, it got a bronze bust of Juancho Gómez to put in the place of honor in its dusty, thirsty plaza. It was to serve as a constant reminder that the "Martyr of the Rehabilitation" had been no ordinary mortal, that he had belonged to a family of super beings whose preoccupations transcended all earthly problems. This paltry gift for a backward, forsaken town whose brawn and sweat and subsoil riches were contributing more to the nation's wealth than all the other towns and cities combined.

In the counting house of the capital, cattle and coffee, once mighty symbols of Venezuela's wealth, were fast receding in importance. Petroleum was king, and it was gushing forth in Zulia in endless rivers of black gold.

It was due solely to petroleum, her greatest natural resource, that Venezuela emerged during the twentieth century as a solvent and

progressive nation. For four centuries the land of Bolívar had struggled through wars and poverty and had lived from hand to mouth. In
1908, when Gómez took upon his shoulders the burden of a whole
century of debts incurred by former governments, no one in Venezuela, least of all the dictator himself, envisaged petroleum as the
new life-blood of the republic. No one could foresee that it would
transform a backward, poverty-stricken land into a prosperous and
healthy nation. It is through petroleum, and through petroleum alone,
that Gómez will earn his niche in history, for without it he could
never have paid off the mountain of external and internal debts and
placed his country on a firm financial footing. Indeed, the saga of
Venezuela's greatest industry is so fabulously impressive, it could
well warrant a volume to itself. It is a story through which weave
swashbuckling adventurers; pioneers from towns like Houston, Tulsa,
London, and The Hague; diplomats and lawyers; titans of industry;
and hostile Indians who lurked in the virgin jungle.

The discovery of petroleum in Venezuela dates back to the time
of the Spanish *conquistadores,* who made special mention of it in their
records. Gonzalo de Oviedo y Valdes (1478-1550) recorded the
peculiar oil stains in the sea off the north coast of Venezuela and oil
seeps in the Lake Maracaibo region. During the early days of exploration some historians called the black viscous liquid "stercus
demonis," (devil's dung), while others referred to it as "petrolio"
and "asfalto." Oviedo y Valdes mentioned that the oil recovered from
the seepages in Venezuela was used by the natives for many purposes,
including cures for various sicknesses. He also reported that it was
being shipped to Spain for medicinal purposes, as it was particularly
beneficial for rheumatism and similar illnesses. This was probably the
first authentic record of petroleum from the western hemisphere being shipped across the Atlantic.

This mention of petroleum, however, did not imply that it was a
discovery known only to the New World. Natural occurrences of
petroleum and asphalt have been known at various places in the
Middle East since the dawn of history. It was Herodotus, the Greek
historian, who first described a salt and oil pool that he saw near
Susa, Persia in 450 B.C. This pool may have been the source of the
flaming oil the Persians successfully used to repulse the Indian war
elephants. History records that flaming oil defeated the soldiers of the

Roman general Lucullus when he attacked the city of Samosatis, and that the ancient Greeks once destroyed a Scythian fleet by pouring blazing oil on the sea.

For centuries in Persian temples there burned powerful white flames, gigantic torches, adored by believers as symbols of the God of Fire, Ormuzd. Though these pillars of fire have been extinguished many years, the ruins of these holy places still remain. Toward the end of the nineteenth century they led an engineer, who had made a fortune in Australian gold, on his now famous trek for oil over the barren plains and hills of Persia (Iran). His name was William Knox D'Arcy.

In the Caribbean area, the pre-Colombian peoples found many uses for the natural asphalts in caulking their boats, in rendering water-tight their baskets, and as a general cement. But to the Spanish *conquistadores,* oil was a poor brother indeed to the other subsoil treasures. When Cortez came to Mexico in 1517, he saw *chapopote* on sale in the Aztec markets of Tenotitlan where Montezuma ruled. It was a black, viscous fluid, for which the gold-maddened conqueror could see little use. Even to Olonso de Ojeda, who discovered Venezuela's Lake Maracaibo in 1499, the finding of petroleum was hardly worth the bother of recording. He did note, however, after a couple of minor skirmishes with the Indians, that his victims covered their wounds with the sticky stuff.

It was treasures of gold, silver, and precious stones that lured Cortez to Mexico, Pizarro to Peru, and Raleigh to Venezuela. The legend of El Dorado—the Gilded Man who bathed once a year in a sacred lake [21] into which his tribesmen threw offerings of gold and emeralds—lured the Europeans on through endless jungle. Hardly had the first decade of exploration passed than El Dorado was sought all the way from Panama to Chile, from the Atlantic to the Pacific. By the time Sir Walter Raleigh sailed up the Orinoco the legend had become a myth. It had shifted to the interior of the Guianas where, so it was alleged, there was the marvelous "Golden City" and Lake of Manoa upon whose shores—to quote the imaginative description of Raleigh—were nuggets of pure gold, "the biggnesse of egges." Like Raleigh's adventurous son, thousands left their bones in the

[21] Later proven to be Lake Guatavita, an extinct crater in the mountains of Colombia, not far from the present city of Bogota.

swamps and jungles of South America, and gullible Sir Walter lost his head upon the block because he failed to find the golden city he sought. So firm a hold did this fantastic tale take that, up to the nineteenth century, all maps of Guiana showed the mythical lake and the golden city.

Twice during the sixteenth century expeditions set out from western Venezuela to search for El Dorado. Venezuela, up to that time, had been found barren of any treasure except pearls. Indeed, so worthless was the territory regarded, that when King Charles V got deeply in debt because of indecisive battles, he granted to the commercial house of the Welsers of Augsburg in 1529 an hereditary fief covering the northwest part of Venezuela. Out of it the Welsers were to repay themselves as best they could. It took but six months for Ambrosius Alfinger, the German administrator, to realize that the Welsers had received a bad piece of real estate; there was no gold.

It was in the year 1529 that Alfinger and his band sailed through the Gulf of Venezuela, through an "S" shaped channel into a landlocked sea, and established a colony on the western shore. In a pitched battle with the Indians, his men succeeded in killing the Indian chief, whose name was Mara. The story runs, that on hearing his soldiers shouting "Mara cayo," meaning that Mara had fallen, Alfinger named his colony Maracaibo. Alfinger did not tarry long in the district; he set forth for the will-o'-the-wisp of El Dorado, and lost his life in the jungles of Colombia.

With Alfinger liquidated, George von Speyer was sent to replace him, but the exploitation of the Venezuelan earth progressed no better. Then came Nicholaus Federmann and a vast concourse of colonists. Imbued, too, with thoughts of treasure, Federmann followed in the footsteps of Alfinger, but his sole achievement was the famous ironical junction with Quesada and Belalcazár on the high plateaus of Colombia.

Twice the village of Maracaibo was razed by Indians, and twice it was abandoned, for sustenance for its inhabitants was hard to come by. When it rose again in 1573 under the name of Nueva Zamora, its residents eked out a poor existence raising goats, fishing in the lake, and trading with the Andeans. From the village north to the Goajira Peninsula the soil of this *tierra caliente* was sandy and semi-arid, unfit for any kind of farming. Around the southern fringes of Lake

Maracaibo, stretching almost one hundred and fifty miles away, rich farms and pasture land were gradually hacked out of the jungle, and the tribe of fierce Motilone Indians residing on the western shore was pushed back into the jungle forest.

It was in the seventeenth century that petroleum first figured briefly in Maracaibo's history. The event was a tragic as well as a romantic one, for it coincided with the sacking of the city by Henry Morgan. It was Cartagena farther to the west which offered the greatest prizes to the buccaneers, for this Colombian city was the metropolis of the Spanish Main where the treasures of the New World were gathered for shipment in the annual convoy to Spain. Maracaibo, nevertheless, fell prey to almost as many attacks as her sister city. First had come the French pirate Jean Daniel Nau; next the Englishman, William Jackson; then in 1669, Henry Morgan, whose cutthroats stripped the city as clean as buzzards picking a bone. Morgan tarried so long on his incursions to outlying haciendas that a Spanish naval force found time to block the channel's entrance and issue him an ultimatum to surrender. His reply was a display of resourcefulness and daring that outwitted the proud Spanish admiral. He rigged up a brigantine with dummy pirates, doused and loaded it with petroleum, and sent it sailing with a skeleton crew at the head of his fleet. The brigantine bore down on the Spanish squadron massed in the narrow channel and rammed its very center. What sprang at the waiting Spaniards as timbers splintered against timbers were not shouting pirates wielding flashing cutlasses, but roaring flames which could not be repelled. The brigantine had been converted into an inferno of destruction. Morgan and his entire fleet escaped unscathed with their loot, while the Spanish vessels either sped toward the open sea or lay burning on the beaches.

By 1899, when Castro's revolutionary army was fighting its way across the Andes, Maracaibo had grown to be a busy, if not prosperous, town of some fifty thousand people. As a trading center it was exporting cacao, coffee, animal skins, dividivi, fine woods, heron feathers, and coconut oil. For home consumption its southern haciendas and farms grew corn, sugar, bananas, plantains, cotton, and cattle. Then, as well as now, the region was not self-sustaining, and Maracaibo derived its principal income from import taxes, mainly from flour, lard, butter, rice, and brandy.

Though the city had a trolley line of "Toonerville" proportions by 1884, and its first incandescent lighting system in 1899, it entered the twentieth century without sewer or water systems or even a paved street. During the dry season from December to May, water was a commodity more precious than bread or salt. The lake no longer served as a source of supply of potable water; it had become contaminated by the filth of the city and the gradual encroachment of salt water from the sea. Only Vichy water was served on the tables of the wealthy, while the rest of the population bought their water from mule-drawn carts. Those who could afford it hired ambulant "experts" and their water witches to locate water on their property. As recently as 1939, windmills for pumping water from private wells were as common a sight as telephone poles.

Guzmán had specifically barred the state of Zulia as a recipient of public projects; he bore the Zulianos as little love as he did the clergy. As for the Zulianos, they cursed his name as well as those who followed him in power. Little did they realize that the fantastic wealth in petroleum that lay beneath their adobe huts and colonial mansions, and even beneath the lake itself, could have paved their streets with gold.

Even as late as 1897, petroleum as an exploitable commodity was looked upon with not a little skepticism. Juan Besson, in his *Historia del Estado Zulia,* records that in that year a private company contracted an American water well expert to study Maracaibo's water problem. For three years the Artesian Well Company of Maracaibo had been searching fruitlessly for a large source of potable water. Stockholders, bemoaning the absence of dividends, were clamoring for an explanation. After the expert had gone over the ground and made some test holes, the company's board of directors gathered to hear his verdict.

"Water," he said, "can be obtained, but with a great deal of difficulty. I am sorry to have to inform you that what abounds here under the earth is oil!"

Zulia's greatest wealth, petroleum, was there, but it was regarded with dismay! The expert was sorry to have to impart the bad news that all was oil instead of water! As the machine age had not yet come to Venezuela, this news caused consternation among the stockholders. Work was suspended and the company was dissolved.

But why this passive indifference toward petroleum when it was being sought after in other parts of the world? Though Edison's electric lamp was fast replacing kerosene as an illuminant, the perfection of the internal combustion engine by Gottlieb Daimler had given petroleum a new lease on life. As far back as 1878, when it granted the first petroleum concession, the Venezuelan government had been led to believe that it possessed hydrocarbons in marketable quantities. What it did not possess, however, were the technicians and capital for development and exploitation, and equitable mining laws that would attract capital from abroad. As custodians of the country's subsoil wealth, the ownership of which has always been invested in the nation, the ruling cliques complacently sat back like the proverbial mountain, waiting for Mohammed. It remained for Gómez to dangle the mountain in front of the Prophet. Yet the early mining codes did not deter a small number of native pioneers from attempting to get at least a toehold in the new industry, though most of them lost their savings in the process.

As chronicled by the early explorers and later by historians, Zulia, especially, was noted for its active oil seeps. Eugene H. Plumacher, United States Consul in Maracaibo for many years, made a list of them in a report to Washington in 1880. One seep in particular intrigued him. Called "The Inferno," it spewed forth both petroleum and boiling water, "making a noise like two or three steam engines." Back in 1825, a large seep in the southwestern part of the state gave rise to great hopes. Thinking that the *mene,* as the Indians called the black liquid, was a new, unknown substance, a small group of investors renamed it "Colombian Oil" and shipped samples to the United States, England, and France to find a market. They found no buyers, for their oil was declared "undesirable."

The first and only successful Venezuelan oil company was the Cía Petrolea del Táchira which started operations near the village of Rubio in 1878. Using only rudimentary tools, a few wells were dug to a depth of about sixty feet. A small "teapot" refinery processed as much as fifteen barrels of oil a day. Only kerosene was recovered, however; the more valuable, lighter fractions were burned as there was no market for them. Some of the crude oil was also used locally as a lubricant.

Venezuelan mining legislation on hydrocarbons developed slowly until 1904. Up to that time the right of exploitation was granted only *after* discovery. The man who claimed to be the discoverer had to make a "denouncement" of his find before the public official indicated by law, and he also had to present a bottled sample as proof. This was followed by the preparation of a map, the payment of certain fees, and the observances of other formalities until the federal executive granted the respective title, which was limited to a small lot. Up until 1904, very few concessions were applied for as only claimants who had stumbled upon a seep from which to take a sample, applied for them. By that year, however, all claims and concessions, with the exception of the one at Rubio, had been forfeited because the interested parties either had failed to draw up a map or had reneged on the payment of taxes.

It wasn't long before one disturbing fact became evident. Though oil reservoirs quite logically might exist in other areas where there were no seeps, no one would drill an expensive discovery well without having previous title to the petroleum the well might produce. Castro, therefore, issued a decree in 1904 which stipulated that henceforth the exploitation of hydrocarbons would be a matter for special contracts. No longer was it necessary to present proof of discovery; any one could obtain a concession provided he adhered to the required formalities and paid the necessary taxes.

Covering minerals as well as hydrocarbons, this mining code carried no special provisions regulating the development and exploitation of petroleum. Its articles, moreover, were loosely worded and as loosely interpreted. Gradually, as the ministry of development acquired technical knowledge of the industry, the code was modified year after year, until finally in 1920 the first "Law of Hydrocarbons and Fuel Minerals" was passed.

The first contract granted under the 1904 Code was to Andrés Espina in the same year. It was of twenty-five years duration and covered 1,214 hectares (2,999 acres) of supposedly oil-bearing land in the Perijá and Maracaibo districts of Zulia. Three years later, fifty-year contracts were granted to four individuals covering a total of four million hectares in the states of Zulia and Falcón.

While the above and all subsequent contracts until 1917 were signed with Venezuelan citizens, four special contracts covering the exploitation of asphalt had been signed with foreign companies. The first foreign group to come into the country were Germans. The name and records of their company are no longer available, but it is known that they worked a small deposit of asphaltic oil near the shore of the Gulf of Paria near Pedernales. By 1900 a narrow gauge railroad five-eighths of a mile long, from the asphalt lake to the gulf, had been built, a refinery had been installed, and asphalt was being shipped. Due to the limited quantity of asphalt and the prevalence of malaria in the surrounding swamps, the workings had to be abandoned. An English company coming into the same region a few years later closed down for similar reasons.

In 1900, the United States & Venezuelan Company obtained from Pedro Guzmán of Maracaibo his rights to the "Inciarte Mine," a small asphalt deposit forty-five miles west of Maracaibo. The largest deposit of its kind in the state, it was merely a surface flow covering fifty-two acres and having a thickness of only a few feet. Starting operations the following year, the company built a refinery and a railroad twenty-six miles long to Carrasquero, a port on the Rio Limón. Packed in bags and barrels, the asphalt was taken down the river in dugouts to San Carlos where it was loaded on larger boats. At the average of eighty tons a day, about one hundred thousand tons of asphalt were shipped over a period of four years. When it was observed in 1905 that the company was operating profitably, the state government found a pretext to seize it. Government management was less successful, however, and operations ceased a year later.

The fourth and most successful venture was by the New York & Bermudez Company with whom the Ministry of Development signed a contract in February, 1909, covering the exploitation of some eleven thousand acres in the northeastern state of Sucre near the village of Guanoco. It is noteworthy to mention that on August 15, 1913, this company (a subsidiary of what is now the Barber Asphalt Company) successfully completed Venezuela's first oil well to be drilled with power tools. Drilled to a total depth of 615 feet, it produced 400 barrels of low gravity oil per day. Although the company continued to drill additional wells during the following seventeen years, its main object was to exploit the world's largest known asphalt deposit. Called the Guanoco asphalt lake, this was a deposit of asphalt two miles long by one mile wide, and one to three meters deep. Lying in the lowlands and swamps between Rio San Juan and the Gulf of Paria, the deposit was the result of the partial evaporation of surface seepages of asphaltic oil. Exploited intermittently by local interests since 1891, 135,569 tons were reported to have been mined by the Venezuelan government between 1904 and 1909.

The Bermudez Company set up a complete asphalt plant, including storage tanks, housing facilities and nine miles of railroad connecting the lake with the shipping terminal on the Guanoco River. Within a short time, asphalt from this lake was being used to pave the streets of New York, Washington, and other American cities. No matter how much asphalt was removed, the lake continued to replenish itself from its underground reservoir.

While the exploitation and export of asphalt was now off to a promising start, for some years that of petroleum had remained at a standstill. The mining code specifically barred the signing of petroleum contracts with foreign powers or with companies in which foreign powers had an interest, but it did not prohibit such contracts with foreign enterprises. Rather, it encouraged them. Yet when Gómez took over the government in December, 1908, not one of the petroleum contracts negotiated in recent years had been activated. The expected exploitation taxes and royalties that would accrue to the government had not materialized. While disconcerting to the dictator, who needed these revenues to bolster his regime and stabilize his country's economy, it was even more so to the contract holder who was obligated to pay an annual surface tax on every hectare of his concession. The feeble efforts of the holders to sell their titles had met with no success.

Just across the border in Colombia, General Barco was having similar difficulty. Granted a promising concession by the Colombian government in 1905, he spent six years trying to find a buyer before it occurred to him that it might be profitable to beard John D. Rockefeller in his own den. Traveling to New York in 1911, the General called at 26 Broadway. Gossip has it that because of his inability to speak English, permission to see Mr. Rockefeller not only was refused him, but he was rather hurriedly ejected from the building by attendants. It was not until several years later that he was able to sell his concession to a group of American promoters.

By 1910 the success of the automobile had created a tremendous demand for gasoline. The navies of the major powers were converting from coal to oil. And in that year, too, the first process for "cracking" oil into its various commercial products was patented. Other events, other discoveries, were to revolutionize the industrial world and cause demand of the black liquid to exceed the supply. With oil fast becoming the most valuable raw material in the world, Clemenceau, at a later date, could say with perfect truth: "A drop of oil is worth a drop of blood."

Yet Venezuela's oil riches still lay untouched. Gómez and the Venezuelan concession holders were perplexed. What had become of the so-called business acumen of the *musiús?* Obviously, the oil titans of the United States and Europe were not interested in South American oil; they were spreading out over other parts of the globe in search of it.

Great Britain, the empire builder, the expert in diplomacy and aggressive salesmanship, was forging her way to the fore in the race for the black liquid. Sir Henri Deterling, a former Dutch bank clerk, had built the Royal Dutch Shell from a lamp-oil concern into a worldwide enterprise that threatened to surpass her strongest rival, Standard Oil. Considered British in spite of its name, Dutch Shell had discovered oil in the Dutch East Indies and in Mesopotamia (Iraq). It had bought control of a French company organized by the Rothschilds to exploit the Baku-Batum oil fields in southern Russia. And it had locked horns with Standard in Mexico. In 1910, its Mexican Eagle Company, through the aid of crafty Porfirio Díaz, who had ruled his country for forty years by granting concessions to foreigners, obtained control of half of Mexico's oil. Following the overthrow of Díaz a few months later, the succession of pistol-toting guerrillas who succeeded him made Venezuela's *caudillo* dictators look tame by comparison.

In 1910, a new British concern, the Anglo-Persian Oil Company, took over the Burmah Oil Company in Persia to exploit D'Arcy's oil concession. Not even Rockefeller knew at the time that fifty-six per cent of its shares were owned by the British Admiralty—the British government itself. The British Admiralty wanted to obtain a steady source of oil for its new oil-burning battleships.

In the Middle East there was a deep-seated hatred against the British. Too, there was smoldering unrest and always the threat of war with the Moslem hatred of Christianity as a potent rallying cry. Arabia, Iraq, Persia brooded fanatically and intrigued dangerously.

If a fanatical war ever broke out in the Middle East, Great Britain would have to look farther away than Arabia and Persia for the fuel to feed the fire-boxes of its navy. With conditions in Mexico just as disquieting, both the Americans and the British turned an apprehensive eye toward Venezuela. At least, while General Gómez remained in power, the country might remain more or less stable. And at fifty-four, the general was in his prime. No need to speculate now what might happen should he die suddenly.

In January, 1912, Dr. Rafael Valladares, a Venezuelan lawyer representing an American group, obtained a contract covering concessions in twelve states of the union and one federal territory. Gómez did not hesitate to grant such a large concession, but he imposed conditions more advantageous for the nation than those of the Castro concessions. The right of the concessionaire to mark out and retain one-half of the parcels of the concessions was limited to two years. In the earlier grants the concessionaire was privileged to make his selections at any time during the long life of the contract, with the result that the remaining parcels which would revert to the nation were not made available for new transactions.

In 1913, Valladares' principals, the Caribbean Petroleum Company, began explorations. By the following year the company had successfully drilled two wells and discovered two oil fields: Totumo, west of Maracaibo at the edge of the Perijá Mountains, and Mene Grande, on the east side of Lake Maracaibo on the present highway from Maracaibo to the Andes. The selection of both drilling locations had been based on the presence of large oil seeps.

The British, meanwhile, had not been inactive. Dutch Shell had bought from General Antonio Aranguren the million hectare concessions in Zulia that he had obtained in 1907. Two companies were set up to exploit these concessions: Venezuelan Oil Concessions, Ltd. and Colon Development Company, Ltd. In 1914 Colon brought in its first well at Rio de Oro in the District of Colon. Situated deep in Motilone Indian country, some one hundred forty miles south of Maracaibo, the Rio de Oro field was never fully developed, due to its remote location and low production.

Straddling the east shore of Lake Maracaibo, V.O.C.'s concession in the district of Bolívar covered an area sixty-nine kilometers long by sixteen kilometers wide. Active oil seeps in the area indicated probable oil beneath the surface and led to the spudding in of the first well in November, 1913. Considerable difficulties arose, however, and the well was not successfully completed until July, 1918. It was not until the V.O.C. brought in a 5,000-barrel-per-day gusher in 1922 that it became aware that it had tapped one of the world's greatest oil provinces.

Dutch Shell was off to such a slow start that for the first few years there were no indications that they would accomplish anything spectacular. On the other hand, the Mene Grande field to the south held by the Caribbean Petroleum Company, looked more promising. Shell's agents were shrewd traders as well as smart diplomats. In 1916 they bought the Caribbean concession from the American owners (Barber Asphalt Company), and in doing so they acquired one of the most prolific oil fields of Venezuela. It has already produced some 350 million barrels of oil and its wells are still pumping strongly.

No one visiting Mene Grande comfortably today, leaving Maracaibo by ferryboat and then driving for three hours on the Palmarejo-to-the-Andes road, can imagine how difficult it was to get there in 1914. It took a full night and a day, riding a launch from Maracaibo to the Motatan River, then another launch up the river, then a burro to the camp site. All materials were transported the same way until the end of 1915, when a pier was constructed at San Lorenzo and a narrow road to the camp was cut out of the jungle. With the successful completion of half a dozen wells, a pipe line, and a refinery of 2,000-barrel capacity at San Lorenzo in 1917, Mene Grande became Venezuela's first producing oil field.

At a cabinet meeting in Maracay in 1917, the Minister of Development reported that an agent for an American company had made an offer for a concession in Zulia. As the conditions asked for would have been less advantageous for the nation than those of the Vallalares contract, the offer had been rejected.

Several weeks after the San Lorenzo refinery went into operation, Gómez, as Venezuela's ruler *de facto*, gave the petroleum industry a thoughtful appraisal. He was not pleased with what he saw. From their entire concessions in twelve states and one federal territory, the Caribbean Petroleum Company had chosen only a relatively small number of parcels, almost all in the single state of Zulia, and had begun drilling in only a few of these fields. Total production for the entire country for the first nine months of the year was less than 100,000 barrels, all of which had been produced in Mene Grande and consumed in local operations. It was evident that if other oil company agents came to Venezuela to solicit concessions, they would offer no better terms than those of the Valladares contract. Perhaps they would demand more, as had been true of the proposition made to the Minister of Development. Yet Gómez could not be swayed from his opinion that the foreign oil companies could be induced to talk business on reasonable terms. Furthermore, he made one thing plain to the cabinet: *The petroleum industry must get going in high gear as quickly as possible; the extra revenues could be put to good use.*

To obtain the results desired, Gómez devised, and President Márquez Bustillos and the Minister of Development put into effect, a plan which was as ingenious as it was practical. Concessions, henceforth, would be given to all who requested them, so that, if possible, the entire surface of the country would be covered. And though the new Petroleum Law of 1920 raised the production tax from ten to fifteen per cent (subsequently reduced by still another Petroleum Law in 1922), it carried one of the most important provisions ever enacted throughout the mining history of the country. It granted to the land owner, for a period of one year, the right to obtain a permit for the exploration of oil and the subsequent right to obtain an exploitation concession over the area covered by his property. This was the first and only time that Venezuelan legislation gave the landowner the exclusive right of exploration and exploitation of oil from his property. This provision of law tended to increase the value of private lands by giving the landowner an opportunity to obtain a concession and then sell it at a profit to an operation company while still maintaining intact his rights over the surface. Moreover, it put the land owner in a strategic position to bargain over rentals for rights-of-way that might be established over his property for the necessary activities of the company.

Of equal importance in this law was the provision which recognized the right of the concessionaire to transfer his concession to third parties, even though these might be foreigners; for the ultimate goal was to have the titleholders succeed in selling them to foreign companies. Gómez was astute enough to realize that sooner or later the landowners would set up a loud clamor for a share of the oil profits. So, while not deviating from his main objective, he devised this way to appease these people at absolutely no cost to the treasury!

During the course of the year 1920, hundreds of landowners throughout the country appeared before the land registry offices to file the required declarations. This resulted in the eventual granting of concessions covering more than eighteen and a half million acres of the country's surface. By 1921, not only the valleys of the coastal and Andean *cordillera* had been covered, but the beds of rivers, Lake Maracaibo, and the sea to a certain distance from shore had been covered as well. And what was gratifying to the country's dictator, the treasury received a considerable return from the sale of stamps and stamped paper used to obtain all these titles.

The next step in this shrewd campaign was to flood the New York and London markets with a vast quantity of these concessions; then the petroleum companies which had not yet decided to enter Venezuela would see that most, if not all, of the most promising regions of the country had been covered, and that consequently there was no longer any hope of obtaining concessions directly from the government. Moreover, as those offered on the market stated clearly the fees to be paid and the formalities to be complied with, the companies would find themselves in the classic dilemma of "take it or leave it." Gómez shrewdly foresaw what the psychological effect would be.

Several of the larger companies bought concessions almost immediately and prepared to enter Venezuela if only as an experiment. It wasn't long before dozens of other companies hastened to follow suit. Once the mad race was on to buy up all the available concessions, a still larger number of companies were formed by stock promoters in get-rich-quick schemes which sought to capitalize on Venezuela's sudden prominence. Waving a concession contract covering acreage that they had never seen, more than one hundred such companies registered in Venezuela as required by law. All of them soon faded out of the picture, though a few were fortunate to be able to resell their concessions.

As for the legitimate enterprises, all was not smooth sailing. The effects of many a shipwreck were felt in many far-off places. As every experienced oil man knows, for every oil company that discovers

an oil field, at least three others fall by the wayside. And though of
late years surer methods for locating oil have been developed, the
finding of an oil field is still three-quarters skill and one-quarter luck.
Due to their limited capital, lack of technical skill, and in some instances worthless concessions, most of the seventy-three oil companies which were established in Venezuela by the end of 1924 were
early doomed to failure. Not more than a dozen are in business today, and of this number the only ones which were really successful
were those which today form the Creole (S.O.N.J.), the Shell Group,
and the Mene Grande Oil Company (Gulf).

While an oil company considers itself lucky if it drills only one
dry hole out of ten, many of the oil companies drilled nothing but
dry holes; it is in the initial stages of exploration drilling that the odds
are greatest against finding oil. Take the Venezuelan Sun, Ltd. as a
sad example. In all, they sank fifteen holes, and every one of them
proved dry. With wildcat drilling costing upwards of a million dollars
a try, some companies folded up after drilling two or three dry
holes. Even for those oil companies which were successful in Venezuela, locating an oil field worth exploiting proved a very expensive
proposition. The Standard Oil Company of Venezuela (Creole), for
example, spent its first three years surveying and studying the geology
of its concessions in eastern Venezuela before spudding in its first well.
Wildcat drilling was initiated in 1924, but it was not until 1928,
after the company had spent more than forty-five million dollars in
exploration work, that its efforts met with success. In that year it
discovered Quiriquire field.

Preliminary to the search for oil was the organization of geologists
and surveyors to make the maps and conduct the geological surveys
necessary to outline structures favorable to drilling. The whole procedure, from the time the exploration concession was applied for,
until oil eventually was pumped into tankers, was a complicated and
long-drawn-out process. There are certain highlights, however, which
merit telling.

The first grant, an exploration concession, did not entitle the concessionaire to exploitation privileges. It merely gave him the exclusive
right for three years to explore the area of his concession (limited to
10,000 hectares), to make geological and geophysical surveys, to
conduct exploratory drilling, and to construct the necessary adjuncts

such as roads, fuel, and water lines, to carry out this work. Before these operations could be started, a right-of-way permit and, later, surface rights had to be secured from the landowner. These in themselves often involved a tedious procedure, as sometimes an intensive investigation had to be made to ascertain the validity of a land title.

Within the three year period of geological exploration the concessionaire had to make a land survey of the concession to accurately locate it on the ground and tie it to a well-known point such as a church or the center of a town plaza. Upon the completion of the exploration work, a topographic map had to be drawn up showing which parcels the concessionaire had decided to retain. Once this map was approved by the Ministry of Development, the parcels retained entered into the stage of exploitation, for which still another concession had to be obtained.

Perhaps the greatest obstacle encountered by the early surveying and exploration parties was the total absence of accurate maps of the country. The old Guayana boundary dispute with Great Britain had shown what could happen when boundaries are not demarcated. Yet neither Zulia nor Falcón, where the greatest portion of the early exploration work was carried on, possessed any scale maps at all. Boundaries were defined by the course of a river, a mountain range or a hypothetical line. The only demarcation markers placed on the ground were at much traversed road points where the soldiery policed interstate traffic. When the British Controlled Oilfields, Ltd. endeavored to establish its concession boundaries, it inadvertently provoked a boundary dispute between Zulia and Falcón that lasted for years. It appears that the Cocuiza River, which appeared on the maps as part of the boundary between the two states, possessed a maze of tributaries. Both states fought each other bitterly in the courts to establish their sovereignty over the disputed land. After old records and maps had been dug up, the B.C.O. still had to go through considerable litigation before the highest court of the land decided the issue.

At the beginning of the exploration for oil, the geology and much of the topography of Venezuela were practically unknown. Only the Andean fringes had been touched by the work carried out by geologists. Gradually, through the work of geologists in the field and in the laboratory, Venezuela's geologic shape became known. Spaced wide apart are three great sedimentary depressions, or basins, which were laid down many millions of years ago when the sea covered the greater part of western Venezuela. The first, the Maracaibo Basin, is situated between two offshoots of the Andean chain of mountains— the Perijá and Trujillo ranges; the second, the Apure Basin, is south of the Andes in the states of Barinas and Apure; and the third, the Maturín Basin in the east, is between the coast range and an ancient land mass called the Guayana shield, which comprises the whole area beyond the Orinoco River. These three great depressions have been intermittently receiving deposits of sands and shales for millenniums. And here, throughout long periods of geologic time, petroleum has been generating and accumulating in great reservoirs.

The Andean mountain system is relatively young, geologically speaking. Several earth movements have elevated these mountains from their original heights (as indicated by several different river terrace levels in the Andean valleys), but erosion has been steadily wearing them down. At one time, a few million years ago, the Venezuelan Andes supported many glaciers. Today only a few "dead" (stationary) glaciers remain, and they are rapidly melting away.

The business of exploring for, or prospecting for, and locating oil was the first step in the long process of producing, refining, and marketing. During the first decade of intensive exploration effort, starting in 1921, surface geology was the only exploration tool existing; the geophysical branches of surface exploration, as well as aerial reconnaissance and photography, were yet to come. As surface seepage was the all-important criterion of oil-bearing territory, exploration work therefore began in the Maracaibo Basin where many seeps were known to exist. Yet a great deal of unrewarding jungle combing had to be carried out, which was not wholly confined to the boundaries of concessions held.

It was up to the early geologists, British, Americans, and Swiss, to decipher the geological history of the country. Traveling over rugged terrain, much of it covered with dense growth, they carried out local stratigraphic and structural mapping. They searched for outcrops, studied the rock strata. They chipped away at rocks and boulders, hunting for the remains of fossils which would reveal something of their age and origin. Theirs was an arduous and often unpleasant task. In a true sense, these men could be classed as pioneers.

Thirty years ago, even fifteen years ago, what could be called roads did not exist in the lake area. Only burro trails led out of Maracaibo, and these were quagmires of mud during the rainy season. Transport of exploration parties was by boat down the lake and up the major rivers, then by burro, and in the swampy and inaccessible areas, by foot.

This was no picture-postcard country. Rather, a varied sort of disenchanting terrain faced the exploration parties: North of Maracaibo were salt and gypsum flats that gave way to great expanses of sand dunes; the periphery of the lake was mangrove swamp which broadened out to scrub and cactus and vast areas of dense jungle; the foothills of the coast range and the Sierra de Perijá were more jungle interspersed with grass-covered savannas; the higher points were rain forests. Each type of terrain presented its own problems and its own particular brand of vicious insect and reptile life.

While transport and terrain presented formidable problems in themselves, there were still others to be reckoned with. Throughout this tropical region disease was rife, and the death rate among the inhabitants was heavy. With dysentery and malaria taking the heaviest toll among the city dwellers, one can imagine the hazards that must have beset the man in the field where malaria swamps and bad water were ever present. It was no wonder that Maracaibo's wealthy spent much of their time in the more salubrious climate of Caracas or the Andes.

From Maracaibo or some other base camp a pair of geologists would set out with several dozen *mestizo* natives, a string of burros, supplies, and equipment. Often it was good-by to civilization for a year at a time. One year of living off the land and eating canned rations. Sometimes pretending that monkey and ant-eating tapir tasted like roast beef. Sometimes running out of water and sucking the moisture of plants.

The chief of a field party was the *jefe* in more ways than one. He had to have the patience of Job and the wisdom of Solomon. In addition to his technical duties he was a combination administrator, bookkeeper, paymaster, supply man, minor mechanic, and practical nurse. He knew how to cook as well as hunt. And he could quickly distinguish a deadly fer-de-lance or rattler from a harmless *ratonera*. Upon him fell the treatment of minor ailments and injuries among his crew, and the responsibility of settling their arguments and allaying their superstitious fears of the unknown. And as if that weren't enough, when the day's work was done and they were gathered around the campfire, he entertained his men with stories and tales of the white men.

Breaking camp at daybreak, these men cut their way through impenetrable, humid jungle, scrambled up and down unshored pits, waded along the beds of streams and rivers, always on the lookout for lurking dangers as well as pay zones. Much of the land they covered had never before been seen by white men. In fact, there is one unexplored area in western Zulia that to this day remains a challenge.

Extending along almost the entire length of the Perijá range and foothills of western Zulia, and south across the Rio de Oro into Colombia, there is a vast tract of forbidding primeval jungle that has never been explored by civilized man. In its deep recesses flourish palms and treeferns, cedar, mahogany, and oak, which hang heavy with lichens, airplants, orchids, and huge python-like masses of lianas. It teems with deer, jaguars, tapirs, and monkeys, raucous parrots and colorful, singing birds. It throbs with palpitating rhythms and it exudes the pungent, death suggesting, yet enticing scent of lush and strange vegetation. Oil men and government agents, farmers and missionaries, have skirted its fringes. Some have traveled across it by plane, but very few men who have ventured into its depths have returned alive. It is a jungle inhabited by the Motilone Indians, the most elusive and fiercest savages known to man, according to anthropologists of the American Museum of Natural History, who spent months attempting to ferret them out to study their culture and language. They not only failed to see a Motilone, but they were nicked by arrows for their trouble. Probably no one has seen these Motilones, certainly no one can describe them, yet they are known to exist there in great numbers. For over three decades oil men have attempted to penetrate this region in search of oil. They have actually gone up its rivers in daring launch forays and have drilled wells on its very edges. In almost every instance each venture has been a costly one; the Motilone shoots a six-foot arrow with deadly accuracy. It is an arrow that can penetrate a steel-mesh jacket that is made to stop a .45 caliber bullet. It is sped on its flight by unseen hands, and it flies to its target when least expected.

No one has tabulated how many oil men have died from Motilone arrows, but it is certain that the number of deaths on both sides of the border have been many. When one Caribbean engineer, heading a field party, was pierced by an arrow, his companions retreated in fright. When an armed searching party found his body hours later, it was minus head and hands and the heart had been cut out. Farmers have been picked off in the fields and even in the doorways of their huts. Not even missionaries have been spared. As in the days of the viceroys, detachments of troops patrol the jungle borders from time to time. Yet, such is the Motilone's craving for salt, he still slips unseen through every barrier, makes off with his loot, and leaves a trail of dead behind him.

Other than that the origin of these aborigines is believed to date back thousands of years, not much more is known of them now than four centuries ago when the Spaniards first charged their jungle stronghold. There are some bows, arrows, loincloths, and aerial photos of their homes. Other than numerous queer footprints, long since erased, there is nothing else. The photographs reveal that the Motilones are not one large integrated tribe, but live in groups in large communal houses set about fifteen miles apart. Set in a clearing planted with corn and yucca, the house is almost all roof, which is round and palm-thatched and slopes down from the center almost to the ground. It is large enough to shelter from fifteen to twenty families.

It was the queer footprints that set the experts to thinking. The big toes were bent almost at right angles to the foot. This furnished the clue as to how the Motilone speeds his arrow with such terrific force. He uses his iron-hard black palm bow like a catapult. Sitting on the ground he braces the ends of the bow between the first two toes of both feet and draws back the arrow and cord with both hands. One Motilone arrow completely pierced a driller working seventy yards inside an electrically charged fence.

There have been tales of cast-off Motilone braves picked up and befriended by missionaries. There have been stories of a Motilone boy picked up many years ago by employees of the Texas Company. It was said he grew up strong and handsome and loved to wear colorful clothes. Where these civilized Motilones are today is anybody's guess. Probably they are figments of someone's imagination. In recent years a group of Capuchin priests with the co-operation of the

Creole Petroleum Corporation have been trying to win over the Motilones with airborne gifts. So far, all attempts to subdue or convert them have been repulsed. The Motilones seem to have only the utmost contempt for the white man's civilization.

From a late start, Venezuela's petroleum industry made rapid strides, and foot by foot, man kept hacking away at the jungle fastness of the Motilones. By the end of 1925, when annual production had risen to over twenty million barrels, the industry was firmly established and growing stronger. However there was more to supplying oil to foreign markets than simply finding the oil. All the thousands of factors involved in producing, refining, transporting, and marketing had to be delicately geared and adjusted.

One of the earliest problems faced by the oil companies in the lake region was transportation through the shallow Maracaibo channel. The shifting sandbars of the lake's outlet to the sea prevented direct entrance by ocean tankers. A depth of eleven feet at high tide was barely sufficient to permit passage of small cargo ships. The companies solved the problem by using shallow-draft tankers to carry their oil to Curacao just off the Venezuelan coast. It was on this barren little deficit island of the Dutch that all of Venezuela's early oil production was refined in Dutch Shell's refineries. It was Henri Deterling's bailiwick. Here Dutch Shell had plenty of cheap skilled labor, low taxes, good relations with the Dutch officials, and a stable government with a future. The setup looked so ideal to Standard Oil that when it was able to set up its own production it dickered for and obtained similar facilities for a refinery on the Dutch island of Aruba.

Many Venezuelans, naturally, resented these arrangements. The Dutch were profiting at their expense. Underhandedly, they accused Gómez of selling Venezuela out to the foreign capitalists. The exploitation contracts, they expostulated, should have stipulated that the oil be refined on Venezuelan soil. But if Gómez was aware of these whisperings, he had nothing to say. Nothing to say, that is, for public consumption. Actually, he had bona-fide reasons for having done what he did, and in private he confided these reasons to his cabinet.

Agitators, he said, were continually infiltrating into the oil camps. Those who were discovered were summarily whisked away to prison, but it appeared there were always others to take their places. It had been reported that there was an undercurrent of restlessness in the laboring element. This had come about just as he had predicted, and it was the reason why he had not countenanced the building of large refineries. It was his reasoning that the massed concentration of thousands of workers in one area would constitute a dangerous threat to his government.

Of course the cunning dictator didn't divulge this fact to the oil companies. On the contrary. He led these companies to believe that he was granting them a special privilege to refine their oil outside of the country, and for this he exacted tribute in the form of additional taxes. Gómez knew more than one way to skin a steer.

It was natural that the dictator would find a way to cut himself and his friends in on a slice of the oil revenues. After all, it had been Castro who initiated him into shady *negocios*. Hadn't Castro forced the closing of the country's cigarette factories so that his own Fabrica Nacional de Cigarrillos could profit from a nation-wide monopoly? The repercussions at the time had been tremendous. At least Gómez had been decent enough to break up the monopoly and restore the free import of tobacco and the right of free enterprise. For this his people had been duly grateful. The national reserves, on the other hand, did not come under this category. They were the property of the nation to do with as he, the federal executive, saw fit.

The most valuable lands in the national reserves became the parcels that had been rejected by the oil companies in accordance with the terms of their contracts. They lay adjacent to the explored parcels that these companies would soon develop and exploit. The government was in no position to traffic in real estate, much less was it prepared to go into the oil business. At least such was the dictator's logic. Following this line of reasoning, what could be simpler than to form a company of patriotic citizens to take these lands off the government's hands for a reasonable figure and put them to good use? So the dictator's friends, those versed in the law and others experienced as smooth land operators, organized the Compañía Venezolana de Petroleo. It was all done legally and above-board. Gomez, Pimentel, and a chosen few subscribed to the bulk of the shares. Then, by a very simple process and through the connivance of subservient officials, this company began buying these parcels for a mere bagatelle and reselling them to the oil companies at a handsome profit.

In the mid nineteen-twenties, a full development of the oil fields began in earnest in several states, but it was in Zulia that activity rose to a feverish pitch. The hiss of steam, the hum of engines, and the roar of bulldozers echoed from deep in the jungle. Vast tracts were cleared, swamps were drained, and piers were built to accommodate the fleets of floating craft and tankers. Buildings and shops sprang up to form new villages and towns which became the hub of networks of new roads to drilling locations. Towering above the surrounding jungle and scrub and extending along the eastern lake shore and into the very lake itself, there sprouted and grew a forest of steel derricks.

The coffers of the state swelled from the added revenue and the multitude of taxes and fines levied on this new industry. Ensconced in the governor's mansion in the Maracaibo suburbs, Gómez's half brother, Santos Matute Gómez, waxed fat and wealthy as an independent sort of chieftain.

CHAPTER TWENTY-FIVE

Oil Boom Towns

In the wake of foreign oil investments in Venezuela, there naturally followed an influx of American oil field workers. The oil industry is a highly technical one, and the amount of skilled labor available from the thousands of applicants who migrated from other regions of the country was practically negligible. As a consequence, the technicians and skilled artisans were brought into the country on contract. Others, from many lands, came of their own accord seeking their fortune. For a decade or more, Americans and other foreigners were employed even for such jobs as clerks, masons, carpenters, welders, and truck drivers. There was no such thing as a labor law restricting the number of foreigners who could be employed, no codes covering housing, minimum pay, medical attention, and accident compensation. Yet the industry's own wage scales were admittedly the highest in the country, if not in all of South America.

Many of the silk-shirted Texans and Oklahomans had drifted down from Tampico following the decline in production of the Mexican oil fields. They had come from a country rich in tales of crime, wealth, and recklessness. Some of the Mexican oil fields in the early nineteen-twenties had been situated in a vast no-man's-land (between the revolutionary and government forces) and the only law and order maintained was at pistol point. Everyone, gringo and Mexican alike, had carried guns, for the Mexicans had shown little hesitation about using them. Gold in Tampico had been so plentiful that throwing gold pieces at the café dancing girls was considered just another amusing pastime.

Maracaibo, a sleepy town of 75,000 inhabitants in 1923, re-

ceived a rude awakening when the first contingents of these wild
bucks descended upon her. To a lesser degree they brought their
shenanigans with them—even to the gold pieces. The guns they had
to leave behind. They piled out of steamers, these tall, fair-skinned
Americans, and they stood upon the docks with their feet apart and
looked at Venezuela's second largest city.

Ninety-three in the shade! They saw a flat congestion of white
buildings brilliant in the tropic sunshine. They saw rutted and pitted
streets, walls stained and cracked, heat waves shimmering over tin
roofs and yard-wide sidewalks. They saw painted Goajira women in
long Mother Hubbards jostled by dirty urchins and old crones hawk-
ing lottery tickets. They saw burros browsing in the garbage of the
market gutters, market stalls and kiosks which swarmed with flies.
They saw unshaven vendors selling *arepas* and sweets, and crippled
and diseased beggars in rags who raised sunken eyes in supplication.
They saw the black caps and faded khaki uniforms of the municipal
police, and dusky *mestizo* females who gave them a flash of gold
teeth.

These were the first things the *musiús* from the north saw in Maracaibo. No glamour of lithesome native beauty and waving palm trees
of the travel posters. It had an air, this city, a gaudy, tropical
indolent air.

Maracaibo, they were told, was almost four hundred years old.
It had given birth to many famous sons of the republic. It had been
the scene of many uprisings against tyranny. It had been sacked time
and again by the buccaneers of the Spanish Main. Proud of its heritage,
Maracaibo now lived on its memories alone. It had no hotel worthy
of the name, no potable water and sewer systems, no refrigeration to
speak of. The men bunked on cots, five and six to a room, and they
paid five dollars a night for the privilege. They drank Vichy water
and lukewarm beer. But mostly beer. And as in Tampico, it wasn't
long before these critical *musiús* came to look upon the dusky females
as luscious blondes.

The coming of the oil men to Lake Maracaibo reacted on the
local population like a shot in the arm. The people awoke from their
deep lethargy and abject poverty to emerge into a bright new era—an
era that gave promise of a chicken for every pot and a pair of shoes
for everyone. Sleepy peons and merchants, accustomed to lengthy

bickering, popped their eyes at *extranjeros* who refused to quibble over a few *centavos*. So profuse became the flow of American gold that payments in Venezuelan currency were generally refused—only silver or American gold was acceptable from Americans. On pay day, therefore, employees were paid off in bags of gold pieces. And by the jingle of their pockets, the merchants heard them coming.

Prices climbed and soared. The United States boom of the late nineteen-twenties was a mild flurry compared with that of the "Roaring Twenties" of Maracaibo. Eggs tripled in price and a fresh cabbage or a can of fruit cost a dollar. One had to pay ten to fifteen dollars for an American hat of low quality, five dollars for a shirt. A fifteen-minute ride in a model "T" Ford cost two dollars.

Avenida Bella Vista, in the northern suburbs, was a wide, treeless avenue—a sand trap in the dry season, a mire of mud in the wet. Set far back from ornamental concrete and picket fences were the century-old *quintas,* or villas, reflecting the opulence of their owners in a profusion of palms, shrubbery and potted plants. They varied from the provincial Spanish to modern in architecture, with some, to humor the owner's whim, borrowing from the Byzantine or Renaissance. It was not unusual to see a Moorish villa next door to a California bungalow. There was even a Norman castle augmented with gray stone towers and battlements whose walls extended around an entire block. It was the common belief that a mark of elegance was achieved by painting the exterior in a variety of colors that would startle the beholder into an exclamation of wonder, if not of admiration; even the tired frames of old Spanish homes were dressed up in hues of violet, tan, and pink.

Viewed singly, some of these quaint old structures may have appeared fascinating to a passing tourist from the north, but appraised with a critical eye, the rotting timbers, falling plaster, and the dank air of decay of a colonial city did not spell progress. What Maracaibo sorely needed was a rejuvenation by a crew of high-pressure real estate promoters. But in that epoch, such harbingers of wealth and suburban face-liftings were a breed unknown to Maracaiberos. The local chamber of commerce functioned exclusively as a protective association for its members, finding it impractical if not impossible to form ties with the civil administration. Political graft and corruption were the order of the day, and the man who profited most was the dictator's half-brother. Santos Matute Gómez made little pretense of carrying out his duties as president of the state; what little work he performed was done in lordly splendor in his private mansion.

Yet, Maracaibo could have been considered a modern and progressive city compared with the oil town of Cabimas. Situated two hours southeast of Maracaibo by launch, Cabimas had once been a quiet little village of small farmers and fishermen. The successful drilling of Well Los Barrosos No. 2 had changed it completely.

On the hot, sultry morning of December 14, 1922, a British crew of the Venezuelan Oil Concessions was drilling Well Los Barrosos No. 2 in the La Rosa field. Dripping with sweat, the crew heard that deep-seated rumble which precedes the first upward rush of oil from its ancient prison. Then suddenly, mud and rocks shot skyward, and a geyser of oil rose to twice the height of the derrick. The most fabulous oil well that Venezuela has ever seen had roared into existence. For nine days it ran wild, spouting one hundred thousand barrels of the churning black liquid a day, before underground sands stopped the flow.

El Chorro—the petroleum fever, the "dance of the millions"—had commenced. Practically overnight Cabimas became transformed into a wild town of frontier conditions. It became a jungle town, not only in fauna and flora, but in the fierce fight for the black gold which attracted prospectors from afar. From Coro and the Andes they came, from the east, the central *llanos* and the remote corners of the earth. Choked with whites, yellows, and blacks, Cabimas became a hodgepodge of races and ambitions, a Babylon of tongues. It became a fantastic, tropical Klondike with all the attendant maladies which had once hit Alaska and also California.

There were the humble whitewashed dwellings, the hovels of wattle-and-daub and flattened out kerosene cans . . . the one-story town hall on the square facing the plaza with its bust of Juancho Gómez . . . the white church with its top-heavy facade of ornate molded cornices . . . the open air *cine,* where Pearl White, Tom Mix, William S. Hart, and other stars aroused shouts of emotion in heterogeneous audiences. There were rutted dirt streets and narrow twisting alleys, along which sauntered on a Sunday newly-prosperous and well-fed workers, trailed by their dusky women in bright-colored cotton prints. There were the unemployed, unkempt and sullen . . .

and the idlers and suspicious characters, shifty-eyed and arrogant, appraising the passers-by from the doorways of *botiquines*. There were the naked brown children, pot-bellied with the swollen spleens of chronic malaria, playing in the dust, happily unaware that such a thing as toys existed. There were the slinking, sickly mongrels sniffing at the charcoal braziers set up on street corners and in perambulating kitchens, from which the odors of *arepas*, fried fish, and *café criollo* permeated the atmosphere already heavy with foreign smells . . . and the country bumpkins, polite but ridiculous figures in their patched and misfit garments, gawking at the wares of the street hawkers and timidly proffering in trade a bleating kid or a brace of chickens. Lording it over the main thoroughfare were a dozen or so more sturdy structures—the emporiums and bazaars of the Syrians and Turks. In the strange-smelling depths of these foreign establishments could be seen the fat, swarthy faces of their proprietors presiding over counters of dry goods, tawdry trinkets, and cheap toilet goods.

When day faded into dusk, the conglomeration of hot, sweaty humanity was swelled by hundreds of professional girls, procurers, gamblers, and foreigners all bent on a boisterous and happy evening. Strings of colored lights along the midway denoted the government-controlled gambling house, the dozens of saloons and brothels, all well nourished by the payrolls of the oil companies. Night after night amateurish orchestras added to the bedlam by blasting the air with off-key renditions of *joropos* and waltzes.

Set apart in fenced-off camps, the foreign contract workers lived in comfortable company cottages with many modern conveniences. The proletariat, in sharp contrast, lived as they had always lived, in miserable hovels with the barest necessities of life. The government income from petroleum taxes ran into the millions, yet none of it ever found its way back to the oil towns in the form of civic improvements. Cabimas became hemmed in by hundreds of producing wells, some of them even in her back yards, yet this town of almost ten thousand souls couldn't claim ownership to a water or sewer system or even a paved street. Ice in this sweltering climate was a luxury almost unheard of. With the advent of the oil men and their new-fangled equipment, ice was first looked upon as an invention of the devil because it was fiery to the touch! The few individual attempts to drill for water had met with failure, and the residents had to buy water that had been brought from distant rivers. The few wealthy *comerciantes* who could easily afford it had water pumped from the lake, but this water was hardly suitable to bathe in and totally unfit to drink.

Here was a fresh water lake one hundred and twenty-five miles long which served only as an artery of traffic and to provide a few edible fish. Water had to be brought from afar or gathered in barrels and tubs during the rainy season. Here were gas flares from the wells, burning into the air billions of cubic feet of gas annually, yet the people were without fuel and had to resort to the *monte bajo* (thickets and low jungle) to obtain their fagots. Here cows and chickens lived by scavenging, and the cows that managed to survive were tubercular and with dry udders; the average child never knew the taste of milk until his father worked for an oil company and brought home a can of it in powdered form. With the soil too arid to grow anything but a poor grade of corn, fresh vegetables were luxury items which were brought in from the distant mountains and sold at ridiculously high prices. Daily scenes at the market stalls were sad-eyed women bargaining for a carrot, a turnip, and a handful of greens to make a thin *sancocho* to vary the daily fare of salted fish and plantains. The irony of circumstances whereby millions of bolivars in oil were being drained from the very soil on which human beings lived miserable lives in the sorriest of hovels, had done nothing but arouse a few wry smiles and phrases of pity. Here, as in the country's largest cities, wealth was flaunted in the very face of abject poverty. It was a wonder that life proceeded so smoothly without undue mishaps. So strong was the dictator's stranglehold upon these oppressed and wretched people they dared not even beg for the crumbs from his overflowing table. They bowed, instead, in utter servility and apparent cowardice. But the time was fast approaching when Juan Vicente Gómez would be summoned to meet his Maker, and the docility of these disillusioned people would give way to a ferocity that could only become satiated with violence and bloodshed.

Even Mother Nature was unkind and added her bit to these people's burdens. Alternately, from one six-month season to the next, she flooded, drained, then baked herself out of all semblance of beauty. Incessant torrential downpours and flash floods played havoc with crops and left morasses of mud and scars of erosion. With the dry season the tropical sun performed its own transformation: its searing fingers baked and cracked the clayey soil and drew a blanket of heat and dust over the countryside.

It was not surprising that some of the townspeople, bitter against both the rich foreign companies and the corrupt officialdom, sometimes took matters into their own hands to secure a few of the necessities of life. Some of the incidents that happened would be very funny if they were not so pathetic. And they were pathetic. The story of the stolen water is a good case in point.

One of the oil companies piped water into its residential camp from a well situated a couple of miles in the interior. When the pressure on the water system decreased at an alarming rate, an inspection of the line revealed the reason. A number of the townspeople had run one-inch lines from their houses and had connected them into the water line. As the available supply of water was insufficient for both the oil camp and the town, the culprits were requested to disconnect their lines. This they refused to do. Thereupon an appeal for action was made to the mayor of Cabimas. That gentleman only shrugged off the company officials and told them to work out their problem as best they could.

One morning, water failed to run out of the town faucets and householders left them open until the supposed repairs would be completed. When they heard the anticipated gurgle and splash they went to turn off the faucets. To their horror, what they saw pouring out was not water, but black, sticky petroleum! The excited outbursts which followed set a good part of the town in an uproar. Loud-voiced threats were heard about suing for damages.

Now it was the company's turn to resort to shoulder shrugging. Turned away from the company's gates, the delegation of angry townspeople marched upon the town hall. No, the mayor wasn't in. He had packed up and left for parts unknown. More angry outbursts. It seemed these good citizens had a score to settle with his honor the mayor, and they wanted so much to lay their hands on him. And they shouted for all to hear that the mayor, that wily rascal, had been charging them a "tax" on the stolen water!

Such despicable practices were not at all unusual in Venezuela during the regime of Gómez; they dated back to the days of Spanish rule. Only then it was the poor Indian who was hounded and exploited.

This mayor, or *jefe civil* (civil chief), as he was called,[22] was the counterpart of hundreds of petty tyrants who ruled their little domains like independent chieftains. They could be likened to the fierce Caribe fish of the Orinoco, a bloated creature with a murderous bite and voracious habits. These officials funneled municipal funds into their pockets instead of spending them on public works. They exacted tribute in every manner and form. From the poor fisherman who donated a small part of his catch, to the wealthy cattleman who paid mythical "taxes," there was hardly a citizen in any walk of life who escaped paying his tithe in cash or goods. As in corrupt China, this local equivalent of "squeeze" was an ingrown habit that took precedence over all other human endeavors. Not content with their high rate of income, these scoundrels coerced drunks and others into paying their way out of jail. One look at a municipal jail cell explained much. It was a dark, stinking pest hole, infested with vermin and the accumulated filth of years. No deference was shown for color, caste, or sex and the common jail cell was always crowded with the dregs of the human race.

More often than not, these officials were illiterate, and of necessity, their secretaries were vested with authority to issue edicts and ordinances and to handle all correspondence. However, there was one man in the history of oil town mayors who was somewhat above the common lot. He was literate, whereas his secretary could neither read nor write. This created an awkward situation, one which this mayor set out to correct. He journeyed to see the governor of the district to complain that while he was obliged to do all his own paper work, his secretary was left to twiddle his thumbs. Certainly, he reasoned, as the governor had made the appointment, he would no doubt be willing to correct his mistake. The governor clucked his sympathy, looked wise, and declared that the matter would be rectified at once. The following day, the looked-for decree was made public. What it said, in effect, was that the complainant had been relegated to the secretary's job and that worthy had been advanced to the post of mayor!

Picked by the higher-ups for his aggressiveness and adherence to the "cause" of Gómez, the *jefe civil* was generally the town bully who

---

[22] This title has since been changed to the more appropriate one of *alcalde* (mayor); and the title of state president to that of *gobernador*.

was privileged to deal out punishment as he saw fit. In truth he could well say: "I am the law!" No one dared to dispute him. No one dared to cross him. For his strength of arm rather than that of character he often rose high on the ladder of promotion. One such man, well remembered in local circles, rose to be state president and an intimate of Gómez. Brute force was his watchword, and black was his record. Once, he personally supervised the punishment of a man who had run amuck in a country settlement and killed his entire family. While the villagers and the police looked on, he compelled the demented wretch to dig his own grave, and then he buried him in it alive.

Not all such scoundrels were civilian officials. There were some who wore the uniform of the military. There has been evidence that cocky and over-zealous officers sometimes caused the arrest of innocent persons merely on suspicion or from personal dislike. One case on record involved a United States citizen. This man was Albert Laborda, a teacher, born in Puerto Rico, who was mistaken for a Venezuelan because he spoke fluent Spanish and atrocious English. Arrested on suspicion, he suffered many outrages at the hands of the authorities, and was held prisoner for six months in San Carlos fortress —a good part of the time in irons. The case came close to an international incident. It was certainly a delicate situation from which— as is usual in such cases—the authorities extricated themselves through sheer Latin bravado. Laborda was the only loser.

The adventures of Albert Laborda began early in 1923, when he set out from Puerto Rico on a vacation and sight-seeing trip into Colombia and Venezuela. He had landed first at Curacao where he took passage to Barranquilla. From there he boarded a river boat to Cienaga, proceeding to Santa Marta, and thence east by schooner to Rio Hache, the easternmost port of Colombia on the Caribbean. In Rio Hache he bought a horse and saddle for sixty dollars, intending to reach Maracaibo on horseback. As the buzzard flies, Rio Hache is some fifty-three miles from the northern Venezuelan border, and from there it is another sixty-two miles to Maracaibo. The route is through barren and desolate country frequented by smugglers, nomadic tribes of Indians and others hardly more desirable—persons without money or passport, down and out Americans tiring of Colombia and heading for the lush oil fields of Lake Maracaibo. But of such matters Laborda was unaware. He wanted to rough it and to see the country. He did not know either that a few weeks before two Americans traveling this route found on the trail some papers which bore the name of a fellow countryman, Edward Connelly. Discreet questions asked here and there revealed that Connelly had been robbed and murdered either by smugglers or by the Goajiras, a supposedly peaceful Indian tribe.

No orthodox tourist would have chosen such a route, and Laborda got rather more of roughing it than he had hoped for. In the hills near the border he dismounted to let his horse drink at a waterhole. He was set upon by some twenty to twenty-five men, evidently a smuggling band. They robbed him of his money, his papers, and his pack of clothes and then sent him on his way allowing him to take his horse.

What followed is best told in the affidavit Laborda signed for the United States Government:

"I tried to arrive at any town or village where I can obtain help of authorities. I came to Paraguaipoa (a village on the shore of the Gulf of Venezuela and some thirty-eight miles north of San Carlos fortress). I recount a brief story to Colonel Sayago, the Chief. He only laugh at me and I was made prisoner. The men of Colonel Sayago take off the clothes I wear and after several hours they bring me military clothes. For three days I was tied with a rope to a post where the soldiers lived. One night on or about ten o'clock of the day 28 of April I was awakened and four soldiers with a sargent bring me to the Colonel. After a trip of twenty hours (barefoot over thirty-eight miles of rough trails) we arrived at the San Carlos Castle. In San Carlos the same day I arrived I was inclosed in a room where was a salt store. In this room grillos [irons] were put on my feet."

For almost four months Laborda was thus kept in a windowless cell without sanitary facilities and was forced to sleep on the damp floor without bedding or covering of any kind. But to continue his own account:

"From the first moment of my arrival I said to the Chief that I was a citizen of the United States, native of Porto Rico, and offered to write the Governor of Porto Rico asking for a copy of my passport. The authorities do not wish to know who I am nor what the purpose of my trip. They wish to have a prisoner and were more glad when I said I was United States citizen. Several times when I ask the Chief to be put in liberty he said with sarcasm: 'Don't dare. Venezuela is rich—more time you spend here more money you shall receive!' These words put anger in me. I think and said to the Chief: 'I appreciate more the liberty than any other thing. Surely I shall try to ask for an indemnization, but one thousand dollars is not sufficient for one day in this prison.' In San Carlos I wrote about twenty letters. I don't think any letters were sent to his destination."

One letter did reach his mother in Puerto Rico, who immediately notified the United States authorities.

"All the letters were with the object that the authorities have a clear idea of my purpose and of the wrong of my detention. I pay special attention to the fact that for the last two months, or from the date that General Jimenez and Colonel Gonzales Pacheco are in charge of the castle I received a more beneficial treatment. I was allowed to walk to the beach out of the fort when I was sick. They let me use a hamaca (hammock) to sleep. But during the first four months I was treated with great vigilance. On November 2nd, General Jimenez, Commander of San Carlos, show me a telegram giving him the order that I was put free, but I do not receive the clothes I wear when I arrived to Paraguaipoa, nor the horse, nor one cent. Several prisoners who work in a shoe factory in San Carlos made a pair of cotizas (sandals) and they gave them to me. One of the generals of San Carlos give me trousers and coat of his property. On the schooner "Commercio" I make the voyage from San Carlos to Maracaibo."

The only justification the local authorities chose to give for the retention of Laborda—and they were careful not to put it in writing—was that he was suspected of being a spy. Yet they blandly ignored the request of the American consul to furnish evidence that led them to that conclusion. It was rumored that political activity was the reason—this was the excuse given to the American Minister in Caracas—but this was entirely unfounded. The only official letter on the case from the Venezuelan government was one from Santos Matute Gómez, president of the state of Zulia. It was dated December 12, 1923. This official admitted that "Laborda's property had been taken from him by the agents of the said Colonel Sayago, a federal officer." There was no mention of redress for the wrongs committed. No apology. This from a government executive, half-brother of the country's dictator, who was known to appropriate all state revenues on which he could get his hands. Recalled from his post three months later, he emptied the state treasury of almost nine million bolivars and fled the country by plane with his two daughters.

It added something to the insult of this last that in 1928 he was permitted by Gómez to return to Venezuela and to resume his former practices. He was then made president of the state of Carabobo. But getting back to the story of Laborda: Santos Matute's curt reply confirmed the suspicions of the United States consular officials, which were that the local authorities realized that a grave error had been committed in imprisoning Laborda and the matter must be passed over as lightly as possible in order to avoid responsibility for the incident. Their report on the case concluded with: ". . . the facts place the Venezuelan authorities in an embarrassing position and justify Laborda in demanding indemnity." Laborda was so advised.

The disillusioned traveler was given back his horse and saddle, but he had to sell them for a hundred bolivars ($19.30) in order to buy food. Due to the generosity of some fellow Americans he obtained passage back to Puerto Rico. There he engaged a firm of lawyers who enthusiastically pressed his claim. It looked like an open-and-shut case. But, as in hundreds of other foreign claims for redress during previous dictatorships, there was no offer of any indemnity. No apology. Only silence.

CHAPTER TWENTY-SIX

The Secret Army

Not much is known of the spy organization established by Gómez save that it was large, intricate, and in no sense haphazard. Through its work thousands went to prison and hundreds to death. There is a clue, however, as to the way in which the system came into existence. Gómez kept abreast of foreign army methods and listened with relish to accounts of the great battles of the past. One of his intimates, the Colombian, Dr. José Rosario García, better known as Dr. Gris, was a great reader. It is known that through this man Gómez became familiar with the exploits of Napoleon and Bismarck. He was particularly interested in the Franco-Prussian War and in Louis Napoleon Bonaparte's surrender to King William of Prussia, and much impressed with the primary reason for Prussia's victory. Bismarck was forewarned of every move made by the French. How? By his secret service division. This was an army in itself, estimated at the then incredible figure of fifteen thousand men and women. Bismarck's secret service chief, Wilhelm Stieber, boasted that there was not a government bureau which did not contain one of his operatives and not a hotel in all of France which did not shelter one. Thus was planted in Gómez's shrewd mind the seed of an idea.

The spy system appealed to Gómez vastly. It was dangerous, it was devious and it was efficient. It was an ugly brain-child, but it grew so strong the wonder was it did not turn on its creator. Another dictator, Adolf Hitler, owed his debt to Bismarck. The first book to influence Hitler was in the one-volume library of his father. This was an illustrated history of Bismarck's war against France!

The Gómez spy system came to be all-seeing and all-hearing. The hired eyes and ears were everywhere that trouble might be brewing.

There were barbers, chauffeurs, waiters, even chambermaids some-times suspected of being on the Gómez payroll. Once, on a steamer plying between New York and La Guaira, a group of Venezuelans met a beautiful woman traveling alone. She had, besides beauty, an air of wealth and culture. She became very friendly, but before the Venezuelans revealed their political sympathies, a steward warned them that the woman was a spy in the pay of the dictator.

Sometimes the system reached into the very homes of persons suspected of revolutionary tendencies. Plans of action thus never got too far, exposure and reprisal being too swift, and the fomenter of revolt never even learned the identity of his betrayer. The success of Gómez at uncovering any intrigue was phenomenal. It was no wonder that the simpler-minded called him sorcerer.

Abroad, the consular service kept Venezuelan exiles under con-stant surveillance. Reports on their movements, contacts, and cor-respondents went into their dossiers which were kept in Caracas. The Venezuelan post offices were another source of intelligence. Letters were steamed open, copied, re-sealed, then sent on their way. For a Venezuelan even to be seen with an exile was dangerous business, as more than one found out.

Vacationing in Trinidad, a Venezuelan university student had lunch one day with an exile in Port of Spain. Upon his return to La Guaira he was arrested. His pleadings of innocence of all conspiracy and the fact that he came from a wealthy family of no political lean-ings were to no avail. He was put in the Rotunda. Seldom were such miscarriages of justice rectified or even brought to the attention of *El Benemérito,* for he was shielded from unwelcome visitors, and written pleas from frantic relatives ended in the waste basket. *"Nada de presos,"* he told his subordinates. Nothing of prisoners. The order was emphatic and decisive, and the man who broke it met with angry silence and a cold stare from the heavy-lidded baffling eyes.

There was one general, however, who insisted on speaking his piece, and *El Benemérito* heard him out, for they were on very cordial terms. There happened to be in one of the cells of the Rotunda, he explained, a man who had languished there in irons for five years. Only now it had been discovered that he was entirely innocent and had been arrested because of some stupid blunder of the police.

Gómez reflected for a moment and then observed, "You say this friend has not been mixed up in anything and yet he has been in prison five years?"

"Yes," said the general. "He is entirely innocent; therefore it would be only just to set him free."

There appeared a trace of a smile under the graying mustaches. *"Anja,"* expounded "The Well Deserving" in his infinite wisdom, "If this be so and this friend, as you call him, already carries irons for five years without having done anything . . . do you believe that to-day he is still my friend? No! It can't be! By now he is probably an enemy of the Cause . . . and for this reason it appears to me that it would be unwise to release him!"

One day while he was in a more expansive mood, one of his retinue asked the dictator if he ever had premonitions of dire things about to happen.

Gómez answered him, "Yes—while in my sleep, as well as when I am awake. All of a sudden I get a hunch that they will try to kill me at a certain spot. And I say to myself—they won't get the chance!

"One day, like those times when General Castro tried to frame me so often, General Galavis told me that some men were going to try to kill me at La Vaquera. (A hacienda belonging to Dr. Torres Cardenas.) I had a feeling that I should go to the place, so I asked for the coach. Galavis tried to stop me.

"It turned out that among the men there were Dr. Eduardo Celis of the Treasury Department and Dr. Carnevali, governor of Caracas

"When I arrived I saw a peon plowing. I thought, this must be the man who is to kill me. So I walked up close to him and asked him, 'Tell me something. Is it possible to plow with two ox-yokes?' Of course this was possible, and I knew it . . . because the thing I know most about is oxen. I am an ox-driver myself. I kept watching him while I talked. I had my hand in my pocket and I said to myself, if you make a move, you bastard, you will drop dead!

"I asked him all this just to make conversation. I told him that I needed peons for one of my haciendas and that was why I was ques tioning him.

"Then I asked him, 'What is going on in the house? I'll bet you there is a cockfight going on because Dr. Cardenas is as fond of cocks as I am of cows, which I have come to see, even though I know there is a plan to kill me!'

"I intended to tell him that I knew everything, but the man appeared scared to death. As soon as I left he told them everything I had said. Afterward, one of them told me that Dr. Celis had said, 'Gentlemen, I am stepping out of this conspiracy. We can do nothing with Gómez.'

"You see, among them I had one who kept me well informed, because in such circumstances, such an arrangement is of great help."

Even Gómez's own family became aware at times that their movements were followed. One evening a grandson, a lad of sixteen, kept an appointment with a friend at a Caracas brothel. They chatted with the girls for a while and then left for the movies. Two days later, when he visited his grandfather to pay his respects, a ritual required of all Gómez children and grandchildren, the lad was greeted with: "Well—so you went to a whorehouse the other night!" Raising his hand for silence, Gómez added, "Oh, I know all about it . . . and I'm surprised that you would go to one of the lowest. *Qué cosa ésa!* You should know better than that."

"Yes, grandfather . . ." The lad was meek. He doubtless was wondering what more the old man could possibly know.

"Here," said Gómez, handing him an envelope, "if you *must* go to one of those places, then go to an expensive one—it'll be much safer." And he dismissed the boy with a pat on the back.

Inside the envelope the young man found one thousand bolivars in bills.

Realizing his danger from a hand of vengeance, Gómez surrounded himself constantly with double cordons of the *sagrada* and detectives and, in public, bulletproof cars and bristling machine guns. He was a dictator, and therefore such protection was routine. No Venezuelan in his right mind ever made an attempt on his life. It would have meant suicide, and one's own life, no matter how forlorn, is much too precious to lose for the imponderable rewards of martyrdom.

Killing the despot in ambush was the only way. But it would need more heads than one to concoct such a scheme and execute it. The surveillance of the Venezuelan secret police was widespread. More heads than one—and could such heads be trusted? Even discussing such a risky business was dangerous. Even with friends it was dangerous. One never could be sure who was an informer and who was not. Besides, shock after shock had thrown the people into a state of lethargy, and Gómez's unbroken string of successes had brought most of his enemies to a paralyzing state of despair. Nevertheless, some thirteen years after he had come into power, a bold plan came forth.

It was a very bold plan indeed, this scheme to assassinate Gómez, evolved by a small group of high ranking naval officers. It would succeed beyond all expectations or—as such plans are apt to go—it would fail miserably. The design was to blow up a Venezuelan gunboat together with Juan Vicente Gómez and his entire retinue in the harbor of La Guaira.

Everything had proceeded according to plan. It was an exceedingly hazardous plan and this handful of officers swore themselves to secrecy. Every possible precaution was taken to prevent even their own families from suspecting what they were doing. An appointment had been arranged for Gómez to make one of his rare visits to La Guaira on the pretext of a naval inspection. Under the cover of night a heavy charge of dynamite had been placed below decks of a sleek gray gunboat. In the morning, after Gómez and his party had boarded her, a violent explosion would rock the entire harbor. At this moment Juan Vicente Gómez would cease to be among the living.

The morning was bright and clear—just the morning for a sea venture. But it was not Gómez who made it. It was the secret police. Like vultures the police swooped down on their unsuspecting prey. Old *Brujo* had discovered the plot, though how he did so the officers never found out. It may, or may not have been significant that only a few weeks previous a Greek torpedo boat had blown up at Piraeus killing fifty-five men.

What was the fate of the unlucky officers? Theirs was a crime of the first magnitude, and under almost any Latin-American dictatorship they would have been lined up against a wall and shot. But for once Gómez displayed a benignity of heart that astonished everyone. That was Gómez—an incongruous mixture of fiend and angel. He was a despot. His punishments were severe. And yet he had his magnanimous moments. Unfortunately, because he was so unpredictable, one could never tell when these would occur, on what day he would be Dr. Jekyll and on what Mr. Hyde.

Of course, all the men were confined in the Rotunda. As was customary, there were no predetermined sentences. They were merely left there with irons on their legs until it became evident that they had learned their lesson. But the wonder was that their confinement was comparatively short. Not one of them served more than five years' time. One of them was released after fifteen months and was given a job in the government service! It is difficult to reconcile such leniency with the countless and hoary legends of this dictator's bruising and truculent tactics. Yet there are many persons living in Venezuela today who will vouch for the fact that leniency and a sort of cool reasonableness often ruled the man's actions.

That the punishment meted out to the plotters was as cited here has been attested by the son of one who spent five years in the Rotunda. The son's account of his father's imprisonment is a moving story of conditions as they existed in the Rotunda during Gómez's time. As related to this author it seems worthy of repetition, even though its narrator must remain unnamed. Both he and his father, who is still alive, might be taken to task should the Gomecistas ever rise to power again. The story is not wholly of prisons, but it must be told—if at all—as it was told to the author.

"I never could figure out why my father became involved in that plot. None of my family had any personal grievance against Gómez. I think that father, like many young fellows of his time, just acquired subversive ideas. In those days, officers were always up to some mischief. Several times they tried to put over revolutions with the aid of the university students in Caracas.

"Some of the men involved in the harbor plot with my father are still living. Two of them are good friends of his and I often listened to their stories. Life in prison under Gómez was unbearable for most. Often the prisoners were not as lucky as these two friends. I mean, they did not live to tell stories, but died quite suddenly. Putting powdered glass in the food, or arsenic in the coffee, was the most common way of getting rid of them in a hurry.

"Sometimes they would be chained to the floor. There were many forms of torture, including the *pela* and the water cure. This last was the most dreaded of all. It cured all right! There was a four by four pit about seven feet high which was filled with stagnant water to a height of about four feet. They'd stand a man in it with the water up to his waist and the ceiling not far above his head. They'd give him enough food to keep him alive, but no water, and there he'd stay. The idea was to get him to talk. Sometimes he would talk and sometimes they'd just be carted out—one week, two weeks, maybe three— a sickening mass of bloated flesh.

"What the jailers called food was just slop. Some men who could afford to pay for it managed to get food sent in from outside after the guards helped themselves to most of it. In the patio or compound they'd build a charcoal fire in a brazier and hang their cans of food over it. Some of the men shared their meals with those less fortunate. Each man was allotted one small can of water a day and had to buy a crock in which to store it. This was fine except when the head jailer announced there would be no water for several days because the system was being repaired. That was his idea of a joke. Remember, too, these men couldn't walk, but had to shuffle around with heavy irons on their legs. These irons were fastened with a rope over the shoulders to lessen the weight, but this didn't help much. They slept on the bare floor with only their jackets for a pillow. Blankets were hard to get. No wonder there was dysentery, tuberculosis, and plenty of other diseases. And no doctor when a man was so ill he couldn't move. He died alone in his cell.

"For a while the group of which my father was one had a young Negro to do certain menial chores. He was a prisoner but was not accepted as one of the clique. But they never forgot him. Years later when he showed up in dire straits they helped finance music lessons for him. He played the flute. They secured a place for him in the Sunday concert band on the Plaza Bolívar.

"One day my father found a watch spring. Someone must have thrown it in from the street. He fashioned a crude file out of it and spent weeks trying to file through his irons. There were no locks on these, they were forged to his ankles. The weeks of trying left little impression on the metal.

"My father never mentioned it but I learned of one murder plot which was carried on right in the prison. Colonel Rascanieri told me about it. The colonel was one of that little band of patriots in prison with my father. They were very serious about carrying out this murder, though there was a certain grim humor in their failure, looking back at it in after years.

"There was a fellow prisoner who used to join them in their quiet talks in the patio. They would whisper about possible means of escape and of getting messages in and out and a file smuggled in. This old fellow, a well-educated and pleasant chap, was also in 'indefinitely' and just as anxious to escape as they were. He became overly anxious, his worries preying on his mind, and gradually his mind gave way. He did queer things. No matter what a man held in his hand he would grasp it for himself and sometimes just as quickly tire of it and throw it down. He took to muttering to himself, and finally to denouncing his friends and screaming their plans to everyone within earshot. He'd scream from his cell at night that they were trying to escape and to stop them. My father and the others kept clear of him and worked out new plans they thought he wouldn't know about. But he learned of these somehow—possibly while pretending to take naps in the patio. One night they were all awakened by his hoarse cries giving all the new details. The guards got the whole story from him and the men were put on short rations for punishment. It was after this that the murder was plotted.

"There was a man there who was known to have sleeping tablets. They secured several and dissolved them in a little coffee in a tin cup. When the old man appeared one of them was holding the cup as though to drink it. The old man grabbed the cup, just as they had thought he would, and drank it down—every drop. When he began to get drowsy they took him back to his cell. They neither saw nor heard from him the rest of the day. It was good riddance—quite justified as things were—and no one the wiser.

"The next morning they were having their ration of coffee, all grouped around the patio fire, and all—in various degrees—feeling guiltier than they would have thought possible. After all, the old wretch had at one time been their friend. Their guilt was short. The wretch appeared among them, not a ghost, a little heavy-lidded perhaps, but as alive as ever. The sleeping tablets were old and had lost some of their potency. No further plans for murder were projected. The old man failed rapidly, both mentally and physically, becoming a good deal of a nuisance to the guards. Whether it was these last who finally put him out of the way, or whether he came to his end naturally was never known. All this happened during the first year or so of my father's imprisonment.

"It has been said that Gómez, during his occasional moments of being magnanimous, would grant a general amnesty to prisoners. This seemed a mere legend, but it was true that individual prisoners were sometimes released. When this happened friends of ours always managed to get wind of it and they would immediately notify my mother in El Valle where we lived. I recall a number of occasions when our hopes were raised. The house would be put in perfect order, my father's favorite dishes prepared, the children dressed in their best. Seated at the grilled window in front, our hearts would jump every time a car chugged up the street. But the big clock would ring the hours and by night we knew he would not come. Five years passed. I did not even remember what my father looked like.

"One Sunday morning my mother started off for church at six o'clock as was her habit. Those Sundays are very clear to me still because they were the only time when the power company left the current on during the daylight hours. We would all go in and romp on my mother's big bed and turn on all the lights. This particular morning she had gone about three blocks when she saw a carriage jogging up the street. We had no carriages in El Valle and she told us afterward that something made her stop dead in her tracks, with a sense which seemed near fear. As the carriage drew nearer she recognized it as one of the type that parked by the plaza in Caracas. Slumped on the rear seat was a familiar figure. Mother didn't reach church that morning . . . father had come home."

CHAPTER TWENTY-SEVEN

The Propaganda Machine

After the Mexican revolution which overthrew the government of General Porfirio Díaz in 1910, the Venezuelan press endeavored to convince Venezuelans that a happy life in Mexico was impossible because of anarchy and disorder. What a contrast, it pointed out, to conditions in Venezuela, where Union, Peace, and Work were producing such remarkable results under the benevolent guidance of "The Well Deserving." Gómez's propaganda organization, at this period, was already functioning with machine-like precision. It portrayed the dictator as a sort of deity. It turned out systematic falsehoods to lull Venezuelans into a sense of security and contentment.

Down through the years, governing cliques have worked ceaselessly to persuade their public to see things the way they did. The methods in use today have changed but little. Batteries of research workers work hand in hand with hired penmen. Newsmen and magazine writers are handed just the right material to help them make up their minds a certain way. Speeches are turned out in reams, and corps of speakers are ready to go into action at the flip of a policy. That's about as far as official propaganda goes in a democracy. Under a dictatorship, further techniques and refinements are added: the propaganda budget is huge so as to cover radio, trade unions, pamphlets, and other media; decorations and other awards go to faithful and outstanding writers; there are subsidies for favorite newspapers that follow the official line, paper quotas and strong-arm squads for those who don't; and always present is the omnipotent censor whose every whim is law.

Molding public opinion was a small, efficient enterprise under Gómez. He could see no need for developing a huge propaganda organization. The iron fist encased in a velvet glove had only to move, and the press performed like an automaton. The dictator had one subsidized newspaper, the *Nuevo Diario,* whose editor, J. A. Cova, a brilliant and prolific writer, never missed his cue. By 'phone calls or written directives, the other newspapers received the signal on what to say, what not to say. In his younger, ruthless days, Gómez closed down a newspaper for one brash article, sent its entire writing staff to prison. In his latter-day role of glorified statesman, cool reasoning rather than senseless anger ruled his actions. But it was a serio-comic kind of reasoning. Only the writer of the offensive piece (generally the owner-editor) atoned in a cell. Other private papers quickly learned what was expected of them.

One of Gómez's daily rituals was to have his secretary read to him a condensed report of what the foreign press was saying of him. If a paper disparaged him or his policies, a 'phone call would go out to Cova and other editors. "Tell the Doctor I shall expect him to answer this." Or "Tell that Doctor . . . What's his name? . . . Tell him I haven't seen any of his work in the paper lately. Tell him to get busy. *Sabe?*" Always the reply would have to be written in a firm but conciliatory vein. That was the *Jefe*'s explicit order. Gómez had the good sense to realize that to retaliate in kind would only provoke his attackers to greater anger. If his diplomatic representative abroad indicated that a newspaper owner might be susceptible to a bribe or flattery, he used a subtle and more persuasive method. Through diplomatic channels he sent the man the decoration of the Order of the Liberator.

In his letter to Dr. Márques Bustillos in 1920, Gómez had written one of the first analyses of atheistic Russian Communism.[23] A decade later the subject of communism was again brought to his attention. Some Spanish priests had been circulating in Caracas a missionary magazine published in Barcelona, Spain. One of its articles, headed "The Horrors of Soviet Russia," depicted the desolation of the Russian earth, starving children, bodies stacked in the streets, gallows,

[23] The first communist cells in Venezuela were established sometime during 1929. The initial group consisted of several ex-university students, a dozen or so civil employees, and a few of the laboring class. Due to the extreme vigilance of the secret police, their activities (which had been restricted to the reading of Marxist literature) were soon broken up, the leaders were imprisoned, and the others went underground or into exile.

and the arrogant, brutal police. A report of the magazine's contents
was relayed to Maracay.

The following Sunday when General Elías Sayago, the Caracas
prefect of police, stood before him, Gómez asked him, "Is it true
that in Caracas some priests are handing out a paper that speaks of
communism?"

"Yes, my General," replied Sayago. "That is so. I permitted its
circulation because it speaks badly of communism. That is good;
it opens the eyes of the people."

Gómez fixed the prefect with a solemn stare. "I don't agree. Tomorrow tell the priests not to bring this paper into the country any
more. It is not of interest to me that they speak badly of communism,
but that they speak of it at all. Enemies—like the dead—should
never be mentioned . . . whether it be good or bad. No, General,
whether it be good or bad . . ."

The one deep thorn in the dictator's side was the defamatory
campaigns that were continually being waged by Venezuelans living
abroad. There was no way to retaliate. They had at their service skilled
writers and newspapermen who turned out not only pamphlets, books,
and ephemeral sheets but also newspapers which fired broadside after
broadside at him. At one time so many Venezuelan exiles were residing
in New York they published two papers simultaneouly—*La Joven
Venezolana* and *El Venezolano*. Both papers were devoted to the cause
of building up morale among the exiles as well as attacking the Gómez
regime. Among the short-lived patriotic societies founded by them in
the great metropolis was a secret society that went by the name of
Orden Calaveran Croquis. Taking a cue from the Ku Klux Klan, its
members used the skull and crossbones as their symbol and they met
in secret session at midnight at the statue of Simón Bolívar in Central
Park.

In Havana appeared the weekly *Venezuela Libre,* and in Panama
a group of Venezuelans published *El Republicano*. Always, these
Venezuelans wrote with the wishful thought that foreign governments
might break off diplomatic relations with Venezuela. With one exception they failed.

In Mexico City, Humberto Tejera and Guillermo Egea Mier, Jr.
published *Pativilea* with such success that they won the sympathies
of the Mexican politician José Vasconcelos, who wielded some in-

fluence with President Alvaro Obregón. Vasconcelos, swayed by undetermined emotions or purposes, lost his sense of discretion in the smear campaign he undertook against Gómez. He not only ridiculed and reviled him in public speeches, he went so far as to accept articles for the magazine of the University of Mexico (of which he was rector) urging his assassination.

Gómez, who had acquired some fame for his ability to handle his foreign policies with skill and prudence, employed every means at his disposal to avoid friction with other countries. Protests through diplomatic channels having failed to still Vasconcelos, he attacked the fiery Mexican in the Venezuelan press. From this stage it was only one step farther to depict Mexico as a land of anarchy and disorder. Moved by an unscrupulous rancor and insensible spite, Gómez stepped up these attacks with a vengeance. No one could reason with him. No one could stop him. Mexico became his pet hate. Yet there were no ringing phrases of a Guzmán or Castro performance. Gómez bore himself with the dignity befitting his position. Though the *Nuevo Diario* was his mouthpiece, he did not permit it to qoute him. Like the dictator in the Kremlin, he was aloof, remote, a man on a pinnacle, a general who was above the battle but also in it.

This phobia of hate against the Mexicans invoked stiff protests from Mexico's diplomatic representatives in Caracas. Ignored or rebuffed at every turn, first one then another of these diplomats left the country in a huff. As an inevitable consequence, Mexico initiated her own press campaign in retaliation. And José Vasconcelos joined in with a will. After making a vitriolic speech during the Columbus Day celebrations in 1920, he led the university students on a march through the streets of Mexico City, inciting them to shout, "Death to Juan Vicente Gómez!" These sentiments were echoed in the Mexican press.

In his turn, the Venezuelan Consul General in Mexico City sent a note of protest to the Mexican Chancellery. There was a polite reply, and the lamentable incident was passed over but was not forgotten. Gómez could not forget, nor could he forgive.

Came his day to retaliate. The Wimer Company, a troupe of Aztec comedians, had been contracted to play at the Municipal Theater in Caracas. Proceeding from Costa Rica, the troupe was not permitted to disembark at La Guaira and was obliged to transship to a cargo vessel, which left it at Curacao. The Mexicans had been refused entry to Venezuela because they were regarded as "undesirable elements."

The troupe appealed immediately by cable to President Obregón. Cut to the quick by this insult to his fellow-countrymen, Obregón acted at once, but his efforts met with no success. Inflexible, unyielding Gómez would have no truck with him. Mexico renewed her press attacks and talked threateningly of breaking off diplomatic relations. This she did on October 7, 1923. Declared Obregón, along with other things: "Mexico severs relations, not with the people of Venezuela, but with the government of Venezuela, because tyrants do not represent the people."

Said in the true style of a Latin dictator, for Obregón, too, was a revolutionary *caudillo* who had risen to power by force of arms. Here are two classic examples of heads of state who regarded themselves as indefectible and worthy to conduct government, but who were, nonetheless, fettered with the inevitable frailties of human beings. At a word, either of these militant dictators could have called a halt to their campaigns of hate and slander. But no. Their vanity hurt, they cast patriotism aside and resorted to recriminations. Their respective countries suffered the consequences. But why this public display of weakness on the part of the affable diplomat from the Andes? Was he just an egoist with a flair for drama and the grand gesture? Was he becoming inept and overconfident as his enemies now claimed? Subsequent events do not bear this out. But it was obviously true that Gómez did what seemed best for Gómez in any given situation. His people were in chains, their bodies controlled by the weapons of a dictatorship, their minds deluded by its propaganda. So strong was this dictator's power, he could buy and sell legislators like a sack of coffee. What rankled in him was that he could not buy the Venezuelan exiles who needled him unmercifully.

It has been said that the first defense of weak minds is to re-criminate. But even vigorous minds can be goaded to recrimination; there is always a limit to human endurance. Enemies, like the dead, should never be mentioned. That was one of Gómez's codes and he lived by it most of his lifetime. Just this once he broke that code, but for all the trouble he caused he was bothered not at all by the twitching pangs of a guilty conscience. Lord and monarch of all he surveyed, he answered to no man for his actions.

CHAPTER TWENTY-EIGHT

Romulo Betancourt, Student and Revolutionist

Although Vasconcelos had contributed to the break in relations, that was as far as his influence went. He could not obtain for the Venezuelan exiles the vessels, munitions, and money which they were hoping for. The exiles had begun to despair of making new and better alliances when, to make matters worse, history played one of its malignant and gloomy jokes. First, Vasconcelos lost favor with the Mexican President, then Obregón was assassinated. If this news wasn't enough to tickle the cockles of Gómez's heart, what followed was. Vasconcelos fled into exile to escape the wrath of the new regime.

During the following few years, penned attacks by the Venezuelan exiles died down. Occasionally a pamphlet or handbill was circulated, but these caused the dictator no great concern. Through the efforts of the Venezuelan Ambassador in Washington, the Venezuelan societies and newspapers in New York were suppressed by the American authorities. It was the same in Paris, Havana, and other cities where the exiles operated. The Venezuelan diplomats worked untiringly at exporting the Gómez ideology (though not always successfully) and maintaining friendly relations.

In 1928 the smear campaign was revived, although much less violently, as a preliminary to the armed invasions which Román Delgado Chalbaud and Rafael Simón Urbina were plotting and which failed the following year. What gave impetus to the strong revolutionary movement which swept the country from 1928 to 1931 were the activities of a group of university students. There was one student in particular who did much to stir the masses to revolt. He was

Rómulo Betancourt, a burning, bitter, sardonic radical with a glib tongue in his head and a clever head on his shoulders.

In exile today, Betancourt has remained a controversial figure, both loved and hated and never fully understood. By some he has been called a harmless socialist reformer, and by others, a full-fledged revolutionary communist. The lower stratum of Venezuelan society came to know him as a golden-voiced spellbinder who preached the struggle of the proletariat against their overlords and offered panaceas for all Venezuela's ills. Successive government regimes, from that of Gómez to the present, thought they knew him for what he was—a rabblerousing radical who was not above using the vocabulary of Marx and the tactics of Hitler to achieve the power and glory he aspired to. It was only a few years ago that Betancourt, disavowing any allegiance to the Kremlin, attained that power through the backing of the army. But, said his backers, he deceived them in more ways than one, and when he began to evolve as just another breed of dictator, they cast him out. President Rómulo Gallegos, who was merely the tail of Betancourt's kite, went out with him.

Rómulo Betancourt was born in the little town of Guatire, Miranda, some twenty-five miles east of Caracas, on February 22, 1908. Like many another disillusioned Venezuelan, his father, a struggling newspaper owner, had found out too late in life how futile a writer's career can be. When his precocious offspring began to display a quick wit and loquacious tongue, he resolved that the boy should become a lawyer. As Guatire's schools taught only to the fourth grade, Luis Betancourt moved his family to the capital. Caracas, he told his wife, was the seat of learning, and he wanted Rómulo to have the best that he could afford. It was in the Colegio Andrés Bello that the future leader met and studied under Rómulo Gallegos, the gifted educator and writer, whose novel, *Doña Barbara,* was going to make him famous. Scorning the classroom for the library, Rómulo developed into an avid reader and, more so, a prolific writer. He cut his literary teeth on a short story which won him first prize in a Caracas contest. This success so overwhelmed his doting mother, she cried with joy, but his father took a sober view. "Don't mess with writing," he counseled his son gravely. But the heady visionary had read Anatole France's *The Gods are Thirsty,* and it had set him to thinking.

Upon graduating, Rómulo served for a time as the substitute

teacher of literature at the Colegio. In 1927, at the age of nineteen, he enrolled in the Central University as a law student. It was, one of the students later recalled, a year of unrest for the students and the citizenry alike; subversive literature was finding its way into the class-rooms and was being passed from hand to hand.

It was in the student debates that Rómulo, the short, spectacled lad with the disarming smile, found his forte; he was an eloquent, almost brilliant speaker given to ardent, sometimes belligerent, dis-course. No need for him to memorize a script; he spoke extemporane-ously. How stimulating to the mind! And how intoxicating the ap-plause! Yet there was so much more this dynamic young orator wanted to say to his eager audiences, but the laws of the land stayed his tongue.

Within a matter of weeks, he had learned about Marx. So Marx, the law student, had turned from law to philosophy. Why not he as well? Why forsake the dais for pleading dull law cases behind the closed doors of a judge's chamber? Something to think about here. And he liked the striking phrases of the Communist Manifesto which Marx and Engels flung into the face of the European bourgeoisie.

The attention of all Caracas first focused on this volatile young man when he tried to disseminate some of the theories he had learned. Early in 1927 there happened to be visiting in Caracas the talented Spanish writer María Alvarez de Burgos, reputedly a lady of Bohemi-an pursuits. It appears that she shared some of Betancourt's views, for at his urging she agreed to give a lecture on one of the doctrines that was at that time being diligently practiced in Communist Russia—free love. Enthusiastic about his plan, Betancourt arranged for the lecture to be given at the Club Venezuela under the auspices of the Law Students' League. The subject, he said, would be "Woman and Love." To the strait-laced *Caraqueños* this was a delicate subject to be sure, yet quite naturally the lecture drew a capacity audience.

As one of his fellow students later phrased it, the occasion was Rómulo Betancourt's début as a revolutionary figure and as a gallant with a roving eye for the fair sex. Perhaps it was fortunate that Betan-court's introductory remarks were not recorded, for it is said that they were audacious and even insolent. Burgos, herself, on commencing her talk, warned that her subject dealt with matters which were *muy delicado*. When it was over, the students, the faculty and a large segment of Caracas society went away stunned. If there had been any doubts as to which path Betancourt was going to follow, those doubts were now dispelled; he had veered sharply to the left, and in doing so he was courting disaster. Before the night was out, one more dossier had been added to the police files. Rómulo Betancourt, *estudiante de derecho,* was a man to be watched.

Almost a year passed and nothing more was heard from Rómulo Betancourt. Having convinced themselves that the young man was going to continue behaving himself, the authorities had relaxed their vigilance. All was tranquil at the university. His madcap venture, however, had filled Betancourt with a strange exhilaration and he was only waiting an opportunity to make another sortie. His chance came just before Carnival.

The students were celebrating "Student Week." Starting on February sixth the Federation of Students went about raising funds for the founding of a "Casa Andrés Bello del Estudiante." Andrés Bello, a *Caraqueño* who had taught Bolívar, had been a famous philosopher, educator, and political theorist. Business houses and individuals contributed generously to hallow the name of this illustrious son. So too did the father of one of the students, a brigadier general by the name of Eleazar López Contreras. Now forty-five and graying at the temples, López had spent the past five years as commandant of the Caracas garrisons. Persuaded by his son, he proceeded to solicit contributions from among the forces under his command.

Their permits in good order, student speakers addressed crowds in various sections of the city: Jóvito Villalba at the National Pantheon; Pío Tamayo in the Municipal Theater; Joaquín Márquez on the Plaza de la Pastora; and Rómulo Betancourt in the Rívoli movie house. The speeches ended in emotional outbursts against the government. That of Betancourt was the most vehement of the lot.

Why did these speakers turn a financial rally into a political harangue? Certainly they must have compared notes beforehand and known what they were about.

On Ash Wednesday, four of the students were arrested. The Rotunda at this time was closed and they were taken to the Cuño barracks. Betancourt was singled out for special attention. The *grillero* put double irons on him and took away his glasses. "You won't need these," he said. "You're not going far and there's nothing interesting to see here anyway!"

In the office of General Rafael Velasco, governor of the Federal District, Raúl Leoni, president of the Federation of Students, listened to a stern reprimand. He would be held personally responsible, Velasco told him, for any further incidents or seditious words. Leoni was thoroughly cowed.

At the university, the students formed a delegation which went to see Velasco and pleaded for the release of the prisoners. Velasco glared at them. "You call them students?" he bellowed. "They're not students. They're Communists!"

It was much the same at the office of Pedro Arcaya (Minister of the Interior) and other places. The four youths were guilty of sedition and disrespect of authority. The law decreed that they must be punished.

Heated debates were held at the university. How to obtain the release of their fellows? Various plans were offered and all were turned down. Two days passed. In desperation they thought of one more recourse and voted to act on it. A delegation would go to Maracay and plead with General Gómez. No groveling. No tears. They would bear themselves with dignity. But some of the students were not so distraught that they couldn't think of their pride—a true requisite of a Latin gentleman. At the word, the students took fresh stock of themselves. Better to suffer indignities, yes, even tortures, than to beg at the feet of the dictator. So, chins uplifted and pride intact, they voted to deliver themselves en masse as prisoners as a sign of protest and solidarity. The vote was unanimously in favor.

That night two hundred and ten university students delivered themselves into the hands of the police. The following dawn, before the city stirred to wakefulness, they were taken in trucks to the fortress of Puerto Cabello. Betancourt and the others were taken along with them.

A few hours later, General López conferred with General Velasco, the rector of the university, and Colonel Pedro García, the prefect of police. López had passed a fitful night; García had telephoned the night before to say that his son had appeared in the prisoner line-up. López tried to brush the problem from his mind as he attended to the business at hand. Velasco, one of the *Jefe*'s grizzled warriors and a veteran of the Restoration Campaign, was for taking strong preventative measures. He foresaw trouble, principally from the other students who were meeting at the university. He asked that a battalion of troops be posted around the building. López refused. This would only make the situation appear more serious than it actually was. What he would do, he said, would be to cancel all leaves and confine the men to their barracks; the same for the Military College and *La Sagrada*. The men would be supplied with extra rounds of ammunition from the national arsenal and rifles would be kept at the ready. If there was going to be any trouble he would be ready for it, but he didn't think it would be wise to show any signs that might be construed as fear.

Day after day other students voluntarily surrendered to the police in small groups and were taken away. Day by day tension in the city mounted as muttering crowds milled through the streets in passive protest. On Wednesday, February 22, the multitude converged on the Plaza Bolívar. Unable to break up the assemblage, the police called upon General López for troops. He ordered out half a battalion under the command of a lieutenant colonel.

Still the people would not move on. A barked command. The soldiers raised their rifles. A last appeal from the officer, which was met with sullen defiance. Another command. Then a thunderous volley which echoed long and loud across the plaza. Almost a dozen men, women, and children dropped to the pavement, dead. Panicstricken, the multitude streaked for the side streets.

In the government telegraph building an operator sat beside his key and clicked the latest intelligence to Maracay.

"*Recibido,*" acknowledged Maracay. That was all. No comments. No orders.

The situation, López agreed, had taken a turn for the worse. Now the populace really had cause for censure. Knots of angry citizens continued to congregate in the thoroughfares. The efforts of the police to disperse them were ineffective. With a heavy heart, López ordered out the cavalry to clear the streets. As the mounted soldiers charged with flashing sabers, the groups broke ranks and ran.

All through the night the clatter of horses hooves echoed weirdly along the rows of silent buildings.

Thursday the business district was silent and deserted. All Caracas was on strike. Not a trolley car or automobile moved. The telephone exchange was closed down. Velasco need not have sent a call
for troops; López had already acted. From the four *cuartels* under his
command details were being sent out to patrol the Plaza Bolívar and
to guard the Casa Amarilla, the capitol building, the Presidential
palace, and the Banco de Venezuela. Another detail moved into the
telegraph and telephone building to prevent disruption of communications with Maracay.

In defiance of authority, more people than ever thronged through
the streets the following day. Mumbling insults and veiled threats,
they marched past the homes of López, Velasco, and other high government officials. Fearful lest this harmless parading might develop
into mob violence, López posted troops at these trouble spots and
strengthened the guard at public buildings. It was impossible to try
to disperse the crowds without resorting to force and bloodshed, and
López simply didn't have enough troops to make a display of strength.
If at this moment the people only knew that each *cuartel* with its park
of arms and ammunition was garrisoned by only twenty men, they
would have overwhelmed the garrisons by sheer weight of numbers.
They were in that frame of mind.

In the telegraph building a formidable array of military chieftains
sat down to a grim conference. Besides Velasco, López, and García
there were Generals Galavis, Fernández, Briceño, Gimón, Eustóquio
Gómez, the generalissimo's brother-in-law Colmenares Pacheco, and
the Colombian, Dr. García.

Pacheco addressed López: "In view of the serious situation brought
about by the student strike, we have gathered here because we are
all responsible to the government for its defense . . . and it is up
to us to take whatever measures we deem necessary. First of all, we
must know what orders you have received from General Gómez . . .
and what you have done to safeguard the city. We believe that men
like Eustóquio, Fernández and others of us here should share full
responsibility."

"General Gómez has given me no special orders," López replied.
"As for what I have done . . . I've taken every measure for the
security of the bank and other buildings within the limits of my

capacity—of which General Gómez, the minister of war, and the inspector general of the army are aware."

"You mean," spoke up a general, "you have no more troops?"

"That is correct."

"In that case," said Dr. García, "we will all sign a telegram to General Gómez requesting reinforcements."

"I regret," said López, "I cannot sign any joint telegram . . . because my prerogatives and responsibilities are explicit and preclude such a step."

It was after López left the building that the telegram was dispatched without his knowledge. Upon receiving it, Gómez, puzzled, is said to have remarked, "General López is the one who has the better right to request reinforcements, and he hasn't done so . . . strange . . . *Bueno, pues,* let them have one battalion."

The next day, Saturday the 25th, saw the greatest concentration of people ever seen on the streets of Caracas. Hour after hour they marched in silent accusation. There were no mounted troops patrolling the streets. To send them out into that mass of humanity would only provoke clashes and bloodshed. Yet all these demonstrations were building up to a climax. If these people were up to mischief, if they meant to overwhelm the representatives of authority, the crisis would come soon. To the resolute commandant, the next move was his and he wavered not an instant. Machine guns were set up at the four *cuartels,* the Ministry of War, Miraflores, the telegraph building, and other strategic spots. Fortunately for everyone, the populace made no hostile moves, but disbanded before the day was out.

That same morning a censor in the telegraph building read a telegram directed to General Gómez at Maracay. The two-hundred-and-sixty-five-word message was signed by Arévalo González, the former newspaper publisher who had suffered imprisonment thirteen times under three regimes. Still the fearless patriot, González was now pleading for the release of the imprisoned students.

". . . I do not beg on bended knees," he had written, "nor with grace, because that would be an offense to them. I beg it with due respect, but on my feet, as one exercising the right to demand justice . . ."

That afternoon a detail of thirty-three soldiers escorted a batch of prisoners to Puerto Cabello. Among them was Arévalo González. He was put into prison for the fourteenth and last time, for this time he died there.

The student incident had now grown to national proportions. In Maracaibo, Valencia, and other cities there were waves of strikes in sympathy with the students. A statement from the President of the Republic was long overdue. What were the crimes of these students? Did the dictator intend to keep them imprisoned indefinitely?

Aware that the eyes of the nation were upon him, Gómez, in his good time, issued a statement for the press. From Los Teques, on Monday the 27th he wrote:

". . . I have opened the doors of the university to them and secured and paid magnificent professors that they might learn honorable professions . . . but they do not care to be anything but politicians. Since they do not wish to study, they can learn to work. I have treated them as a severe parent. I have sent them, temporarily, out to the roads . . . There they will reflect and understand their errors.

"I do not consider these boys my enemies. For the true enemies, for those who disturb the order and the social well-being, they know that I have methods of true severity."

Those who were with Gómez that day in Los Teques vouch for his state of mind when he wrote that statement. He was visibly distressed rather than annoyed that he was impelled to punish youths. It had been his henchmen, not the commander-in-chief, who had instigated the arrest of Betancourt and his brethren. Yet his men had done exactly what he would have done had he been in their places. Castro, Crespo *et al* had been fearful of being called despots, so they had done nothing to correct an unpleasant and sometimes embarrassing situation. They, too, had been harassed by insults and childish pranks. The core of the matter, however, lay deeper than that. If one is to believe historians and disinterested observers of bygone eras, the students of the university regarded politics as an extra-curricular activity. In this they were encouraged by revolutionary elements which sought to undermine the dictatorship of the period. This the students knew: they were minors in the eyes of the law and as such they could not be (legally, that is) punished for their acts. As neither their professors nor parents could curb them, Gómez, his *paciencia* having run out, took the matter personally in hand. The punishment he meted out to them was harsh and for good reasons; these youths would have to learn the error of their ways, and a searing example must be set for the younger generation.

It was about the middle of February that a column of open trucks bearing the students and their guards left Puerto Cabello and wended its way south through the rolling hills and rich farm lands of Carabobo. Sounding its horns, it roared through the tree-shaded Avenida Principal of Valencia, then turned east along a narrow concrete highway which skirted the southern shore of Lake Valencia and the dictator's model farm and cattle ranch at Güigüe. At the crossroads village of Magdaleno the column left the concrete strip and swung south along the hard-packed dirt road toward Villa de Cura, the scene of Gómez's triumph over General Luciano Mendoza twenty-seven years before. Passing the water resort of San Juan de Los Morros, the column crossed the last brown hills and descended to the shadeless plains of Guarico. It was the dry season, and the relentless sun beat down from the cloudless sky on the parched prairie grass, clumps of *chaparros,* and solitary moriche palms which stood like lonely sentinels in the vast dreary wastes. Trailing a cloud of dust which hung in the still air like the smoke of a prairie fire, the grimy caravan rumbled through the sunbaked village of Ortiz. An hour later it drew up at another cluster of huts sitting forlorn on the banks of the Río Guarico, now shrunken to a mere trickle. This was El Sombrero, the base of operations for the road builders. Beyond lay the convict labor gangs and the new ribbon of road which was inching its way toward the village of Palenque.

Facing the plaza in El Sombrero is an old two-story colonial house of many rooms. The largest building in the village, it had once been the home of a Spanish rancher. Now it is a school of arts and crafts, but at the height of Gómez's road-building program it served as a shelter for some of the slave laborers who slept in packed rows on its tiled floors. A jail the villagers called it, and a jail it was, with iron bars at the windows, guards at the doors, and always the clank of chains and shackles.

Shackled in pairs, the students were herded into trucks before daybreak and taken out to the *llanos* where they were given picks and shovels and put to work. There was no attempt at rehabilitation here. It was strictly punishment. The colonel in charge of each gang was like the captain of a slave ship that plied the Spanish Main three centuries ago. It was he who decided the fate of the prisoners in his charge. Whether they lived or died depended on his whim and pleasure. When they failed to keep up with their quota of labor, even boys and frail old men were lashed with a bull whip by guards possessed. They toiled from dawn to dark, and after wolfing a bowl of *sancocho,* they dragged their exhausted bodies and their heavy shackles into the dry prairie grass for the night.

They were a motley crowd, these prisoners. Chained to the pale, city-raised youths were hardened criminals, sometimes a dying wretch who at one time had been a gifted poet or a brilliant lawyer. Among them were debased and dangerous murderers escaped from French Cayenne. There was one pathetic *mestizo* who had been a chauffeur in Caracas. He was paying with his life for having collided with a Gomecista's car.

For most of these wretched beings toiling under the hot *llanos* sun, their days were numbered and they knew it. Daily the combined mental and physical tortures, malaria, dysentery, and starvation diet took their toll. Day after day the students witnessed it. Aching, emaciated bodies, teeth chattering from the fever of malaria, were forced to wield a pick or shovel until the very last; and diabolical guards laughed as they dumped the corpses into a hole by the roadside. So many hundreds died in the building of this gravel road that the natives of the region called it *el camino de los muertos*—the road of the dead. There were others like it, built at the same appalling expense in human lives—the road between Barcelona and Aragua in Anzoátegui, and the long, tortuous one that ran the length of the Cordillera from Trujillo to Táchira.

It is hard to believe that human beings can be so degraded, yet in the prison camps of Dachau, Buchenwald, and Belsen the world has seen ample evidence of what inhuman barbarities civilized men are capable of inflicting on their fellow beings. Dictatorships are synonymous with cruelties and tortures, and so long as a people tolerate a dictator, they will also have to bear with chambers of horrors like the prison of Carabanchel in Spain, or Venezuela's dungeons and its roads of the dead.

Gómez's motto, long publicized with appropriate fanfare, was "Union, Peace, and Work." Union, yes, mocked an oppressed people, but it is Union in jail, Peace in the cemetery, and Work in the chain gangs.

"The Well Deserving" had hoped to instil in the minds of these rebellious students fear of God and Gómez. What he accomplished was quite the opposite. Just when the students had begun to despair that there was no God and were expecting an early death and burial in the prairie soil, they were taken back to Caracas and set free. This was in early March. The university being closed, they were left to their own devices, and idleness bred mischief. The student incident had awakened a large part of the country and especially the Venezuelans in exile to possibilities (until then considered non-existent) of overthrowing the regime. In this group of students who had returned from the *llanos,* the potential revolutionists saw a useful ally who could do much to topple the regime from within. As for the students themselves, their experience had fired them with new ambitions. They now craved excitement, glory, and above all, revenge. Their hands itched to grasp the butt of a gun.

Up to this period, the twentieth year of Gómez's dictatorship, there had been but few disturbances in the country. What bellicose *caudillos* remained outside of the official family were too wary to venture a try at armed rebellion. Gómez's prowess on the field was still fresh in their minds. What attempts were made to break the peace were led mostly by men who had no military experience whatever and relied on a spontaneous uprising of the masses to give weight to their movement. On this front they obtained almost no help at all, and the net result was dismal failure in every instance. The first rebellion, in eastern Venezuela in 1914, was led by General Horacio Ducharne. It was quickly put down, and Ducharne, who managed to escape, was later killed in Maturín. Several times small bands of exiles crossed the Colombian border into Táchira. With the exception of the attempts led by Dr. Roberto Vargas and General Juan Pablo Peñaloza, the old Andean warhorse, these were merely hit-and-run engagements which smacked strongly of bandit forays.

Up until 1928, the only revolutionist to earn a name for himself as such was Emilio Arévalo Cedeño, who made numerous incursions into the country over a period of fourteen years. He was never caught. Perhaps no other man gave the army so much to do and caused the dictator so much annoyance as this tenacious rebel. A self-styled general, Arévalo actually was a telegraph operator who fancied himself a modern Robin Hood. Carrying on a shrewd guerrilla warfare, he never lacked for followers, and his exploits made him the unsung hero of the people. One of his first acts upon venturing on Venezuelan soil was to tie his telegraph key to a government line and send a taunting message to Maracay.

"Have just caught the famous General Arévalo Cedeño," he once wired Gómez from the southern *llanos,* signing the name of an obscure *jefe civil.* "What shall I do with him?"

Back came a command from the generalissimo: "Well done. Bring Arévalo here to me."

Beside himself with mirth, Arévalo tapped out another message: "But I don't want to go, my General. Why don't you come for me yourself," and added his name.

Gómez tried to pass off these taunts and forays by painting Arévalo to the Venezuelan people as a bandit bent only on pillaging and murder. He was vexed because Arévalo kept by-passing the mountain stronghold of Táchira where strong government forces waited to come to grips with him. A product of the *llanos* and therefore an agile horseman, Arévalo dispensed with foot soldiers as being too cumbersome and slow. Avoiding the natural barrier of the Andes, he and his band confined their raids to the open, less populated regions toward the south, and they routed many village garrisons by their surprise attacks. In 1924, after Arévalo had captured the capital of the federal territory of the Amazon for the second time, Gómez asked for and received permission from President Ospina of Colombia to send Venezuelan troops through Colombian territory to attack the guerrillas from the rear. But Arévalo, who had eluded a special detail of gunmen who had trailed him for years, could not be located, Shrewd *llanero* that he was, he knew how to hide in the thick *monte,* lose himself on the wide, winding rivers, and devour distance on the back of his horse. In 1928 he turned up in Paris where he began plotting with the Venezuelan exiles.

Toward the end of March, 1928, Alfredo Arvelo Larriva, commissioned by Román Delgado Chalbaud and other exiles then living in Paris, arrived in Caracas on a revolutionary mission. Barely a year had passed since Chalbaud had been released from the Rotunda after fourteen years imprisonment. Now he was putting to fulfillment his sworn ambition to war to the death, and he was seeking allies for his coming invasion. In Caracas, Larriva began to extend cautious feelers.

Independent of Chalbaud's movement, the students and several army officers had formed a coalition to seize the Caracas garrisons. Juan José Palacios was the liaison man for the students, and Captain Rafael Alvarado, of the San Carlos barracks, was the military leader. The initial plan was to seize simultaneously Miraflores Palace, the Military College, and San Carlos. In the latter barracks was stored a park of six thousand rifles and five million rounds of ammunition. Once these arms were in their hands, the plotters were to arm the waiting students who in turn would pass out rifles to the citizenry. From San Carlos the rebels would go on to storm the telegraph building and the other *cuartels* of the capital. From that point on, however, their plans were rather vague.

At his home on the evening of Saturday, April 6, General López received a surprise visit from Colonel Sayago, Director of the Military College, and two officers. They brought ill tidings. Only a few minutes before, a cadet had revealed to Sayago some of the details of the plot. What he was unable to learn was the hour the insurgents would strike. Rather than go through the telephone exchange, where there might be a leak, they had brought the news in person.

López immediately phoned the commandants of the various *cuartels* to be on their guard. To Colonel Díaz Peña, commandant of San Carlos, went a special order. Alvarado and his lieutenants were not to be arrested but were to be kept under surveillance. But Alvarado was not in the barracks.

Came a call from General Velasco. He had it from a reliable source that the insurgents were going to strike at any moment. He had so advised Maracay by telephone, but General Gómez happened to be out attending a fiesta.

López called Miraflores. Ramón González, captain of the palace guard, had retired early and answered the telephone in his pajamas. He was told to station his men around the building, that the insurgents would attack soon.

Then another call to San Carlos. *"Quién habla?"* asked the voice at the other end.

"General López Contreras. Who is this?"

López heard a click. The party had hung up.

Accompanied by his orderly, López hurried out to the street and walked toward police headquarters at a fast clip. He arrived just as a call was coming in from the telephone exchange. It was reported that the sounds of gunfire could be heard coming from Miraflores.

Jumping into a taxi which was parked at the door, López and his orderly headed for San Carlos. It was now a quarter to one in the morning. Nearing the Plaza del Panteón they passed several groups of men walking in the same direction. Somewhere out there was Rómulo Betancourt with a revolver in his pocket. Peering out into the shadows, López spied Captain Alvarado walking alone toward Dos Pilitas. Stopping his car he called to him to halt. But Alvarado, recognizing the general's voice, ran off into the darkness. López ordered his orderly out after him and continued on alone.

CHAPTER TWENTY-NINE

Invasions

The streets of Maracay were silent and deserted, the Plaza Girardot shrouded in darkness. In the vestibule of the presidential residence, moths fluttered around a globe of light which threw its faint rays on two soldiers sitting guard at the entrance. In the tiled corridor that skirted the patio, Dolores Amelia, trailed by her two eldest sons, Juan Vicente and Florencio, strode back and forth like an enfuriated jaguar, her words falling over each other in a shrill crescendo. She had rushed over from her home on Calle Santa Michelena as soon as she heard the news. To the officers and aides who were waiting both for the generalissimo to return and the telephone to ring, the suspense was nerve-racking enough, but the woman was so distraught from fear that the air became vibrant with excitement.

At last the presidential car purred to a stop at the entrance, and the dictator, looking the picture of confidence, strode calmly into their midst. Admonishing his almost hysterical woman to be quiet, he asked an aide to put through a call to General López. Then he went into his office, sat down behind his desk and waited, unruffled and serene.

When the gold telephone jangled, Gómez himself picked up the receiver.

"I am informed," he said to López in his slow but businesslike voice, "that some elements have started an armed uprising in Caracas. Is this true?"

"Yes, my General. My men are attempting to quell it at this moment."

"Very good. Use strong measures, you understand? Call me later in the morning and give me the details." And he hung up.

Walking to the patio, Gómez casually bid the waiting group good-night and went to his bedroom.

At a reasonable hour Sunday morning, López phoned in his report. He had arrived, he said, at the San Carlos portal just in time to arrest Lieutenant Fernández, one of the leaders in the plot. Within a matter of minutes, the *cuartel* had been stormed by over two hundred soldiers, civilians, and students . . . a pitched battle ensued which lasted half an hour . . . one hundred and thirty of the insurgents were captured and were now in prison. His orderly, Miguel Sanabría, had captured Captain Alvarado who was now undergoing question-ing . . . Several men on both sides had been wounded and there had been one killed at Miraflores. The insurgents had crept up upon Captain González while he was putting on his shoes and they had cut him down with machetes. But the uprising had been quickly put down with the aid of the cavalry . . . All was quiet in Caracas.

Other than to order the Military College and the Central University closed permanently, the *Jefe* issued no special orders. There were, to be sure, a number of details to be settled. These his hench-men would handle as a matter of routine. They knew that the *Jefe* did not like to be bothered with trivial matters, even less if they were unpleasant ones.

In Caracas, his henchmen were busy. The Rotunda, which had been turned into a storehouse for the Department of Public Works, was re-opened and put to its old use. The dragnet was out to gather in the rest of the students, the army deserters, the young government clerks, and all the others who were known or suspected of having been involved in the uprising. But most of the birds had flown.

Given all the ready cash his father could lay his hands on, Rómulo Betancourt had been driven to Puerto Cabello in the dead of night, where he embarked on the steamer *Tachira* of the Red D Line. Also on board were Lieutenant González Méndez and a group of wanted students. They had booked passage to Maracaibo but none of them had any intention of going there. They all disembarked at Willemstad, Curacao, without passports and in the guise of tourists. Some managed to work their way to Barranquilla where they made a living of sorts peddling fruit. Betancourt obtained a minor job in a Venezuelan commercial house and began plotting anew in the refinery labor camp with Colonel Simón Betancourt, a guerrilla who had fought under Ducharne.

Despite the failure of the uprising, another insurrection was born a few weeks later. In this one the plotters utilized the gullible owner of a photographic shop who permitted them to use the back room of his establishment for their meetings. Their first objective was to seize the San Carlos barracks, even though they were aware that its park of rifles and ammunition had been transferred to Maracay. As they recognized in General López an adroit foe to be reckoned with, they evolved a scheme to get him out of the way. The photographer was induced to invite the general to come to the shop and pose for a picture. The time that López would choose to appear would be the hour for revolt. As luck would have it, before the invitation reached him, the secret police picked up one of the plotters, and under grilling he confessed everything. Before the night was out all of the men involved had been picked up and locked in the Rotunda.

At this time General Chalbaud's invasion was still in the embryo stage, but just over the border in Colombia, General Peñaloza, the old Andean warhorse, thought the time ripe for another invasion. Taking heart because of the recent rebellion, he rallied his guerrillas around him. Peñaloza was the general who had held San Cristóbal against Castro's troops in '99, and had then gone down to defeat in the Battle of Tocuyito. In the early days of Gómez's regime he had tried to collaborate with him but had been bitterly disillusioned. He had spent the last eighteen years in exile. An old man now, he was withered and gray, but he still commanded respect and the loyalty of the few men who were willing to fight tyranny. His opponent, General Juan Alberto Ramírez, was also old in years, but in contrast he commanded far superior forces which he knew how to deploy around the strategic mountain passes.

Peñaloza was never to know the taste of victory. Bravely he and his band fought until they were overwhelmed. The popular uprising he had hoped for never materialized. Captured, he was taken to the fortress of Puerto Cabello, and there he died four years later, a mass of bones lying in his own filth. Informed of his death, Gómez is said to have remarked, "Too bad! He still owes us something!"

The year 1928 ended tranquilly enough. Up to now there had

been nothing spectacular in the way of uprisings, but perhaps it was only the calm before the storm. Perhaps at long last a national spirit of liberation was born.

The new year started off with an ominous warning. In January, great stretches of the country shook in the throes of an earthquake. More than two hundred people were killed, and the damage to property was considerable. In February, congress passed Venezuela's seventeenth Constitution. Its most important change was the abolishment of the offices of First- and Second-Vice President.

To the casual observer, Union, Peace and Work appeared to be reaping benefits. The national revenues were threefold what they were when Gómez assumed power. Petroleum production was twenty-five per cent higher than 1928, when 104,875,706 barrels were produced. Venezuela had now passed Russia for second place in world oil production. Exports, too, were on the increase, surpassing the record established the previous year, of 609,554,962 bolivars. Although coffee was no longer king it still ranked as the major agricultural export. Coffee, too, was big business with Gómez. From his hacienda El Trompillo (bought from Antonio Pimentel) and the others in Táchira and Colombia, he shipped from twenty-five to thirty thousand bags yearly. In the Venezuelan pavilion at the Trade Exposition which opened in Seville, Spain, in May, café "El Trompillo" was the featured attraction.

In Caracas, work had finished on the reconstruction of the National Pantheon and the new Avenida de la Paz, and in the state of Carabobo, on the site of the great battle of that name, the generalissimo inaugurated with great pomp and ceremony a sumptuous monument to commemorate the Heroes of the Revolution.

With many trained ears to the ground listening for any revolutionary stirrings, the dictator and his official family looked forward to a prosperous if not too peaceful future.

"Thanks to the untiring efforts of *el Benemérito* General J. V. Gómez," crowed the *Nuevo Diario,* "Venezuela is enjoying a well-earned prosperity. We are at peace with each other and the world, not fighting among ourselves to the death as are the bellicose Mexicans in their senseless civil war." [24]

[24] General J. G. Escobar's Mexican revolution, which started in March and ended two months later, cost four thousand lives and eleven thousand wounded.

When, in the early days of May, the first rumblings came from over the hills in Portuguesa, Gómez was not taken by surprise. General José Rafael Galbadón, a wealthy rancher, had risen in revolt. And in Miranda, far to the northeast, three guerrilla chieftains joined his banner.

Gómez, the grizzled warrior, was too old now to go out at the head of his troops on punitive expeditions. He was nearing seventy-two and was bothered with attacks of uremia. Though he took short rides on horseback as often as his health and his doctors would allow, he didn't have the stamina to sit all day in the saddle. So he delegated the task of subduing these rebels to his state presidents, generals all of them. Eustóquio Gómez, having been reinstated in his good graces, had been appointed president of Lara on January 18. To him and to Pedro María Cardenas in Táchira, Leon Jurado in Falcón, and Félix Galavis in Yaracuy, went a telegraphic order on May 12 to "wipe out this vile plague the same way I did at Sierra de Carabobo. The blow should be swift and well aimed so that not one shall escape."

The blow fell hard and true, but it was not as swift as the *Jefe* would have wished. It took forty-five days to annihilate these rebels and capture Galbadón, their leader.

An election year was 1929. At the opening of congress on April 19, its president had read the *Jefe*'s annual message on the state of the nation. It terminated with the declaration by Gómez that he would not be a candidate for re-election. It left the senators and deputies in the chamber stunned. They had taken it for granted that he would run again, that he would insist on being President as long as he could stand on his own two feet. The fact that "The Well Deserving" gave no hint as to who he wished to succeed him only lent confusion to the issue. Nor had the leaders of congress been enlightened beforehand as to just what was expected of them. He had told them nothing. After taking several days to mull things over, the group of frock-coated puppets who constituted this supine body arrived at one conclusion. The cunning horse-trader of La Mulera had set a trap for them in much the same manner as Castro had tried to trick him. Either they were sincere in their saccharine tributes which painted him as the one indispensable man, and would draft him for re-election, or, believing him impotent and unfit to fill office, they would ignore him and elect a man of their own choice. Those among them who may have entertained hopes of electing a more worthy and patriotic citizen could not ignore the fact that to the powerful military men who surrounded him, Gómez was still an idol. Though he might be failing in health if not in mind, the army was his strength and buttress against treason.

As not one man in congress possessed the gumption to ignore the threat and speak his mind, they felt they had no choice. The whole sovereign congress jointly sent off a long-winded telegram to "The Well Deserving" at El Trompillo where he happened to be communing with nature. It behooved the legislators to draft *el Benemérito* General Gómez for the Presidency as he was indispensable to the peace and welfare of the nation.

El Benemérito was duly flattered but regretful. He reiterated his stand. He had served the Fatherland long and well. The country was at peace and was prospering mightily. It no longer needed him. He now wished to devote his full efforts to the soil that he loved so well.

The members of congress were completely baffled. Again they discussed the matter and finally they decided to do what "The Well Deserving" probably had expected of them in the first place. On May 15 they repaired en masse to the official residence in Maracay where they were ushered into the carpeted front *sala* which served for affairs of state. Awed and apprehensive, they stood gazing at the huge equestrian portrait of the Hero of La Victoria at the end of the room, until the Hero himself walked in leisurely and took his seat beneath it. There was an empty chair on each side of him. On such occasions, Vicentico, once the heir-presumptive, would have sat beside him stiff and erect and stroking his mustache, looking like a younger image of his father. Vicentico was gone now, cast out of his father's heart and mind, and there was no other son to take his place.

After the khaki-clad patriarch had bestowed a bland smile and warm words of greeting, the president of congress made his little speech. Gómez listened approvingly, smiling benignly, and nodding his head from time to time at the recounting of his triumphs.

When it was over, the congressional reporter who had accompanied the group turned a page of his notebook and poised his pen expectantly.

Still sitting—a privilege that was his due—the affable patriarch fingered his cane, coughed nervously, and began to speak.

"Your visit really surprises me because I thought I had made myself clear in my message that I would not accept the Presidency.

"I had said in my message that I had found the country like a house in ashes, and that I had rebuilt the house on solid foundations . . . And what is needed to take care of a house? You need a caretaker, but you don't need me. My work is finished. My energies are being devoted to the task of doing something good for the Fatherland . . . and so I have chosen work . . . work to cultivate the soil.

"I am a farmer and a stock-raiser, and in these pursuits I believe I have obtained good results. I have a great deal of experience in farming and cattle-raising, and because of this I desire that you comply with my wishes, although I shall always be heedful for the welfare of the Fatherland. (Loud applause)

"The Fatherland before everything . . . nothing else matters . . . not even life. And when you need me, I shall not fail you. For this you can count on me. (Loud applause)

"But for the rest, I have to repeat . . . that I do not accept the Presidency. Look for the method that will give you a solution to this matter. And now permit me to say to you what you can do. Will you permit me? (Cries of *Sí! Sí!*)

"Well, then, many enemies have said, 'What that gentleman wishes is that they go and beg him to accept the Presidency.'

"I do not wish that you come and beg me, because I am not accustomed to beg nor to being begged. I say to you that we should come to an agreement on this matter. I do not accept the Presidency, but I do wish that you name me commander-in-chief of the army. (Loud applause) . . . because for me the army is my life. There are two things that I love—the Army and work.

"Therefore you will have to choose a man who, in exercising the functions of President, will be in accord with me in everything. He will respect the army under my command and will guarantee the tranquillity and peace of Venezuela . . . and when the enemies know this, they will refrain from any action against the republic. The individual whom you select will have to work harmoniously with me in every way . . . and with this understanding, everything will go along smoothly.

"If you agree, then, proceed with the nomination, which I calculate should be made on the twenty-third of May. (Loud applause)

"If you agree, I will give you a candidate whom I shall select . . . but I will have to search for one, as this candidate will have to work in harmony with me. If you authorize me, then, I shall find him for you. (Cries of *Sí! Sí!*)

"That which we have resolved here should be proclaimed this very night because it is important that everyone within and outside of the country shall know the arrangements made and the motives and reasons why I have accepted the nomination of commander-in-chief of the army rather than the Presidency of the Republic." (Loud and prolonged applause)

So, by guile and artifice, Gómez accomplished his aim to thrust on to a subservient congress the candidate he had in mind all along. Though he still lusted after women, he was feeling his years now and lost all desire to sit in the Presidency; the burdens of office were too heavy on his tired shoulders. Rather, in the usual Monagas and Guzmán tradition, he would hand over the reins of government to an inconspicuous proselyte, one who could not conceivably jeopardize his own power and material wealth. He would have to be a man of the same mold as his brother Juancho—colorless, plodding, loyal, and obedient, without rancor and unscrupulous ambition, without a following, yet of a mien to command respect. In short, a man of clay who would attend to all the tedious details of administration while the master relaxed on his broad green acres and made all the decisions.

The man Gómez palmed off on congress and the Venezuelan people, Juan Bautista Pérez, was the personification of innocence, the embodiment of all attributes that any truculent dictator could have wished for. A tall, gaunt man addicted to wing collars and canes, he is aptly described by Jorge Luciani as follows: "A native of Caracas, a mediocre, obscure lawyer; innocuity that passed for merit. Irreproachable in his private life, virgin in politics, always apart from the world, very gentlemanly, very serious, very gentle. One of those creatures who do the same things every day with chronometric punctuality, who eat, sleep, bathe, and defecate at fixed hours, who keep the Sabbath, carry umbrellas and salute the most humble with a deep bow. Inheritors of a modest estate that endures and grows without assistance; much addicted to etiquette; very respectful of the government that imposes taxes and orders imprisonments; without intellectual curiosity and without spiritual unquiet of any kind; . . . who, on clear days, pronounce in magisterial tone, 'It is a fine day,' and on cloudy days, discover, very pompously, that 'It is going to rain'; who give alms publicly on Saturdays but who are incapable of inconveniencing themselves for anything or anybody. More than good-natured, they are egoists who will not permit their mode of life to be disturbed. And there, in the bosom of their tranquil homes, they are petty tyrants."

That was the man who, at the behest of the dictator, was elected President of the Republic on May 30 by the national congress.

Propelled into the limelight much against his will and somewhat bewildered by it all, Pérez made a conscientious effort to perform his job to the satisfaction of his mentor if not to his people. Pérez turned out to be a mere figurehead who looked and acted his part, and what glimmers of hope had first arisen that he might be the long awaited Messiah who would lead his people from the bondage of tyranny, were quickly dissipated. Not so in Curacao, however. Apprised by radio and the press of the dictator's retirement from the Presidency, some of the Venezuelan exiles in Willemstad deduced that the moment of liberation was close at hand, and they counted on Pérez for support. With the dictator's crack troops still tied up in Portuguesa and Miranda tracking down Galbadón and his followers, these exiles reckoned the time propitious for a coastal invasion.

With both Betancourts off on a junket through the Caribbean islands to procure arms for the coming Chalbaud expedition, the exiles in Curacao had been left without a leader. At this juncture, Rafael Simón Urbina, an ambitious exile of thirty-one, took charge. A native of Coro who had been expelled from school in his youth because he would not submit to discipline, Urbina was a frustrated egoist who proclaimed himself a zealot for democracy. He had no military training whatever, but what he lacked in experience he made up for in energy and imagination. Always an opportunist, Urbina quickly evolved a bold plan in which he figured as the leader, and thus acquired for himself the grandiose title of "general."

The island town had less than one hundred policemen, and the

Dutch governor wasn't very vigilant. The Venezuelans, on the other hand, numbered in the thousands. Most of them were Corianos who had migrated to the better paying jobs at the refinery and on the quays. Perhaps a hundred or so, which included several students and the present Communist leader, Gustavo Machado, were impoverished political exiles. All of the latter fell in with Urbina's plot as did about a hundred of the others.

On the afternoon of June 9, just ten days after the election of Pérez, Urbina and his band kidnaped the governor and captured the fortress which guards the approach from the sea. From its arsenal they supplied themselves with arms, ammunition, and a cannon which they pulled down to the quay, a few yards away. In the affray two Dutch policemen lost their lives. Taking the governor and some of his aides with them as hostages, the revolutionaries commandeered the American passenger and cargo vessel, *Maracaibo*, of the Red D Line, and ordered its captain at pistol point to put to sea and head for the Venezuelan coast sixty miles away.

Before daybreak the next morning the expedition disembarked at La Vela, Falcón, the bailiwick of General Jurado. Then the governor and the ship were set free.

All had gone well so far with the rebels and all perhaps would have gone well in the Venezuelan phase of the adventure if Urbina had been practical instead of visionary, or if he had been as rich and cunning as Gómez. Instead of buying off in advance most of the influential officers and citizens, he uttered long speeches about liberty and tyranny—which would doubtless have had its effect in the long run on the peons, but hardly on generals and officials whom Gómez had rendered subservient with money and haciendas.

Thanks to his spies in Willemstad, Gómez had been forewarned of what had been going on and of the impending arrival of the *Maracaibo*. He had telegraphed the state presidents up and down the coast to be prepared. Thus when Urbina and his luckless band tramped over the sand dunes toward Coro, Jurado's soldiers were waiting for them. The fighting was over in less than an hour and most of the invaders were taken prisoner. Urbina, who knew the territory well, managed to escape and return to Curacao, where his late prisoner, the governor, placed him in jail. The workers in the Shell refinery, sympathizers of Urbina, threatened to sabotage their company's plant if harm came to their idol, so Urbina was allowed to go into exile in Santo Domingo. Fortunate for him that he was not made to enter the dread portals of La Guaira.

The precipitated planning of Urbina's expedition was typical of many of the ill-fated invasions and internal uprisings that had occurred up to this time. What had been lacking in all of them was proper co-ordination and the element of surprise. Lack of funds, of course, presented a serious problem in itself, but this was compensated for somewhat by the simple expedient of piracy. Where there's a will there's a way seemed to be the favorite axiom of these determined rebels, but they failed to take into full account the preying eyes of Gómez's spies and the speed and acumen of his generals. What doomed these movements to failure was a combination of factors, some of them unforeseen. Undoubtedly, a far greater number never even reached the launching stage, sometimes because of a last-minute betrayal on the part of a timorous partisan or a stupid blunder by one of the leaders.

One instance of utter stupidity, which provoked not a little mirth in Maracay, wrecked an attempted uprising by General Gregorio Segundo Riera soon after he resigned in disgust from the federal council and returned to his native Coro. No soonei had he begun to hatch a plot involving the garrisons of the state than he discovered that he was being kept under surveillance. Before journeying to Maracaibo, ostensibly on business but actually to throw Gómez's agents off the scent, Riera briefed a lieutenant for his part. He was to continue lining up adherents among the state garrisons and was to wire him on a certain date using a prearranged code. When referring to the number of recruits he could count on he was to use the word "goats," and for the number of rifles available he was to use the word "cigars."

At the appointed time, Riera received the following telegram: "HAVE FIVE HUNDRED AND FIFTY GOATS AND SIX HUNDRED CIGARS STOP WILL NEED SHOES AND HAMMOCKS FOR THE GOATS AND AMMUNITION FOR THE CIGARS."

Maracay, situated eighty kilometers west of Caracas as the buzzard flies, was the hub of Gómez's military machine. The macadam roads stretched north, east, south, and west—north to the Caribbean, east to Caracas, south to the great plains, and west where they met the trails that led into the Cordillera and Colombia. Crack troops, stationed at well-stocked arsenals, could radiate in any direction to meet a sudden emergency. Speed was the thing, and it was with speed that Gómez's generals exterminated, before they could grow and flourish, the many "vile plagues" that germinated along the length and breadth of a prostrate land.

In far off Paris it was obvious to General Ramón Delgado Chalbaud that if his invasion was to succeed it would have to strike far to the east, out of reach of Gómez's main forces. He laid his plans accordingly.

Chalbaud, one of the Restorers under Castro, and "Admiral" of the fleet and director of the government shipyard under Gómez, had been involved with his brother Miguel in a conspiracy to assassinate the dictator in 1912. A cultured, mild-mannered man, his fourteen years in the Rotunda had converted him into an emaciated and hollow-eyed fanatic who lived for nothing but revenge. In his cell in 1921 he had said to a fellow prisoner, José Rafael Pocaterra, who lived to become Ambassador to Washington under a more liberal regime, "If we both get out, let's go to war; if you get out first, wait for me." In December, 1927, Chalbaud had been released. His brother had died in prison. What wealth he still possessed was in a bank in Paris. Gómez had confiscated his three haciendas and all of his stock in the *Compañía de Navegación Fluvial y Costanera.* With a rough plan formulated in his mind Chalbaud went to Paris to join his wife and son Carlos, who was expected to obtain his engineering degree at the Sorbonne the following year.

There began for Chalbaud the long, tedious task of writing letters to all the exiles scattered over half the globe, enlisting their aid. Chalbaud was willing to risk his life and all he possessed for his cause. What had they to offer? At one time or another all of them had been outspoken in their censure of Gómez and his tyranny. Were they willing to fight for their beliefs? Were they willing to risk their necks as well as their wealth to overthrow the tyrant?

One by one the letters began to trickle in from New York, Havana, Panama City, Barranquilla, Willemstad, Port of Spain and a dozen other cities. In general the replies were affirmative and almost all of them offered money, though in most cases it was pathetically little. On the roster that Chalbaud compiled began to figure such names as José Rafael Pocaterra, Leopoldo Baptista (Gómez's former

Secretary General), Dr. Santos Dominici (who had refused an appointment in 1922 as Venezuelan Minister to Washington), Rómulo Betancourt, Colonel Simón Betancourt, Generals Carabaño and Blanco Fombona, Doctors Alberto Smith, Pedro Jugo Delgado, Néstor Luis Pérez, and Atilano Carnevali, plus a host of lesser luminaries.

Through a contact in the Parisian underworld, false passports were secured so that emissaries could carry out special missions. One such individual reached Caracas without mishap in March; another contacted the exiles in New York in July. A month later, Leopoldo Baptista and other exiles held a meeting at Rouses Point, New York, near the Canadian border. In December, another meeting was held at the Cadillac Hotel in New York. In the spring of 1929, still another was held in Port of Spain. A year had passed in careful preparations, and at last Chalbaud could say that he had set up a business-like organization. Still, the scheming went on.

On May 15, 1929, at a fiesta in Caracas in honor of General Emilio Fernández, who had just been appointed president of the state of Sucre, General López was ushered into a private room by a man he hardly knew. Seated there were a well-known lawyer, a banker, and a high government official. First made to swear that he would not divulge their names nor what they were about to discuss, López was invited to join Chalbaud's conspiracy.

López was astounded. What was there about him that would inspire such confidence? What had he ever said or done that would lead anyone to believe that he was open to treachery? As to what he thought of their chances of success, he had better not say. Stiffly, he declined their invitation. The meeting ended on a sour note.

Time and again López had sworn his fidelity to his commander-in-chief. Almost as often Gómez had let it be known that he trusted him implicitly. There was little likelihood that López would turn traitor. As events turned out, there was little chance that he could be of help to *any* conspiracy. López had incurred the ire of Colmenares Pacheco and Dr. García for his recalcitrant attitude during the student rebellion. With evil forces at work against him, he soon found himself holding a minor post in Táchira.

Through the efforts of a friend in Paris, Chalbaud was introduced to Felix Kramarski, a partner of Felix Prenzlau & Company, a banking firm of Hamburg. Kramarski was sympathetic to Chalbaud's plan, and after assuring himself that its chances for success were good, his firm arranged for the purchase of a vessel and a park of arms and ammunition. The vessel they found in the Polish port of Gdynia was the *Falke,* an old coal-burning hulk of two-hundred-and-forty-foot length, but seaworthy enough for the voyage that lay ahead. It was delivered to Danzig where Kramarski attended to its outfitting, the hiring of a German mercenary crew of thirty-five men, and the storing of arms and ammunition. At Chalbaud's request, the vessel was renamed *General Anzoátegui.*

Jubilant that their plan of attack was soon to be put into action, the exiles formed their *Junta de Liberación de Venezuela* in Paris on July 5. Two days later the pact was signed in Geneva to avoid (in the event the document was discovered by the French police) any pretext of charges of violation of neutrality. The avowed aim of the *Junta* was to take over the Venezuelan government once the invasion was successful, and for this purpose the following officers were elected: Dr. Santos Dominici, President; Dr. Alberto Smith, Vice-President; José Rafael Pocaterra, Secretary General; Dr. Jugo Delgado, Treasurer; General Delgado Chalbaud, Director of War; and General Leopoldo Baptista, Chief of Staff.

One man who was bitterly disappointed because he did not figure in the *Junta* was Antonio Aranguren, the same individual who had sold the million hectare concessions in Zulia to the Dutch Shell. This deal had made him a millionaire and formed the basis of an even larger fortune built up through commercial and real estate transactions. Thwarted on several occasions by restrictions imposed on him by the Gomecistas, Aranguren decided to throw in his lot with Chalbaud. Journeying to Paris, he offered to finance part of the expedition —for a price. His parting words to Chalbaud denoted what he had in mind: "Don't forget, Román," he had said, "I am to be President!" Had he been a modern-day Bolívar, he would have been welcomed with open arms, with or without his millions. But Aranguren was not the zealous patriot he pretended to be. He was an avaricious opportunist, and as such was denounced to Chalbaud before the *Junta* was formed. Brooding over his disappointment in Caracas, Aranguren withdrew his support but kept up his flair for intrigue. He proceeded to form an alliance with Urbina, which never amounted to much, and

culminated twenty-one years later in disaster for both of them; Chalbaud's son, Carlos, the leading member of Venezuela's Military *Junta,*
was brutally assassinated by Urbina in his last desperate attempt at
rebellion.

Carlos Chalbaud had graduated from the Sorbonne in 1928. Serious and unassuming like his parent, this lad of twenty-one had persuaded his father to let him join the expedition. Together with the
other exiles, numbering ninety-nine in all, Carlos boarded the
Anzoátegui in Hamburg. There on the river Elbe they were forced to
remain for several days due to complaints of the crew against the
captain, which led to an investigation by the authorities and the discovery of the nature of the cargo. So once again Gómez was forewarned of impending danger, not by spies this time, but by the German
Foreign Office.

Chalbaud had gone to great stealth and trouble to conceal his
plans. When the vessel sailed from Hamburg shortly after the middle
of July, only one man besides himself, Leopoldo Baptista, knew their
exact destination. Emissaries had been sent on ahead with sealed
orders to contact the various waiting groups of revolutionaries.

Pedro Aristiguieta, one of the *Junta* members, went to Port of
Spain to take charge of the group there and to arrange for a sailing
vessel to land them near the port of Güiría. There in his native province he was to round up his friends and partisans and march overland to attack their objective from the rear.

Another emissary handed his orders to Rómulo Betancourt in
Santo Domingo. Betancourt's group (which included fifty Dominicans
drafted by golden promises) was to head south in a schooner and he
was not to open his orders until he had been under way twenty-four
hours.

It was on August 10 that the *Anzoátegui* made her rendezvous
with a small sailboat near a barren island off the Venezuelan coast.
Two hundred rifles and several cases of ammunition were transferred
to the bark, which sailed south to land the cargo in a deserted cove
for Aristiguieta. Turning due west, the *Anzoátegui* steamed on for
several hours, then turned south to pass the western tip of the Araya
Peninsula. It was past midnight. Directly ahead, shrouded in darkness,
lay the municipal pier of the town of Cumaná and the mouth of the
Río Manzanares, now swollen by the rains. A thousand yards to the

east, which brought her into the Gulf of Cariaco, the *Anzoátegui* dropped anchor a half mile off a lonely stretch of beach.

So far, all appeared to have gone well, and Chalbaud was confident that Cumaná, his first objective, could be taken by surprise. Betancourt was expected to join him at any moment, and after arming his men from the *Anzoátegui*'s store, they were to attack the town together at 5 A.M. At precisely the same time, Aristiguieta's band was to attack along the east coastal road.

As the crucial hour neared, Chalbaud sat there in the dark in his cramped quarters, grimly optimistic. He was never to know that fate was playing him a cruel trick, that his carefully-laid plans already had gone completely awry. To the west, Betancourt's dilapidated craft had sprung leaks and the captain had refused to go on. The boat had turned back to Santo Domingo. Aristiguieta, too, had suffered misfortune. He had misjudged the time it would take to cover the rough and hilly terrain, and was still many miles away.

Unaware of these mishaps, Chalbaud gave the order for action. In pitch darkness the lifeboats of the *Anzoátegui* were lowered into the calm waters of the gulf. Ninety-six guerrillas, double bandoleers over their shoulders and revolvers strapped to their waists, eased into them and rowed toward shore, one boat separating from the rest and heading west past the river mouth toward the pier. Left aboard with the crew were José Pocaterra, young Chalbaud, and a guard. In the lead of the group that headed for the beach was General Chalbaud who kept glancing at his radium-dial watch and scanning the darkness for a sail that would denote the arrival of Betancourt.

His timing was perfect. It was bound to be, for Chalbaud was methodical in all that he did. He knew the general layout of the town. Beyond the river to his right stood the customs house, the objective of the other group. From this building the Avenida Bermudez led straight to the bridge, one kilometer away. This bridge, the only one which crossed the river and led to the town proper, would be easy to reach and hold. Ahead of him, beyond the sand flats and its few scattered adobe huts sprawled the residential section. Two and a half kilometers inland and slightly to his left *el Castillo San Antonio* frowned down upon the town from the nearest of a series of rolling hills. He knew almost to a man the strength of its garrison—about one hundred and thirty-five men, he had been told. He knew too, that Cumaná had not yet fully recovered from the earthquake of January past, that the fort had suffered considerable damage. There was still plenty of rubble lying about and many abandoned buildings in which to take refuge should the fighting turn against them. As he had planned it, he and Aristiguieta were to arrive at the foot of the hill about the same time.

The revolutionists pulled their boats up on the beach, crossed the sand flats by the light of the stars, and filtered through the dimly lit streets toward the fort. Hardly had the first contingent reached the foot of the hill than the sound of shots was heard coming from the customs house. Immediately, the *cuartel* alarm sounded. It was five o'clock and there was no sign of Aristiguieta.

Outnumbered, the revolutionists abandoned their plan of attack and took cover as best they could to await the onslaught of the garrison. When it came, it was from around the two sides of the hill as well as from above. Bursts of flame punctuated the darkness as they sought each other out by the dim light of the street lamps. After the first assault was over, Chalbaud, the gallant warior, lay dead in the street. Eighteen of his men were either killed, wounded or captured. Of the government dead, one was General Emilio Fernández, the commandant.

From then on it was retreat for the invaders, retreat to the west to join their fellows at the bridge. From doorway to doorway they fired, and block by block they withdrew under punishing volleys. When at last they were within a few yards of the bridge they ran for it, leaving behind their wounded. Barely forty of them managed to cross it in safety.

As the sun rose over the hills, the revolutionists took up positions with their companions on the other side. The river, swollen by the rains, was a natural barrier across which the government soldiers could not cross except by the bridge. This the revolutionists intended to hold until either Betancourt or Aristiguieta appeared on the scene. From the rooftops they could see the *Anzoátegui* riding quietly at anchor in the shimmering gulf. But no sign of a sail.

Time and again the soldiers attempted an assault across the bridge. Each time they were repulsed with heavy losses. After two and a half hours of sporadic firing the revolutionists heard a hum in the sky coming from the west. They waited apprehensively as four army biplanes from Maracay winged in low over the town and appraised their positions. This was a new kind of warfare, one which these old-style guerrillas felt they were unable to cope with. Were these infernal machines going to bomb or strafe them as they lay exposed on the rooftops? Fearfully they glanced out at the gulf and saw their last hope fading away. The *Anzoátegui* had weighed anchor and was heading out to sea. Their only chance of retreat cut off, the revolutionists reluctantly raised the white flag of surrender.

What prompted Pocaterra to abandon his fellows has never been fully explained to everyone's satisfaction. He claimed afterward that the captain had threatened to hand the vessel over to the government forces, that rather than submit to capture, he had thrown the remaining arms overboard and had persuaded the captain to put to sea. With only one day's supply of coal in her bunkers, the *Anzoátegui* headed for the British island of Grenada.

Aristiguieta's band, three hundred and five strong, was quickly spotted as it came along the coastal road. The government forces, strengthened by reinforcements brought in by truck from Barcelona and Puerto de la Cruz, went out to meet it. The rebels, weary from their all-night march, and harassed by the planes which strafed them unmercifully, surrendered after several short skirmishes. Several men on both sides had been killed. Pedro Aristiguieta, mortally wounded, died on his litter as he was being borne to town.

Thus came to a disastrous and speedy end the Chalbaud expedition, the only revolution, in any way deserving the name, ever to seriously threaten Gómez's rule. With it died all hope that the dictator could be overthrown.

Urbina and Aranguren, however, refused to be convinced. They nourished the fond hope that the fortunes of fate would turn. Encouraged by Aranguren, who sent him small sums of money regularly, Urbina plotted anew in Mexico. It was not until October, 1931, that he evolved another one of this bold schemes. He was aided by Colonel Preve, a renegade Mexican officer who had murdered Senator Field Jurado in Mexico City.

In Paris two years before, Preve had made a proposition to Generals Chalbaud and Cedeño. He offered to hire himself out as a mercenary provided a group of his Mexican friends were included in the expedition under his command. His offer had been refused. To Urbina in Mexico he made the same offer and it was quickly accepted.

In the guise of workers headed for the oil fields of Tampico, Urbina, Preve, several Venezuelans, and some two hundred Mexican guerrillas boarded the steamship *Superior* at Vera Cruz. Hidden in their duffle-bags were arms and ammunition. Once out at sea, Preve and his men drew their revolvers and made the captain set his course for Venezuela. Two days later they disembarked at La Vela in Falcón and marched on Coro.

There on the sand dunes the invaders clashed with the forces of General León Jurado. The Mexicans, all experienced in guerrilla warfare, put up a stiff resistance, but after Preve and several of his officers were killed, the band surrendered the following morning. Urbina was not among them; foreseeing defeat, the elusive rebel had slipped away during the night.

Told of the prowess of the Mexicans, Gómez ordered that they be brought before him; also the captain of the *Superior,* which had been captured by a Venezuelan gunboat. Looking like a motley array of cut throats, which they were, the Mexicans stood forlorn and apprehensive while they answered questions and suffered the scrutiny of the generalissimo and his aides. They fully expected to be taken out and shot. But Gómez, the "Founder of Peace," as he liked to be called, was in a benevolent mood. He ordered that the *Superior* be coaled and provisioned and turned over to the captain. To each of the men he gave a sum of money, then let them all embark to return freely to Mexico. If the ship owners or the Mexican government wished to press charges of piracy and kidnaping against the guerrillas, that was their own affair. He would not make any charges on his own account.

To use a Venezuelan idiom of speech, Gómez regarded Rafael Simón Urbina as just a "mosquito," meaning that he was a mean-spirited dastard who was not to be taken seriously. Not so Rómulo Betancourt, however. The former *estudiante de derecho* had matured into a dangerous adversary whose words were listened to avidly by the proletariat of several Latin American nations. From soapbox orating in the Dominican Republic he had gone on to Colombia where he did more of the same. When the Colombian government awarded Gómez the Cruz de Boyacá, Betancourt, incensed, made the most virulent speech of his career, in which he flayed not only Gómez but Olaya Herrera, the Colombian President, as well. Booted out of the country, he went to Costa Rica where the cost of living was ridiculously cheap and Venezuelan exiles were received with sympathy.

After the death in 1931 of the Peruvian dictator, Juan Leguía, Betancourt and the Venezuelan poet Gonzalo Carnevali turned up in Lima. Betancourt gave a "lecture" at the University of San Marcos which produced such a popular manifestation against the tyranny of Gómez, that Sánchez Cerro, the Peruvian dictator, told the youths to get out of the country or he would jail them in the dreaded prison of San Lorenzo.

Back in Costa Rica, Betancourt joined the *Junta Libertadora de Venezuela,* an association of Venezuelan exiles which was looked upon with favor by the Costa Ricans. His first job, a temporary one, was as *Jefe Fiscal* at a voting booth in the hinterland where he was entrusted with "supervising the purity" of the presidential election. Somehow he obtained the wherewithal to found his newspaper *El Trabajo* in San José and to marry Carmen Valverde, a Costa Rican girl of a good but impoverished family. His editorials immediately began to reflect his communist leanings.

To Valmore Rodriguez, Ricardo Montilla, and Raúl Leoni, former students then living in Barranquilla, Betancourt began to write a steady stream of letters preparing the groundwork for insurrection in Venezuela. He wrote on January 27, 1932: "Parties follow where their leaders direct them, and the leaders of our Party will be us and those of the group who have our decided socialist filiation . . . We will take the course to the extreme left at the opportune moment, with the assurance that the majority of the Party will follow behind us. This amorphous, God-fearing segment (the Venezuelan masses) of which Valmore speaks is but cannon fodder which will serve to give us weight, and it matters not to me that they will be left behind. Ballast is always thrown overboard . . ."

And again on August 15, 1932: ". . . Once inside the country (Venezuela) we will unite in a leftist congress and will found—call it what you will—a Communist Party, in an open fight against imperialism, the *caudillos* and the other native and foreign representatives of capitalism . . ."

As Betancourt himself admitted, there didn't seem to be any doubt in Costa Rica as to the color of his banner. "Here, publicly and openly," he wrote, "I have been called a communist, and I have acted like a communist. I believe it would be better if we proceeded more cautiously for awhile . . ."

Sotillo Picornell, another exile who worked with Betancourt in San José, wrote of him: "It is easy to say that anybody is a communist, but of Betancourt you have to say it twice; that is to say, he is a double communist—in his brain and in his heart."

Although it was never proven that he held a Party card, Betancourt followed the traditional Marxist methods of revolt among the masses and he chose Costa Rica as a proving ground. Having aroused the ire of the United Fruit Company and the Electric Bond and Share by his inflammatory articles in favor of the downtrodden worker, Betancourt proceeded to organize Costa Rican labor, concentrating on the workers of the United Fruit Company.

On May 22, 1933, the workers and *desocupados,* armed with tools, clubs, and stones carried out a demonstration in the streets of San José, contrary to the wishes of the authorities. As proven later in a government investigation, the movement had been instigated by Betancourt and four other communist leaders. The police (there was no army) were unable to disperse the mob, and in the clash that ensued, one policeman was killed and several were injured. Being the first of its kind, the incident caused great consternation in San José. The result was a cabinet session the same night at which it was decided to deport Betancourt and four others of his ilk because they were "undesirable elements who constitute a danger to the security of the state." So read the decree signed by President Ricardo Jimenez on May 25. However, it was easier decreed than done, for no country's consul would issue Betancourt a visa.

In a conversation a few weeks later in the presidential palace between President Jimenez and Dr. Luis Alejandro López, the Venezuelan consul, the latter admitted that if Betancourt were deported to Venezuela, it would probably mean his death in one of Gómez's dungeons. In view of Betancourt's defamatory campaign against the dictator and his status as a communist, Gómez was insistent that he be extradited to Venezuela.

To which Jimenez replied: "By all the concepts of international law, I do not have to sanction the extradition of this man if I have reason to believe he will meet his death at the hands of your government. We have been watching Rómulo Betancourt closely and I am informed he has begun to abandon his communist tendencies. Therefore we will let him remain here for the time being."

Observed the Venezuelan consul, dryly, "Your Excellency, I don't believe the leopard can change his spots."

"Perhaps not," countered the President, "but the snake can shed his skin!"

CHAPTER THIRTY

The Mellow Years

The airfield of Maracay, with its broad hangars, shops and *cuartels,* lies on the nothern fringe of the town, just a few minutes walk from the Plaza Girardot. In the early nineteen-twenties a concrete road was laid down from the airport to the Caribbean, thirty miles away. It crosses a narrow green valley, winds over treeless, eroded hills, patches of savanna and torrent-spanning bridges, and climbs up steep jungle-clad slopes and cliffs to the cool floor of Portachuelo Pass, almost three-quarters of a mile above the sea. For miles in every direction the moist green slopes and gorges are dense rain-forest, full of creeping, crawling, and flying things. Here is the "High Jungle" of William Beebe, a treasure-house for scientists who collect and press plants, and trap and preserve strange animal and bird life.

Guarding the pass are two peaks, almost continuously shrouded in mist and low-lying clouds. During late summer and early fall the pass is used as a highway by flocks of birds, as diverse as warblers, hawks, and swallows, which migrate from the north to the southern continent.

Occasionally, when the mist clears, one can look back across the intervening ridge of La Trampa del Tigre and the range of mountains to island-dotted Lake Valencia lying in a palpitating heat haze. To the north, the ribbon of road hairpins around deep, narrow gorges as it descends and branches off to the villages of Ocumare de la Costa on the sea, and Turiamo on the shore of a small, sparkling bay.

The entire four-mile-long valley beyond the airport had previously belonged to the De Armas family of old and honorable lineage. Many was the time the dictator and his retinue took a canter along the tree-shaded road past their hacienda. The ancient trees—ceiba, samán, almendra, and candela—alternated in their flowering so that month after month there was always perfume and color and the hum of bees. Sleek horses and cattle grazed in the meadows and fields. It was indeed a beautiful valley to behold, and Gómez coveted it. What an ideal retreat, so close to the crowded plaza and yet offering the secluded atmosphere of the country. So, with the exception of the De Armas hacienda and a few surrounding acres, the dictator acquired the valley, converted it into a veritable feudal estate, and built the road as an escape route to the sea.

In a shaded grove, three and a half miles from the airport, Gómez built his house and called it Las Delicias. The last nail was hammered in on the third of May, 1922. As a human abode it was an architectural monstrosity, unlike anything seen in Venezuela, before or since. Of two stories and built entirely of wood, it had a front and rear outside staircase leading to the upstairs veranda which ran completely around the structure. From the guarded iron gates a driveway and raised walk bordered with flowers and shrubs led to the simple front door. A murmuring stream meandered nearby.

It was not until 1930 that the owner moved in, bag and baggage. The room he chose as his bedroom—it measured only ten by thirteen and a half feet—was a corner one in the rear. With him came a mongrel bitch named Fifi (an affectionate and intelligent animal, according to her master), and a large collection of framed photographs, which were promptly hung up on the outside walls. The safe he left behind in the town house, which still retained its status as the presidential residence.

It was about this time that other houses and structures were completed in the valley, all of them fronting on the fine road. Close to Las Delicias was a zoo, and next to it an imposing dance pavilion. Just beyond was the *quinta* of Juan Vicente, who moved in with a mistress and started a family of his own. Next to him lived his mother, Dolores Amelia, and her two youngest, Berta and Juan. As they married into prominent and wealthy Caracas families, her daughters Belen, Christina, and Hermenegilda moved into the valley also. It was Belen who chose the *quinta* Franchet D'Esperay after the French Marshal returned to France.

When the feudal lord began to lapse into fond memories of his early years at La Mulera, he sent an engineer to Táchira to take the measurements of his birthplace. In 1931, an exact replica was completed on the road to Las Delicias and put into use as a guest house.

In April of that year, Gómez suffered another attack of uremia. It was serious enough to cause undercurrents of intrigue to stir anew. He was seventy-four now. He had lost much of his paunch and his cheeks were lined and hollowed, yet up to the day he was put abed he had mounted the scales daily "to watch" his weight. One day he got into an imbroglio with his doctors. They came upon him sitting out on the veranda. "But I can't look at those four walls all day long!" he complained. The solution was a hospital-type bed on wheels. When the urge came upon him to look on Mother Nature, or the hour drew near for visitors, he was wheeled out to the veranda and a servant cranked him up to a sitting position. Stretched out on the white bed, he looked like a tired old man whose days were numbered. He seemed to live in a half-real and half-dream world of protocol, farming statistics, and past military glories.

During those days of suffering and forced idleness, he had given much thought to a serious problem. Doubts had begun to assail him that, should he die, the country might fall into the hands of a tyrant more ruthless than he. He was fooled not a whit by the fawning, scheming generals and *políticos* who came to pay him court. Before the machinations of fate struck him down he must designate a successor, a man if not worthy enough to take his place, at least honest and sincere, and above all a patriot. Who, among those that he knew well, filled these qualifications? There was Pedro Arcaya, the bibliophile, for one; the learned Foreign Minister, Pedro Itriago Chacín; his old cronies from Táchira, Generals Ernesto and Rafael Velasco; and there was that up and coming soldier from Independencia—Eleazar López Contreras.

Only four months before, he had recalled López from Táchira and appointed him acting chief of staff. Lean and ascetic, López exuded strength and assurance. Though punctilious to a fault, Gómez knew him as a leader who commanded respect. It so happened that General Tobías Uribe, the Minister of War and Marine, was then preparing to leave for Europe for reasons of health. Gómez decided to install López in his place on an acting basis to try his capacities further. The appointment was made official on April 21.

In far-off Barquisimeto, where he reigned as president of Lara,

Eustóquio Gómez received this news with much misgiving. It was clear to him that the position which his cousin had given López was tantamount to an appointment as his successor. If Gómez should die when congress was not in session, it would fall on the cabinet to elect a president from among its members. The most logical choice would be a military man—the Minister of War and Marine. Ratification of the appointment by congress would be a simple formality. Eustóquio was bitterly disappointed that his cousin had let him down. By blood ties and seniority the appointment should have been his, especially in this trying crisis. Hadn't he reformed and rendered a fairly good account of himself? Eustóquio was very much a dandy now instead of a reprobate, and he had lost much of his ferociousness. His beard was gone, and his hair and mustache were as white as snow.

Eustóquio packed his bag and journeyed to Las Delicias. He was the affable relative come to palaver with his cousin and be solicitous about his health. Having assured himself that that worthy was not yet ready to die, he went into conference with Antonio Pimentel, the dictator's crony. He was looking for strong backing in his stealthy climb to power.

Pimentel aranged a meeting at the Hotel Jardín in Maracay and called in General López to sound him out. Eustóquio was there, as was also Dr. López Rodríguez, president of Aragua, and a few others. López was not very talkative and wanted to know what the meeting was all about. Pimentel fidgeted for a moment, then came out with it.

"Well, it's like this, General López," he began. "I have just talked with my *compadre* Juan Vicente on behalf of Eustóquio who asked me to explain the convenience of putting the Ministry of War and Marine in the hands of a relative as the only way of protecting . . . ah . . . the government. I told Juan Vicente that you were a good man but that we felt Eustóquio would be a better man for the job . . ."

"And . . .?"

"Well . . ." Pimentel gave Eustóquio a baleful look, "Juan Vicente listened to me all right, but all he had to say was that you were the better man . . . that Eustóquio, because of his violent nature, would alienate all of his officers."

"And you called me here to tell me this?" López was surprised and angered.

Pimentel forced a smile. "I thought you would like to know what the General thinks of you."

Once again Juan Vicente Gómez recovered, and in a surprisingly short time was feeling spry and cheerful as before. He decided to try out an experiment that had occurred to him while watching the chickens of Las Delicias.

One day he ordered that no food be given to the chickens for twenty-four hours. The following day he walked among the flock with his retinue and a group of friends. "Here I have a grain of corn," he said. "Now watch!" He threw it to the chickens and it vanished.

"Now *señores*," said the Great One with a wry smile, "can any one of you tell me which chicken ate the corn?"

The group looked on bewildered. "No one? Well, that is what is going to happen when I die. The national treasury is going to disappear, and nobody is going to know who took it!"

The old soldier was still the crafty tactician, shrewd and calculating. His unhurried manner and stubborn peasant logic contrasted notably with the more fluid demeanor of the government career men who surrounded him. The members of his suite followed him like courtiers, in a carefully fixed order of precedence. They hung on his every word, and every statement of his was made to appear as a milestone in history. He enjoyed listening also to the learned men who came to pay him homage. His intellectual curiosity was immense, and he took all knowledge to be his province. He moved among scholars, lawyers, economists, artists, soldiers, speaking to them with authority and erudition in their own fields. His memory was such that he seemed to have spent considerable time in reading. In reality, however, he seldom picked up a book; either his lawyer-secretaries read to him or quoted from the vast storehouse of their knowledge. And he never forgot a pertinent fact, figure, or homily that would serve good purpose when it came his turn to speak.

With the exception of an artist and poet and Dr. Rafael Requena, who was a physician, most of his secretaries had been lawyers. His present secretary, Dr. Enrique Urdaneta Carrillo, was a lawyer, as was his father before him, who had served General Gómez for over a decade. Enrique Urdaneta was the ideal secretary, though a serio-comic one. He wore high button shoes and stiff collars and was extremely shy with girls. He never missed mass on Sundays or holy days, nor the weekly visit to his father's grave. Efficient and industrious, he could spout law and history like a savant, and his devotion to his master was like that of a dog.

Gómez summoned Urdaneta one day and asked him to compose a letter. This was in March just before his illness. It was to be a very special letter to the members of the National Congress in reply to their written request that *El Benemérito* sacrifice himself and return to the Presidency. With an economic depression engulfing the world, the country was tottering on the brink of ruin. Only he, they said, could save it. Gómez felt inclined to hearken to the call, but there was one deterrent. By Venezuela's seventeenth Constitution of 1929, the office of President had been stripped of its powers and these had been vested in the congress. Were Juan Bautista Pérez to go and be elected to his place under the present Constitution, he would be subservient to that body. This would never do. "What I want you to say," he told Urdaneta, "is that I will serve as President provided that I remain in command of the army and they grant me my old powers. That means that they'll have to change the Constitution, but put it diplomatically. Tell them that I have never failed them, that I will do my best. You know what to say."

The letter which Enrique Urdaneta prepared and Gómez signed and sent off, read as follows:

It is with patriotic interest that I have taken notice of your letter dated two days ago, in which you insist on the expediency that I assume the direction of the national destinies as President of the Republic as being the only solution for the salvation of the nation.

"To persuade me in this respect, you have invoked the Fatherland. I have never hesitated to serve it; I have never failed to watch over her greatness and prosperity. It is my thought, however, that the difficulties which have resulted from the present crisis would continue were I to accept this magistracy which lately has been an unhappy one.

"The established precedent which makes the President of the Republic so closely dependent on the sovereign congress of the nation, wholly precludes any solid authority for the position; the eloquence of accomplished facts proves that an authority so fragile should be eliminated.

"If I remain as commander-in-chief of the army, assuming all administrative duties, rights and responsibilities, and with ample powers to organize the republic, I would hold myself responsible for whatever you wish; thus, I would have a wider base—already made solid and firm—upon which to guarantee peace and rights with their precious attributes: order, prosperity, the effectiveness of guarantees, security, and everything necessary for the greater glory of the nation and the happiness of my compatriots.

"The rest (revamping of the Constitution) is for you to organize, as it is you who are solely responsible for the outcome.

Your friend,
J. V. Gómez

It behooved the National Congress to accept "The Well Deserving" on his own terms, and the wheels were put in motion to draft a new Constitution. However, due to Gómez's illness, matters reached an impasse for several weeks, and it was not until June 13 that Juan Bautista Pérez's "resignation" became effective. Congress named Dr. Pedro Itriago Chacín, the Foreign Minister, to occupy the Presidency provisionally until June 24. On that day, to a flurry of fanfare and grandiloquent orations, the Father of Peace, the builder of roads and of commerce between nation and nation, was solemnly inaugurated as President of the Republic.

What made the saga of Juan Vicente Gómez so remarkable was his uncanny ability to maintain himself firmly in power for twenty-seven years. By all the rules of fate and chance, he should have suffered defeat and perhaps ended his days in prison as did Augusto B. Leguía, the dictator of Peru. The years 1930 and 1931 were disastrous years for many Latin American dictators. In the short space of a year and a half, no less than eight Latin American governments [25] were overthrown by revolution.

Until overthrown by Commander Sánchez Cerro in August, 1930, Leguía had enjoyed the longest dictatorship (eleven years) in the history of Peru. Having risen to power on a measure of genius, he had been accepted into the brotherhood of tyrants through the protocolic friendship of official notes and greetings exchanged across the Andes.

[25] Argentina, Bolivia, Brazil, Chile, Panama, Paraguay, Peru and Salvador.

He and Gómez had much in common; in fact, their regimes were similar in many respects. Leguía had seized power in a bloodless coup, had smothered opposition, political parties and civil liberties, and had ruled with his friends and kinsmen. He believed in force and knew how to wield it, but there the similarity between the two men ended. In temperament they were as unlike as their professions implied. Leguía, a former bond salesman, was a dapper little man, high-strung and quick of wit, who loved the elegant social world of balls and society salons. Though he showed a distinct penchant for administration, he became more and more a determined pursuer of life's pleasures, and expected blind loyalty as a matter of fact. And therein lay the reason for his downfall. He failed to appease and align the discontented army squarely behind him. The consequence was the military coup which landed him in Lima's prison, where he died lonely and abandoned within a year. In turn, Sánchez Cerro was overthrown (March 1, 1931) and sought sanctuary in Venezuela. But Gómez regarded him as a contemptible upstart and denied him permission to disembark when his ship docked at La Guaira.

Unlike Leguía, Gómez realized his power rested basically on the army, that without at least its passive support, no Venezuelan president could remain in power even a day. So he nursed and pampered the army—the high brass, that is—and gave it everything it asked for, and more, to make it happy. He was a connoisseur of men. *"Conozco a los hombres"*—"I know men," he once confided to a subordinate. He knew what his generals wished, and he gave generously and spontaneously—cars, expense accounts, *quintas* in the city, haciendas in the country, and any number of other gifts. In 1926 he gave, through the Minister of War and Marine, an outright gift of thirty thousand bolivars to all generals commanding troops. For writing his book *El Callao Histórico,* which commemorated the battle of Ayacucho, General López received twenty-five thousand bolivars. For another on Bolívar he received twenty-four thousand bolivars. When López married for the second time (his first marriage ended in divorce), Gómez gave the bride one hundred thousand bolivars as a wedding present. In such a roseate atmosphere of brotherly love, it was no wonder that the army's loyalty was assured.

If any incipient rebellion occurred in the ranks, his well-fed generals quelled it with dispatch. The one problem child, however, was the junior officer, especially the *mestizo* who came of a poor family. His new authority went to his head. He began to imagine himself in his commanding general's boots, ordering everyone about, sitting back in his shiny car, and drinking champagne with very important people. His goal was fixed and clear; he was going to be a general, but he didn't see any sense in working and waiting years to get there. This problem child, with an automatic on his hip and his cap cocked at a jaunty angle, was always ripe for intrigue and caused his superiors no end of worry.

One day in 1932 it reached the ears of the generalissimo that a certain young lieutenant of a Caracas garrison had been trying to foment a conspiracy among his fellow officers. To the surprise of everyone, instead of ordering the man imprisoned, Gómez arranged his transfer to the Maracay garrison so that he could meet and observe him.

One Saturday afternoon, in the Hotel Jardín, in front of all his friends, he heaped attentions on the young officer. He inquired as to his financial problems, his aspirations in life, in fact everything that would give him a slant on the man's character. Finding nothing wrong with him that money couldn't cure, he promised to improve his financial and social position. Then he introduced the dazed young man to a pretty señorita and suggested they dance.

Julio Anselmo Santander, chief of the aide-de-camps, who was in on the secret, had listened in astonishment. Such velvet-glove treatment of an insurrectionist was beyond his comprehension.

Driving off together, Gómez turned toward him and flashed a toothy smile.

"Julio Anselmo—you were surprised, weren't you? But don't get me wrong. The youth is still an unbent sapling. What he wants is not power—which is difficult to handle—but what power can give him: a car, women, money, servants. And now that he is going to have these things, he won't cause any trouble. You'll see . . . You'll see . . ."

Gone forever were the sneering disdain for pain and suffering, the brutal directives of the truculent despot who once ordered every prisoner given fifty lashes. The soldier-statesman-farmer with the chilled steel nerve had mellowed with the years into a tolerant, affable patriarch who enjoyed expounding homilies on the value of work and patriotism, and performing little acts of kindness. Though his power was still supported by an apparatus of terror, he appeared as a man without personal grudge and rancor. To the repentant enemy he offered peace and security; he was willing to forgive and forget. His ingratiating smile, his down-to-earth talk that put listeners at their ease, his air of modesty and good-fellowship, evoked confidence and admiration. There could be no denying the warmth of his personality and no mistaking the look of veneration on the faces of those who served him. Though coin-of-the-realm may have bought the loyalty of many an ambitious *caudillo,* most of those who surrounded him loved this man Gómez for himself alone.

What was so extraordinary about him was the air of plainness and even austerity in which he lived. To look at this benign and slow-moving man of Spanish-Indian blood, or watch him at his day's work, it was almost impossible to believe that he had amassed one of the greatest fortunes of his time, that he was the richest man on the continent. This was certainly a remarkable feat for an unschooled peasant in an impoverished country of less than four million people. He himself admitted that his yearly income ran into the millions. He had long ceased to bother keeping records of his wealth. The profits which he did not plow back into his new and visible sources of revenue were generously handed over to his favorite sons and relatives. Not a little of it found its way to numerous girls and deserving persons. Santos Matute Gómez—for one—sent so many millions to the banks in Costa Rica that further deposits were refused, and he was obliged to open accounts in Mexico City. When he settled in Costa Rica after Gómez's death, he acquired the questionable distinction of becoming that country's richest and most despised resident.

During their heyday, one member of the Gómez clan drew up to a Caracas bank in a truck loaded with boxes. He would speak with no less a personage than the manager. This individual, accustomed as he was to seeing large sums of money, was somewhat taken aback to find the boxes packed solid with gold, silver, and currency. But no sooner were they unloaded from the truck than a disagreement arose over the proper formalities for depositing the treasure. Thereupon the owner abruptly changed his mind and ordered it loaded back upon the truck. He drove off, leaving the astonished manager stand-

ing on the sidewalk. The man had yet to learn how many millions those
boxes contained and the identity of the prospective client who had
eluded him.

Gómez never maintained any large deposits in Venezuelan banks.
Not that he lacked faith in banks. Quite the contrary. It was just a
matter of being able to get his hands on plenty of cash in a hurry. In
a revolutionary coup, moments are precious to both sides and vital
objectives may be cut off very suddenly. That was why he kept a
safe well stocked with cash. In it were millions of bolivars, all in one
hundred bolivar bills. The whole sum would fit nicely into a couple
of large suitcases. There must have been many more millions kept
elsewhere. Just where no one could tell. Rumor had it that they were
buried in shallow ground in the vicinity of Maracay. Gómez's secretary would know. And so would Eloy Tarazona. So people thought.

It would seem, however, that Gómez preferred to invest his wealth
in tangible goods. Besides his many business enterprises, his residential properties in Maracay were so numerous that persons passing
through the little town were jokingly reminded that they were tres-
passing on private property. And so it was made clear to such strangers
as were questioned on the streets. If they could not give a satisfactory
account of themselves they were told to get out of town—and quickly.

Juan Vicente Gómez was also a man of vision. In the nineteen-
thirties, at the little deep-water village of Turiamo on the Caribbean,
his dream of a great free port was being translated to reality with the
building of concrete piers and great steel warehouses. European
engineers, employed to survey and submit plans for a cargo railway
from Turiamo, were in their talks with the dictator astounded by the
shrewdness of his discernment.

By 1934 Gómez was seventy-seven years of age. Rather than
make the tiresome trip to the Municipal Theater in Caracas, he ordered his engineers to build in Maracay the finest theater in the country—at government expense of course. Construction came to a standstill upon his death.

He liked music and the opera. Whenever the impresario, Adolf
Bracale, visited Venezuela with his opera company he would first pay
his respects to the dictator and inquire of him, "General, what opera
would you like us to perform for you?" To which Gómez would invariably reply, "Put on that one where the man kills the woman!"

He was referring to *Carmen*. He was also fond of *Hamlet* and, especially, *Barber of Seville,* which Titto Ruffo sang to Gómez and his court for four thousand dollars a performance.

He possessed his private cockpit, which was frequented every Sunday morning by his cronies and their friends. Upon his entrance a hush would descend upon the throng. But after he had bestowed his smile of indulgence and a nod of the head to proceed, the excitement would rise to fever pitch and bets of thousands would change hands.

Cockfighting was the national sport, but he had a great respect for the royal sport of Spain—bullfighting. "A manly sport," he called it. In Maracay he built a bull arena in the exact likeness of the ring at Seville and invited the best toreadors from Spain. However, bullfighting in Venezuela is, at best, a dull, depressing pastime, for the bulls raised on the Venezuelan *llanos* are so sluggish and docile that the sport degenerates into little more than public butchery.

There was also a little matter of five or six luxury hotels, all within a few hours drive of Maracay, which provided Gómez and his cronies with food, rest, and enjoyment. He had his choice of the famed mineral springs at San Juan de los Morros, the salt sea air at Macuto (where he occasionally took a dip in the sea), the cool air of the hills, or perhaps just an evening of dawdling at the bar at the Hotel Jardín in Maracay.

On Sundays, he generally proceeded from the cockfights to a barbecue at some hacienda. *Carne asada* (barbecued beef) and filet mignon were his favorite foods, but the usual fare at Las Delicias was the simple dishes of his native Andes. Other than a sip of champagne to celebrate a birthday or a wedding, he did not drink. For some years he had smoked an occasional cigar given to him by Tarazona. Later, he took to chewing these cigars, but in 1930 he discarded tobacco altogether and turned to eating caramels, the only sweet he ever cared for. He had an inordinate fondness for eau de cologne, which his daughters on their trips to Paris bought for him by the gallon.

For three days each year the Hotel Jardín was the scene of the famous *Las Ferias de Maracay*. Two orchestras alternated, playing continuously in the grand ballroom. Diplomats, government officials, officers of the army, their families, their friends, and just hangers-on —all were welcome. No invitations were necessary, but formal attire was *de rigueur,* and hefty individuals would stand guard at the entrances to see that strangers did not intrude. Tables would be loaded down with delicacies, plates heaped high with caviar. Champagnes vintage wines, and brandies were always provided in abundance. The pop of corks would sound all day long and far into the night.

After the three days of revelry were over, after they had gorged their bellies full and swilled themselves to the gills with expensive champagne, intelligent but impressionable young officers would wend their weary way to their barracks, firm in the conviction that Juan Vicente Gómez was not such a bad fellow after all.

During the last year of his life, Gómez, now an austere though garrulous old man of seventy-eight, was still a stickler for a long formed habit. He rose at five every morning to deal directly with his foremen, farm hands, and peons, grunting with satisfaction as he surveyed the produce from his plantations—the corn, beans, coffee cocoa beans, sugar cane, rubber, and cotton. He continued to be an agriculturist in constant touch with the land, and was full of ideas and maxims: "The land weeps when it is not cultivated," he would tell visitors. Seven o'clock was his breakfast hour, and he would preside at a simple table—as at all meals—without pomp.

Especially welcome were his grandchildren, many of whom would troop in from their neighboring homes to share with him the plain fare of *café con leche* and *pan de guayas* (a whole wheat bread). A very touching scene! After breakfast he drove to his office on the Plaza Girardot. Here he would receive the less distinguished visitors. These would be kept waiting for a time in a small bare reception room whose high and only window opened on an adjoining guard room. The rattle of arms and the quiet talk of the soldiers of the guard carried easily to those sitting on the straight-backed chairs. Ambitious and avaricious callers, reasoned Gómez, would thus be given cause to ponder and perhaps to modify their petitions.

Life at Las Delicias was enlivened by nightly motion picture shows. When Hollywood began sending sound pictures to South America, Gómez was one of the first to install sound equipment. And he seldom missed a show. In fact, he personally censored all films to be exhibited in Venezuela. If he thought a picture unfit or too enlightening for the Venezuelan public it was banned. This ban did not apply to his own relatives and progeny. To the young ones it was an incentive to attend all the shows in droves. Gómez would sit on the upper verandah with a few friends while the family and the children would sit below. After the show they would all file upstairs to say their good-nights. Then Gómez's personal physician, Dr. Rafael Requena, and his son-in-law, Dr. Ramón Ignacio Mendez Llamozas, surgeon general of the army, would take his pulse. The verdict, chanted in unison, would invariably be, *"Esta bien, General,"* meaning that grandpa was in fit condition to go to his bedroom to meet his paramour for the night.

During the show the girl had been kept hidden in the background. But those who knew of these arrangements would comprehend the whispers and rustling of feminine garments that emanated from the adjoining room, and would know, when they had departed, that the young lady would be ushered into the bedroom. His mustaches twitching with anticipation, Don Juan would arrive a few minutes later, purring and smiling and bestowing little compliments. He had finished with being dictator of Venezuela. Caracas might revolt, the exiles invade the country, and a tunnel, already dug, be discovered between the Rotunda and the palace of Miraflores, but His Excellency was not to be disturbed.

This sort of thing went on until the very last year of Gómez's life. Judging by the arrival of little Gomecistas at various cottages in Maracay, the old man remained potent until almost the very end.

Always on the premises, sometimes beside Gómez, sometimes in the background, could be seen a short, squat figure usually in an ill-fitting khaki uniform. Bow-legged and ugly, of plainly evident Indian origin, this was Tarazona, Gómez's one-time bodyguard, who had been with him since his days in exile. Now a colonel and aide-de-camp and one of the few confidants of Gómez, he wielded almost unlimited power—to the extent that he could make or break almost any officer in the army. Gómez was his god and he tried to imitate *el Jefe* in every way. Like his boss, he managed to appropriate for himself his share of the spoils—some seventy-two houses, three haciendas, and a saw mill. And like Gómez too, he acquired a bevy of young maidens. But there the similarity ended. It appears he lacked the virility of the *Jefe,* for no one remembers having seen any bow-legged little Indians strutting around Maracay. Instead, his girls—all of them beauties between fourteen and eighteen years of age—complained of mistreatment and perversion. Naturally, attempts were made by romantic but

rash young officers to rescue at least one such damsel in distress. But
Tarazona assigned a special detail to guard against such occurrences.
Not a few smitten officers were transferred, cashiered, or even imprisoned—the penalty varying with the degree of their success. Tarazona was a tough hombre to be reckoned with. And for all his uncouth and repulsive ways it was conceivable why the entire army
kowtowed to this lowborn and illiterate Indian.

Curiously enough, although he permitted his subordinates to use
the most brutal of tortures, Gómez himself often meted out punishment in smaller doses, sometimes revealing a Solomon-like wisdom
when chastizing an erring subject. The story of the "fish tax" is a
good illustration of his ability not only to correct an evil but—at the
same time—to win a friend.

One sunny afternoon, one of Gómez's grandsons was returning
with a companion from the seaside resort of Macuto. As a rule he
drove his own car, which bore no license plates—nor did the cars of
other members of the Gómez family—but on this occasion he was
riding in his friend's car. He happened to be dressed in dirty old
clothing, as he had been assisting with some boat repairs. At a road
alcabala (road station) they were ordered to halt while the guards
searched the interior of the car for fish. The explanation, curtly given,
was that the young men might be hiding fish to evade the "fish tax."
The guards' effrontery was taken good-naturedly. The young men
kidded them, suggesting that they better search under the seats, in the
spare tire, and so on. Then the grandson remarked in an offhand
manner, "You know, if we *had* brought any fish they would be intended for the Gómez family." One of the guards innocently asked
what he meant by the remark. When the soldier was enlightened and
the grandson of Gómez identified, the guards became quite frightened
and begged that no report be made of the matter.

A day or so later, however, when the usual visit of respect was
paid to grandfather, the young man casually mentioned the incident,
telling it only as a joke upon himself. But Gómez took more than
a casual interest in the story and asked for details. It developed that
he had never heard of any "fish tax." A thorough investigation immediately followed.

A couple of days later the grandson sat in on the interrogation
of the petty official who headed the racket, and who was made to

cool his heels for a spell in the reception room. By the time he was told to take a seat in the Great One's office and explain the so-called fish tax, his confidence had ebbed considerably. Thoroughly ill at ease, he fumbled through some kind of a prepared story, the gist of which was that the "tax" was to protect the legitimate fishermen in the district. It had no official sanction.

"Mm—mm-mm, *muy interesante*," said the Great One. "Now tell me your story again . . . from the very beginning."

The man stammered through his story a second time . . . then a third and fourth time. His ordeal was now becoming increasingly more trying. And, although the day was not a bit too warm, he was perspiring profusely.

As Gómez had expected, each version was altered somewhat in its telling. And each time he would say, with undue emphasis: "Ah, ha! *Muy interesante. Por favor*—repeat once again what you have told me."

After the *fifth* version—which bore practically no resemblance to the first—the man was told he could go. However, the cheering words had to be uttered once again, for the poor fellow was not sure he had heard correctly. It was difficult to conceive that he would not be led away, that there would not even be a thunderous reprimand, that he was now a free man. He rose, hesitated a moment, then bolted for the door like a frightened rabbit, when suddenly a roar of laughter filled the room. For the petty little dictator, now humble and dejected, had undergone a thorough fright and had wet his pants!

No action was taken against the man, for no action was necessary. As Gómez predicted, no one was ever bothered again with a "fish tax." Instead, the man who invented this lucrative racket tried hard to reform. In time he became one of Gómez's staunchest supporters.

CHAPTER THIRTY-ONE

The Patriarch of Las Delicias

Whenever a prominent foreigner set foot on Venezuelan soil he was given a royal reception. Often it was headed by the President in person, flanked by his sons Juan Vicente and Florencio and a large suite. Conquered by gifts, banquets, guided tours, and saccharine tributes from adulating guides, these visitors returned to their own country praising Venezuela's splendid hospitality and eulogizing its ruler. Writers were given preferential treatment. They were put up at the Hotel Jardín, furnished with servants, a car, and chauffeur—all at the expense of the government. As if that weren't enough, they were given handsome gifts in cash for "expenses."

Visitors were always welcome to Gómez's domain, but his preference was for those in a position to write for publication glowing accounts of the grand old man at Maracay and the wonders he had performed for Venezuela. Most writers were willing to oblige. Nemesio García Naranjo, an exiled writer from Mexico, lived in luxury in Maracay for many months and received varying sums totaling something like twenty-five thousand dollars for writing a short book and a few articles. The Spaniard Francisco Villaespesa wrote a drama on Bolívar, and a sonnet in which he compared the dictator with Bolívar. He received a like amount. There were numerous others. Almost everyone left the country with the firm conviction that the gracious dictator with the winning personality was the savior of his country and the personification of everything that was good. Not once was a foreigner given the chance to visit one of the dreaded prisons and confirm for himself the stories he must have heard of injustice, mistreatment, and tortures.

380

If one can believe as truth the articles he wrote on Venezuela and Juan Vicente Gómez, even such notable writers as Thomas F. Lee [26] were completely taken in. Naranjo's material, much of which found its way to foreign publications, could be called outright propaganda. His *Venezuela and Its Ruler,* in which he paints Gómez as something of a deity, is a masterpiece of hokum as well as prose.

In all fairness to these writers, however, some idea should be given of the manner of reception and interview which were accorded to such visitors to Venezuela. A typical official visit in 1935—the last year in the life and reign of Juan Vicente Gómez—would have been a veritable Cook's tour with all incidentals paid, with well-educated guides speaking the language of the visitor, whose job would be to show in their most charming manner only the things the government wanted seen.

For years the tour has always been the same. The visitor would be driven from his ship at La Guaira over the winding, mountainous road to Caracas. He would see the museums, the restored house where Simón Bolívar was born, the view of the capital from El Calvario, and the Pantheon where Venezuela's famous dead are enshrined. A few minutes drive from the hub of the city was the rambling Country Club where he would enjoy a leisurely lunch and would meet the elite of the capital. Then came the long smooth ride over a macadamized highway to Maracay.

Approaching the town the car would stop for a moment at an old samán tree growing in the very center of the highway which forks around it. It is the historic "Samán de Güere," under which, it is said, the fierce *cacique* Maracay once fought a hand to hand battle with a brave Spanish captain. Bolívar once spoke to his troops from under its spreading branches, and on another occasion conferred there with Miranda. The spot is hallowed ground now, thanks to the patriotism of General Gómez, and though the tree is gnarled and crippled with age, it stands as a monument with several Spanish cannon behind a fence of old muskets. The General held it in such high regard that he had a small replica of it, complete to the muskets, in his house in Maracay.

In Maracay the guest was put up by the Venezuelan government in the Hotel Jardín. After a pause and a refreshing drink at the

[26]*A Close Portrait of Gómez,* Mentor Magazine, November, 1925.

bar he would be whisked north past Las Delicias and up the winding road to Portachuelo Pass. Here, three-quarters of a mile above the sea, a huge niche had been excavated out of the moist green slope and it was filled with a white three-story building over one hundred yards in length. Almost two hundred workmen were rushing to complete the Hotel Rancho Grande, and the visitor might well wonder what whim impelled the ruler of the country to select this lonely site for such a great structure. He would barely have begun to enjoy the vista of green jungle stretched out before him and the melodious trills of birds hidden in the dense foliage, when the tour would commence again. If there was time it would continue straight on until, suddenly, the road ahead tapered to a narrow ribbon. Nestled at the foot of the hills, with a wide expanse of sparkling Caribbean and a porcelain blue sky framed above them, were the twin sleepy villages of Turiamo and Ocumare de la Costa.

Perhaps, instead, the drive would be south from Maracay through the wide, gently rolling valleys of Lake Valencia and Aragua in the direction of Gómez's hacienda El Trompillo near Güigüe. In colonial times one of the principal landowners of the region was the Marques de Mijares, who possessed vast holdings in the cultivation of indigo, tobacco, and sugar cane. Though the lake that met the visor-shaded eyes of the first Spaniards has shrunk to a fraction of its former size, the land is still highly productive. The road leads past orange and lime groves, rich bottom lands rippling with sugar cane and corn, fields of cotton, and slopes where shining green coffee trees are planted with rows of shade trees between them. Here and there, horses and cattle graze in deep, rolling meadows, and clear streams appear and are quickly lost again in the high grass. Set far back from the road, half hidden by trees and colorful hibiscus and bouganvillea, are the old haciendas where life is leisurely, elegant, and secluded. In the early summer when the rains begin to fall, Mother Nature dabs the country-side with splashes of color from her hidden palette. The apamate trees are masses of gold, and the samáns accentuate the black-green of palms and almendras with their billows of new white leaves which glisten like spun glass. Purple-blue morning glories lace the roadside and neat fences and flamboyant blossoms dot the landscape with splashes of vivid red.

What the guides would fail to tell the visitor would be that this pastoral scene that delighted the eye and soothed the mind had been built up and maintained by the toil and sweat of peon labor. All these fine haciendas belonged to the Gómezes, who rule over their vast estates like feudal lords of old.

All the while the guides would have been giving a running account of the marvels that had been accomplished by Juan Vicente Gómez. In Maracay they would point out the fine theater under construction, the bull ring, the mills and factories and the school for girls —all built by the country's benevolent ruler. In no time at all the visitor would get the glorified impression that this man Gómez had brought fabulous prosperity to a country that had known nothing but corruption, bankruptcy, and stagnancy. He would have no way of knowing that he had seen only a gilded false front, that behind all this thin veneer of wealth and contentment were unbounded poverty, misery, and disease.

In the principal square of Maracay he would see a man hang a bunch of bananas from a tree limb, and inquiring the reason would be told, "It is a daily offering that General Gómez makes to the birds of Maracay." And as the visitor watched the birds flock around this feast he would not know that other eyes were watching also, and that those eyes saw in that same peaceful scene only repulsive buzzards feasting on the bones of Gómez's victims.

He would be reminded, with every appearance of sincerity, that General Gómez was regarded with veneration by his people, that many foreign nations had honored him with awards and that the congress of Venezuela awarded him the title for life of *el Benemérito*. It was with understandable trepidation that the visitor would approach Las Delicias to keep an early appointment with the Great One.

The house had been provided with every comfort and convenience. Along the outside walls and in every room were photographs of the owner—dozens of them—depicting him in every conceivable pose and variety of dress uniform, with friends, foreigners, diplomats, and famous visitors. But he hadn't stopped there. Puffed up with inordinate self-exaltation, his vanity had long since burst its seams and there were *four* imposing busts of "The Well Deserving" in marble and bronze.

As the visitor approached, the old man would rise from beneath the shade of an ancient ceiba in greeting. Wearing an olive drab uniform, with high tan boots, a loose tunic buttoned up to the neck, and a broad-brimmed Panama hat, his face was gaunt and deeply lined; a gray drooping mustache all but covered his mouth. Behind horn-rimmed glasses his small, heavy-lidded eyes gleamed with quizzical brightness. Despite the debilities of old age, the visitor would feel that this man was still a leader of men.

He would put his guest quickly at ease. Switching his cane to his left hand, he would extend a firm gloved hand in greeting, *"Cómo está? Cómo está? Me alegro mucho!"*

Hoping to see some members of his family, the guest might glance around, but there were only the guards, some gardeners puttering in the gardens, and perhaps Tarazona, impassive as the head on an old copper penny. "The Well Deserving" would soon take his cue, and the soft, well-modulated voice would begin: "Yes, we are very proud of our country. For one thing, we have no internal or external debts . . . Venezuela is in debt to no one. As a matter of fact," and he would emphasize each word with a nod of the head, "our treasury is full—full almost to overflowing." And he would sit back to let the weight of his words sink in.

Invariably the visitor might ask, "I am told that Venezuela is obliged to import most of her foodstuffs. Is that so?"

"Import foodstuffs?" he would snort, glancing in feigned surprise. "Haven't you seen our farms, *señor?* Ah! Sure you have. And where have you seen finer rice, sugar cane, corn, or coffee? I have always been a man of the soil, *señor,* and I assure you, growing all these things . . . and many other agricultural products also . . . has been for me a labor of love. Yes, Venezuela once had to import most of her foodstuffs . . . but now," and he would say it believingly, "she is self-sufficient."

The guest might comment favorably on the broad macadam highways that crisscross Maracay.

"Quite so, quite so," he would say, vastly pleased. "The excellent roads you have just seen are but a small part of an extensive network of fine highways." And he would make a mental note to warn the guides to make sure visitors venture no farther than yesterday's junket.

"And revolutions—aren't there ever any revolutions in Venezuela?"

"There has been," he would say, adroitly evading the question, "peace in Venezuela for thirty-two years." He would discreetly omit to mention the many embryonic revolutions and the snuffing out of thousands of lives to preserve the *status quo* of the Gómez clan.

Then he would boast of the battles he fought and won when Castro was President. "Since then," he says, "there has been peace in Venezuela. After I fought the last battle and telegraphed President Castro that peace was at least established, he wrote me a letter which I have never divulged to anyone." And he would recite from memory, as if he hadn't done it a thousand times before, the flattering message Castro sent him after the battle of Ciudad Bolívar.

Gómez would note that the visitor's interest was wandering, so he would rise from his chair and offer a little diversion. On the property he had an aviary and a zoo of which he was very proud. In the aviary were beautiful tropical birds, all typical of Venezuela. In the zoo were many fine specimens of Venezuelan animal life, from the soft-eyed deer and wiry jaguar, to the ugly tapir and shaggy-haired sloth. There were foreign animals also, some of them gifts from admirers abroad. His favorite was a rhinoceros for which he reportedly paid eight thousand dollars. Not without a sense of humor, he nicknamed him *Buenmozo*—Good-looking. He would approach *Buenmozo*'s cage, a daily habit, and say a few friendly words of greeting, for he was genuinely fond of animals.

Only one interruption would Gómez permit while he was conversing with "distinguished" visitors of the journalistic profession. That was to grant immediate audience to those of his subjects who came bearing gifts—but who sought no favor. A humble peon offering spontaneously to his ruler some choice produce of his little farm or something of his own handiwork was a poignant scene which spoke more eloquently than a thousand words. Whether visitors were present or not, he made it a practice to give to the donor a sizable sum of money—quite often as much as a thousand bolivars.

One of Gómez's favorite anecdotes, which he related often, concerned one such gift—a potato. It was not just an ordinary potato but a tuber which had, by some caprice of nature, grown to gigantic proportions. It had been presented to him by a poor peon who had trudged all the way from a small village in the state of Yaracuy—a good hundred kilometers distant. Gómez had accepted it graciously

enough and, according to his own version of the story, had given the
man in return a thousand bolivar bill. A week or so later another peon
appeared, this one convoying a burro upon which was proudly displayed another freak of nature—an enormous cabbage. A little polite
questioning disclosed the fact that he also was from the same little
village in Yaracuy. Gómez surmised, perhaps correctly, that this wily
fellow had heard of his compatriot's windfall and was bent on the
monetary reward rather than the honor of meeting him. And he noticed, not without considerable amusement, that the fellow could
hardly restrain himself and was fairly watering at the mouth with
anticipation.

"Your state of Yaracuy," said Gómez blandly, "must produce
many extraordinary things."

"Ah, *sí, mi General*—it is very fertile."

"So I have observed. Mm—mm-mm—such a gift as yours de-
serves a suitable reward. Come—follow me. I have something special
to give you."

He led his delighted visitor to a room whose walls and tables were
covered with many varied gifts from admirers—pictures, amateurish
portraits, coarse tapestries, pottery, vases, handcarved canes—and
the huge potato.

"Here—hold out your hands," said Gómez to his astonished
visitor. And he deposited therein the enormous potato. "Please accept this extraordinary potato I received from a countryman of yours
. . . It is worth every bit of a thousand bolivars!"

Standing in the center of that room, musing on its odd assortment
of "Indian gifts," stacks of canes, white elephants and gewgaws,
Gómez would often remark to his aides or members of his family,
"What people won't do for money!"

His sole enjoyment was derived from the gifts of animals and
birds. He had no less than half a dozen parrots of gorgeous plumage
in the patio at one time, each on its individual perch. The donors had
taken the foresight to drill into the skulls of their birds honeyed words
of flattery for them to recite; nearing the patio was more like approaching a local political rally, what with shrill cries of *"Viva el General!"*
"Viva General Gómez!" and other such phrases emanating therefrom.
One would think that *el General* would have been goaded to the

limit of his endurance and would have wrung the birds' necks. But that would have been expecting too much—for what they sang was like music to his ears. One parrot in particular—a rare yellow variety —fascinated him. And thereby hangs a tale.

Returning to Caracas from a trip to the interior—so the story goes—a Señor González, a commercial traveler, brought with him a pretty yellow parrot which he had received under rather unusual circumstances. It had been presented to him, cage and all, by a pair of total strangers as he was on the point of leaving a small pueblo. Why not, he thought, pick up a few extra bolivars by selling the bird in the Caracas market? So he took it along and arrived in the evening at his home in the suburbs.

The next morning Señor González was found dead in his bed. There were no visible signs as to the cause of his death. No autopsy was ordered, and by sunset the remains of Señor González had been carried to his grave.

There was a younger brother, Rafael, who lived in the same household, and it was he who succeeded to the ownership of the bird. The next morning he too was found dead in bed; and again, there was no indication as to the cause of death. Pandemonium reigned for awhile until finally the traveling man's widow calmed down sufficiently to remember something sinister that her husband had told her: *The owners of the bird had appeared unduly anxious to dispose of it.*

A state of emergency was declared and the family called a pow-wow to decide the parrot's future. The majority were convinced that they had a lethal instrument on their hands and voted down a proposal to kill the bird lest they bring disaster down on them all. Some one timidly suggested giving the bird to the landlord (a sweet, penny-pinching old codger) who lived not far away. The protesting bird was presented forthwith to that astonished gentleman without further delay. As they expected, the scouting party which reconnoitered the enemy camp the next morning picked up the following distressing intelligence. There had been no need to enter the house—the shrieking and the wailing on behalf of the departed (may the Lord rest his soul!) could be heard for many *cuadras.*

There no longer remained any doubt in anyone's mind in the González household; whoever possessed the yellow parrot never lived to see the light of another day. They held another confab and this

time all the male relatives participated. After devising a scheme to recover the parrot, there followed a heated discussion as to which enemy
should be exterminated next.

Finally, up spoke crotchety grandfather Manuel, the patriarch of
the González clan. *"Un momento, muchachos*—now it is my say . . .
and listen well to my words. I say, let us do a service . . . a patriotic
service . . . for our country. It will—as you will soon find out—
be a deed which will redound to us all. It will bring us freedom . . .
happiness . . . and glory! Right now, let us discuss only one man
who should be done away with—the tyrant, Juan Vicente Gómez!"

The proposal stunned the gathering. "Juan Vicente Gómez, *el
Presidente?"* they gasped collectively. Such an undertaking had been
beyond their conception. "But such a venture," they argued, "could
only be one of great magnitude—it would call for artful strategy—it
would be most dangerous—it would . . ."

"Ay, Dios! What fools!" and the old man's brow furrowed with
displeasure. "For years now no one has been able to kill this tyrant
. . . and here we have the means to do away with him at practically
no risk to ourselves. I tell you, *muchachos,* it is all so beautifully
simple. Let us go about it in this way . . ."

A few hours later, Alejandro and Ignacio, the two emissaries
chosen by lot, alighted from a hired car at Las Delicias. Grasped
firmly between them was a handsome new cage. On its bottom rung
perched a pretty yellow parrot which eyed the world speculatively and
mused (in all innocence) on the strange habits of man.

Yes, his Excellency, *el Presidente,* was at home said the guard.
What? The señores had brought such a lavish gift and did not even
wish to *see* the General? *Bueno,* he shrugged, it would be as they
wished. He would see to it that the gift was delivered.

Alejandro and Ignacio fairly fell over themselves in beating a
hasty retreat.

Back in the suburbs of Caracas a certain crowded household
fairly vibrated with nervous excitement. Now that the bodies of their
loved ones had been consigned to God and the cemetery, feverish
preparations were started—for tomorrow would be a momentous day
—a date to go down in history.

Starting at dawn, Carlos would act as monitor at the radio in the
corner shop of Pablo Sanchez; when he heard the news flash he would

blow two loud blasts on his whistle. Ramón (he of the long legs) would haunt the nearest newspaper offices and would run home post haste with the special edition. To scholarly Gilberto was assigned the delicate task of writing grandfather's speech—a speech which would be applauded throughout the world by all men who treasured freedom.

No one in the González household slept a wink that night. And no one—except grandfather Manuel, who dozed fitfully—slept the following night either. For word of the demise of the tyrant had failed to come through. On the second day tension mounted by the hour, but still no news; nothing on the radio, nothing in the papers. Somehow, somewhere, the scheme had miscarried.

On the morning of the third day it became all too obvious that grandfather Manuel was on the verge of a nervous breakdown. Against their vigorous protests, Alejandro and Ignacio were again sent off to Maracay—this time to scout the field.

At Las Delicias, Alejandro and Ignacio proceeded to stroll along the road as nonchalantly as their trembling limbs would allow. At the gate was the same guard leaning on his rifle. As they feared, he recognized them.

"Say, aren't you the same men who brought a parrot here the other day?" The tone of his voice portended important news, and the men began to quake.

Alejandro, the leader of the two, gulped and finally found his voice. "Yes," he said weakly, "we are the ones." And the two men awaited the worst.

"*Conchale!* Have you no shame giving a parrot like that to Genral Gómez! It died the next day!"

Actually, Gómez's yellow parrot lived for several months. He mourned its passing as if he had lost a favorite son. No amount of luscious young maidens could restore him to his normal self. Only another yellow parrot could appease him.

So the command was flashed over the wires to the far corners of Venezuela: "*El Benemérito* desires a yellow parrot—*lo mas pronto posible*—and hang the expense." After an impatient wait of several weeks a yellow parrot arrived at Las Delicias under special convoy. It naturally followed that a generous reward wended its way over the return route—but wherever it changed hands it diminished alarmingly in the process. It had taken the concerted efforts of eight state presidents, their army garrisons, the *jefe civiles* of numerous towns and villages, their municipal administrations, and entire civilian populations to comb the jungles to procure that one bird.

Set back from the road at Las Delicias is a life-size likeness of a bull in bronze. His label reads: *El Cacique de los Llanos*—The Chief of the Plains. It was the bull to which Gómez likened himself for his voracious virility, and when his cronies greeted him with a *"Cómo está, General?"* he would bellow, *"Como un toro*—Like a bull!"

On his deathbed there was no bellow left in him, but jokesters say that the dictator tried very hard to live up to his life-long habit. When an old friend bent over him and whispered, *"Cómo está, General?"* there was an immediate response in the tired old man's eyes, but the only sound that he could force from his dry lips was a faint but clearly discernible "Moo-oo-oo!"

He often had said, "I shall live to be a hundred," and not many doubted that he would. Some had never known any other ruler, while the oldsters, in their apathy, believed for a certainty that they would never outlive him—that like the rains, the droughts, and the plagues his cursed rule would go on year after year.

Even the press published subtle propaganda against him. The Caracas newspaper, *El Universal,* founded only a few months after he rose to power, often printed a poem, the first letter of each line spelling *"Muera Gómez*—Gómez should die!"

The grim Reaper was not one to overlook such a transgressor as Juan Vicente Gómez. His day of reckoning had already been scheduled for hearing in that Higher Court from which there is no appeal.

"He cannot last much longer," an aide whispered one day to a foreign envoy. "Perhaps a year. Maybe two. He's a very old man now. Seventy-eight."

The envoy, who knew the true story of Venezuela's subjugation and suffering, thought of the revenge that must have festered for decades in the minds and hearts of many of her downtrodden people. He thought of the pent-up fury and hate that would surely burst its bonds on the day that life ceased to exist in the body that was Juan Vicente Gómez. He asked the aide, "I wonder what will happen when the General dies?"

"Anything can happen," was the ominous reply.

CHAPTER THIRTY-TWO

The End of the Road

At seventy-eight, the dictator's once massive frame was thin and wrinkled, but he bore himself erect like a venerable old soldier. He had acquired the idiosyncrasies of old age, musing on events of the past and assuming a paternalistic attitude to visitor and servitor alike. In his heyday, he seemed to have as many phases as the moon and was an unrelentless taskmaster whose very voice was enough to strike fear in the hearts of his underlings. In his dotage, though he still claimed for himself the obeisance due him, he spoke in calm and measured accents and was a meditative old bachelor whose demeanor was as placid as Lake Valencia at sunset.

The dictator now appeared in public only on very rare occasions. In December, 1934, he had reviewed for the last time the Army of the Republic (eight thousand strong) on the field at Maracay. General López had pinned on his Bolívaresque jacket the medal, "Francisco de Miranda, First Class" [27] awarded him by the senate, and had made a little speech about his "patriotic work as a talented statesman and outstanding soldier." The generalissimo, properly grateful, but his *amour propre* not one bit deflated by the years, had replied in kind.

As early as 1933 there had been considerable speculation in official circles as to what candidate Gómez would propose for the Presidency for the term beginning in April, 1936. By 1935, when he was often confined to his bed due to illness, there was a great deal of conjecture that the new President would outlive his sponsor. The out-

---

[27] Awarded for thirty consecutive years of meritorious service to the republic.

standing candidate discussed at the time was Dr. Pedro Arcaya, the sociologist, jurist, politician, and historian. Twice premier of the cabinet, he was now in Washington as Minister Plenipotentiary to the White House. He had just published a book, in both English and Spanish, entitled *Venezuela and Its Ruler,* which was a vehement defense of the Gómez regime. The well-informed began to talk of him as the candidate *bien visto* by the White House and North American interests. As for the General, he said nothing. If he disapproved of the talk going around, he gave no sign. The "Sphinx of La Mulera" was not one to express his thoughts until the moment for action arrived.

Dr. Arcaya had a brother, Camilio. A university graduate, he was an honorable gentleman of the old school, and had no political ambitions whatsoever. At this time he was the administrator of the customs house at Puerto Cabello.

When Pedro Arcaya made one of his periodic trips to Venezuela, there was great speculation about his expected visit to Maracay. Would General Gómez welcome him with open arms? Would he give some sign that Arcaya was his chosen candidate?

The day that Arcaya appeared at Las Delicias, the dictator was surrounded by a group of friends and officials. When Arcaya's name was announced the atmosphere suddenly became electric.

Gómez greeted him with a toothy smile. "A pleasure, Dr. Arcaya. How is the customs house? And how is Puerto Cabello?"

Had Gómez forgotten his old friend, Pedro Arcaya, or was this just a subtle innuendo to stifle political gossip once and for always? The subtleties of the dictator being well known, the members of the inner circle were inclined to believe the latter. Suffice to say that from then on the candidacy of Pedro Arcaya was no longer talked about.

The last few months of Gómez's life were marked by a decreasing lack of activity. His visits to his office on the Plaza Girardot were short, as were his rides about the countryside. He seldom visited his latest lady-love, *la Española,* as she was known about Maracay. A raven-haired beauty, this Spanish girl had borne him a son two years before. Her father lived apart, discreetly attending to the flourishing commercial establishment that the dictator had bought for him.

December marked the beginning of the dry season. Though the streams and irrigation ditches kept the fields and meadows of the valleys green with vegetation, the eroded hills were becoming parched and brown. The thick layer of gray rain-clouds had changed to huge snowy-white banks which hung in the northern sky in fantastic shapes. The tropical sun beat down with greater intensity, covering Gómez's little valley with a palpitating heat haze, causing man and beast to hug the shadows. In Maracay and other large towns and cities, merchants and street vendors had put out their Christmas wares, and the thoroughfares were thronged with shoppers. Day by day, to both Venezuelans and foreigners alike, the very air grew buoyant with the festive promise of Christmastide. But for many, including Juan Vicente Gómez, it was a promise that would not be fulfilled.

It was the ninth of December that the old patriarch suffered an attack of prostatitis which became complicated by uremia. His doctors shook their heads over his condition, but said nothing. They did what they could, quickly and efficiently, but to those who were permitted to hover for a few minutes over the sick man's bed, it was obvious that he would never get up again. His cheeks were more sunken and pale than ever, his lips dry and cracked with fever under the scraggly gray mustache, his hands that lay inert on the white sheet were thin almost to transparency. He had his lucid moments, moments when he chatted briefly with members of his family and officials of his government and patted the heads of the children who stared with round uncomprehending eyes. But most of the time his small, heavy-lidded eyes remained closed. He lived in a half-dreamy world of his own.

As he lay prostrate on his bed of death, shielded from worldly noises and always guarded from possible attacks against his ebbing life, Juan Vicente Gómez perhaps for the first time in his life took time to pause and reflect. What a rush of thoughts must have flitted through that tired, enfeebled mind! What a desperate clinging to fond memories! If only once again he could see the cool, green valleys of Táchira . . . run his hand through freshly threshed wheat . . . inhale the virile, pungent smell of the cattle . . . approach Buenmozo's cage for a last farewell. And his children and grandchildren! The scores and scores of them! He strove to recall their joyous laughter, their childish sayings . . . if he could partake with them all one more breakfast of *café con leche* and *pan de guayas*. But it was not to be. Never more would he greet Buenmozo . . . there

would be no more childish laughter . . . no more fond scenes that
he loved so well. The reckoning was fast approaching, but he dare not
look ahead, he could only look back . . . back into the dim hall of
memories to recall misty vistas of earthly pleasures . . . and perhaps weigh them against the misery, suffering, and death that during
his lifetime he had dealt out relentlessly and without compassion.
Had it been worth it?

Day by day the condition of Juan Vicente worsened. It became
plain to his doctors that he had only a few more days to live.

The truth has never come out and probably never will come out
about the plots and counter-plots that were hatched around that old
man's death-bed. All sorts of stories are told: that in an interview with
Generals López and Ernesto Velasco, Gómez offered Velasco the
Presidency; that because Velasco considered himself unqualified, he
had turned down the offer, recommending López instead; that Eustóquio had asked for the Presidency and had been rejected as unfit;
and that a few days before his death, Gómez had expressed the wish
to his sons Juan Vicente and Florencio that Dr. Pedro Rafael Tinoco,
then Minister of the Interior, be named to the post. According to Juan
Vicente and Florencio's version, they were fearful of what would
happen in the army ranks if a civilian assumed the supreme command; to protect their interests, they proposed to the cabinet (which
had taken residence in the Hotel Jardín during the crisis) that they
nominate General López, as he was the one man who could maintain order.

There was no concrete evidence that General Gómez had made
a political testament. General López, as a consequence, became the
man of the hour. It was to him that both the administration and the
Gómez clan turned during this time of crisis. Though the seriousness
of the general's condition had been made known to only an intimate
few, the news quickly spread among the upper echelons of the army.
López had long suspected Eustóquio Gómez of aspiring to his cousin's
seat, and now the suspicion was confirmed when reports came in that
he was aligning officers on his side to spring a coup. So, scheming and
conniving was going on right under his nose! It was a dangerous situation to be sure, but the Minister of War thought he could handle it.

Rather than relieve these officers of their command and perhaps
force Eustóquio to play his hand, López had them watched. His spies

were told to be extra vigilant and report anything unusual, no matter how trivial. López did not relish confronting the ferocious Gomecista face to face and accusing him outright of conspiring to revolution. Surrounded by his gang of cut-throats, Eustóquio might have sought some provocation to do away with him. Yet López had to let him know that he would not tolerate any interference with his command nor any attempt to overthrow the legally constituted government. He arranged a friendly meeting at the home of Regina Gómez in Caracas. Perhaps the presence of ladies would curb the scoundrel's tongue and stay his hand.

Besides Regina there was her sister Emilia and her husband General Colmenares Pacheco. Eustóquio had appeared with his two brothers and several officers. López had brought only his aide, Colonel Murrillo. Tall, thin, and bespectacled, López looked more the scholar than the soldier, but he had the steel nerve of a fighter and Eustóquio knew it. He stood there in the front *sala,* straight and confident, and calmly told them why he had called them together. Due to the grave illness of General Gómez, the country was in danger of falling into anarchy if personal ambitions were not curbed and the cabinet restricted from exercising its constitutional prerogatives. López explained his responsibilities as Minister of War in the cabinet, adding that his efforts would be to no avail if certain high political figures and relatives of General Gómez continued to withhold their collaboration and cause dissension in the army. He was speaking, he told them, as a loyal servant of his country, in all sincerity and good faith. He asked to be treated the same way. The Gómez sisters voiced their warm approval, and Eustóquio, though glum, spoke up to say that he was in agreement with whatever López thought best.

Did Eustóquio mean what he said? López wondered about that as he went out to his car where he found his wife waiting for him. Quaking with fear, she told him why she had come. A friend had phoned to warn her that Eustóquio had gone to the meeting armed to the teeth, that the life of her husband was in danger.

Although López did not know it at the time, Tarazona was mobilizing the personnel of the haciendas of Gómez in Aragua and Carabobo to concentrate and arm them in Maracay in connivance with the administrators of these estates. López found out about it the next day. As the leaders involved were either relatives or friends of both

Eustóquio and Tarazona, and as these two were inseparable comrades, it was not difficult for López to figure out who was at the head of this plot: it was Eustóquio.

From then on, the reports came in thick and fast. On the night of December 11 there had been a clandestine meeting at Las Delicias of the servants, neighboring friends, and some members of the local police force; rifles, light machine guns and ammunition had been handed out; Tarazona and his cronies had traveled at night to Ocumare de la Costa, San Juan de los Morros, Gómez's hacienda *El Trompillo* and other spots where Eustóquio counted on contingents of followers; the civil authorities of San Juan de los Morros had had an altercation with the local army commandant because the latter had declared that he would not comply with any orders other than those issued by the Gómez family; the commandant of the battalion Girardot intended to issue arms to the peons; an officer of El Limón was waiting for his uncle, commandant of the garrison in Ocumare de la Costa, so that he could comply with a special assignment, which was to either capture or liquidate General López the moment Gómez died.

Late on the night of Friday, December 13, General López received a fresh batch of reports. Excerpts from some of them: Colonel Tarazona had met with a large group of men in his house in Maracay and had ordered them to spread out in the town; an operator at the government telegraph office in Caracas had submitted evidence that General B——— was working for Eustóquio Gómez; Colonel G——— and Captain L——— were also suspected of plotting with him; the chief of police of Maracay had enlarged his force and had stationed three agents at every street intersection.

The reports on Saturday were just as grave: Three large cases had arrived from El Limón for Commander A———, which he delivered to three battalions; it was almost certain that these cases contained revolvers; all the hotels and streets of Maracay were filled with strangers and characters of ill repute; no compromising evidence had been obtained against Eustóquio; other than spending considerable time at the Hotel Jardín chatting with the members of the cabinet, his movements were above suspicion.

This last item appeared innocent enough on the surface, but López knew full well that Eustóquio was in the plot up to his ears.

He was only trying to throw López off the scent so that he could catch him unawares. But the Minister of War was not so naïve. "Keep watching him," he ordered. "He might slip somewhere. And if he writes anything, get it."

The watchful waiting paid off. Within forty-eight hours, General López had in his possession the following letter:

Sr. Colonel Eloy Montenegro,   Maracay,
Barquisimeto.   December 15, 1935
Dear Friend:

I salute you, hoping that you and your family are well.

Over here, according to what the doctors told the boys (Gómez's sons) today, General Gómez is very grave. This will be the day of judgment. It will be a disaster. Tell the chiefs of the battalions to take great care, to redouble their vigilance and that they are to answer to me, that they obey no one's orders but mine and to be careful not to go against my wishes; even though the Minister of War may give them orders, they are not to move unless I say so.

This is a key: When I tell you "the work is finished," it will mean that the general has died or is dying, so that our people will rise up in arms.

The state of affairs is very vague and who knows what may happen or turn up. General Gómez left nothing organized, which makes our situation very difficult.

Summon Josué and tell him the same thing I am telling you, that he be very careful and vigilant, that in case anything turns up his men are to grab their arms and I will notify you by means of the key. Furnish an express train to (name deleted), telling him the same, that he take great care and that we all be in mutual accord, that what we need today is unity among us, so that we can be invincible at the right moment.

I haven't heard yet what the Royal (Royal Bank of Canada) has decided about receiving the money I told you about.

These matters should be handled with extreme caution so that no one will interfere. Tell Colonel Mendoza to be very careful, to put Colonel Benavidez in charge over there and to come to El Tocuyo, and tell him to add some more policemen so that his vigilance will be tight, and to take care with the enemies whom he knows.

In other words, be careful, very careful in everything.

Your friend who embraces you,

E. Gómez

On Sunday, December 15, at the army hangars and barracks of Maracay, the garrison was electrified by the rapid issue of orders— which had never before been issued on the sabbath. All leaves were canceled and the men were ordered to arm. Around the hangars fronting the road which led to La Delicias, machine guns were placed at thirty-yard intervals and also at the guard posts along the road. The cars that passed were ridden by stern-faced Gómez relatives and high officials. As the soldiers manned their posts, curiosity rather than fear started a wave of rumors.

A motor caravan drove in at the hangars and out stepped General López, the respected Minister of War. He addressed the men lined up in formation, and in a few crisp words reminded them that they had a dominant duty to perform, that as soldiers they must obey their officers implicitly and thus they would faithfully serve their country. Above all, he added, they must bear in mind constantly their illustrious President and commander-in-chief. They must never forget that he is an integral part of the army and that he relies on their staunch support *come what may.*

On that pregnant phrase López turned and sped off as quickly as he came. Although many words had been left unsaid, he had dropped the veiled inference that the dictator's realm had begun to topple. This, coupled with the failure of Gómez to put in an appearance during the past week, gave credence to the rumor that he had died. This rumor spread and fanned out like an unchecked forest fire.

On the morning of the sixteenth tension mounted and the grapevine circulated a new report. Tarazona was going to blow up the hangars and planes with dynamite! The fear was well founded as it was known to the army that Tarazona could not stand the sight of planes.

Tarazona passed the hangars several times that day, riding swiftly by in his black Lincoln, but his thoughts were not on bombing sprees. It had become his habit to drop in on the sick man two or three times each day to see how he was faring and to perform any special *comisiónes* that his master might want done. On this day the old man was not doing well at all. His strength was ebbing fast. Though he smiled wanly at his visitors, he didn't seem to recognize them. There was nothing for the Indian to do but stand around awkwardly, hoping that he might be of some help. For over thirty-six years Eloy Tarazona had served his master faithfully and well like a devoted slave. Now that death was going to separate them, he knew he would have to fend for himself. His alliance with Eustóquio Gómez was one of convenience so that he could climb to greater power and wealth.

Eustóquio had returned unexpectedly to Barquisimeto that morning. Before leaving he had told the Indian what he was to do. It was shortly after 6 P.M., after he had conferred with the doctors on his last visit, that Tarazona went to the phone in Gómez's office and cranked the handle to signal the operator.

Dolores Amelia, sitting alone in the *sala*, heard the ring on the extension phone. Who was calling whom? Was it about the general? The distraught woman, red-eyed and weary from her long vigil, was worried about herself and her children. The death of the general would place them all in a precarious position. Did this call portend ill news? Unable to restrain her curiosity, she went to the phone, lifted the receiver carefully, and listened. Tarazona was putting through a call to Eustóquio in Barquisimeto.

"*Quién es?*" a harsh voice asked faintly through a crackle of static.

"*Soy yo,* Eloy. Listen! Listen carefully! Prepare the knife . . the steer is ready! I'll be right there . . . *Sabe?*"

There was a click. Tarazona had hung up.

Dolores Amelia sat down heavily in one of the wicker chairs to think things over. It didn't take her long to realize that Tarazona was up to no good, that the message was some sort of a key that boded ill for someone, probably the general or her and her children. Or was it Venezuela? That was it! By "steer," Tarazona had meant Venezuela. He and that scoundrel Eustóquio were going to seize the power for themselves!

Envisaging all sorts of dire calamities, Dolores Amelia went looking for someone in whom to confide her secret. Passing the office, she looked in. It was empty. Leaning against the railing of the veranda and looking into the general's bedroom where a doctor and nurse stood on duty, was Gómez's cousin, Isidro Torres Gómez. Dolores Amelia knew him well. He could be trusted if anyone could. She whispered to him what she had heard.

The man's eyebrows went up. "This is indeed serious," he said. "I had better get to General López right away." He hurried downstairs to his car. As he drove off to López's headquarters in Maracay, the leaves of the almendras and ceibas of Las Delicias rustled in the evening breeze. The guards at the gate stood in deep shadow.

López received the news calmly; he had been expecting it. Eustóquio he could not lay a finger on, for obvious reasons, but Eloy Tarazona was not immune. Orders were issued for his arrest and for the officers who were known to be in collusion with him.

A captain and a squad of soldiers went to Tarazona's house just a block away from the Plaza Girardot. A servant said that the colonel wasn't in, that he had driven off with his chauffeur in his Lincoln at seven o'clock.

"Where did he go?" he was asked.

"I do not know, *señores,*" he replied. "He did not tell me. He just said he would be back tonight."

The captain deliberated with his men on the sidewalk. They fanned out and laid in ambush. The big hands of the church clock moved slowly. Midnight passed. One o'clock. Two o'clock.

At ten minutes past two a long chauffeur-driven limousine drove up the street and turned into the driveway of Eloy Tarazona's house. The car was covered with a thick layer of dust. On the rear seat, almost lost in shadow, sat the short, plump figure the captain was waiting for. In the short space of seven hours, Tarazona had been to Barquisimeto and back. His chauffeur had covered the three hundred and forty-four grueling miles of tortuous, dusty road at fifty miles an hour!

The soldiers pounced on the two from both sides. They took Tarazona completely by surprise. It was well they did, for on the seat beside him was a loaded machine gun and a box of ammunition. In the baggage compartment they found a wooden box filled with five-bolivar pieces—payoff money for the peons. Tarazona and his chauffeur were marched off to the *cuartel calabozo.*

A few hours later, as the sun rose over the bare brown hills, there was a great stir in the house of Las Delicias. The old man had lapsed into a semi-coma. He was babbling incoherent phrases. His secretary began phoning his friends and relatives to say that the end was near. The white bed with its frail burden was wheeled into the *sala* so there would be room to accommodate the visitors. The doctors brought in equipment for a transfusion. First Juan Vicente, then Florencio, gave their blood. It was of no use. At one-thirty in the afternoon the old man sank into a complete coma.

As her grief-stricken children and the other relatives looked on, Dolores Amelia, weeping incessantly, placed on a table next to the dying man's bed the cherished Papal blessing which bore the Pope's signature. It was the best thing she could think of to entrust her man into the hands of God. Until his last lucid moment, Gómez had refused to receive a priest and the last rites of the church. The sacrament of marriage likewise was out of the question. To passive Dolores Amelia, his wishes were her command. Though Juan Vicente had committed every mortal sin, he had loved her in his own strange way. Above all, he had been a considerate and loving father. He had made no will but she and the children were well provided for. Their haciendas and other properties were worth millions. There were more millions in cash in the big safe in the other house. He had told her the combination, but in case she forgot it, it was written on a piece of paper hidden in his desk.

All day and until late at night a steady procession of relatives and friends filed quietly into the *sala* to have a last look at the once great dictator. Pérez Soto had flown in from Zulia, León Jurado from Falcón, Santos Matute Gómez from Carabobo, and Eustóquio from Lara. The latter, incensed at the arrest of his chief lieutenant and the other officers, was fierce to behold. From the far corners of Venezuela they had come, all the hundreds of in-laws, cousins, nephews and nieces, sons and daughters, and grandchildren. Tears were shed unashamedly.

While a doctor stood over the inert figure, anxiously watching and listening, the breathing stopped. It was 11:45 by the bedside clock, December 17, 1935, when the long career of Juan Vicente Gómez came to its end.

Strange that Juan Vicente died on this above all other days; it was the anniversary of the death of Simón Bolívar.

CHAPTER THIRTY-THREE

The Cataclysm

Early the next morning, friends of the late dictator carried his mortal remains to the house on the Plaza Girardot. There the body was embalmed, dressed in a grand Bolívaresque uniform, and placed in an elegant casket, to lie in state in the big *sala*. For several hours members of the Gómez clan viewed the body for the last time. When General López walked into the room, Eustóquio, his face a cold mask, stalked out with his two brothers.

Afterward, the casket was carried across the street to the church on the corner to lie in magnificent grandeur amid banks of flowers. While an honor guard of cadets stood the death watch, thousands of curious filed past to view the body.

At 11 A.M. Thursday, the cavalcade of cars stood ready to begin the funeral procession. General Ernesto Velasco, who was to lead the procession on his horse, happened to glance up at the church belfry where he saw a man in white with a dark object in his hand. Velasco ordered an officer to investigate. When the officer reappeared he reported that the man had been caught with a rifle and that he had freely admitted that he had intended to kill the general. He had been taken to the *calabozo*.

The procession set off without further incident, General Gómez's favorite horse, a chestnut-brown stallion, in the vanguard. To the people who lined the streets and stared, it seemed that the horse bore a rider—General Gómez himself, who sat stiffly and erect, looking straight ahead. The people couldn't believe that the dictator was dead.

At the cemetery, six sons bore the coffin from the motor hearse to the mausoleum. Juan Vicente was lowered into the family vault be-

At a fiesta in Maracay. Left to right, front row: Antonio Pimental, Dolores Amelia, daughters Belen and Rosa Amelia, Gómez, his sisters Regina and Emilia. Standing, in mufti, son Florencio, son-in-law Roberto Santana, Eloy Tarazona (behind Gómez).

Inside the Gómez mausoleum, Maracay cemetery. Gómez lies between his favorite son Alí and his brother Pedro. The tomb of José Vicente, whose body was brought back from Paris, lies on the right. The mausoleum has twenty vaults filled with relatives of the dictator.

side his brother Pedro and Alí, his beloved son. Long ago Gómez had once said, "Alí slept next to me many a night. When I go I want to sleep at his side. Remember that, Indalecia." Indalecia had remembered.

Said a foreign diplomat after the ceremony was over, "I believe we have seen not only the passing of a man, but also the passing of an era."

The morning after Gómez's death, the cabinet had elected General López Provisional President. His first act was to call a meeting of the heads of the army and the government at the offices of the Ministry of War in Maracay. Specifically excluded were all members of the Gómez family and their in-laws. A strong guard was posted to make sure that neither Santos Matute Gómez nor Eustóquio would enter. At the meeting, López informed those present that in accordance with the terms of the Constitution, he was now vested with authority as Provisional President of the Republic and would so carry on the affairs of state. On the spot he made various civil and military appointments.

One of his official acts that day was to order the release of all political prisoners and those working on the roads. This move brought a storm of protest from the friends and relatives of Gómez, and especially from Eustóquio, who complained that it placed their security in great peril. Ousted from his position as president of the state of Lara, Eustóquio was also worried about his future.

"What are we now?" he asked López mournfully, referring to the Gómez clan in general.

López's answer hinted at a change in the order of things. "You are orphans!" he answered dryly.

With his bond to the dictator severed, and the eyes of the nation upon him, López released the political prisoners with the full realization that he was incurring dangers for the Gómez clan and all their followers. Before he left for Caracas after the funeral, he ordered the garrisons of Caracas, Maracay, Valencia and La Victoria reinforced in case of a political or public upheaval. Fortunately for him the army was solidly behind him. As one officer later phrased it, "If the army had not been united during the days that followed, who knows but something worse might have happened."

The press had published its obituaries, all flattering to the deceased. Hundreds of messages of condolence poured in to the government and the Gómez family from friends, oil companies, foreign governments, and admirers abroad. Fifteen days of mourning had been decreed; across the land official flags flew at half mast. The dictator was no more, but the only reaction to the passing of a reign of tyranny was a spiritless apathy. The people couldn't bring themselves to believe that the dictator was dead. They were still numb from the apparatus of crisis and terror that had held them bound and helpless for twenty-seven years. For a full day, as the army watched and waited for they knew not what, events followed their tranquil course. It was only the lull before the storm.

It started in the little town of La Victoria on Thursday, December 19. When a man coolly walks away from the scene of his crime he is likely to escape undetected. If he runs, he is sure to be chased. The *jefe civil* of La Victoria, a tyrant in his own right, chose to run. The schizophrenic violence that followed spread to other towns and villages and racked the country from end to end.

In Caracas a mob poured into the Plaza Bolívar, shouting, laughing, "The Catfish is dead! *Viva la libertad!*" They were answered by a volley of rifle fire from the soldiers of General Rafael Velasco, the governor of Caracas. Many fell dead and wounded. López demanded and received Velasco's resignation, and installed in his place General Félix Galavis.

Mobs of youths roamed the streets, carrying hastily-lettered placards, laughing and shouting. The men who joined them were elements of the lowest order, all bent on a spree of destruction, looting, and murder. A wave of looting swept the city, and in the bedlam of confusion and disorder the doors of the prisons were opened wide, spewing their contents into the streets. It was a scene repeated in dozens of cities and towns. Thieves and murderers swelled the surging mobs in search of plunder. Men went armed, anyone who bore a resemblance to a Gomecista was shot at, all sensible men remained indoors. Life everywhere ground to a shuddering halt as mob violence replaced law and order. From the streets of Caracas to the far-off camps of the Zulia oil fields, the atmosphere was one of fear, gloom, and tense anxiety.

For the "Royal Family," it was a frantic flight for their lives. López had repeatedly advised them to get out of the country and they had wondered why he had been so insistent. Many of them arrived at the conclusion that López wanted them to leave Venezuela, not for their safety, but to solidify his own power. He was afraid that the hundreds of Gomecistas would unite under the Gómez sons and remove him from office. "He threw us out of the country," said Juan Vicente and Florencio years afterward.

Since the eighteenth, López had had the gunboat, *Zamora*, anchored at the port of Ocumare de la Costa for just such an emergency. On it embarked for asylum in Curacao almost a hundred of the Gómez clan—Dolores Amelia, her sons and daughters, Gómez's other son Gonzalo, and many of the cousins and in-laws. They took with them what prized possessions they could carry and what money they could lay their hands on. Dolores Amelia had hurried to the safe in the house on the Plaza Girardot. She had stuffed valises with one thousand bolivar bills. One bag alone contained ten million bolivars. When she and her sons loaded their cars which were to speed them to the coast, they had so much baggage that they had to leave one overnight bag behind with a friend. When he opened it later he found in it almost one million bolivars in bills. When General López searched Gómez's house he found the safe locked. He didn't know about the combination written on a piece of paper in the desk drawer, and he ordered the safe burned open with a torch. He didn't find anything in it but a few worthless papers. The safe is still lying half buried in the sand of one of the patios where his men dumped it.

Gómez also had a heavy steel filing case which held valuable and confidential papers. That, too, was broken into and rifled, presumably by López, although it is said that Dolores Amelia and other persons close to Gómez got to it first and removed incriminating documents. Despite the guards posted at the house by López, the gold telephone, the fancy desk set, in fact everything of any value disappeared within two or three days. All that remained was the ornate furniture, the general's inlaid desk, and the French bronze in his office.

Another group of Gómez relatives headed for La Guaira via the main highway to Caracas. Just beyond La Victoria they were halted by a line of cars coming the other way. For a moment it looked as if there would be an exchange of gunfire, but the party turned out to be friends who had come to convoy them to their ship. At La Guaira the group was denied the use of a launch, but after a nervous wait of three hours they obtained small boats in which they rowed out to the liner anchored some distance offshore.

From Curacao, all the Gomecistas scattered to other havens. Rafael Velasco went to his ranch in Canada, Santos Matute and his family to Costa Rica, while others went to Mexico and France. Dolores Amelia and her children went to Santo Domingo, the bailiwick of the dictator, Trujillo. Her exile was one of lonely wanderings and unhappy experiences. On the streets of Madrid she was called vile names and was pelted with tomatoes.

Dolores Amelia had left behind in Venezuela with the Colombian, Dr. Rosario García, her youngest child, Juan. García saw to it that the boy was packed off safely to England and put in a good school. Later, when the youth stated his preference for the United States, he enrolled him in Pennsylvania State College where he was graduated in civil engineering.

Another son, Gónzalo, whose mother was Dionisia Bello, went to New York where he proceeded to squander the money he had banked from the Caracas lottery. Fancy living and legal tangles with Broadway show girls relieved him of a million dollars in little over a year. His short-lived marriage to the actress, Joyce Matthews, ended in divorce.

Gómez's sister, Emilia, her arm broken when she jumped from the rear wall of Regina's house in Caracas, was forced into hiding and was cared for by friends.

After a hair-breadth escape, Dr. Itriago Chacín, one-time Minister of Foreign Relations and Provisional President for eleven days in 1931, reached the Canary Islands with his son Ilario. One day his clothes were found on the beach and his body in the sea. He had left a note in his rooms which gave instructions that in case of his death, his body was not to be returned to Venezuela under any circumstances.

Some of the Gómez clan, accompanied in flight by frightened corrupt government officials, took to planes thoughtfully put at their disposal by López. One plane crashed close to the frontier but the wounded occupants all managed to crawl to safety into Colombia.

General Vincencio Pérez Soto, the millionaire president of Zulia, fled to Trinidad in regal style on his yacht, leaving behind his notorious woman servant to fare for herself. Nicknamed "Chameleon," it was commonly believed she was Pérez Soto's clandestine executioner. It is said she was the one who put arsenic in the coffee and mixed powdered glass in the food of condemned prisoners. Abandoned by her children, she somehow managed to elude capture, and today she roams the streets of Maracaibo, unrecognized, selling lottery tickets and begging alms.

Tough Leon Jurado, a battle-scarred veteran of countless revolutions, stood his ground in Coro. Protected by his subservient soldiers and his gun-toting sons, he chose to remain and fight for his vast properties and enterprises. Other moneyed generals did likewise, while hundreds of less affluent small-fry holed up in mountain retreats or slipped across the border in the dead of night.

Eloy Tarazona, meanwhile, fumed and swore in the fortress of Puerto Cabello to which he had been transferred. He was told that he would soon be deported to Colombia as an undesirable. A friend who was permitted to visit him convinced him that he should marry a Venezuelan girl, that only in this way could he possibly retain ownership of his string of houses and haciendas. Tarazona selected his favorite concubine, an eighteen-year-old girl from the Andes, and they were married in the fortress. A few weeks later Tarazona was deported to Colombia.

Though López had no compunctions about deporting Tarazona, he was loath to lay a finger on Eustóquio. For old time's sake he had resolved to grant safe conduct to every one of the Gómez clan, and that included this *vagabundo* who he figured had been shorn of his lightning. Eustóquio, however, refused to stir from Maracay where he maintained a home and family. As proven by subsequent events, he still entertained hopes of taking over the government. With his best officers behind bars and the army united as a buffer against him, there was not much he could do but search for a weak spot in López's armor. His following had been reduced to a small group of hirelings and renegade officers, all willing to do his bidding, all armed and ready to fight. But what chance had a handful of desperados against a unified army and a people roused to revenge? To Eustóquio's crafty mind, the disorders in the capital presented the situation he was waiting for. It would take daring and nerve but the venture might be worth the risk. Surely a fistful of cash handed out in the right places would work wonders. For money a man would lie, steal, and kill. Every man has his price.

It probably was during the night of the nineteenth that Eustóquio made up his mind, because before daybreak the next morning he was on the road to Caracas with two carloads of henchmen, all heavily armed with machine guns and revolvers. To his wife he had delegated an important duty. Early that morning she phoned General Ernesto Velasco at the Maracay barracks. Would the good General be so kind as to send a truck and some soldiers over to her house to convoy several boxes containing eight million bolivars in cash and silver to her husband in Caracas? Most unsafe to leave that much money lying around the house during these troubled days; her husband wanted to deposit it in a bank. The general, willing to oblige, sent over a truck with four soldiers and a captain, and the treasure was soon on its way.

It was about 8 A.M. that an aide announced to General López in his office in the Ministry of War that General Eustóquio Gómez desired to see him. The general, not a little surprised, said to show him in but not to leave him alone with the man—he was dangerous.

Eustóquio was ushered in and parked his stout figure in front of the Provisional President's desk. If he was disappointed that the aide made no move to leave, he did not show it. After an exchange of polite greetings, he made small talk, saying he had come to Caracas on some personal matters and that he would be leaving shortly for Barquisimeto to settle his affairs there. Invited to take a chair he sat down leisurely and stretched out. Evidently Eustóquio was just paying a friendly call.

López could not help but admire the audacity of the man. The capital at this moment was like a hornet's nest; the streets were teeming with people who would have liked nothing better than to get their hands on this notorious scoundrel and tear him limb from limb. And here he was paying an impromptu call while the rest of the Gómez clan were fleeing the country to save their lives. "Don't you realize," López said to him gravely, "that you are taking undue risks coming to the city at this time? The people have risen up against the old officials of the government and especially the Gómez family. There's no telling what might happen. The situation is serious, very serious . . ."

The President of the Republic, his Minister of War and Marine,
López Contreras, reviewing a parade.

General Isaías Medina Angarita, President of Venezuela,
1941-1945.

Eustóquio favored him with a cynical smile. His eyes under beetle-brows flashed venom.

"Well," López shrugged. "Don't say I didn't warn you. I'm having breakfast sent in. Would you care to join me?"

"*Graçias, no.* Breakfast is waiting for me at my house." Eustóquio appeared in no hurry to leave.

"My advice to you," said López with a touch of impatience in his voice, "is to return to Maracay at once. You won't be able to go to Barquisimeto because the people there have already held demonstrations against you."

"All right, then I'll go to Maracay."

"That's better. Do you think you'll need an escort of soldiers? You can choose the officers yourself."

"I won't need them."

"Maracay is the only place where you and your family will be safe. However, in case any trouble develops there, I'll be glad to put a plane at your disposal to take you to Curacao. Just let me know."

Eustóquio stood up, tidied his natty gray suit and reached for his hat. "*Adios, pues,*" he said curtly, and stalked out. López did not fail to notice the telltale bulge on his right hip.

The Provisional President of the Republic ate his breakfast rather hurriedly. Time was fleeting and many matters awaited his attention. From time to time he gave ear to the rhythmic tramp of feet and the rising babble of voices that floated in through the open windows. The shouts of street rowdies were becoming more numerous.

It was about 9:45 that López received a phone call from General Galavis. Eustóquio's arrival at the Government House with several of his henchmen had caused a great deal of excitement. He seemed to have gone completely *loco*. He had posted two of his men with machine guns at the entrance and was deliberately provoking the crowd on the Plaza Bolívar from an upstairs balcony. The populace was clamoring furiously for his head.

"The fool! Lock him up," ordered López. "Lock him up right away and arrange to send him to Maracay under a strong escort. We'll keep him in the *cuartel* until a plane can take him to Curacao."

Galavis issued instructions to an aide who rushed off, then gathered three officers around him and went looking for Eustóquio. He met him in the corridor. Two of his men were behind him holding machine guns. "I am sorry, General, but I have orders to place you under arrest . . ."

Eustóquio sneered as he reached for his hip. He did not know that a few yards behind him a soldier watching from behind a pillar had raised his Mauser to eye level. In that instant a trigger was pressed and a shot reverberated through the building. The figure in gray dropped to the tile floor mortally wounded.

"It was his life or mine," said Galavis afterward. "Everyone knew of Eustóquio's evil reputation."

The henchmen, cowards now, ran for the stairs. In the excitement Eustóquio picked himself up and staggered off down a corridor. Galavis's men followed the trail of blood. They found him cowering in the men's room. It was there that he met his end. They snuffed out his last breath by holding his head in a toilet bowl.

What happened to the eight million bolivars? Nobody seems to know. By the time the truck arrived in Caracas, Eustóquio was dead. The captain, upon his return to Maracay, reported to General Velasco that he had delivered the money to one of López's officers. López denied any knowledge of the matter. For some unexplainable reason no investigation was ever made and the matter was hushed up.

Meanwhile, the mob in the plaza was pressing forward, ready to enter and overrun the building. They did not know that Eustóquio could no longer hear their shouted demands for his head. On the balconies facing the plaza, lines of policemen appeared with machine guns. An officer shouted to the mob to disperse or his men would shoot. But either the unruly people could not hear or they paid no heed. They surged forward. At the sharp command of "*Disparen!*" the deafening volley of machine guns drowned out their cries. As the guns raked the front ranks and over a hundred fell, the mob disintegrated like an exploding rocket. Like red blossoms fallen from flamboyant trees after a heavy *chubasco,* patches of crimson lay splashed over inert bodies and along the walks and grounds of the plaza. His handkerchief held to his wound, one man stumbled toward the equestrian statue of Simón Bolívar. With one last desperate heave he threw the dripping piece of cloth, then dropped to the pavement. The handkerchief landed on the mane of Bolívar's horse, and there it remained to fade day by day in the Caracas sun and ask the mute but poignant question, "What price liberty?"

It is said that the gutters ran red with rivulets of blood and that men and boys returned to dip their handkerchiefs into it and write in blood on the statue's base and on the walls of buildings bitter remarks about the liberty that was denied them and the death they received instead. It was the massacre of 1928 all over again, only this time the blame could not be charged to the tyrant, Gómez.

It was then that frenzied mobs roamed through the streets converting everything that looked and smelled of Gómez into a holocaust. Stores and buildings which still displayed pictures of "The Well Deserving" were pillaged and wrecked. Juan Vicente died again a thousand deaths in effigy as his portraits were burned on bonfires in the streets. A theater belonging to Pimentel was wrecked, as was also a club where the Gómez sons held their carousals. Everywhere there was the glint of forbidden arms, the flash of steel as machetes flailed the air and chopped furniture to bits. The police had disappeared from the streets or stood by helpless to interfere. All law-abiding citizens remained indoors behind bolted doors.

On Saturday morning after a mob of hoodlums had wrecked the plant and offices of the *Nuevo Diario,* the government newspaper, General Galavis addressed the citizens of Caracas on the radio. He warned them that unless such acts ceased immediately severe measures would be taken.

Said the Caracas manager of an American oil company in his cabled report to his home office: "THERE IS NO DOUBT BUT THAT THE GOVERNMENT CAN AND WILL ABSOLUTELY CONTROL THE SITUATION IN ANY EVENT."

But the hoodlums and youths of Caracas either did not hear or paid no heed. Armed bands tramped out to the suburbs and picked the houses of the Gomecistas clean. The elegant *quintas* of the Gómezes, Velascos, Pimentels and Santanas, Pacheco, García, Itriago Chacín, Cárdenas, Tinoco and Arcaya, were looted and wrecked. Pedro Arcaya's library of rare and valuable books was dumped in his garden and burned. Paintings, silver trays, chinaware, cases of liquor, even chairs, statuettes, and chandeliers were lugged through the streets and sold to anyone who offered a few bolivars. Cars were stolen, loaded with loot and driven away. Others were left smoking skeletons in the streets and driveways. Ragged urchins, searching through the litter and rubble, scampered off with less valuable trophies. Sporadic pistol fire mingled with shouts, and then columns of smoke rose into the sunny, clear sky.

In the Plaza Juan C. Gómez, the bust of Juancho, the "Martyr of the Rehabilitation," lay shattered on the pavement.

Again the voice of General Galavis boomed over the Caracas radios. Martial law was going to be declared; the people had one hour to get out of the streets.

Though the shouts and rattle of small-arms fire continued, from one end of Caracas to the other there was a mad dash for safety. Here and there, faces, eyes round with wonder, pressed against window grilles; lone figures clung closely to doorsteps, ready to flee inside at the slightest danger. In every home dwindling supplies of foodstuffs were jealously guarded, for there was no telling how long the siege would last.

When the hour was up, Galavis's cavalry poured into the streets from the city barracks to augment the ineffective police force. As the mounted soldiers charged with flashing sabers in pursuit of fleeing men, their horses' hooves clattered on empty streets and the sounds echoed weirdly along the rows of silent buildings.

Citizen Germán Quintero, standing behind the locked door of his home near the center of the city, listened intently to the sounds of conflict that filtered through from outside. From up the street he heard through the sporadic gun fire the rhythmic sound of swiftly fleeing feet, and from a distance the faint clatter of the pursuing cavalry. The footfalls grew ever louder. Then he heard the thundering roar of the horses. They had turned a corner and were bearing down his way. The running feet were just opposite him now. Suddenly they halted and Germán Quintero was startled by a frantic pounding.

"Please open in the name of God!" shouted a frightened voice. "I am a priest and I beg your protection!"

What did Germán Quintero do? Quintero was a God-fearing man and if he hesitated it was for only a second. He unbolted and opened the door. The figure which confronted him was short and squat, dust covered his black cassock and perspiration bathed his dark *mestizo* face. But he was a priest. Señor Quintero stepped back to let him enter but he could not hold back the people who pressed close upon the priest's heels. They brushed him aside as they crowded in, and someone closed and bolted the door. There was a breathless moment as they waited for the cavalry to gallop by, then they took stock of their situation. Altogether, including the Quintero family, there were twenty-nine of them—twenty-five adults and four children. There were only six small rooms and the stock of food was not plentiful. There was no telling how long they would be forced to remain together, but, having granted asylum to the priest, Señor Quintero could not bring himself to refuse sanctuary to the others even though they were all strangers. As long as the riots and shooting lasted he would shelter and feed them all.

For three uneasy nights they slept wherever they could rest their heads. For three feverish days they shared the rationed food. Before each scanty repast they bowed their heads in unison while the priest said grace. Between meals, while death stalked the streets outside, he soothed them by quoting from the scriptures.

Today, if one should come upon Germán Quintero at Sunday mass, he will be seen fingering a gold rosary—a remembrance from a grateful priest—and by the shining light in his face it is clear that he is at peace with God and his conscience. For Germán Quintero is a God-fearing man.

What happened in Caracas was repeated in almost every town and hamlet in the country. Mobs inflamed went on a rampage of destruction and killing under the pretext that they were exacting revenge. They were composed of *mestizos* mostly, men and youths who lacked the sobriety and self-restraint of the Man of Iron; the *gente decente,* that is the middle and upper strata of society, could only stand back in horror and resign themselves to the disgrace their country suffered. Looking back, almost everyone had rather expected violence, but there was not much that could be done to prevent it; with the authorities in flight, the mobs took the law into their own hands. There had been a halfhearted hope that the death of the tyrant would be celebrated with music and sober speeches. Instead, the masses, willingly caught up in a maelstrom of passions, had revealed their basest instincts. They had clamored for personal liberties, that will-o'-the-wisp that Bolívar fought and died for, that Gómez had called "the most foolish of all human hopes." Did they deserve it? Liberty does not grant one the right to vilify and destroy, to loot and kill. Wanton destruction and indiscriminate killing are not just retribution for the sins of a regime.

Of all the states of the republic which fell prey to death and destruction during those dark days of December, Zulia suffered the greatest, for here in the heavy heat of the lowlands dwelt the majority of the conglomeration of races that were being fused into the new race of *mestizos*. Here were poverty and disease, discontent and misery, and the host of problems that went with them. The presidents of Zulia, perforce, had all been men of the army; they were men who maintained the peace by brute force and threats, and achieved a semblance of prosperity by putting malefactors and champions of freedom into chain gangs to slave for the state. Yet there had been some, like General Vincencio Pérez Soto, who displayed suave manners and restraint and bestowed small favors, albeit with a benign and lordly gesture. While he ruled, Pérez Soto was depicted by the press as a true *servidor* of the people; when he fled after the death of Gómez he was called the vilest of despots. He had been a little of both, a sort of *Padre* Borgas, who committed a sin one day and regretted it the next. When he donated a statue of Christ to the Maracaibo Church of Santa Teresita, he had the plaque on it inscribed: "Offering from a repentant sinner."

In the still, burning heat of the lowlands tempers run high. A phrase spoken in anger is like setting a match to dry tinder. The Zulianos knew this. So did the *Americanos*, the Englishmen, the Dutchmen, and all the other foreigners and their families who sought refuge behind the flimsy protection of cyclone fences of the oil camps. Maracaibo and the oil towns that dotted the lake shore were tinder boxes which were touched off with a few fiery words of hate and rebellion shouted through radio loudspeakers.

The youths of the city took the law into their own hands. They seized the radio station. They broadcast petitions to General López in Caracas. They swayed the masses with strident shouts to overthrow the civil authorities. Almost immediately the people began to gather and parade through the streets. A youth harangued a crowd in the Plaza Bolívar. At the height of his fury he smashed an officer in the face with the butt of his revolver. His death, at the hands of a policeman, converted him into a martyr.

Tempers flared, inflammatory leaflets were passed around to incite revenge. A parade of citizens clashed with the police. Eighteen on both sides were shot to death.

From that hour on, howling mobs milled through the streets, looting, killing, and wrecking. Criminals from the city prison were turned loose to join the mobs in the streets. Policemen who ventured near the plundering hordes were shot to death or cut down with machetes. Two whole blocks of business houses were sacked and burned to the ground. Fifteen looters perished in the flames.

There had been conflicts and jealousies between the police force and the army. The police had fired on the army. The army had fired on the police. Now the populace fired on both of them. So the army and the police remained in barracks and returned the fire.

When the mobs found out that the city and its environs were left without any authority or official protection, they roamed through the suburbs, sacking and destroying the homes of government officials and all their petty functionaries and followers. The home of the late dictator's nephew, Gustavo Gómez, on the main boulevard was stripped and raked with gunfire, his Club Golfito across the street was left a shambles. Armed men prowled the streets searching for their personal enemies and shot them down in cold blood. There would be no official accounting for these acts, for that would be impossible to accomplish. Justice was in the hands of the people and each and every one of them dealt it out as he saw fit.

Somewhere about the streets of the city on the afternoon of December 21, the American consul and the U.S. military attaché from Caracas were convincing themselves that what the managers of the foreign oil companies had told them were facts; that considerable street fighting was taking place between the subaltern authorities and the populace, that large-scale looting and wanton destruction were increasing in intensity hourly,[28] and that all semblance of order and authority had vanished from the city. The next morning the military attaché left by plane for Caracas to report on conditions in the west and to transmit requests that the American Embassy bring pressure to

---

[28]At no time, it may be said, did any demonstrations occur in Maracaibo against American citizens. Although the offices and residential camps of the American oil companies fell within the city limits, they remained outside of the zone of disturbance due to their relative inaccessibility.

bear on the provisional government to provide full protection for American interests and to allay tension in the oil fields.

The cataclysm struck the oil fields on Saturday, the 21st. Thousands of workers failed to report to work that afternoon. Men straggled, but with a purpose, toward the plaza and the *jefatura* of Cabimas. At dusk, a mob brandishing weapons and rumbling with threats overflowed the plaza and spilled into the square facing the one-story town hall. Inside behind closed shutters were the *jefe civil*, the chief of police, the governor of the district, and a number of others of lesser importance. Theirs was a desperate desire for survival and freedom.

The mob shouted for them to come out and give themselves up. But those inside were made of tougher stuff. Suddenly the single door swung open and the heavy window shutters, propelled by rifle barrels, slammed against the wall. A hail of bullets raked the mob and men dropped in the street. Volley after volley shattered the air until the last of those citizens who remained on their feet had disappeared from the square and the plaza. Then the Gomecistas emerged and ran to the rear of the building where they had parked their cars. They sped north, pausing enroute to pick up their families who had been left in hiding in outlying shacks. They cut the telephone and telegraph lines and farther on destroyed two small bridges. Beyond La Rita their trail disappeared in the wild and desolate wastes. They had headed for Falcón and the coast.

The citizens of Cabimas came out of hiding. They poured back into the square and carted off their wounded. The dead they carried into the corner barber shop and stacked like cordwood in tiers against the wall. Then they grabbed their weapons and began hunting down and killing every man who had maintained even the remotest connection with the past regime.

An American personnel man of one of the oil companies received instructions to go into the village to see what was going on and to render any assistance within his means. Outside the company gate he hailed the Venezuelan owner of the village light plant who was driving by to have a look on his own account. They parked in front of the white church. Its doors were bolted shut. Next door a the *jefatura* men were ferociously tearing the offices to pieces. The pair looked in at the barber shop. The American started counting the bodies. Suddenly he stopped. He had seen one of the bodies move!

"Good God!" he exclaimed. "That one on the bottom is still alive!" The American was nauseated by the dreadful sight but he steeled himself to say, "Let's get those bodies off him and take him to a doctor."

The Venezuelan held him back. "No," he said. "If we interfere, those men outside would be on us like a pack of wolves. Come, we had better go."

They drove back down the street from whence they had come. The sound of shooting was coming from all directions. They came upon a group of men standing around a body in the street. A man with a gun in his hand held up his arm for them to halt. "Take this back and deposit it with the others," he ordered.

The men heaved the body into the car. The American asked to be driven to his camp. He had seen enough and he was worried about his wife and children. When he arrived at his house he could hear the whine of bullets, some of which struck the zinc roofing of a warehouse next door. For several agonizing hours the family lay prone on the floor until the shooting died down.

All night and during the next day the wounded streamed into the dispensaries of the oil companies. The exhausted doctors worked frantically against time. On an operating table a huge Trinidadian Negro lay conscious while a doctor probed the wound in his abdomen. Suddenly the doctor straightened and beckoned to a nurse. "I can't find the bullet," he said hopelessly. "Have him put over there . . . he's going to die anyway . . . and bring me another!"

The Negro raised his arms in a gesture of supplication. "Doctor!" he wailed, "don't let me die! I want to live!"

The doctor turned away.

Sunday morning the situation took a turn for the worse. The villagers were taking revenge for personal grievances. An oil camp watchman was tied to a tree in the plaza and left there for two sultry days. He had refused the villagers entrance to company property to fill their water cans. Another watchman was thrown into a cell of the *jefatura* together with a live rattlesnake. At Lagunillas, an oil village farther south, two men were burned alive in the village incinerator.

That morning the captain of one of the oil tankers was handed a message to be relayed by cable from Aruba to New York. It read: THIS MORNING ALL AUTHORITIES INCLUDING CUSTOMS MOVED OUT OF

CABIMAS AND LAGUNILLAS LEAVING THESE PLACES WITHOUT PRO-
TECTION SITUATION SERIOUS STOP CONSIDERABLE SHOOTING TOOK
PLACE CABIMAS LAST NIGHT MANY NATIVES KILLED STOP SO FAR NO
MOLESTATION PROPERTY AT EITHER POINT STOP REPEAT SITUATION
SERIOUS.

At the gate of the largest oil camp, what at first had been a knot
of silent, sullen men had grown in the matter of a few hours to a
huge threatening crowd charged with mob hysteria. They shouted
names—American names—of men they thought they had good reasons to hate. They were in a killing mood and now was the time
to settle old scores. "Send them out here," they shouted, "or we will
go in and get them!"

Inside the cyclone fences the foreign oil workers patrolled the
grounds with shotguns and revolvers. Inside the cottages, frantic
women packed their bags for hurried flight. At the oil loading piers
of the different oil companies tankers stood ready to carry men and
families to safety. Commented one woman wearily, who was due for
confinement momentarily, "I wonder where my baby will be born."

On Monday, the new president of Zulia arrived in Maracaibo
with two hundred soldiers. He was none other than General Leon
Jurado. A strong man for a serious situation. The American consul
and representatives of the oil companies went to see him and requested that troops be sent to the oil fields. Jurado agreed to send
one hundred and fifty men immediately.

Jurado restored calm to Maracaibo in short order. In the fields,
however, the situation showed no noticeable improvement; there were
not enough troops to go around. The mobs had intimidated the company superintendents into permitting small groups to roam the camps
"to search for Gomecistas." They also demanded and received from
warehouse stock hundreds of machetes "to restore order." One Venezuelan was slain on company property. Another, a doctor, fled to a
tanker dressed in his wife's clothes. Another, a petroleum inspector,
escaped his pursuers by hiding in the narrow space between the ceiling
and roof of an American's cottage. The Americans the mobs had first
searched for had fled two days before on a tanker. When the marauding bands could not find any more Venezuelan officials to kill, they
left the oil camps quietly.

On Tuesday morning the situation in Cabimas and Lagunillas appeared to be getting more tense and families of foreigners were advised that they would be safer in Maracaibo, Curacao, or Aruba. The tankers would sail that afternoon. The employees themselves were told to make up their minds and could go too if they wished. Almost all chose to stay.

At dusk, as lights started to twinkle on the shoreline, women and children were put ashore in Maracaibo. Others remained aboard the tankers which ploughed north through the gathering darkness to make the tide at the bar. It was a clear, starry night. From the north came the cooling breezes of the trade winds which dispelled the heat of the day. In the southern sky could be seen one of Venezuela's many strange phenomena—eerie flashes of light which intermittently lit up a bank of clouds; it was the seamen's beacon, the Catatumbo Lights.

It was Christmas Eve. Peace on earth, good will toward men.

On Christmas day the cable lines hummed with messages. One of them read: ALTHOUGH TROOPS WERE COMPELLED TO FIRE INTO MOB AT LAGUNILLAS YESTERDAY NOON SITUATION THIS MORNING HAS TAKEN DECIDED TURN FOR BETTER STOP LAST NIGHT APPROXIMATELY FIFTY PASSENGERS SENT TO ARUBA MOSTLY WOMEN AND CHILDREN STOP AUTHORITIES LAGUNILLAS HAVE TOLD LABORERS TO RETURN TO WORK AND HAVE GUARANTEED THEM FULL PROTECTION STOP AGITATORS HAVE BEEN ARRESTED STOP ARE HOPEFUL LAGUNILLAS WILL BE SEVENTY-FIVE PER CENT NORMAL TOMORROW PRODUCTION STILL CLOSED IN BUT NORMAL EXPORTS HAVE NOT CEASED AND WILL NOT CEASE STOP RUMORS THAT GENERAL JURADO IS ONLY PROVISIONAL BUT WE HOPE HIS AUTHORITY WILL BE PERMANENT STOP WILL ADVISE PROGRESS TOMORROW STOP MERRY CHRISTMAS.

CHAPTER THIRTY-FOUR

The New Regime

During the years since the death of Gómez, the rulers of five regimes have sat in the chief executive's chair in the Casa Amarilla—placed there through election by congress, the people, or by revolutionary coups. Beleaguered by grave problems and the same jibes and vicious attacks of subversive propaganda that ridicule and harpoon all Latin American regimes, these leaders often bemoaned the fate that brought them to their vulnerable positions. There have been times when every one of them has fervently wished that he had the fortitude of a Gómez. Dissension in the ranks, plots and counterplots of scheming *ambiciosos* who aspired to rule have toppled more than one from his high place, have banished others into ignominious exile, and have ended the life of one by assassination. The political life of most of them has been stormy, though not without its compensations. In recent years Venezuela has come a long way along the path of democracy with the full enjoyment of its attendant rights. To a greater or lesser degree, each ruler has made his contribution to the nation's welfare. Whether any one of these men has been lecherous or incompetent in office will remain a question for the Venezuelans themselves to decide.

In recent years the men in power have made veiled charges of corruption and incompetence against their predecessors. Always these charges have been quickly relegated to political oblivion. The law dealing with calumny is explicit and allows stiff penalities, which explains the absence of mud-slinging in the Venezuelan press and political campaigns. Wary of raking up the past and paying dearly for it, the press and officialdom alike sensibly look toward the future.

General López's tenure in office (1936-41) was a trying one in many respects. He had to rid himself of the stigma of *Gomecismo*. He had to switch overnight from a dictatorship to a democracy. He had to fight off the corrosive effects of Communism. He was faced with the stupendous task of literally lifting the country by the bootstraps from backward colonialism to the social and industrial level of the twentieth century. Bread, education, respect for individual liberties, equal justice, and workers' legislation were all demanded at the outset.

The job that awaited the Provisional President would have been a challenge to the intellect and stamina of Bolívar. It disconcerted López but little. He had risen through the ranks not as a heady visionary but as a man of action and foresight. He knew what was right and he knew what was wrong, what was honest and what was not, what was just and what was unjust; and by these firm convictions he governed. He steered Venezuela through the unchartered seas of resistance, overcoming the vicissitudes of skepticism and lethargy, and the prejudice against those who were thought to be tainted because of association with the past regime. It was Venezuela's great good fortune that her President acquitted himself nobly and guided the ship of state safely into her new port.

The first few months were difficult. The people were skeptical. To demonstrate good faith and that he was not a *caudillo* out for plunder, López, though living in Miraflores Palace as befitting his position, shed his uniform and became "citizen López." After his formal election in April, 1936, he had congress amend the Constitution, shortening the presidential term from seven to five years, and announced his intention to serve for only five years although he could have remained in office until 1943.

The people were impatient for new faces, a new era. For lack of capable new candidates at the beginning of his administration, López was obliged to use such Gómez hold-overs as Jurado, Perez Soto, Galavis, and Tellería until he could put into office some of the liberal elements selected from the released prisoners and returning exiles. Even the National Congress which elected him to the Presidency was the same old Gómez congress. As the old militarists in the federal and state governments were replaced by young and aggressive liberals, López found himself alienated more and more from the old favored clique. Some of these men had been his friends since '99. Yet he remained steadfast in his purpose to wipe the slate clean and remain aloof from any tainted political ties.

The memory of many broken friendships caused López to remark in later years: "My grief was sincere and profound upon the death of that man (Gómez) who in his last years offered me trust, kindness, and affection, and so I told his sons Juan Vicente and Florencio. These sentiments have not diminished, though relatives and former followers of the general have spoken of ingratitude and inconsistency. My duty as chief of state obliged me to serve the country and to effect a change in that system of private politics developed by General Gómez which thrived not entirely of his own volition but because it was encouraged by all of us who served under him and was countenanced by the greater part of the country which, willingly or not, accepted such a situation."

As with Gómez twenty-seven years before, López began his administration without a party banner. Harkening to the old exhortation of Pedro Arcaya that "political excitement (i.e., political parties) necessarily brings on civil war," he made it clear that he would not sponsor any political party. When Dr. Márquez Bustillos asked him what name he would give to his regime or party which he was about to head, López replied: "I am not going to be the head of any party but the head of the Venezuelan State, and there will exist only the regime of the Fatherland."

The people wanted political parties, a free press, personal liberties, the struggle of ideas, of interests. Always abreast of world affairs, López knew that free criticism and frank discussion are considered the bulwark of democracy. He knew too that Venezuela was not yet ready for an outright democracy, that to permit the free play of ideas and passions would bring on anarchy.

The idea of a Messiah, which has excited the masses and even the intelligentsia in Venezuela during every political change, was hailed at the beginning in a thundering chorus of hope that something new and great was about to begin. Was this spare, ascetic-looking man, now fifty-two and looking like a scholar in his gray business suit, the promised Messiah who would lead his people out of bondage?

The President responded to the expressions of national consciousness with generous acts. Within a matter of weeks he found reason to regret his generosity, and he could only console himself with the thought that a new democratic government must learn by trial and error. Never could he be charged with being just another brand of dictator who suppressed the rights of the people.

One of his first acts was to talk to the nation by radio. This was a novelty, the President of the Republic in the role of servant of the people, addressing each citizen personally and rendering an account of his genuine humanitarian program. He had, he said, freed all political prisoners and had granted amnesty to all political exiles who were willing to recognize the new government. Political prisons and their *grillos* would be destroyed. Venezuela would have freedom of speech, of the press, of assembly, liberty of conscience, restoration of the suffrage privilege, and free elections for a new congress. Meanwhile the old congress would function. He promised sanitation, new hospitals, new schools, new transportation facilities, agricultural advancement, and a just labor law for the masses. Venezuela would soon assume her rightful place in the society of respected nations.

The new era, however, began under a cover of dark clouds. While the government busied itself with plans and surveys for the new program, Juan Bimba (Mr. Ordinary Citizen), the intellectuals, and the returning exiles aired their grievances in the press, on the air waves, and in public gatherings. All the pent-up hatred of years poured out in the form of vitriolic tirades against the officials of the past regime. The air waves throbbed with detailed accounts of crimes and sufferings. While most of the heartrending stories were founded on fact, insults and calumny were often heaped on the heads of innocent persons. Untrained in the art of journalism, the long-censored press knew nothing of a code of ethics; it printed anything and everything without any attempt to verify facts.

The courts, too, were turned into instruments of irresponsible passions. With a nod of approval from the federal executive, the attorney general attempted to annul several contracts dealing with the sale of certain real estate holdings to the nation by General Gómez, and to recover over one hundred and thirty million bolivars which had been spent in "public service commissions" during the previous ten years; all these, the attorney general alleged, were illegal. He sued the Gómez heirs, former presidents, and the ministers of the interior and of the treasury for that period, but he soon realized that he had no case in court because the contracts had been properly drawn up.

Checkmated on that score, the attorney general left in abeyance the court proceedings he had instituted and resorted to congress, asking it to pass a constitutional amendment authorizing the confiscation of the estate left by Gómez. Congress, after much hesitation, passed the amendment, enlarging the authorization to include, if it should be deemed advisable, the confiscation of property belonging to all former presidents, cabinet members, governors of Caracas, and presidents and general secretaries of the different states who had held office since 1922, as well as to all such officials in the future when congress (or the state legislatures, as the case may be) finds them guilty of "crimes against public property."

This was precisely what many of the state administrations were waiting for, and once their plans of action were legalized, they confiscated estates *in toto*. No accountings were published nor were any reports presented to show who robbed whom and for how much.

Congress itself decreed the confiscation of only the Gómez estate and through diplomatic channels sought the confiscation in Colombia of the three haciendas Gómez had bought long before he held any government office; this the Colombian government naturally refused to do. The confiscation in Venezuela was carried out with no court hearing, no investigation to ascertain facts of any kind. Under these conditions the entire proceeding, as more than one member of the Venezuelan judiciary has admitted, was null, both morally and juridically. It proved nothing concrete against Gómez; rather it was full of tremendous implications as being the first step in South America in the way of general confiscation of private property as preached by Communism.

What was thought to be a wise law that would be a deterrent to the embezzlement of public funds by high officials, boomeranged against the men who signed it. Their own properties, as well as those belonging to officials of the succeeding Medina administration, some one hundred and sixty in all with a worth of nearly eighty million bolivars, were seized without notice by the revolutionary *junta* which swept Rómulo Betancourt into power in 1945.[29] Having set a precedent, López and his colleagues had cause to reflect why they were not presented with formal charges or even granted a hearing. No seri-

[29] Decree No. 113, signed by the revolutionary *junta* two months after its successful coup, made it obligatory for members of the *junta*, the cabinet, state presidents, and other officials, on taking and relinquishing office, to make a sworn declaration before a judge of their personal wealth.

ous charges were ever proven, and we can only assume that Betancourt's strategy from the beginning had been to reduce the opposition to penury and a state of impotency, or that the justification for the confiscations was based on too loose an interpretation of the law; the charge "guilty of a crime against public property" could just as easily have been made against the citizen who trampled on the plaza lawn, so broad are the law's possible interpretations. It was not until 1950, two years after Betancourt and President Gallegos were ousted, that a new revolutionary *junta* set up by decree a Restitution Commission, which reviewed each case and subsequently restored the properties to their rightful owners.

For years the charge was repeatedly made that Gómez forced many persons to sell him valuable real estate at low prices, but it is significant that no one has ever demanded the nullification of any sale on these grounds. In the civil claims presented against the Gómez estate the claimants declared only that they had been illegally arrested or imprisoned without trial. Claims of this nature were taken out of the courts and turned over to a special political commission which adjudicated them and paid awards with part of the confiscated Gómez estate.

Though it was officially announced that an inventory had been ordered of the estate and that 25 per cent of its value would be allocated to the settlement of claims, no inventory or figure of estimated worth was ever made public. Comprised as it was of many forms of property ranging from coffee plantations, farms, ranches, hotels, residences, factories, dairies, abattoirs, and power plants, to diverse securities in other enterprises, the work of appraising and disposing of these holdings which represented a total value of something like several hundred million bolivars, must have been a long, drawn-out process.

Several money-making properties, such as hotels, factories, and ranches, were retained and managed by a government agency (*Corporación Venezolano de Fomento*) because they provided steady sources of revenues which were needed to help finance the government's many projects. Other land holdings were set up as experimental stations for the benefit of farmers and stock raisers. Part of Gómez's model farm and ranch at Güigüe was subdivided into twelve-acre farms which were allotted to married men with children.

Twelve acres was insufficient to make farming profitable, but with industry and thrift it would yield enough to feed a family, with a small surplus of garden truck, hogs and fowls for market. The three-room house that went with the farm was financed by the Worker's Bank, to be paid for over twenty years at a low rate of interest.

In 1936, the reconstruction era held the stage. Industry expanded. Jobs multiplied. New life coursed through the nation. But all was not milk and honey at the outset. With only 120,000,000 bolivars in the Treasury, basic needs came first, and Juan Bimba was impatient. The exiles that had flocked home were also restless. They were debating Mexican socialism, Russian communism, Trotskyism, the chances of emulating New Dealism. They thought everything was possible, including nationalization of the oil companies, free land for the farmers, taxation of the rich to give to the poor, woman suffrage, trial marriage. The country was yeasty with speculative talk, and in the thick of things could be heard the shrill voices of the students. What was wanted was a Utopia, and it was wanted right away.

Hungry people, crushed for centuries between exploitation and illiteracy, are prey to demagogues who promise a better life, more food, more security, a higher standard of living. The soap-box orators that appeared in the ranks of labor made promises that could never be answered with realities. Gómez was in his grave barely a week when rabble-rousers appeared in the Zulia oil fields implanting outlandish demands, and requesting the organization of labor. To avoid trouble, an increase in wages was granted immediately and several agitators were put under lock and key. Laws covering labor reform and the legalization of unions were not yet in the blueprint stage.

Though trade unions had been allowed in England as early as 1825, it was not until the mid-nineteen thirties that labor unions found government acceptance in Latin America. As in Venezuela, attempts to organize labor in the Latin American republics and the Caribbean colonies had been met with ruthless suppression. Gómez associated labor unions with communism because he realized they both fed on the discontent of the have-nots. Their very existence, he maintained, would engender anarchy and lead to the inevitable overthrow of government.

Organized labor appeared in Venezuela for the first time in 1936 as a result of the Labor Law enacted the same year. The Labor Law reflected the best modern thought and was far ahead of most modern practice. It forbade child labor, regulated working conditions for women, provided for an eight-hour day and forty-eight-hour week, housing and medical attention, arbitration of labor disputes, and the establishment of minimum wages, profit sharing, and the right of labor to organize. The faults and omissions found in the legislation during the following years were corrected through amendments passed in 1945 and again in 1947. As it stands now, the Venezuelan Labor Law has been accredited by the International Labor Offices as the most advanced social legislation in the world.

While it would seem that organized labor in Venezuela has achieved all that could be desired short of owning industries outright, some labor leaders continue to encroach in a forbidden field—politics. During the early stages of union organization, labor leaders, aided by Communist agents [30] and provocateurs, carried on aggressive campaigns against the government; using the unions as a weapon and shield they fomented strikes and incited rebellion. To protect itself against "certain elements (radicals and Communists) who abuse the privilege of democracy," the López administration incorporated into the Labor Law a handy provision: unions were allowed to establish industrial and commercial schools, libraries and clubs, but the Labor Law specifically barred them from engaging in political activities and empowered the government to dissolve any union so engaged.

Many labor leaders, nevertheless, continued to use the union hall to make harangues against the government as well as the "foreign imperialists." After a three-day nationwide strike in the oil fields in 1950 (which was nothing more than a political demonstration by Rómulo Betancourt's outlawed Democratic Action Party), the present military *junta* outlawed the Communist Party and dissolved forty-five oil unions because of the "persistent campaign of political agents who had infiltrated the ranks of labor." Since then, several of the unions have been reinstated in the good graces of the government, but union activities, generally, are still kept under surveillance.

[30] One of them: Joseph Zack Kornfeder of Detroit, who testified before the House Committee on Un-American Activities in Washington in 1949, that as a graduate of the Lenin school in Moscow, trained in "political warfare," he had been at one time a representative of the Communist International in Venezuela and Colombia.

While Communism has never become part and parcel of the Venezuelan labor movement, observers have long detected in certain union activities the obvious influence of Communist and radical leaders. Foremost among the early radicals to carry any influence with labor was Rómulo Betancourt. Betancourt, deeply conscious of the Latin's inability to grasp the full meaning of democracy, preyed on this failing with considerable success. He learned from his travels that all Latins are fundamentally the same, that as far as democracy is concerned, the Latin is still a political novice; impatient and irrational by temperament, he will follow any leader who will promise to change things his way. As one harried Venezuelan official humorously put it: "If the Latin doesn't like something, he'll immediately say '*el gobierno no sirve*' and want to change the government by force; if there are holes in the street, '*el gobierno no sirve*,' if the boats do not arrive on time, '*el gobierno no sirve*,' and if it rains too much, '*el gobierno no sirve*.' And the only way to change the government, of course, is by revolution."

For a long time, Betancourt dreamed of revolution because "*el gobierno no sirve*," but it was not until 1945 that his wish became an accomplished fact. At the beginning, his tirades against Gómez made sense for his campaign was against an unwanted dictatorship. But what he gave out for public consumption was one thing and what he confided to his cohorts was something of a different color. The real reason behind his proposed rebellion, which he made the mistake of putting in writing, was "to conquer the Venezuelan masses and incorporate them in the ranks of Marxism." How he proposed to accomplish this is explained in a letter he wrote to Raúl Leoni in 1932: ". . . As the Venezuelan masses have parliamentarian and constitutional illusions, faith in a civil and changing government, personal liberties, national suffrage, etc., we will fight for these conquests, and we will cast them aside when it suits us."

The Venezuelan decree of 1936 granting amnesty to political exiles found Betancourt still in Costa Rica. Seeking to return to the land of his birth, he was informed that due to his political affiliation he was considered *persona non grata*. Unabashed, he tried to obtain a visa to some other Latin American country, and was refused at every consulate. Returning to the Venezuelan consulate, he entrapped the consul with his infectious grin and hard-luck story. The result was a conclave with the Panamanian and Colombian consuls, both of whom agreed to issue Betancourt a visa on condition that he would not remain in their countries longer than thirty days. So Betancourt had his choice, Panama or Colombia, and he chose Panama. Once in Panama he made some discreet inquiries and learned that the Venezuelan consul there had not yet received any instructions concerning his status. He lost no time obtaining his visa and taking a plane to Venezuela.

Arriving in Venezuela in March, 1936, Betancourt found the political situation pregnant with possibilities. The government had just ended a politically-inspired strike by proclamation. Though several radical papers had been closed and there was now some censorship of the press, the magazine stands were ablaze with radical publications and translations of Marx and Engels. There was still freedom of movement and speech. Radical labor leaders were raising such a clamor for more reforms, that López, desiring to introduce the discipline of reason instead of force, invited their counsel to help draft the new labor law.

The students, too, had formulated a platform, which was immediately denounced as being Communist-inspired. Their first demand was for free elections. They wanted agrarian reform—the end of the vast estates, which enabled a few men to control most of the land. They demanded that lands taken by force or fraud be confiscated by the government and rented to the people on fair terms. They wanted a strong labor law. They were opposed to imperialism—the foreign oil and mining companies who "exploit our resources for their own benefit and who are always unfair to labor." The full-fledged Communists maintained that these proposed measures were halfway; they were for nationalization and the revolt of the underprivileged masses.

Soon a new demagogue was in their midst, inciting domestic unrest with a golden voice and spewing forth clandestine propaganda from a prolific pen. Cloaking his revolutionary teachings in Aesopian language, Betancourt, more the burning, bitter radical than ever, set out to woo and win the poor down-trodden masses who had parliamentarian and constitutional illusions. He joined *Orve (Organización Venezolana),* one of the new political parties, in which he quickly rose to leadership. Before the year was out, Betancourt and his fellow-travelers put their power to the test by calling a general strike. The strike lasted forty-five days.

Caracas, 1937: Scathing press editorials criticize the government. Strict censorship is imposed. Protests from the populace. Another big strike and sabotage in the oil fields. A mob storms Miraflores Palace. A fusillade of bullets. Many killed. From the harassed bureaucracy a poignant cry: "What are we going to do with these people? We offer them an olive branch and they want the whole tree!"

Progress is poison as well as food; personal liberty is the most foolish of all human hopes. Doubtless the new President cogitated on the old general's sage advice. While observers wondered in what direction Venezuela was headed, the conservatives were convinced that López was a strong man who would not let himself be stampeded by agitators. Obviously, Communism had made inroads in the social system, even in the very government itself. Of the new congress elected by the state legislatures in 1937, almost one-fourth of its members were radicals. López took stock of the situation and called for drastic action.

The few radical congressmen were made the test case. The elections of four of them were annulled on the ground that they were Communists. Bitter attacks on the President in the press. More papers closed. The students go on strike, become involved in an imbroglio with the police and are arrested in numbers. Then on April 8, the newspapers published a proclamation of the governor of the federal district: twenty-three Venezuelans, Communists, are to be banished from Venezuelan soil. Heading the list are Rómulo Betancourt and four elected representatives to the National Congress.

Betancourt, however, could not be found, though the police searched from one end of Caracas to the other. He was in the oil fields of Zulia, hiding in a worker's house, hanging up his hammock each night like a lowly peon. Relentlessly, the police widened the search. Repeatedly, the fugitive moved from one *obrero* house to another. On one of his sudden flights Betancourt remembered that he had left a book on a table, and he rushed back for it. It was *Napoleon* by Emil Ludwig.

Every three or four months he saw his wife and daughter for a few moments. It was a simple encounter of two automobiles which met on a back road in the dead of night. His daily stint was an "Economy and Finance" column, which friends mailed to the Caracas daily, *Ahora*. Day after day, month after month, his food and shelter were provided by the very elements that Betancourt some day expected to cast overboard like so much ballast.

In 1939, an automobile sped away from a police patrol after an exchange of gunfire. The vehicle, riddled with bullets, was found in a garage and the owner was put under surveillance. The trail led to Betancourt, who was exiled at once to Chile.

Betancourt, at thirty-one, was one of those rare Latins who had the patience of a philosopher; neither time nor exile would stay him from his life's work.

With the radical king-pins dispersed, the rehabilitation of Venezuela forged ahead without further disturbances. Minor incidents during 1939, however, augured the coming of a new menace. Japanese and German emissaries arrived in Venezuela to dicker for the purchase of large petroleum shipments. They were sent away empty-handed. Grinning Japanese "tourists" were observed clicking their cameras at vital installations as well as at everything else. The Nazi swastika was being prominently displayed by German nationals, and bund meetings had come into being. The Italian Minister was denied a permit for uniformed Italian Fascists to parade through the streets of the capital.

Then came an arrogant demand from the German Minister, who was promptly rebuffed. In smooth diplomatic language he had asked the Venezuelan government to accede to the request of the German Chancellery that "because Adolf Hitler wished it," Germany be allowed to choose the Venezuelan to be appointed Minister to Germany.

With war clouds in the offing, Venezuela looked to her defenses. Nationals of the Axis block began to be looked upon with suspicion. The forces of the *Seguridad Nacional* were augmented and instructed to watch for sabotage. Caution was the watchword.

In September, with German armies on the march, it became obvious that the narrow channel connecting Lake Maracaibo to the sea was Venezuela's Achilles heel. Petroleum, the life-blood of the nation's economy, must continue to flow uninterruptedly from the lake. Assuredly, the Axis would make an attempt to block the channel and thus stop the flow of oil so vital to England's and France's war machines. The feat, if it could be called that, looked ridiculously easy; a cargo vessel loaded with cement or scrap iron and scuttled crosswise in the channel would halt oil shipments for weeks and close down wells that were producing over 300,000 barrels a day.

It was in October, after Russia and Germany had partitioned Poland, and one month before the invasion of Finland by Russia, that the Finnish tramp steamer *Daphne* tied up at the Maracaibo wharf. To all outward appearances the *Daphne* was a harmless little vessel of a neutral country. Having discharged her cargo she proceeded to take aboard a new consignment. It was the nature of this new cargo that aroused suspicion, for it was a product that Venezuela had never been known to export; *it was cement.* As there were no legal grounds on which she could be detained, the *Daphne* was permitted to sail. But until she crossed the bar and the Gulf of Venezuela, she was kept under the watchful eye of an armed escort.

Though spies and counter-spies began to swarm over the land, the end of López's term found Venezuela at peace with herself and other nations. López had continued to address the people by radio, and his last message to congress in April, 1941, was broadcasted. In it he rendered an account of his stewardship and the accomplishments of his administration. The nation was solvent. Total revenues for his five years in office amounted to 2,049,252,785 bolivars compared with 3,158,185,429 bolivars for the entire twenty-seven years of Gómez's rule. He had kept his pledge to restore to the republic its political decorum and legal rights. Liberal laws had been passed to aid the working man and farmer. Huge sums had been spent to improve health, hygiene, and education. The working classes were now enjoying a happier, healthier life and a higher standard of living than ever before. Then he went on to list the new roads, schools, and higher centers of learning for teachers, nurses, agricultural teachers, veterinarians, and experts in animal husbandry, low cost housing projects for workers, and experimental farms. There had been grave problems. There had been attempts to convert the labor organizations into fighting elements of reaction against the state. Certain measures had been taken in the interests of public security. He was confident, however, that the great majority of the Venezuelan people repudiated violence, revolution, and demagoguery as leading only to the disruption of order and the decay of the social and political systems. Although given power to govern by force, he had preferred to govern as head of a state of free men.

López had suppressed sinecures, had done away with military rule and the system of *jefe civil* cut-throats in the country's towns and villages. Guided by foreign experts, he had instituted agrarian reform, reorganized the army, built hospitals, schools, and workers' housing, improved and opened roads, pre-occupied himself with public health, and introduced the scientific accounting of public funds. He had tried to solve in one term one hundred years of aggravated social problems. He had instituted more industrial and social progress than all previous administrations put together.

The reaction of the masses to this splendid record was only stolid indifference. There were no huzzas from the lower echelons of society. Most, bent on a soft security, had expected that López would ease them into Utopia from a supposedly inexhaustible treasury. Honesty, integrity and devotion to duty, practiced for the first time by a president in the republic's history, counted for naught. Only time would convince the Venezuelan masses that a good is not appreciated until it is lost, that golden promises of false prophets are but hollow phrases.

López always had great prestige with the army. He realized that without at least its passive support no Venezuelan president could remain in power for even a day. In all probability congress would choose his successor from its ranks. Though he made no move to intimidate that body, López had been grooming for responsibility an officer who exuded strength and assurance. He was General Isaías Medina Angarita, his Minister of War and Marine and the only active full general left on the government payroll besides himself.

In contrast with López's lean frame and austere and professional bearing, Medina, stout and balding, had a disarmingly frank manner, a rough wit and a quick laugh. He was born in the Andean town of San Cristóbal on July 5, 1897. His father, a federal general, gave his life four years later on the battlefield while fighting the enemies of Cipriano Castro. After graduating from the military school as a second lieutenant at seventeen, Medina rose rapidly through the ranks. Undoubtedly, his rise was given added impetus because he was born a *paisano* of the ruling oligarchy. By July, 1935, when he was thirty-eight, he was made a member of the general staff. Eight months later he was appointed Minister of War and Marine, which post he held (with time out to head a military mission to the United States in 1940) until 1941. On March 9 of that year he left with the blessing of his patron on a leave of absence to campaign for the Presidency as the candidate of the conservative Nationalist Party.

Medina's strongest opponent was the *Caraqueño* Rómulo Gallegos, ex-school teacher, political exile, and one-time Minister of Education under López. Author of the classic *Doña Barbara* and other best-selling novels that sublimated the lowly peon and ridiculed the large landowners, Gallegos was the champion of the underdog and the favorite of a few of the intellectuals as well. As leader of the *Partido Democrático Nacional,* an underground group leaning toward the left, he was nominated as its candidate.

After outlining his platform, in which he declared himself to be a middle-of-the-roader, General Medina toured several states, court-ing the arch-conservative *hacendados,* big business and the press. By the time congress convened on April 28 to elect the next President, its senators and deputies had been deluged with petitions and even a weighty pamphlet which extolled the virtues of the indispensable man who was "not compromised with anyone." The result of the voting was a walk-away for Medina: one hundred and twenty votes to Gallegos' thirteen; two votes went to Dr. Escalante, Ambassador to the United States and senator to congress.

To a flurry of fanfare and speeches, General Medina was in-augurated on May 5. As is customary at such ceremonies, the outgoing President was at his side when he visited Bolívar's shrine in the Na-tional Pantheon and pledged allegiance to the Bolivarian doctrines and the republican principles of government.

CHAPTER THIRTY-FIVE

The Barranquilla Plan Succeeds

Petroleum production in 1941 reached the unprecedented figure of 625,000 barrels a day, and government revenues from royalties increased with it. The government judiciously embarked on a five-year public works program to construct roads, bridges, airports, aqueducts, and sewer and drainage systems. The estimated cost of these projects, the new President informed the nation by radio the following January, would amount to four hundred million bolivars, almost one-fourth of the expected government income for the five-year period.

The day after the Japanese attack on Pearl Harbor, the President in indignant terms publicly condemned Japan's aggression and pledged Venezuela's friendship and solidarity with the United States and the other nations of the continent. Putting her words to deeds, Venezuela severed relations on December 31 with the governments of Germany, Italy, and Japan, and impounded several German and Italian freighters then tied up at her docks.

At the Pan-American Conference, the United States had promised Pan-American countries help in protecting themselves. President Medina made a formal request for military aid. The result was a pact, later ratified by the Venezuelan Congress, whereby the United States was to send a military mission and to construct the necessary air bases to patrol Venezuela's lifelines to the Dutch Antilles. Similar aid was rendered to the Dutch government in exile for the protection of the large refineries located in Aruba and Curacao, thus relieving British troops that had been shouldering the burden alone. American armed forces and the required technical manpower were permitted to be stationed in Venezuela "for a reasonable length of time and in limited numbers." The agreement also called for the co-operation of agents of the Federal Bureau of Investigation with the Venezuelan security corps (*Sección de Vigilancia y Coordinación Federal*) estab-lished in 1941 for the tracking down and apprehension of spies and saboteurs within the country.

Another pact covering the exchange of military missions and the patrol of territorial waters was worked out by Venezuela with the Dutch officials of Aruba and Curacao, but before it could be put into practical effect, the Germans made a bold move.

Barely had the first contingent of Americans landed in Aruba than a Nazi submarine opened fire on the refinery installations and harbor on the night of February 16, 1942. No damage was done to the refinery, but torpedoes sank one tanker in a sea of flames and damaged another. Aruba immediately put on drab battle dress. The tall towers of the refinery units lost their silver sheen; the white storage spheroids were camouflaged with elephant gray. The island went under blackout. Prowling submarines sank several tankers in the months that followed, but with American patrol planes on constant guard, there was no further attack on the Dutch islands.

In his message to congress in April, 1942, President Medina apologized for the suspension of constitutional guarantees for labor and industry. This action had been necessary, he said, to give the Federal Executive power to mobilize the economic forces of the na-tion during this hour of peril. Yet all Venezuelans were free to unite by means of political parties. During the previous year there had not been one political prisoner. Not one Venezuelan living in exile need fear reprisals should he decide to return to his homeland.

Betancourt and the other exiles, granted amnesty, returned home Strikes and labor agitation being *prohibido,* politics became the forte of these young intellectuals. Their choice of a party was decided easily Medina's *Partido Democrático Venezolano* (PDV) was out, Medina being regarded as their arch-enemy. Ignored also was the out and out Communist Party, *Unión Popular Venezolana* (UPV). Though Marx was their bible and Stalin their hero, most of the former exiles refused to serve as jackals of the Kremlin. That left Gallegos' party which had been granted sanction the previous September under the new name of *Acción Democrática* (AD). One time teacher and mentor to Betancourt, and a leftist in his own right, Gallegos welcomed his protégé and his friends to the ranks of AD.

It was not long before Betancourt became the dominant figure at the secret meetings to discuss policy and strategy. The "Barranquilla Plan" (social revolution, wholesale confiscations, etc.) adopted by the students in exile in 1931, was thrashed out, then shelved until the opportune moment. As the new driving force of the Party, Betancourt, edging out the aging Gallegos, set the pace in the Party's demands presented to the government.

Complete nationalization of the oil industry was one of the Party's aims. As such an objective would have no chance of fulfillment while the war lasted, AD modified it by asking for a greater government share in the oil profits. Medina, still the middle-of-the-roader, but mindful of the government's slipping war-pressed economy, countered by passing a strong income tax law, which went into effect on January 1, 1943. Based on a sliding scale, starting at 2 per cent of annual income of 9,000.01 bolivars (which left the earnings of the average wage earner untouched), the tax rose to $9\frac{1}{2}$ per cent on incomes of 2,000,000.01 bolivars, and so on upward. The hardest hit were the oil companies, whose incomes ran into the hundreds of millions.

AD's persistent demand, in congress and in the press, met with considerable sympathy in some government circles. The popular trend appeared to be in the direction of more social benefits for more of the people, with the privileged oil worker group as a model and the rising income of the oil industry as a source of revenue. Finally agreeing to the principle that royalties and other general taxes should give the nation an oil income equal to the net income of the companies, the government employed the services of a United States consultant firm headed by Herbert Hoover, Jr., to work out a formula. Based on the results of this study, the government concluded that a blanket 16 2/3 per cent royalty would ensure a fifty-fifty split, and incorporated it in the new petroleum legislation that was presented to congress. The loudest opposition in congress came from the AD delegation, which argued for a higher percentage. The legislation nevertheless was passed, and became the Petroleum Law of 1943, the basic legislation governing the oil industry today.

In the fall of 1944, the Medina Administration was put to the test by the voters in the election of municipal councilmen and members of state assemblies in seven states and the federal district. The electoral battle was between a recently formed coalition of Medina's PDV and the Labor-Communist UPV on the one hand, and the only organized opposition party, AD, on the other.

Both groups sounded the keynote of social liberalism. The administration campaigned on its record of social reform, including the income tax and social security laws. The AD, somewhat embarrassed by the unwelcome support of many rightists who feared Medina's new liberalism, called for still more extensive royalties.

Both sides attacked "La Reacción." This was the popular name for the unorganized forces of the right as well as all opposition in general. The PDV slogan was: "With Medina Against the Reaction." The AD countered with: "Against the Reaction Wherever it is Found."

The heaviest campaigning was carried on in the capital. Rival squads roamed the streets pasting up election posters, each trying to cover up the displays of the other as quickly as they appeared. Mass meetings were often highlighted by unscheduled features—stink bombs and fist-fights. Monster meetings on the last two nights climaxed the campaign.

The result was a vote of confidence in the administration of President Medina. The government was victorious in six out of seven states. The AD was barely able to hold on to its two seats in the Caracas municipal council. The crushing blow for AD was the defeat of Gallegos for a council seat by only seventeen votes.

The AD retired in silence to lick its wounds. Defeated at the polls, the party chieftains plotted a different strategy—that of force. The Barranquilla Plan was taken from the shelf and dusted off. Insidious propaganda first prepared the ground.

In July, 1945, a short article written by Rómulo Betancourt and Valmore Rodríguez appeared in the AD paper *El País*. It listed in minute detail the estimated wealth of ex-President López. There was no *exposé* of malfeasance while in office. The implied accusation, left to the reader to deduce, was that no life-time employee on the federal payroll could accumulate a fortune of eight million bolivars if he were honest. Since López's fortune has never been proven to be worth more than a third of this figure, obviously the story was fabricated out of whole cloth, but it was successful in its aim of planting the seeds of suspicion. No one, not even López, surmised at the time that something was stirring within the AD Party.

The first evidence that real trouble was afoot was the appearance in *El Nacional* of an article charging that if congress failed to elect López President, he would seize power by a military coup. This was on October 12, the same day that a convention was to convene to propose López for the Presidency.

This propaganda enfuriated López, who published his protest saying that he would remain faithful to state institutions. However, the damage was done. López's popularity with some of the army gave way to distrust, and rumors began to fly of discontent in its lower echelons.

What AD accomplished by artful scheming was a coalition with the *Unión Militar Patriótica,* a group of officers, none above the rank of major and none more than thirty-five years old. For both it was strictly a marriage of convenience to achieve the overthrow of Medina. The plan of revolt seems to have been aimed at accomplishing by force what it would have been difficult to accomplish in any other way—elimination of the Andean dynasty of military presidents which had governed Venezuela since the time of Castro. Assuredly the Medina administration was a liberal one, but it was part of a well-entrenched and self-perpetuating machine which AD had little hope of ousting at the next presidential election. The dynasty was safe while the army remained loyal, but now a rift had come about because of talk that López had presidential aspirations. The younger officers, bitter because of favoritism and inequalities, grew more restless, making revolt possible.

The alliance between the military and the AD was arranged in haste after two or three surreptitious meetings. The only points they found time to agree on were the complete divorcement of the armed forces from politics, the election of a president by popular vote instead of by congress, the prosecution of all government officials deemed to have misused their offices for private gain, and "a government by the people and for the people."

The coup was planned for the early part of November, but on the morning of October 18 one of the conspiring lieutenants was overheard talking of the plot in his barracks and was arrested. Although Medina was informed of the plot, he failed to take preventative measures in time. The military insurgents decided to act at once and so informed the AD, who had no other choice but to go along with them.

To the cry of *"Viva la revolución!"* the first shooting began in the San Carlos barracks of Caracas at 2:05 P.M. the same day. The fighting quickly spread to other barracks of the city and to Maracay. President Medina escaped from Miraflores Palace when the first blow was struck and took refuge in the Ambrosio Plaza barracks. General López was captured on the street by a squad of soldiers as he neared the palace. By nine o'clock the rebels had forced their way into the strategic military school and had taken Miraflores.

In Maracay, the rebels captured the main barracks after a short artillery barrage. Taken also was the military airfield with all its planes. As there was no cessation of small-arms fire, the wives and children of officers of the American military mission were evacuated by plane to the United States army base in Curacao.

Fighting raged on through Caracas' steep, narrow streets the next day. Pro-government Communists broke into a depot, appropriated guns and uniforms. From a new six-story housing project they sniped at roving bands of rebels. Loyal cavalry galloped into the fray. Rebel planes circled over the city dropping leaflets, then swooped low to machine gun the sectors of resistance and drop grenades and medium-calibre bombs on the barracks. By noon, the insurgents had won police headquarters and four of the city's five garrisons. The Ambrosio Plaza barracks surrendered four hours later and President Medina was taken prisoner.

While light tanks and armored cars hammered at pockets of resistance, portable transmitters and captured radio stations repeatedly called on the people for volunteers. What followed was December, 1936, all over again. Foreigners and law-abiding citizens remained behind barred doors while unruly mobs roamed the streets bent on plunder and violence. Above the din could be heard the shouts of the students. Mobs cleaned out police headquarters and San Carlos barracks of their guns and ammunition. Urchins peddled machine guns and rifles for whatever they could get. Cars left in the streets were stripped or driven off. Stores in the El Silencio section were looted and wrecked, as were the homes of government officials in the suburbs.

The first revolutionary junta of Venezuela, 1945: Left to right: Dr. Raul Leoni, Dr. Edmundo Fernández, Dr. Luis Beltran Prieto, Col. Carlos Delgado Chalbaud, Col. Mario Ricardo Vargas, Sr. Rómulo Betancourt, Dr. Gonzalo Barios.

The government junta of Venezuela, 1952: Lieut. Col. Luis Felipé Llovera Páez, Lieut. Col. Marcos Pérez Jiménez, Dr. Germán Suárez Flamerich.

Staccato gunfire sounded far into the night. Belatedly, loudspeakers blared exhortations to the people to restore law and order and turn in their arms.

Desultory fighting continued throughout the third day as armed Communists and national guardsmen loyal to Medina tried to counterattack the rebels. In other parts of the country, government opposition was limited to skirmishes. By nightfall the National Guard had surrendered. The next day, Sunday the 21st, the remaining points of resistance throughout the country were liquidated.

It had been one of the shortest, successful revolutions in Venezuela's history, bettered only by Gómez's bloodless coup of 1908. What was significant was the new style of revolutionary fighting brought on by the mechanical age and modern weapons: the radio had replaced the telegraph and mounted courier; the machine gun and repeating rifle had replaced the Mauser and machete; the armored car had replaced the horse and burro; and the light fighter-bomber had replaced cumbersome artillery. Old-style guerrilla warfare had been rendered obsolete, for the armored might of the defenders could span distance and natural barriers with cyclone speed, and inflict devastating damage at close range. Like the coup of October, the Venezuelan revolutions of the future would have to bore from within the army juggernaut to achieve success.

Betancourt had scored a complete triumph. The AD Party had come through unscathed while the army had taken the brunt of the battle. The cost in lives had been high, higher than the victors cared to admit. Three state presidents had been assassinated. Many garrison commandants had been shot down in cold blood. Eighty per cent of a company of four hundred troops from Guarico that had gone to the defense of Maracay had been wiped out. In all, some six hundred military personnel and civilians had been killed and fifteen hundred wounded.

The revolutionary *junta* that took over the government was composed of seven: Major Carlos Delgado Chalbaud (son of the revolutionary general killed in Cumaná) and Captain Mario Vargas of the army, four officers of AD, and a physician, Dr. Edmundo Fernández. President of the *junta* was Rómulo Betancourt.

In Miraflores Palace, under a portrait of the great Bolívar, the Provisional President worked like a frenzied Robespierre promulgating

a series of decrees and appointments. Now that the old guard's heads
had fallen he could again play the Jacobin orator, this time to the
visiting delegations of idea-bearing citizens, sheepish rightists and
Communists who came offering peace.

After outlining the *junta*'s program to the press, Betancourt had
added: "We are not going to make a million promises, nor promul-
gate programs as long as Chinese laundry lists, but we hope that
when we leave Miraflores within a few months, it may be said that
Venezuela had a government which did not misuse public funds and
did not violate the citizens' conscience."

The "few months" turned out to be over two years, and the mis-
management of public funds came to be known as "The Dance of the
Millions."

To keep its promises to labor and win its loyal support, the new
regime started off with a blast of decrees that sent lawyers scurrying
to their law books and set big business wondering where the next
blow would fall. In the first five months alone, two hundred and
twenty decrees were issued that affected Venezuelans in every walk
of life and gave rise to enthusiastic huzzas for the new liberal, democratic government.

The revolutionary *junta* had been installed in office but two days
when Dr. Raúl Leoni, AD member of the *junta* and Minister of Labor,
summoned representatives of the oil companies to a special meeting.
Only the day before, Betancourt had announced to the foreign press
that the rights of the oil companies would be respected, but now his
minister informed the oil companies that they would be expected to
grant new concessions to labor. It was labor, he said, that brought the
new government into being, and it was labor that formed the greater
part of the membership of the AD Party. It was "important that certain reasonable concessions to labor be made promptly to demonstrate the provisional government's sincerity as regards the labor
group."

The oil companies bowed to the inevitable. Though the petroleum
worker was already the highest-paid worker in the land, new benefits
were granted which raised him to a still higher level.

Most of the early decrees dealt with lowering the cost of living
and bettering conditions for the working classes. The duties on wheat

and flour, for example, were lowered, and the prices of flour, bread, and meat were rolled back, as were also electric rates and rentals of houses leased at under four hundred bolivars a month. Prices on gasoline and kerosene were reduced, notwithstanding the loss it entailed to the oil companies of several million dollars a year.

The wages of the police and teachers were raised and the pay of the common soldier was increased from two to eight bolivars per day. The salaries of federal employees were raised also, whereas those of the Provisional President, cabinet ministers, ambassadors, and other high ranking officials were reduced to an even four thousand bolivars ($1,200) a month.

To discourage graft, army men and government employees were prohibited from accepting the usual Christmas gifts from business houses and seekers of favors. Instead, all government workers were granted a Christmas bonus of one week's pay.

One of the earliest decrees froze the funds of former government officials. On November 27, a decree created a "Tribunal of Civil and Administrative Responsibility" to try these officials, but before the legal machinery could be set in motion, twenty-four of the accused were exiled "for reasons of public security." Generals López and Medina and ten others left by plane for Miami on November 29, and twelve others left the country a few days later.

Against these men both vague and sensational charges were made. They had defrauded the government "in different ways" and had appropriated millions of bolivars from the secret "slush-fund" formerly controlled by the Ministry of Labor. Medina was specifically charged with having paid out the equivalent of seven million dollars in promised bribes to insure his election, and with obtaining from the Foreign Ministry budget forty thousand dollars a month which he spent on lavish entertainment, jewels, and gifts for his friends. His private residence, appraised at two-and-half million dollars, was a mansion laid out in an extensive park and furnished in regal taste. There was a banquet hall for state dinners, a luxurious bar with dozens of cases of rare liquors, fixtures and ornaments of silver in every room including the bathrooms and kitchen. On every table and on every wall, even to the bathrooms, were handsomely-framed photographs of the owner—ninety-six in all. Not counting the government guards who patrolled the grounds, a staff of twenty-three servants had maintained the establishment, and their total wages alone almost equaled the salary Medina earned as President.

Assuredly, it took more than honest toil and lucky investments to live like a multimillionaire on a salary of $7,500 a month.

After several months of thorough house cleaning, in truth it did seem that all the grafters had been swept out and that the government was vested in men of high moral integrity. In its dicta the seven-man *junta* presented a united front. Nary a word of dissension reached the public. Behind the scenes, however, close observers perceived widening cracks in the *junta* foundations; the AD faction was deviating more and more from the avowed aims of the original agreement, the outnumbered army members were being slowly maneuvered into the background.

Betancourt had reneged on his promise not to form a one-party government. As he grew in stature so did the membership and power of the AD Party. Although army men headed the ministries of war-navy and communications, and the governments of various states, it was AD that gained complete control of the federal and municipal governments. Favors and political appointments went to party adherents, though in the beginning their numbers were few; clerks became chiefs of police, youthful lawyers became *jefe civiles* and district governors. Not to be "of the party" was to be a political outcast. In matters that went through litigation, or even minor traffic collisions, most often it was the non-party man who paid the bill.

From party headquarters in Caracas, non-uniformed, armed squads known as the *Guardia Móvil* were assigned to roving duty throughout the country, ostensibly to supplement the police and National Guard in maintaining law and order. For months, until a shocked congress looked into the matter, AD henchmen operated a house of tortures to wring confessions from obstinate political prisoners.

As labor joined AD in droves, it was encouraged to "fight capitalistic enterprises." The Ministry of Public Works set the example by signing a closed-shop labor contract with a construction union. By December, 1946, 542 new unions had been formed, bringing the total throughout the country to 757. To pool their strength, employers also organized. Others, realizing on which side their bread was buttered, joined the Party, hardly demurred when they were coerced into buying out newspapers to disseminate party propaganda.

Betancourt had seen to it that labor got almost everything it wanted. Yet business enjoyed no surcease from harassment. New taxes were imposed. Two German import-export firms were dissolved by executive decree and their assets taken over by Venezuelan business groups. Lawyers, spurred by an old law which allows the informer half of the proceeds, pored over old records and instigated suits against oil companies for alleged evasion of taxes and illegal occupancy of lands.

In 1947, the oil companies were dealt still another blow. In his New Year's message in January, Betancourt announced a new decree whereby corporations and individuals with yearly incomes of over 500,000 bolivars would be subject to an excess profits tax, scaled upward to a maximum rate of 26 per cent for incomes of 28,000,000 bolivars or more. The tax would be exercised for one year only, *but it was retroactive to January of the previous year.* Betancourt, sworn foe of all foreigners, made no secret of the fact that this tax measure had been aimed principally at the oil companies.

Though still proclaiming to the world his staunch adherence to democratic principles, Betancourt had now emerged as an absolute dictator. His executive orders, more onerous than those of the Gómez period, proclaimed, in effect, the words of the ill-fated Louis XIV, "I am the State." And no one could dispute him. To a well-known lawyer who protested to the *junta* against the use of force and dictatorial edicts, Betancourt, with all the arrogance of a dictator, answered in a public statement, "Naïve is he who imagines that a government such as ours, strengthened by collective faith and backed by a unified army immune to destructive maneuvers, is going to permit the legality of its actions to be disputed in any judicial court. It would be a hazardous undertaking for those who would take this road of insolent provocation."

Betancourt had built up a callous, blatant party machine which operated with the full protection of the law. And like its leader, it too was inviolable. When a lengthy anti-*junta* article in *El Universal* rebuked "the tropical fascists of *Acción Democrática*," its author was imprisoned.

"Today," the weekly *El Demócrata* editorialized, "Venezuela lives under the disgrace of being dominated by a group of traitors to the principles of democracy. They have trampled upon public liberties and the rights of citizens, have bloodied and mocked the principles of justice, have instituted tortures, and are now preparing to imitate Mussolini by establishing in Venezuela 'special courts' to ruin the opposition."

Among the opposition to be reckoned with was the Catholic hierarchy, which had become active in the Andean states proselyting for the Catholic *Copei* Party. Betancourt was an atheist. That in itself was enough to incur the enmity of the Church. But the AD faction in congress, abetted by the two Communist delegates, had committed an unpardonable sin. In the preamble of the draft of a new Constitution which appeared in the local press, the name of God had been omitted. Admonished by the horrified prelates of the Church to rectify this fault, congress debated the matter hotly an entire day and half a night. God won by a narrow margin.

According to ex-President López, it was the aim of Betancourt and his party to nullify what little influence the Church still exerted over the individual. "To carry out the Plan of Barranquilla," relates López in his book *El Triunfo de la Verdad,* "and to follow faithfully the directives of the Communist International, Betancourt made the attempt to divide the Catholics of Venezuela, and he used the renegade priest, Castillo Méndez to create the scandal."

What Betancourt is said to have had in mind was the creation of a Venezuelan Church, independent of the Holy See, to be controlled by the state. Some sixty years before, a similar proposal by President Guzmán had been voted down by congress. Sensing that even in these progressive times, such an idea might again be rejected as preposterous, Betancourt assigned the project to a willing ally.

Actually, Castillo Méndez had never been ordained, though he did attend various seminaries both in Venezuela and Spain. He had been expelled from all of them for entertaining a "distorted conception of the priesthood." Frustrated in his ambition to become a priest, he took to posing as one, and was once jailed for impersonating a priest of Táchira.

Simultaneously with the coup of October, he reappeared on the scene attired like a priest. Trailed by two figures in white cassock (one a barber by profession; the other an ex-peddler of newspapers) he spoke openly and boldly to all who would listen. Fingering a gold cross given to him by Betancourt's wife, he made a statement to the press with the air of a man who had at last found the true faith: thirty-three priests were preparing to submit a project to the forth-coming Constituent Assembly calling for the establishment of a Vene-zuelan Apostolic Catholic Church. Foreign priests? They would be barred. Latin? It was so much mumbo-jumbo and would be eliminated from all rites. Women? They would be admitted to minor orders. Free love? It would be condoned. Marriage of priests? Of course! "After all," the pseudo-priest added with a mundane air, "the chastity oath is not being observed by the Venezuelan priesthood and is a constant source of demoralization."

The church paper, *La Religion,* and the Catholic hierarchy took bitter exception to these charges. For heresy and apostasy, Castillo Méndez was speedily excommunicated by the Archbishop of Caracas, as were five priests from among his followers who were discovered to have taken themselves wives.

Shortly after the project had been submitted to the Constituent Assembly in February, 1947, Castillo Méndez was "consecrated" a bishop by another self-styled bishop from Brazil. It was a beautiful ceremony, marred only by the new "bishop's" speech to the press. He spoke of the enemy with a Savonarola-like eloquence, but his words, to some, had a familiar ring: "Our program is to give battle to the papacy, to extortionist Romanism, and to imperialistic capitalism on all fronts."

There was little doubt that Castillo Méndez had been groomed as a mouthpiece for AD. "All the activities of this man," states López, "were financed by *Acción Democrática,* and it was Betancourt who oriented the ideology of the new schismatic Church."

After preaching a few sermons to curious throngs, Castillo Méndez was taken into custody and stripped of his ecclesiastical gar-ments. When he was released, it was with a warning to take up a more orthodox profession.

For once the army faction of the government had put its foot down. The orders for the arrest of Castillo Méndez had emanated from the Ministry of the Interior headed by the *junta*-member Mario Vargas, recently promoted to lieutenant colonel. For months, though the public had no inkling of it, the military had been chafing under the digression and rising power of AD. Dissident officers and bureaucrats suspected of revolutionary leanings were shifted about or sent on missions abroad. Embryo revolts in far-flung barracks were thwarted and the leaders put in prison.

One of those under suspicion was Lieutenant Colonel Julio Vargas, Inspector General of the Army and brother of the Minister of the Interior. Sent on a mission to Belgium, Vargas returned home hurriedly when his name was openly discussed after an abortive revolt in Maracay. Suspended from his post, he wrote Lieutenant Colonel Delgado Chalbaud an open letter and distributed copies to the press. The main points of the missive were: the AD leaders had reneged on their promise not to form a one-party government; the army plotters of October, 1945, had shed their blood for Venezuela, not for *Acción Democrática*. His bitterly-worded letter denied categorically any attempt to incite the army to revolt. He could not resist however the urge to add, "My point of view is shared by many Venezuelans in positions of great responsibility."

When the order was issued for his arrest, Vargas had already obtained asylum in the Colombian Embassy, and he later secured safe-conduct abroad.

Vargas had the courage to air publicly what many other influential persons deemed prudent to leave to the realm of the mind. Nevertheless, conspiracies to overthrow the government did persist, and *El País*, organ of AD, attempted to soft-pedal these incidents by laying them at the door of political exiles and the dictator Rafael Trujillo of the Dominican Republic. The better to foil such plots in the future, the Constituent Assembly passed a law which was incorporated directly into the new Constitution. This statute, which started a flurry of controversy, stated that the President, provided he notified congress within ten days of his actions, was empowered to order the "preventative detention of persons who there is reason to believe are implicated" in plans to overthrow the government.

The new Constitution, the twenty-second since independence was achieved from Spain, was formally promulgated on July 5, 1947. Considered by many observers as the most leftist in the Western Hemisphere, it provided specific guarantees for labor, such as paid vacations, pay for Sundays, pensions, layoff indemnities, profit-sharing, and the right to strike.

Patterned after the Constitution of the United Sates, in other respects, the charter granted the state wide powers for planning the national economy. It guaranteed the right of private property and the establishment of employer associations; and, while monopolies were held to be illegal, capital was entitled to a "fair return."

As provided in the Constitution, the government was to consist of a Senate, Chamber of Deputies, and a Supreme Court empowered with jurisdiction over the constitutionality of all laws. For the first time in the history of the republic, the Chief Executive was to be elected by "direct universal suffrage" for a term of four years, but he could "not succeed himself for the two following terms."

If anyone was impatient for a legally-constituted government and the election of a president by popular vote, it was the military. A clause in the revolutionary pact of October, 1945, ratified by decree in 1947, disqualified any member of the governing *junta* from holding presidential office. Yet, though the army had put its stamp of approval on Gallegos as a candidate, it was Betancourt whom the Party appeared to be grooming for high office. For two years, three months, and twenty-seven days, the time Betancourt was in power, it was he who basked contentedly in the limelight. Given to invective and flamboyant rhetoric, but nonetheless knowing when to punctuate an irrelevance or an ambiguity with a smile, he enjoyed his role to the full. Like the smart cutaway and striped trousers he took to wearing almost daily, his role of statesman fitted him becomingly. In fact, he was one of those rare humans who have a talent for public life, for living naturally and even comfortably in the public gaze, like a goldfish in its bowl. It was no secret that Betancourt harbored presidential aspirations and that he was assured of party backing to succeed Gallegos to the Presidency.

Not until the electoral machinery had been set in motion did Betancourt permit his mentor to come on stage and take the spotlight. Having donned the immaculate tunic of "nationalism," Gallegos made a few campaign trips through the interior smearing the ousted regime. These junkets, however, were only window dressing; neither friend nor foe doubted the outcome of the election. The party chieftains had carefully cultivated labor as a political force, had seen to it that Juan Bimba received almost everything he demanded. Now, by the eve of the election, labor had outgrown the army as a power. And

with the election of Gallegos assured, Betancourt could be expected
to be the tail that would wag the dog.

Provisional President Betancourt had promised that the elections
would be "more democratic than that of the United States." In that
he kept his word. The October, 1946, elections for members of the
Constituent Assembly had set the electoral pattern. On election day,
December 14, 1947, the army was again out in full force to prevent
fraud and to maintain order. But there was no fraud or disorder to
speak of, and the soldiers could just as well have remained in barracks. In truth it was the fairest and most orderly election Venezuela
had ever known. The care with which the election was organized was a
large factor in its success. It was conducted, not by government, but
by a Supreme Electoral Council on which each political party was
represented. For the first time in their history, the people of Venezuela, men and women, rich and poor, literate and illiterate, without distinction of creed or color, were choosing directly their own
President, senators, and deputies.

To make doubly sure that calm would prevail, campaigning and
the sale of liquor were forbidden starting twenty-four hours before
the people went to the polls. To foil repeaters, each voter was required to dip a fingertip into a green stain. For the convenience of
the illiterates, ballots were cast by colored cards: White [31] for AD,
green for *Copei,* brown for URD, red for the Communists, and black
for a dissident Communist group.

Though the other presidential candidates were considered capable,
it was sixty-three-year-old Rómulo Gallegos who carried the most
popularity with the electorate. The final returns of the balloting
showed some strength for the Communists in Zulia, and for *Copei*
in the mountain states of Mérida and Táchira, with the AD slate riding to victory with over seventy per cent of the votes. One-sided as
the vote was, it represented the choice of the people.

---

[31] The official color of the AD Party. A few months preceding the elections,
the red brick Gómez mausoleum had been refinished in white, which gave rise
to the quip: "Even Gómez has changed to *Acción Democrática!*"

CHAPTER THIRTY-SIX

The Army Giveth, and the Army Taketh Away

What was noteworthy in the festival of the inauguration of Gallegos the following February was not the unusual number of diplomats in attendance, or the military parade with its contingents of American, British, and Dutch marines and sailors, or the squadron of American planes that flew in formation over Caracas. What was noteworthy was the presence in the capital, at the invitation of the AD faction, of a considerable number of the principal writers and intellectuals of Latin America. Rómulo Gallegos, a man without political, military, or business experience was still and always would remain an intellectual who believed, if not in outright Communism, in the upheaval of modern Socialism. For Gallegos, the occasion was an historical moment. It meant that at long last he could transform with legal sanction his ambitions and those of his Party from the realm of wishful-thinking to the realm of fact.

To the left. That had been his goal. Once in 1936, when he served three months as minister of education, he expressed to General Contreras his approval of the way the President was carrying out his administration, but added reprovingly, *"If only you would take your stand on the side of the leftists."*

A few months after the smoke of the October revolution had cleared, the fact came to light that López had been condemned because "he was manifestly inferior to the historical hour in which he happened to live."

To quote Gonzalo Carnevali, a party spokesman, in his written rebuke to a Colombian newspaper editor for sympathizing with López in his exile: "History will have to judge them (López and Medina), not for what they have done . . . but for what they failed to do . . . because of the possibilities they had in their hands."

And now the famous novelist and President, acutely aware of the enormous possibilities at his command, makes his inaugural address and indicates clearly in which direction his administration will travel. He will adhere to the policies "already begun" by Rómulo Betancourt. Significant too, is his added statement that he will not include members of the opposition parties in his cabinet, "since this measure is usually resorted to only in times of crisis or danger."

Thus the new President, imbued with the confidence of a man who knows what he is about, embarked on his great venture to fulfill the avowed aims of the Party. But he proceeded cautiously and by devious means lest he bring down the wrath of his enemies and the scorn of free nations upon his head. If there were moments when he was torn between a desire for fair play and loyalty to the Party, Betancourt was always close by to prod and encourage him. "I am a creation of *Acción Democrática,*" Gallegos reassured a delegation of party men four months after his inauguration, "and it is toward this Party that I should turn . . . I will never leave the line of my Party . . . and if ever the occasion should arise when I would not be in agreement with that line, I have sufficient courage to retire from politics rather than act against the AD program . . ."

In synthesis, the "program" was the brain-child of Rómulo Betancourt, and it was to him, as the titular head of the Party, that Gallegos looked for instructions and guidance. As one of the Master-Mind's critics phrased it: "If ever there was a king who could say with propriety, or without it, 'I am the State,' Betancourt can say without any doubt that the Party is he. And it is no lie or exaggeration. *Acción Democrática* without Betancourt would be a body without soul, a sky without stars."

When the head of the revolutionary *junta* stepped down from power, the Caracas newspapers announced that he would return to his Party and the "political fight" in the capacity of a simple citizen. *El País* imparted the news that he would soon become its leading columnist, but the looked-for articles never appeared. Instead, the master of the spoken and written word became a sort of roving spokesman without portfolio for the government's foreign and domestic policies. Though he had no official place in the government and no visible means of livelihood,[32] Betancourt still moved about, surrounded by flunkies, secret service men, and a motorcycle escort, as if he were still President.

When it was announced in March that Betancourt had been chosen to head the Venezuelan delegation to the forthcoming ninth Inter-American Conference at Bogotá, there was a storm of protest from the opposition. Why, the question was raised on all sides, had the choice fallen on a man of leftist leanings when everyone knew that one of the most important topics for discussion in Bogotá would be a mutual defense agreement against the encroachment of Communism? "With a feeling of sympathy for American defense," states the anonymous "Mister X" in his pamphlet *Rómulo Betancourt, Statesman and Diplomat,* "we ask if Rómulo Betancourt, renowned for his Communist activities on the continent, expelled from more than one country for subversive acts, a social agitator by trade, and skilled in Soviet artifice, is qualified to preside over the Venezuelan delegation? It is true that there exist decrees which put on record his anti-Communist position, but this is insufficient reason to validate his appointment as head of our delegation to the Bogotá Conference . . . It has not been difficult for us to always find him mixed up in curious ideological contradictions, sustaining with equal warmth two counterpoised theses—Communism and anti-Communism. Suddenly we hear him say: 'We do not work for the corrupt bourgeois democracy, but for the Soviet power; we look for indoctrination, not in Bolívar but in Marx; and we claim as our teacher, not Robespierre but Lenin. That is why we do not speak the sugar-coated language of the liberals but the uncouth proletarian language of Engels, Trotsky, and Rosa Luxemburg.' And then we hear him exclaim with equal warmth: 'I reject the Communist Party with all the force of my intransigent patriotism, because its dependence on Moscow converts it into a simple appendage of the Soviet State.' . . . He should not go to Bogotá!"

A careful review of Betancourt's political activities since the death of Gómez offers no irrefutable proof that he is an absolute Communist subservient to Politburo orders. Yet, gathered together, the

---

[32] When he declared his financial worth, as now required of retiring presidents, Betancourt stated under oath that his net assets exceeded his debts by only 1,144 bolivars ($343).

threads of his latter-day activities can be woven into a symmetrical pattern that lead to this inevitable conclusion. He claims he recanted Communism, yet he has continued to mouth Marxist doctrines advocating hatred, class struggles, and a "last-ditch fight against imperialism." On one occasion he said to the foreign press: "We are against Communism." But once in ignominious exile he admitted in writing: ". . . the anti-Communist policy of AD was only 'for export' . . . AD has always used the Communists as allies in national politics." He made public tirades against the regimes of Trujillo in Santo Domingo, Somoza in Nicaragua, and Franco in Spain. Not once did he openly condemn the despot in the Kremlin. AD journalists slanted the news so that, for example, some obscure phrase uttered by a native fanatic in far-off Delhi became a banner headline depicting the United States as a warmonger bent on world conquest. When news dispatches mentioned the possibility of a war between the United States and the Soviet Union, Betancourt, instead of making a timely statement for the side of democracy, issued an ominous warning which revealed just where his sympathies lay: "(In the event of war) . . . not one drop of petroleum would leave the country." When the anniversary of the Red Revolution arrived, he further showed his sympathy for Russia by happily posing for pictures with comrade Trevlin the Soviet Ambassador and drinking champagne with him in his luxurious mansion. To the surprise of even many Venezuelans, the AD government granted the Soviet Union special permission to maintain in Caracas the largest embassy staff of any foreign power; and although Russians had no stake in the petroleum industry, they brought into the country numerous "technicians," several of whom, strange to say, found their way into positions in Venezuelan government bureaus. Of the immigrants AD officials screened in Europe supposedly for farming and related pursuits, it has been estimated that twenty thousand were Spanish Republicans and nationals from behind the Iron Curtain. It was these same twenty thousand men of dubious repute who obtained Venezuelan citizenship with astounding dispatch, though their activities bore no relation whatever to the planting of potatoes. For what sinister purpose these men were destined was not made clear until after the overthrow of Gallegos.

Both Venezuelan and Colombian journalists have charged that Betancourt was involved in the Bogotá riots of 1948. That he was a

master of intrigue who employed a strategy of infiltration and provocation through agents and provocateurs had been demonstrated in
Costa Rica in 1933. That he had also been a key figure in the Bogotá
incident has been widely suspected but never proven.

Colombians and particularly the people of Bogotá, will long remember the fateful day of April 9, 1948, when the assassination of
the liberal leader, Jorge Gaitán, set off the upheaval that broke up
the ninth Inter-American Conference of American States and threw
the capital into sixteen frenzied hours of anarchy. The death of Gaitán
was the spark that touched off the bloody and destructive civil war that
raged in the back areas of the sprawling mountain country for almost
six years. Actually, the revolt was not a spontaneous outburst of
popular fury as was first supposed. It was, as charged by President
Mariano Ospina Pérez, a premeditated plot by Communists to wreck
the conference. Following the severance of relations with Russia, it
was proven to the satisfaction of the Colombian Conservative government that the Reds were exceedingly active among leftist elements.
The Liberals have admitted their connections with the Communist
Party. What they dare not admit, say informed Colombians, is that a
coalition of turncoat Liberals and Communists existed prior to the
April 9 outbreak.

Gaitán, the idol of the Colombian masses, had leftist leanings, but
he happened to be a bitter foe of the Communists. Having been selected by the powerful Liberal Party as its presidential candidate for
the 1950 election, it appeared likely that, once elected, he would
suppress the Communist Party. By destroying him at the opportune
moment, the radical coalition could conceivably achieve, not one, but
three objectives: shift of the leadership of the Liberal Party into the
hands of the Communists; a popular uprising against the Conservatives, which might culminate in a Communist victory; and the disbandment of the Inter-American Conference before an anti-Communist pact could be signed.

According to United States intelligence reports, which were
studied by a Senate investigation committee, "several Latin American
countries" knew weeks in advance that a Colombian revolution was
afoot. One dispatch from Bogotá to Washington reported that the
Liberals were storing throughout Bogotá arms and even uniforms
identical to those worn by the Colombian army and police. Another

dispatch, dated March 10, reported that a foreigner in Bogotá, in the service of a certain Latin American government, aided the Liberals in bringing contraband arms into the country. The Department of State was fully aware that disturbances and possibly violence were expected in Bogotá while the conference was in session, and Secretary of State George Marshall had been so informed.

And here is further evidence, circumstantial if not incriminating, that indicates that the conspiracy was international in scope and *Acción Democrática* leaders may have been involved. Though Betancourt often reiterated his stand of strict neutrality and adherance to international pacts, the AD press conducted a subtle propaganda campaign against President Ospina and his party. For what purpose? The Venezuelan delegation to the conference was composed entirely of AD partisans. Why were representatives of the opposition, especially the Catholic Copei Party, excluded? Other party men preceded the delegation to Bogotá on the pretext of "taking a vacation." What was the real reason? What business was it that also led the Venezuelan Communist leader, Gustavo Machado, to travel to Bogotá? Was it the same business that also brought the Chilean Communist leader, Salvador Ocampo, to the capital? *"AD has always used the Communists as allies in national politics."* So they were all allies if not birds of a feather. That is known. It is known also that all of them aspired to the overthrow of Ospina and his government. Yet more coincidences, if they can be labeled that, continue to pile up. Within one hour after Gaitán was shot down, armed radicals rose up throughout the Colombian Republic. Who alerted them? Who supplied them with arms? Even as the mobs of Bogotá began their rampage of terror and destruction, a radio commentator on the AD payroll broadcasted from Caracas a vitriolic tirade against President Ospina and incited the Colombian people to join the revolutionists in civil war. Was it a coincidence that radio time had been contracted for in advance by *Acción Democrática,* that the commentator spoke from a prepared script, and that AD party men were present at the broadcast?

The most important question that has never been answered concerns the whereabouts of Betancourt when the riots began. Declared a Venezuelan cabinet minister to the press upon his return from Bogotá: "When the rioters started to occupy the building, the Venezuelan delegation made preparations to leave. The crowd made way for the small group. In front, carrying the flag, unperturbed, impassible, marched Rómulo Betancourt." Contradicting this is the report of a Venezuelan journalist that it was Luis Lander who carried the flag; Betancourt was not with his delegation, having left the city early that morning "to attend a cattle exposition." When pressed for comments by Caracas reporters, the delegates declined to talk. But an explanation was unnecessary. Those who knew Betancourt were positive that when important issues were at stake, he had as much interest in cattle as a farmer has in law books.

With the Bogotá assignment over, Betancourt enjoyed a short respite, then took off for the United States, ostensibly on a vacation. Though President Gallegos had already preceded him at the invitation of President Truman, he appeared to act as an unofficial spokesman for his government. The former delegate who in Bogotá had taken a stand of moderation against Communism, assured apprehensive big business and the White House that the small group of Communists in Venezuela exerted very little influence, and that the door was open for American investors. Upon his return to Caracas after an absence of two months, he took over direction of his party and led the week-long celebrations in September on the seventh anniversary of its founding. Observed *El Nacional* in a flash editorial referring to the event: "Ordinarily, one becomes responsible at the age of seven."

Betancourt let it be known that the Party not only had come of age, but that it exerted a strong influence in shaping the republic's destiny. Moreover, he was still Venezuela's most powerful man. No one was made more aware of this than the opposition, who were considerably irked that the country's most gifted orator continued to voice the government's policies without legal sanction. Declared more than one thoughtful citizen after Betancourt spoke of an audacious program of social reforms to benefit the nation, "How many Presidents do we have in Venezuela?"

Though it appeared that "the silent one in Miraflores" was bothered not one whit that this former protégé kept stealing his thunder, it was not so with the military. The officers who engineered the October revolt had cause to ponder the sorry state of affairs. Through government dictums and strong-arm methods, *Acción Democrática* had ham-

strung the opposition, its insidious propaganda was creating antago-
nism between labor and industry, and its incessant inroads into private
enterprise had all but cowed businessmen into submission. President
Gallegos, an idealist who looked at the world through rose-colored
glasses, was, to quote a spokesman of the present government, the
"innocent but indifferent dupe" of Rómulo Betancourt and the leaders
of his party. "His government paid no attention to administrative
matters, perhaps because they were beyond its comprehension. Its
plans and promises contained more impressionistic phrases than the
knowledge of what had to be done and could be done. The outcome
of three years of endless talk and procrastination was the return of
demagogic quackery to government and the gradual decay of all
existing structures until they became unserviceable. Funds appropriated for public works were expended in partisan propaganda among
the workers without demanding any labor in return. The workers
were paid to keep them happy and to secure their votes at election
time."

Of greatest concern to the army was the discovery that not half of
the arms ordered from abroad by the war ministry were reaching their
destination; the missing arms were being diverted to two arsenals
under the control of AD; arms and ammunition were being issued to
loyal adherents throughout the country in anticipation of a clash with
the disgruntled army.

Resolved to correct an intolerable situation, a military group
headed by Lieutenant Colonel Delgado Chalbaud urged the President to set matters aright, form a nonpartisan cabinet of military and
independent members, make some changes in garrison commands,
and send Betancourt into exile. When Gallegos demurred, the demands
were pressed again and again, with negative results. "My die is cast,"
said the aged President coldly. "You will have to throw me out—
either dead or as a prisoner."

Day by day rumors flew and tension mounted in the capital. On
November 17, Gallegos suspended constitutional guarantees, a sign
of impending trouble. On the 22nd, when a strict censorship was imposed on press services going out of the country, the military group
issued an ultimatum: Gallegos had forty-eight hours to accede to its
demands. On the following day, the government issued no official an-
nouncements other than that the cabinet had resigned. The President

failed to make a public appearance. All during the day and far into the night, seven clandestine radios, one of them in the oil town of Cabimas, broadcasted a continuous alert to AD followers. The army knew then what the final answer would be: a test of strength between the outnumbered military forces and the members of the AD party, half a million strong.

Came Thursday the deadline and no answer from Gallegos. Promptly on the hour, Sherman tanks rumbled through the narrow streets of the capital, trucks full of steel-helmeted soldiers screeched up before Miraflores. In a matter of thirty minutes, troops had occupied every important building and intersection in the city. It was the same throughout the country; every garrison had supported the military *junta;* hardly a shot had been fired. Juan Bimba had declined to risk his neck over an issue that was beyond his comprehension. The result was the sudden disintegration of the once omnipotent people's party.

Though docile, easy-going Gallegos permitted himself to be locked up, not so Betancourt. The wily political schemer spent six fretful days dodging from one hiding place to another before he obtained refuge in the Colombian Embassy. A number of deposed bureaucrats likewise found sanctuary in foreign embassies, but the vast majority of the Party's politicians and labor leaders were rounded up and put in jail. Quipped a neutral observer when the excitement died down: "The Army gave, and the Army taketh away!"

Long weary of Latin American military coups, Washington took its good time in recognizing the *junta* headed by Delgado Chalbaud. President Truman, having reviewed the documentary film of Gallegos' speech made at Bolivar, Missouri the previous July, decided that it was a sincere exhortation in praise of democracy and that the *junta* members were only predatory upstarts. But those solid citizens who knew scholarly Delgado Chalbaud, knew him to be a zealous patriot willing to fight for the democratic principles that his father had fought and died for. Those citizens who might have doubted the more serious of the charges hurled at the old regime were soon convinced.

For weeks following the coup there were disclosures of defalcations of funds in federal and state treasuries. The army and secret service kept uncovering caches of arms, dynamite, and bombs in private homes, local party headquarters, and even in the patios of schools. Clandestine radios and printing presses were seized. But the most incriminating evidence was found in Betancourt's home in Altamira. Two file cases of highly confidential documents proved just who had been ruling the country: there were daily secret service reports covering movements of the military and of civilians considered to be enemies of the Party; there were long tabulations showing the sums that had been paid to nationals and immigrants who were to form "shock brigades" for the expected battle with the army; the army, as revealed in other papers, was to be disbanded and supplanted by AD militia; there was voluminous correspondence outlining the intricate setup for an absolute dictatorship—a dictatorship that would be Marxist as well as anti-American; and there was a plan of action to be followed, in the event of an armed conflict between the United States and Soviet Russia, which would deprive the United States and her allies of Venezuelan oil.

Like the ill-fated Robespierre, Betancourt had overestimated his strength and had failed to look to his own head. How true the phrase, "He who is in power today, may be out tomorrow!"

Depressed and forlorn, the fugitive paced his cramped quarters in the Colombian Embassy like a caged animal and schemed anew. He wrote, in three scrawled messages smuggled out to his "Companions of the Central Committee": "I have decided to try to go abroad. I have made this serious decision coldly and serenely, eight days after the coup . . . To go into hiding would create the illusion that we will immediately regain power. We will, but after long labor, not by magic . . . I am depressed, for reasons which several party companions know. This state of mind makes it impossible for me to analyze the events serenely . . ."

And when time had tempered his troubled mind: ". . . It is time to organize a campaign of political slogans on walls, sidewalks, etc. . . . The women should organize protests against the high cost of living and the deficiency of public services . . . All contact with officers should be avoided . . . Our return to power cannot be the product of a lucky coup but the consequence of a process of national disintegration which will oblige the army to summon us to Miraflores. Then we would allow the crisis to worsen, until the army has virtually disappeared, and we would arm the people . . . To insure success, it is essential that there be a sole command which would have access to the army . . . Through the unions, sabotage should begin by pacific means. Violent destruction is dangerous because it would cause mass dismissals and the outlawing of the unions . . . Strikes should be submitted to the study of the Central Committee . . ."

And his parting words of instruction just before he and Gallegos went into exile: "I will establish contact with Cuba. Prepare the apparatus for an underground movement . . ."

Thus ends and thus begins again yet another step in the vicious cycle of revolutions that have intermittently smoldered and flared for over a century of Venezuela's history. As in the past, every ruler of the future will have his pitfalls, his hour of reckoning in the eyes of his critics; whether he be a Gómez, a Medina or even a López Contreras, there will ever be ambitious men who will call him unworthy, brand him a tyrant, and challenge his power through force; for in so doing they will be exercising what they consider to be the time-honored "sacred right of insurrection."

Of the razor-tongued radicals who vilified and pilloried Juan Vicente Gómez, it was Betancourt who labored the most to turn him into a scapegoat for the economic ills of a whole century. Yet given the power to do better, say his peers, both he and Gallegos proved they were only capable of doing worse. Dr. Arturo Hidalgo summed it up succinctly when he wrote in his *Balance de Dos Epocas*: "When we observe the undeniable accomplishments of Gómez, which are now almost unanimously acknowledged, and the tragic and ridiculous failure of his detractors, we are left with the impression that we have received a stern lesson in reality . . . having learned that though he is given every means including power to do what he wishes, a twaddling charlatan is good for nothing."

Such is power; envied by those who do not have it, abused by those who possess it.

EPILOGUE

The books of the Gómez era have been closed for almost two decades, and time has tempered burning memories. Much good has been accomplished in Venezuela since she was freed from her chains. Progress has reached over mountains, plains, and rivers, and the drive against poverty and illiteracy goes on unceasingly. Due to her vast underground reserves of oil and iron, the country is riding a wave of prosperity. As in the time of President Guzmán, Caracas is still the hub of everything new. No longer the quaint city of red roofs, its new tall buildings and broad boulevards have transformed it into a modern metropolis. Now more than ever, it is the Mecca which every Venezuelan wishes to visit before he dies.

The inevitable proletarian movement is now a reality, and Juan Bimba still demands a better place in prosperity's sun and an obliging administrator who will place him there. The underground movement is also a reality, but in these days of firm military rule, it appears to exert no influence to speak of. The catchword of the outlawed *Acción Democrática* that *"el gobierno no sirve"* is fast becoming a trite phrase. The rambling diatribes of distortions and lies that occasionally appear in subversive handbills and pamphlets are so much hogwash. As a pamphleteer and revolutionist, Rómulo Betancourt appears to have lost his magic touch and popular appeal. Yet this bitter exile still writes and schemes with the same drive and purpose as the revolutionist of old.

Of the power and glory that was Gómez, all that remains is his lonely tomb in the Maracay cemetery, a few historic monuments, an unfinished opera house, and the shell of Rancho Grande shrouded in

462

mist and all but hidden by the encroaching jungle of what is now known as the Rancho Grande National Park. At Las Delicias, visitors still gape at the animals in the zoo, but they ignore the weatherbeaten wooden building in the background half hidden by trees. Now a country school, Gómez's former residence echoes these days to the laughter of little children; teachers' cots crowd the room where he died.

The house on the Plaza Girardot is also a school. Pathetic looking mementos still lie about in it unnoticed and unattended: the dictator's inlaid desk, now marred and worn; the French bronze gathering dust in a corner; the velvet drapes, faded and frayed, hanging in the front salon; a huge but worthless oil painting; and the safe lying rusted and half buried in the sand of a far patio.

Maracay is no longer the little town of quiet charm that Gómez loved. It too has felt the impact of the boom. The roar of trucks and the noises of new construction go on unceasingly. Its streets are crowded with soldiers, workers, shoppers, even tow-headed American youngsters in bluejeans. All is hustle and bustle and talk of innovations—skyscrapers, jets, automatic washers, and television.

For some, Maracay still carries fond memories. Dolores Amelia, who refused to be dislodged during the period of confiscations, still lives behind the secluded walls of her old house. Her married daughter Cristina lives nearby. So does her youngest son Juan, a graduate engineer from Pennsylvania State College, who works for the municipality. Daughter Belen lives in far-off Lisbon with her husband, Roberto Santana.

Sons Florencio and Juan Vicente occasionally commute from their Caracas homes to oversee the plantings and harvests on the haciendas that were restored to them by the military *junta*. Now gentlemen of leisure, but no longer the playboys of old, they are staid respectable married men who have no interest in politics or revolution.

Of Gómez's brothers and sisters, all have passed on but Regina, now a lonely spinster in her eighties who lives in sunny Trinidad.

The white Gómez mausoleum dominates a dry and dusty area of the Maracay cemetery. As the old caretaker will attest, few people visit it. "Only his relatives and a few of the poor come . . . those for whom he did favors during his lifetime. . . . Those whom he helped to get rich fear his tomb."

Stained glass Moorish windows cast purple, blue, and red hues on the tombstones. That of the head of the clan is distinguished by a wreath of iron leaves and two Saviours on crosses. Nearby is a marble slab inscribed:

To Papa Gómez
His Grandchildren

And on a wall a tarnished silver plaque bears the legend:

To General Juan Vicente Gómez
Eloy Tarazona, who accompanied him in life for 36 years, renders a permanent tribute of admiration and loyalty and maintains before this tomb the most treasured remembrance and the most devoted affection of his lifetime.

Today, Eloy Tarazona is a lonely pathetic figure. Once a millionaire who commanded respect and attention, this Colombian Indian is now a wizened old man without money or friends. Before being deported by President Contreras, he married one of his concubines so as to safeguard his vast real estate holdings. But the girl was young and naïve and was fleeced of the properties by a corrupt lawyer.

Recently Tarazona returned to his old haunts, which renewed the rumors of Gómez's buried treasure. "Yes, I know where General Gómez's treasure is hidden," he answered inquiring reporters. And with a guileless smile the sly old Indian added: "I have long talks with General Gómez every night. He has told me I must never let anyone know where the treasure is hidden. And I have promised."

From the story of Eloy Tarazona, the people of Venezuela can draw an object lesson. Like this Indian who was but a poor peon on a hacienda when his benefactor befriended him, the land of Bolívar was an impoverished and humiliated nation when Gómez took over the reins of government. Its treasury exhausted, its foreign debts long unpaid, its population decimated by countless civil wars, the country was beset by economic chaos and its coast blockaded by hostile warships. When death removed the strong hands that held the reins, the republic was solvent, prosperous, and respected, but it was still young and inexperienced.

Whatever else he was, Juan Vicente Gómez was a pillar of strength who never knew the humility of defeat. A leader of great wisdom who never reneged on his word, he would rather proffer the hand of friendship than the iron fist. Whatever the charges impartial history may make against him, he stamped out the last vestige of semibarbarous militarism, warded off the specter of Communism, and unified his people. He could scarcely be expected to search his own soul to weigh his shortcomings against his glorious deeds. In the glitter of his own victories and accomplishments, he could not be expected to count the cost in human lives and suffering. Continually confronted by grave problems and heavy responsibilities, he could not stop to realize that after all he might not have been such a kind father to the great host of Venezuelan children. His tragedy was the tragedy of absolute power embodied in one human being, the tragedy of a man who lifts a nation beyond its innate capacities, and who perforce must compromise with the strong at the expense of the weak, who must suppress liberties to protect his own interests, until power supersedes patriotism as the motivating force. He was Caesar, the accuser, the judge, the warden, the maker and breaker of laws.

The Latins are fervent worshipers of national heroes. Given time, they are prone to overlook the foibles and sins of a man if he has left his mark of achievement for posterity. Padre Borges is a prime example. It was only recently, twenty-two years after his death, that both Church and State paid him solemn homage as a great orator and brilliant poet. Even the great Simón Bolívar was execrated and vilified during his lifetime. The last years of his life were spent in exile, and his death in nearby Santa Marta aroused no tears or emotion in the land of his birth. Twenty years were to pass before the great movement began to exalt his memory. Today there is hardly a hamlet in all of Venezuela that does not have a monument that bears his name. In the National Pantheon, where he was buried, a ceiling fresco depicts Bolívar just "one step to the rear and one step to the right" of Jesus Christ. This adulation is not for Bolívar the man, but for Bolívar, the national hero.

Time heals all wounds. No longer is Juan Vicente Gómez execrated and pilloried as a bloodthirsty scoundrel. The hoary legends that relegated him to the nadir of degradation have become myths that pay tribute to his prowess and wisdom. There are increasing signs that not many years hence he may be metamorphosed into a national hero. Sentimental historians will probably want to place a halo around his head. They will hold him up as a model of everything that is great and noble in human life. They will call him the Father of Peace, the builder of roads and of commerce between nation and nation. Though condemned to oblivion, just as Lima can harbor a statue of Francisco Pizarro, the cruel conqueror who subjugated the Incas and kept a gibbet in the city's square, so the day will come when the statue of Gómez will stand in his country's capital.

BIBLIOGRAPHY

Angell, Hildegarde, *Simón Bolívar, South American Liberator*. New York, 1930

Arcaya, Pedro, *The Gómez Regime in Venezuela and its Background*. Baltimore, 1936

Besson, Juan, *Historia del Estado Zulia*. Maracaibo, 1951

Brandt, Carlos, *La Epoca del Terror en el Pais de Gómez*. Caracas, 1947

Cordoba, Diego, *Venezuela Agonizante*. Caracas, 1936

Creole Petroleum Corporation, *El Farol*. Caracas

Cutright, P. R., *The Great Naturalists Explore South America*. New York, 1943

Dance, Charles D., *Recollections of Four Years in Venezuela*. London, 1876

Davis, Richard Harding, *Three Gringos in Venezuela*. New York, 1896

Dennison, L. R., *Caroni Gold*. New York, 1943

Ediciones Caribe, *Rómulo Betancourt, Semblanza de un Político Popular*. Caracas, 1948

Freebody, Captain James H., *Heat, Hell and Humour*. London, 1935

Gallegos, Gerardo, *Guancho Gómez, Un Drama de la Realidad America*. Caracas, 1937

González Guinán, *Historia Contemporánea de Venezuela*. Caracas, 1924

Hanighen, Frank C., *The Secret War*. New York, 1934

Hidalgo R., Doctor Arturo, *Balance de Dos Epocas*. Caracas, 1948

Lee, Thomas F., "A Close Portrait of Gómez," *Mentor Magazine*. New York, November, 1925

Liddle, R. A., *The Geology of Venezuela and Trinidad*. Ithaca, 1946

López Contreras, Eleazar, *El Triunfo de la Verdad*. Mexico D. F., 1949

——. *Páginas para la Historia Militar de Venezuela*. Caracas, 1945

Loreto, Rafael, *Gen. Isaías Medina Angarita, Un Año en el Poder* Caracas, 1942

Ministry of Mines and Hydrocarbons, *National Petroleum Convention*. Caracas, 1951

Mister "X" (Anonymous), *Rómulo Betancourt, Estadista y Diplomático*. Caracas, 1948

467

Mosqueda, Miguel A., *El Padre Borges, La Vida de un Romántico.*
  Caracas, 1946

Otero Silva, Miguel, *Fiebre.* Caracas, 1939

Pepper, José Vicente, *Nos Vamos a Pique.* Caracas, 1939

Perera, Doctor Ambrosio, *Historia Orgánica de Venezuela.* Caracas, 1943

Pocaterra, José R., *Memorias de un Venezolano de la Decadencia.*
  Caracas, 1937

Quintero Quintero, J., *Muros.* Caracas, 1942

Rohl, Eduardo, *Fauna Descriptiva de Venezuela.* Caracas, 1949

Rondon Marquez, R. A., *Guzmán Blanco, El Autocrata Civilizador.*
  Caracas, 1944

Rourke, Thomas, *Gómez, Tyrant of the Andes.* New York, 1936

Royal Dutch Shell, *Tópicos Shell de Venezuela.* Caracas

Standard Oil Company of New Jersey, *The Lamp.* New York

Tell, Arturo H.. *En el Bajo Orinoco.* Caracas, 1945.

INDEX